# THE FORGOTTEN COMMISSIONER

# THE FORGOTTEN COMMISSIONER

*Sir William Mildmay and the Anglo-French Commission of 1750–1755*

❖

## Enid Robbie

Michigan State University Press
East Lansing

∞ The paper used in this publication meets the minimum requirements of
ANSI/NISO Z39.48–1992 (R 1997) (Permanence of Paper).

Michigan State University Press
East Lansing, Michigan 48823–5202

Printed and bound in the United States of America.

08  07  06  05  04  03   1  2  3  4  5  6  7  8  9  10

LIBRARY OF CONGRESS CATALOGING-IN-PUBLICATION DATA

Robbie, Enid
    The forgotten commissioner : Sir William Mildmay and the Anglo-French
    Commission of 1750-1755 / Enid Robbie
        p.  cm.

    Includes bibliographical references and index

    ISBN 0-87013-683-0 (cloth : alk. paper)
    ISBN 0-87013-651-8 (paper)
        1. Mildmay, William, Sir, 1705-1771. 2. Treaty of Aix-la-Chapelle (1748).
    3. Diplomats—Great Britain—Biography. 4. Anglo-French War, 1755-1763.
    5. Great Britain—History—George II, 1727-1760—Biography. 6. Great
    Britain—Foreign relation—1727-1760. 7. Great Britain—Foreign relations—
    France. 8. France—Foreign relations—Great Britain.

    DA501.M55 R63 2002
    327.41044/092 B 21

Book design by Michael J. Brooks
Cover design by Ariana Grabec-Dingman

Visit Michigan State University Press on the World Wide Web at:
*www.msupress.msu.edu*

# Contents

# A Biographical Index:
# The Main Characters

❖

*Jean Baptiste, Comte de Machault, Sieur d'Arnouville, 1701–94*
Appointed controller general (finance minister) from 1745 to 1754 and keeper of the seals from 1750 to 1755. In 1754, Machault was appointed secretary of the marine and held that position until 1757. Machault was a protégé of Madame de Pompadour and, consequently, the political enemy of Marc, comte d'Argenson (1696–1764). The latter was the secretary of state for war from 1742 to 1757; together with his brother, the marquis d'Argenson, he actively sought to overthrow the marquise.

*Roland Michel Barrin, Marquis de la Gallissonière, 1698–1756*
Governor of Canada from 1745 to 1749. The military governor of Canada, based in Quebec during King George's War (1744–48), and a distinguished admiral in the French navy. Appointed the senior French commissioner to the Anglo-French Commission in 1750.

*Gaston Charles, Marquis de Mirepoix, 1699–1758*
Created the duke de Mirepoix in 1751. Ambassador to Venice from 1737 to 1741. During the War of the Austrian Succession, he served in the French army in Bohemia, Italy, and Flanders. He was appointed French ambassador to London in 1749. Mirepoix was recalled to Paris in 1755, but during his six-year tenure as ambassador he was well regarded by the British government.

*Robert Darcy, Fourth Earl of Holdernesse, 1718–78*
Sent as British envoy to Venice from 1740 to 1751. Appointed British ambassador to The Hague from 1749 to 1751. Appointed secretary of state for the Southern department to replace the duke of Bedford in June 1751. He remained in that cabinet post until March 1754 when he was appointed secretary of state for the Northern department. He became the stepson of

Benjamin Mildmay, earl of Fitzwalter, when his mother, the widow of the third earl of Holdernesse, married Fitzwalter in 1724.

### George Montague Dunk, Second Earl of Halifax, 1706–71

Appointed to the Board of Trade as first lord in 1748 and became the president of the board in 1753. The chief supporter and founder of the new colony and town of Halifax in 1749. A strong advocate in the cabinet of an active British military policy against the French encroachments in Nova Scotia, New England, and Virginia.

### Etienne, Marquis de Silhouette, 1709–67

The second French commissioner on the Anglo-French Commission in Paris from 1750 to 1755. His other appointment was on the King's Council as the controller general of finance in 1759. As a personality, Silhouette was so retiring and diffident that his name has become synonymous with something fleeting, one-dimensional, and shadowy.

### William Anne Kepple, Second Earl of Albemarle, 1702–54

A major general at the battles of Fontenoy and Colloden, 1746, and commander in chief of the British forces in Scotland after the departure of the duke of Cumberland. Had extensive military experience and was well regarded by both George II and the duke of Cumberland. Appointed the (absentee) governor of Virginia, September 1737. Appointed the British ambassador to Paris in March 1748, and died there in December 1754.

### Benjamin Mildmay, First Earl of Fitzwalter, 1672–1756

Appointed one of the Lords commissioners to the Board of Trade from 1735 to 1737. Became Baron Fitzwalter on the death of his brother, Charles, in 1728. Created earl of Fitzwalter in 1730. Married Frederica, dowager countess Holdernesse, in 1724 and became the stepfather of the four-year-old Robert Darcy, fourth lord Holdernesse. Appointed treasurer to the royal household in 1754. A distant family relative and the patron of William Mildmay.

### Henry Pelham, 1696–1754

Pelham became the first lord of the treasury in 1743. At the same time he also became the chancellor of the exchequer. He proposed and carried out a restructuring of the national debt, which had the effect of lowering the interest rates, and also developed a more equitable method of administering the national revenue. He died unexpectedly in 1754 at the age of 58.

### Thomas Pelham-Holles, Duke of Newcastle, 1693–1768
Stepbrother of Henry Pelham. He took the name of Holles as the requirement of a wealthy man with no descendents before he named Thomas Pelham as the heir to his fortune. Created the duke of Newcastle by George I in 1715. In 1743, Henry Pelham, first lord of the treasury (or prime minister), appointed Newcastle to be secretary of state for the Northern department in his administration. On the sudden death of Henry Pelham in 1754, George II asked Newcastle to form a government. He was first secretary of the treasury from 1754 to 1756, and again from 1757 to 1760.

### Sir Thomas Robinson, 1695–1770
First secretary to the British embassy in Paris from 1725 to1726. Appointed the British ambassador in Vienna from 1730 to 1748. Helped to negotiate the Treaty of Aix-la-Chapelle in 1748. Made a lord commissioner of the Board of Trade in 1748. Appointed to be secretary of state for the Southern department from March 1754 to November 1755.

### Antoine Louis Rouillé, Comte de Jouy, 1689–1761
Minister of the Marine from April 1749 to July 1754. Appointed minister of foreign affairs in July 1754 and held that position until June 1757.

### John Russell, Fourth Duke of Bedford, 1710–71
Appointed secretary of state for the Southern department in February 1748. Submitted his retirement from this cabinet post to George II in June 1751 at the insistence of the duke of Newcastle, his political opponent.

### Ruvigny de Cosne, 1720–78
Arrived at the British embassy in Paris as a personal secretary to Lord Albemarle in 1748. Appointed first secretary of the British embassy in 1751. Became the senior official in charge of the embassy on the death of Lord Albemarle in 1754. Returned to London when the embassy closed in 1755. Served as first secretary at the British embassy in Madrid from 1755 to 1760. Following the departure of William Shirley, appointed as the second British

commissioner to the Anglo-French Commission in May 1752 under William Mildmay.

*William Shirley, 1694–1771*
Born in Sussex, England, and educated as a lawyer at the Inner Temple, London. He immigrated to Boston, Massachusetts, in 1731 and became advocate general to the government of Massachusetts in 1733. He was appointed to be its governor in 1743. Shirley was appointed senior commissioner to the Anglo-French Commission in Paris in 1749 and returned to London in 1752. After he returned he was appointed a member of the Board of Trade from 1753 to 1754. He returned to Boston in 1754. Shirley was named the military commander of the Massachusetts forces from 1754 to 1756, but was replaced as governor of Massachusetts in 1756. He was appointed as the governor of the Bahamas in 1759 and returned to Boston in 1767.

*Daniel-Charles Trudaine, 1703–69*
A councillor of state. In 1752, Trudaine became an *intendant* of finance at the Department of Finance under the direction of Jean Baptiste Machault, controller general of finance from 1745 to 1754. The director of the Department of Roads and Bridges. A friend of William Mildmay since 1751.

*Joseph Yorke, 1724–92*
The third son of Lord Chancellor Hardwicke. Sent to Paris as the first secretary of the British embassy from 1749 to 1751. During the absences of the ambassador, Lord Albemarle, Yorke acted as the embassy head of mission. In October 1751 Yorke was appointed the British ambassador to The Hague, where he remained until 1761.

❧

# Introduction

ON MONDAY, 31 AUGUST 1750, four men met in Paris to negotiate some still disputed clauses of a peace treaty that, in 1748, had ended the War of the Austrian Succession. As the main parties to the Treaty of Aix-la-Chapelle were France and Britain, Louis XV appointed the marquis de la Galissonnière, late governor of Canada (New France), and the marquis Etienne de Silhouette to the commission. The two British members named by George II as his representatives were William Shirley, governor of Massachusetts, and William Mildmay (later to be Sir William Mildmay). After five years were spent holding lengthy commission meetings, writing numerous reports, and issuing ten memorials—six British and four French, which stated the position of each government—the negotiations failed. As a direct result of this diplomatic failure the Seven Years' War (1756–63) began between Britain and France. The war was to have immense consequences not only for both countries, but also for the subsequent history of the world.[1]

There have been extensive examinations of the war that ended the French presence in North America and created the conditions for the birth of the British Empire, the latest and most comprehensive of which is by Fred Anderson, published in 2000.[2] Curiously, the history of the commission whose diplomatic failure led to this war has been of relatively little historical interest. Only Max Savelle, in *The Diplomatic History of the Canadian Boundary, 1749–1763* (published in 1940), has studied this commission in detail. However, a great many of the manuscripts that I use were not yet available for study in 1940, and much of the evidence in William Mildmay's commission reports, his private and official letters, and his personal journal appears to contradict Savelle's conclusions on the purpose of this commission. Without a critical examination of these manuscripts, not only does the work of commissioner William Mildmay become completely overshadowed by that of his more celebrated colleague, William Shirley, but there is a distortion of the history of this fateful commission: namely why it failed and who may have been responsible. This present account of Mildmay's diplomatic work will not only present a different perspective on this five-year commission, and of the intent of its personnel, it will also introduce William Mildmay (1705–71) as a skillful British diplomat whose present obscurity is quite undeserved.

When Mildmay went to France in 1748, he was a London lawyer of forty-five who, from necessity, had lived a prudent, frugal life, supplementing his modest income by carrying out minor administrative duties for members of the British government. In 1750, this skill gained him a place on an Anglo-French commission in Paris and for the following five years his position as a diplomat gave him constant access to French legal and political society. The contents of Mildmay's letters, his private commission journal, and his official commission reports not only provide a remarkable first-hand insight into the torturous process of eighteenth-century diplomacy, but they also raise the fascinating possibility that in the early summer of 1752 a successful end of the treaty negotiations might have been possible. It can, of course, be argued that such a peaceful result would have been only a temporary post-ponement of an inevitable conflict between Britain and France in North America, but such a postponement would have produced a new cast of char-acters, and thus a potential change in the outcome. A war begun in 1766 might therefore have had a very different end result from the one that broke out in 1756.[3] Given the importance of the Seven Years' War for Britain and its empire, Mildmay's detailed description of the work of this commission, recorded over its entire five-year life, is therefore a remarkable and, indeed, unique chronicle of a crucial episode in British and French diplomacy.

Despite Mildmay's valuable information both on mid–eighteenth-century diplomacy and on French society, he is still almost unknown as a source. Even though his documents have been in the public domain for the past sixty years, they have been largely overlooked by modern historians. In 1934, seven volumes of William Mildmay's papers were placed at the William L. Clements Library in Ann Arbor, Michigan, and his diplomatic letters to one of the secretaries of state, Lord Holdernesse, are in the Leeds Papers in the British Library, London. Since 1955, a substantial number of his documents have been in the general collection of the Mildmay family papers in the Manuscript Department of the Essex Record Office, Chelmsford, but very little use has been made of his material in any of these collections.[4]

A great deal of Mildmay's information on diplomacy, French politics, economics, and society was given in letters to his relative, patron, and friend,

Benjamin Mildmay, earl of Fitzwalter. Throughout his residence in France, Mildmay sent Fitzwalter regular letters: 129 in all. These were written to a man who had been a chief commissioner on the Board of Trade and Plantations and who, in 1750, was the treasurer to the royal household of George II.[5] Beyond his contact with Fitzwalter, Mildmay gave further information on France in letters to Lord Holdernesse, Henry Pelham (First Lord of the treasury and government leader until 1754), the duke of Bedford (secretary of state for the Southern Department until 1751), and Sir Thomas Robinson (secretary of state for the Southern Department after 1754). These letters are either in the Leeds Papers in the British Library or in the D/DM series of the Mildmay Papers in the Essex Record Office.

Mildmay's correspondence is in two, distinct categories—one official and the other private—and the considerable number of letters that he sent to Lord Fitzwalter and Lord Holdernesse have a candid quality that stems from his long-standing association with both men. Mildmay was related to Fitzwalter and Holdernesse, either directly or through marriage. By 1750, he had been a friend of Fitzwalter for thirty-four years and Holdernesse for twenty-five.[6] Mildmay's letters thus reflect his confidence that, within bounds, he could write with an open frankness to a member of the Privy Council (Fitzwalter), and to a British government minister (Holdernesse). His qualifications as a diplomat were excellent. He not only lived in France from August 1748 to May 1755, but he was also fluent in spoken and written French, had a wide circle of influential friends, and had considerable experience with the customs of French aristocratic society. He was a careful man, however. His writing was small, neat, and evenly spaced: the hand of a man who was consciously in control of himself. He was intelligent and well read but he never forgot that although he was the equal of Lord Fitzwalter and Lord Holdernesse in foresight and analytical skill, they were his social superiors, his patrons, and his masters. The tone of his letters to both men was carefully deferential and he always put forward his proposals as delicate suggestions that could be withdrawn at the earliest sign of any disapproval.

After he had returned to England in 1755, Mildmay wrote and published two books: *The Police of France* in 1763, and *An Account of the Southern Maritime Provinces of France,* issued in 1764.[7] Despite the large amount of his published material, however, the existing record of Mildmay's life and work consists of brief, unrelated, and in some cases inaccurate fragments of information. Only Max Savelle has used any part of the varied contents of the

Mildmay Papers in the William L. Clements Library, but his study was limited solely to a discussion of the North American boundary disputes and did not use the detailed and important information that is in Mildmay's private commission journal. Both of Mildmay's books on French society in the mid-eighteenth century are in the British Library, but the only historian to make use of the material contained in *The Police of France* is Alan Williams. Mildmay's second book on the south of France has not been used in any economic or social study of eighteenth-century French history.[8]

When Alan Williams wrote *The Police of Paris 1718–1789*, he gave numerous citations from Mildmay's book on the French system of police but he did not mention that Mildmay was also a lawyer and was working as a British diplomat in Paris. When Max Savelle discussed Mildmay's diplomatic work he was apparently unaware both of Mildmay's legal career and of his books on the police and economy of France. The only historian to consult Mildmay's papers in the Essex Record Office has been Hilda Grieve. In the second volume of her book *The Sleepers and the Shadows, Chelmsford a Town, Its People and Its Past*, she noted that Mildmay had been a diplomat in Paris and had written books on the French police system and on the economy of Languedoc and Provence. Grieve's entire interest, however, was in the activities of the newly created Sir William Mildmay after he had inherited Lord Fitzwalter's Chelmsford estates in 1756; in her history of Georgian and Victorian Chelmsford, she did not go into any details of Mildmay's earlier work in Paris or of the content of his books.[9]

Apart from the information in his letters and books, in 1743 Mildmay also contributed a detailed monograph on the civic administration of the City of London at the request of his friend Sir Richard Hoare, who had been a sheriff of the city in 1741 and in 1743 was a city alderman.[10] This manuscript was first published by Mildmay in 1768 and a copy of this edition is in the Buhr Collection in the University of Michigan at Ann Arbor.[11]

When he left Paris in May 1755,[12] Mildmay brought back to England his memoranda on the commission negotiations, his copies of the letters he had written from Paris between 1750 and 1755, and the information he had been gathering on the French economy and system of police over the past seven years. In 1756 he inherited Lord Fitzwalter's Essex estates and in 1765 he was knighted. When he died childless in 1771, this collection of all of his papers was inherited by his wife, Anne.[13] On her death in 1796, they then passed to her niece, Jane Mildmay, who was the sole heir to all of Anne and William

Mildmay's property. Jane Mildmay was married in 1786 to Sir Henry Paulet St. John, who then took the name of Sir Henry Paulet St. John Mildmay.[14] The family estate of Sir Henry was Dogmersfield Park, in Hampshire,[15] and although Jane St. John Mildmay inherited William's house of Moulsham Hall in Essex, she and her husband continued to spend the majority of their time in Hampshire. In 1809, Moulsham Hall was demolished and the land was sold.[16]

William Mildmay's papers were taken to the St. John Mildmay family archives in Hampshire,[17] but in 1879 the Historical Manuscript Commission stated that a part of these archives was now owned by Captain Hervey G. St. John Mildmay, R.N. of Hazelgrove House in Somerset.[18] In 1913, Henry A. St. John Mildmay used these family documents, which included extracts from Mildmay's travel journal, in a book that he wrote on the history of his family called *A Brief Memoir of the Mildmay Family*.[19] Early in the 1930s, a member of the St. John Mildmay family sold a part of Mildmay's collected papers to a bookseller at the Museum Book Store in London. It was from there that the William L. Clements Library purchased the papers in 1934.[20]

The rest of William Mildmay's papers remained in the possession of other members of the St. John Mildmay family until they were given to the Somerset and Hampshire Record Offices in 1936. Since they related directly to the history of Essex, in 1955 the Somerset Record Office transferred these papers to the Essex Record Office at Chelmsford as a reclaimable loan and in the early 1970s, the Hampshire Record office similarly transferred their holdings.[21] The Essex Record Office has now catalogued William Mildmay's papers and they are included within the general collection of the Mildmay Papers at Chelmsford. As an undisputed provenance is such a vital aspect of any evaluation of a collection of unpublished manuscripts, it is therefore fortunate that a complete history of the ownership of William Mildmay's documents can be clearly traced by the Essex Record Office and the William L. Clements Library.

The originals of the correspondence between William Mildmay and Lord Holdernesse were initially in Holdernesse's possession as a part of his own records as a government minister. In the mid-eighteenth century, it was not yet the custom for the papers of a minister to become the property of the State, and on leaving office all of his papers remained his private property. When Lord Holdernesse died, his papers were thus inherited by his daughter and sole heir, Lady Amelia Darcy. She married the marquis of Carmarthen, who was the eldest son of the duke of Leeds, [22] and her father's documents became a part of the muniment collection of the dukes of Leeds. The Leeds Papers were subsequently acquired by the British Library and Mildmay's correspondence with Lord Holdernesse in this collection is now in the Egerton Additional Manuscripts volumes in this library.[23]

The British Library and the William L. Clements Library have bound William Mildmay's letters into volumes. His letters in the British Library are individually catalogued and foliated; those in the Mildmay Papers at the William L. Clements Library, although they have been bound in date order, are neither individually catalogued nor foliated. Mildmay's documents in the Mildmay Papers at the Essex Record Office are still in their original bundles, but most of the contents of these bundles have been individually catalogued. His letters in the British Library and his documents in the William L. Clements Library are in good condition; however, the condition of his documents in the Mildmay Papers in Essex varies greatly.

Mildmay wrote his letters on sheets of approximately 11 inches long by 16 inches wide (28 by 40.5 cm) and folded in half, lengthwise, to form four pages of 11 inches by 8 inches (28 by 20.25 cm). He always wrote on the inner two of these pages and left the reverse sides blank to form an envelope cover. On the originals of Mildmay's letters, the recipients have used this cover side to record both their names and, in some cases, a brief description of the contents, but in his copies of his own letters Mildmay did not write on this cover. If a letter was too long be contained on the inner two pages, a second double sheet was inserted into the first and similarly folded. Mildmay wrote in a small, semi-script hand, with no copperplate elaboration, and he kept carefully to a straight line. Most of his paragraphs were separately spaced and he also left a regular margin on each side of the page, but he rarely wrote in these margins. He always signed his letters as "Wm Mildmay," with the "m" in lowercase and written as a superscript at the top of the "W." Following the normal eighteenth-century writing practice, he used capitalization throughout in a somewhat arbitrary manner and sometimes wrote contractions of certain words. In the quotations, I have changed the format to modern punctuation and have written the contractions as complete words. I have also retained most of his original spelling, but where it seems appropriate I have given a modern interpretation in parentheses. As Mildmay was not created a baronet until 1765,[24] I have chosen not to use his title when referring to any event that took place before that year. For the majority of this book, he is thus referred to as William Mildmay.

In those few letters where an exact comparison between the dates in London and Paris is an important factor I have quoted the double dates of the New Style, used in the rest of Europe, and the Old Style, used in Britain until September 1752, both of which Mildmay wrote on all on his letters from Paris until the British dating system was changed. The Act 24 Geo II c 23, passed in March 1751, ordered that 2 September 1752 [this date style is preferred by CMS, so I have not changed it throughout] would immediately be followed by 14 September 1752 and, accordingly, Mildmay dated his first letter under this new convention with the single date of 19 September 1752.[25] Except where the double date is necessary to establish their chronology, in most of the letters that Mildmay wrote from Paris before September 1752 I have cited their New Style date and, similarly, I have used the single Old Style date that headed the letters written by his correspondents in London. The letters written to Mildmay are the original letters from his correspondents. Those letters that are from Mildmay to others are his own copies, and his memoranda, journal, and notes are also in his handwriting. The books by Mildmay that are now in the British Library were all published during his lifetime, under his supervision, and none has been edited by others at a later date.

A portion of this book is based on my Ph.D. thesis of William Mildmay's French observations, and I would like to thank my thesis supervisor, Professor Julian Dent of the University of Toronto, for his invaluable help and criticism. I also owe a great deal of gratitude to Miss Janet Smith, the assistant county archivist at the Essex Record Office, and to Dr. Robert Cox, curator of the Manuscript Department at the William L. Clements Library, for their assistance in helping me to locate the documents I have used in this book. I would also like to acknowledge the constant, ongoing guidance and friendship I received from my editor, Martha Bates, of the Michigan State University Press. Above all I would like to thank my husband, Rod Robbie, without whose patient support and encouragement this book could never have been written.

# I.

# WHO WAS WILLIAM MILDMAY?

❧

FOR A MAN WHO WAS AT the center of a piece of critical eighteenth-century British diplomacy, remarkably little has been said about William Mildmay. In the existing analyses of the 1750–1755 Anglo-French Commission, he appears simply as the second name on the royal warrant and is portrayed as a passive, superficial participant whose presence, supposedly, had no effect on the conduct of the negotiations. As this sparse, erroneous information has remained the only account of his work in Paris, it is essential that before examining Mildmay's diplomatic activity he is first put in the context of the family he came from, the events of his childhood, and his training and professional experience.

William Mildmay was born in 1705. At the beginning of the eighteenth-century, the Mildmays of Essex, England, were a large, extended family with a three-hundred-year history of social and political influence in the county. Many of their members were prominent landowners, but William's family was not a part of this group of landed gentry. At William's birth, his father was a chief agent of the British East India Company; he died when his only son was five years old, leaving a modest inheritance to his two young children. Over the next fifty years, the large Mildmay clan was to experience the misfortune of many landed families whose estates were entailed—a failure of male heirs in the direct line of succession—and in 1756, William Mildmay, as the last surviving son from a cadet branch, inherited almost the entire Mildmay family holdings in Essex. For the first half of his professional life, however, he had been merely a lawyer with expectations of an inheritance, but with comparatively little income.

The family's landed fortune was founded at the beginning of the six-teenth century from the entrepreneurship of a Thomas Mildmay, who left his Essex village of Great Waltham in 1505 and moved to the nearby town of Chelmsford to become a mercer, or market trader. Ten years later Thomas had not only acquired a house for his family of eight children, but had been able to buy his own stall in the Chelmsford marketplace from which he sold fish.[1] Over the following thirty-five years his business prospered, and before he died in 1550, Thomas Mildmay had become a prominent burgess and a major owner of land in and around Chelmsford.[2] Despite his wealth and status, in his will Thomas still described himself as "merchant and yeoman," although his sons called themselves "esquires" and considered themselves to be gentlemen.[3]

Thomas Mildmay was succeeded by three daughters, and four surviving sons: Thomas, William, John, and Walter. He left various parts of his business and estate to the three eldest sons,[4] but by 1550 Thomas Mildmay [II] and the youngest son, Sir Walter Mildmay, had already taken the family far beyond the commercial life of Chelmsford. Thomas Mildmay [II] began this upward mobility when, in 1536, he was appointed one of the ten auditors of the Court of Augmentations. Henry VIII had initially set up this court to sell the land and assets of those smaller monasteries whose annual income did not exceed £200, but in 1540 its mandate was expanded to dispose of the property of the larger foundations. Thomas, as a senior court official, was able to benefit from the large redistribution of land that took place in this total dissolution of the monasteries.[5] His brother Walter was equally fortunate. In 1540, Walter joined Thomas on the court as a surveyor and receiver and in 1545, he was promoted to be chief of the general surveyors.[6] In 1546, Walter—now Sir Walter Mildmay—became joint auditor with his brother for four counties and the City of London, and the sole auditor for the Duchy of Lancaster.[7] On the accession of Queen Elizabeth in 1558, Sir Walter was appointed treasurer to her household. Ten years later, in 1568, the Queen made Sir Walter Mildmay her Chancellor of the Exchequer: it was a post he held with considerable distinction until his death in 1589.[8]

Sir Walter was the most illustrious of the Mildmay brothers, but it was through the efforts of Thomas the Auditor that the family acquired its large Essex estates. In 1540, four years after Thomas Mildmay [II] began taking an inventory of the Essex religious houses, he was able to buy a property that had belonged to the Abbey of Westminster in the village of Moulsham, just across the river from Chelmsford. This was an estate of 1,300 acres, with 200 tenants, and having acquired a leasehold grant from Henry VIII, Thomas demolished the dilapidated dwelling once owned by the Dominican Priory and built his new manor house of Moulsham Hall.[9] In 1553, "Thomas Mildmay . . . alias Thomas Mildmay Esq." was able to purchase the freehold and the lordship of the manor of Moulsham in a Crown grant of sale,[10] but it took until 1563 before he was able to buy the royal manor of Chelmsford (Bishops Hall), which carried with it the lordship of Chelmsford, the right to hold a Court, and the presentation of the Rector to the parish of Chelmsford.[11] Before he died in 1566, Thomas the Auditor had also been able to marry his eldest son, Sir Thomas Mildmay, to Lady Frances Radcliffe, daughter of Henry Radcliffe, second earl of Sussex and Baron Fitzwalter.[12]

As Thomas was determined to preserve his manors of Chelmsford and Moulsham intact as a unit, in his will he left them entirely to his eldest son, Sir Thomas Mildmay, and his male heirs. If Sir Thomas died without a surviving son the next inheritor was to be the Auditor's other son, Henry. If both of these direct lines failed, however, the will then ordered that the successive reversions of these two estates were to pass to the male heirs descended from Thomas the Auditor's brothers: beginning with those of his youngest brother, Sir Walter, followed by the heirs of his second brother, William, and finally to those of his third brother, John.[13] Two hundred years later the consequence of this strict entail on male heirs was to have an unexpected effect on the life of William Mildmay, the diplomat, who was a direct descendent in the male line of Thomas the Auditor's brother, William.[14]

During the following century, the family directly descended from Thomas Mildmay [II] moved slowly upward in society. In 1640, the direct line of male heirs to the Barony of Fitzwalter failed and Thomas the Auditor's grandson, Sir Henry Mildmay, claimed the title in right of his mother, Lady Frances Radcliffe, but his attempt did not succeed (another member of the family descended from Henry Radcliffe, the second earl of Sussex, was judged to have the better claim).[15] It was not until 1670 that Sir Benjamin Mildmay, Thomas the Auditor's great-grandson, was able to obtain permission from Charles II to assume the rank of the seventeenth baron Fitzwalter.[16] In 1730, the Mildmay family briefly achieved a place in the peerage when the nineteenth baron Fitzwalter, Benjamin Mildmay (1670–1756), second son of the seventeenth baron, was created earl of Fitzwalter.[17] Unfortunately, Benjamin's earldom of Fitzwalter ended with his death, as his infant son and only child had died in 1726.[18] Since all the surviving children of his sister, Mary, were girls, the earldom thus became extinct, but, in accordance with the terms of the entail established by Thomas the Auditor, on Lord Fitzwalter's death in 1756 his landed property was then inherited by William Mildmay, who was the next and, ultimately, the last direct male heir of all the families that had descended from the original four Mildmay brothers in the sixteenth century.[19]

The relatives in William Mildmay's branch of the family had been more modest landowners. From the sixteenth to the mid-seventeenth–century, they lived on their family estate of Springfield Barns, near Chelmsford, but at some point in the mid-seventeenth century William's grandfather sold this estate. In 1768, the eighteenth-century antiquarian, Philip Morant, wrote his second book on the history of Essex and in it he mentioned the sale of Springfield Barns; but although Morant and the newly created Sir William Mildmay were neighbors when it was published, and Sir William was one of the book's advance subscribers,[20] Morant did not give the reason. This sale, however, was to have a considerable effect on the life of Mildmay's father, another William Mildmay. No longer able to inherit Springfield Barns, William Mildmay senior went into trade as one of the agents of the British East India Company, and at the beginning of the eighteenth century he was sent to the company factory at Surat, north of Bombay, where his only son, William, was born in 1705.[21]

At the time of his son's birth, William Mildmay senior was the "Chief of Surat" (the president of the East India Company community) and he had married a Sarah Wilcox, daughter of Judge Wilcox of the Queen's Bench.[22] In the will that William Mildmay senior made in Surat in 1707, his wife was not named as a beneficiary and three of his merchant friends were appointed guardians of his two infant children, Mary and William. Sarah Mildmay also does not appear in any of the existing documents in the Essex Record Office on William's immediate family, all of which date from after his return to Essex as a child,[23] so it seems that Sarah Mildmay must have died either in childbirth, or else in Surat when her son was very young.

As the only son of the president of Surat, William Mildmay spent his early childhood in considerable luxury. The East India Company factory of Surat was established in 1612 at Swalley, at the mouth of the river Tapti, on the Gulf of Cambay.[24] In his book *A Voyage to Surat in the Year 1689*, John Ovington, who was the chaplain on the East India Company ship *Benjamin*, recorded life at the Surat factory in that year. He described a prosperous and important trading company, where the senior company employees lived an opulent life. He said their factory house was an impressive, forty-room structure once owned by the Mughal ruler of India, which contained a large private apartment for the president and his family. The compound walls enclosed several warehouses, a large water tank, a private garden that led down to the river, and even a "humhum" (*sic*, from *hamman*), or Turkish bath. In the cool of the evenings the senior officers and their wives strolled along the banks of the Tapti, and on Sundays and ceremonial occasions they dined on "deer and antelopes, peacocks and partridges, all kinds of persian fruits . . . and persian wines [which] are drunk with temperance and alacrity." When they left the compound, the president and his wife were carried in palanquins on the shoulders of native servants, and the saddles of the factors' horses were "all of velvet, richly embroidered. The Head Stalls, Reins and Croupers are all covered with solid wrought silver."[25]

In his early childhood William Mildmay thus lived the life of a young aristocrat, but at some point after the year in which the will was made (1707), his father's contract ended and this secure, cosseted existence was replaced by the hazards and discomfort of a long voyage home on a company ship. Ovington's return voyage from Surat to London took nine months and he described a difficult and dangerous journey across the Indian Ocean and around the Cape of Good Hope, where their ship was threatened by violent storms. As they neared Europe they were fortunate to be able to outrun two French privateers, and they finally reached Gravesend on 5 December 1690, having left Surat on 14 February of that year.[26] William Mildmay did not write anything about his childhood, but the unexpected hardship of this journey from his sheltered, familiar world of Surat to an unknown existence in England must have been bewildering and traumatic for a young child.

His father brought William and his elder sister Mary to the village of Little Baddow, near Chelmsford; in the bond that Mildmay signed when he entered the Middle Temple as a student in 1723, he stated that his father had been "William Mildmay of Little Baddow, Essex, deceased."[27] There is no record of the year in which William's father died, but attached to the bottom of his 1707 will is a codicil, dated 5 February 1715, that appoints Edmund Waterson as the guardian of "the infants Mary and William Mildmay, named as the beneficiaries of the property of their father, William Mildmay, now being dead." Waterson was a wealthy London merchant who, in 1696, married Elizabeth Mildmay, the daughter of Henry Mildmay of Graces and a cousin of Benjamin Mildmay (later to become Lord Fitzwalter.)[28] Waterson and his wife looked after the five-year-old William and his eight-year-old sister for the next six years, but in 1716 Waterson died, and in a bundle of bills that were sent by a Mr. R. Poole, solicitor, and dated 26 February 1718, are Poole's fees for the appointment of "Mrs. Waterson [as] guardian to the infants William and Mary Mildmay," and for the probate of the will of Edmund Waterson.[29]

Although by February 1718 Elizabeth was now their sole legal guardian, she did not pay any of these bills from Mr. Poole on behalf of her wards; at the bottom of each Poole recorded that they had been paid by "the Honourable Benjamin Mildmay."[30] This payment pattern continued and it was with this constant financial help from her cousin Benjamin that Elizabeth brought up William and Mary Mildmay until William entered Emmanuel College, Cambridge, in 1721.

From 1716 until 1722 William and Mary were involved in a legal battle to obtain a proper accounting of the inheritance left to them by their father, and of a further sum given to them in the will of Edmund Waterson. Waterson had been a Freeman of the City of London, and on his death the lord mayor and city council therefore assumed their legal responsibility to administer the inheritance of any orphaned minor heirs of a Freeman until they came of age. In 1716, the money left to William and Mary Mildmay by their father and by Waterson was now being held in trust in the Orphans Account of the City of London, and the city alderman in charge of its administration was a Robert Atkins.[31]

The other two beneficiaries of the Waterson estate were the infant son and daughter of Edmund Waterson's widowed sister, Margaret Bonnell, but Robert Atkins was also Margaret Bonnell's brother-in-law, and thus had a conflict of interest in this matter.[32] Since they were legal minors, the lawsuit to force Atkins to give a full statement of his accounts was prosecuted on behalf of William Mildmay and his sister by Elizabeth Waterson and Benjamin Mildmay, and Benjamin paid out over £500 of legal expenses during the seven years that it took to get a satisfactory settlement.[33]

On 14 July a "Statement of Settlement of Suit" was issued which stated that William and Mary Mildmay had now received from Mr. Atkins the sum of £1,869 as the final balance of their joint inheritance, together with an acknowledgment from William that eighteen months earlier, on 16 January 1721, he had also received a partial payment of £4,416.[34] In the same bundle of documents as the settlement statement are a series of legal bills and over forty invoices from tradesmen. These cover the repair of carriages, the cost of servants' livery, various items of clothing and material, the supply and trimming of men's and women's hats and shoe buckles, and numerous invoices for items of food, together with the cost of their carriage by the carter. All of these bills are marked as purchases made for the use of Elizabeth Waterson and her wards and all of them are discharged as paid by Benjamin Mildmay.[35]

Benjamin Mildmay gave a copy of the Statement of Settlement to Elizabeth Waterson on 24 July 1722,[36] and on 17 November 1722 the sixty-year-old Elizabeth wrote a letter to her forty-three-year-old cousin, Benjamin. It was an intimate, family letter in which she inquired after the state of his health, gently suggesting to her bachelor relative that she wished "he would not keep late hours abroad . . . on the diversions of the town." She also thanked him "from whom I have received abundant obligation" for all the years of trouble on her behalf.[37] William Mildmay had also the same "abundant obligation" to Benjamin Mildmay, Lord Fitzwalter, as his financial guardian during his minority, but he gradually developed a close friendship with Fitzwalter as his patron and mentor. This friendship was valued by both men and it lasted throughout Mildmay's working life until Fitzwalter's death in 1756, at the age of eighty-six, when William Mildmay was fifty-one.

In 1724, Benjamin Mildmay married Lady Frederica Darcy, widow of the third earl of Holdernesse, and her four-year-old son, Robert Darcy, the fourth earl of Holdernesse, came to live with her at Moulsham Hall. William Mildmay, now nineteen, became a family friend of Benjamin's young step-son and he was later to find this friendship with Holdernesse during his Lordship's childhood and adolescence was critically important to his career as a commissioner in Paris. On 18 May 1751 Holdernesse was appointed secretary of state for the Southern Department, with a responsibility for France as part of his ministerial portfolio, and Mildmay reported directly to Lord Holdernesse for his commission work.[38] This family connection is a significant background to the letters that Mildmay exchanged with Holdernesse between 1750 and 1755.

Six months after he had received the first part of his inheritance, on 1 July 1721 William Mildmay, aged sixteen and the "son of William, of the East India Company," entered Emmanuel College Cambridge as a pensioner.[39] He matriculated in 1723 and in 1728 he was awarded the degree of Master of

Arts at the University of Cambridge, but between his first and second degrees Mildmay left Cambridge. On 25 January 1723 he was admitted to the Middle Temple as a student, under membership bond number 6017,[40] and he was called to the Bar of the Middle Temple on 16 May 1729.[41] The records of the Middle Temple show that on 14 February 1727 William Mildmay took out a right to a life interest on a set of chambers on the second floor of 3 Essex Court, Middle Temple. He paid a £2 partial payment for this right and on 21 November 1728 he completed the transaction with a further sum of £30.[42] Mildmay continued to live in these chambers for the next twenty years, as two of his letters written during this period were headed "Essex Court": the first to Lord Fitzwalter on 24 May 1738 and the second to Henry Pelham on 12 November 1747.[43]

It appears that by November 1728 Mildmay had begun the practice of law, at least as a law clerk; in his papers are the notes he made on 28 November 1728 for "A submission for the accounting of the estate of Sir John Scattergood, by William Mildmay."[44] Sir John Scattergood had been a London merchant trading to the Far East and Mildmay gave a detailed valuation of the goods Sir John had held in his warehouse, his shares in the East India Company, the money owed to him, and the annuities Sir John owed to his lenders. In the accompanying notes Mildmay explained that Sir John's widow was disputing the executor's valuation and this list was being made for the purposes of a future lawsuit.

Although Mildmay practiced as a lawyer in London during the 1730s and 1740s, there are only three other references to his legal work. The first of these records shows that on 29 October 1736 Richard Hoare, jeweler, banker, and later to be the lord mayor of London, employed William Mildmay as his solicitor in the sale to the Masters and Benchers of the Middle Temple of some property that Hoare owned in Devereux Court, Middle Temple.[45] The second refers to the briefing notes that he made in 1741 to assist the defense council for now Sir Richard Hoare and his brothers in their appeal to the Court of King's Bench against a judgment to pay damages to a Sir John Hartopp.[46] The last of Mildmay's legal documents is a statement of protest that he presented before the Middle Temple Masters and Benchers in 1745, and in which he argued the case for the barristers and students against some recent actions of the Bench.[47] Mildmay was the elected speaker of the Middle Temple Parliament, or the official proceedings of the Benchers, and in this long denunciation of the recent practices of the Masters and Benchers he vehemently objected to their attempts to limit the Parliamentary rights of the barristers and students.[48] From his argument it appears that the Middle Temple officers were illegally denying the junior members their right to hold a Vacation Parliament and to have the use of the Middle Temple Hall.[49] Among their other offences, Mildmay also charged that the Masters and Benchers had allowed the library to deteriorate, they had permitted "an interruption of strangers," and they had monopolized the allocation of Chambers.[50]

In August 1748, three years after Mildmay represented his fellow barristers to their society, he left England to spend eighteen months traveling in southern France in the company of his friends, Sir Richard and Lady Hoare.[51] On these travels Mildmay's interests were never those of a simple tourist. He had a considerable interest in the development of British trade and commerce, particularly in any advantages that could be gained from observing the economic practices of France, and he was always careful to record any military advantages that Britain might have gained from the War of the Austrian Succession. On his journey to and from the south of France he therefore sent Lord Fitzwalter detailed information on various French trading activities, and on how this recent war appeared to have affected the French economy.

Mildmay returned to London at the end of 1749 and in April 1750, he was appointed by George II to the Anglo-French Commission in Paris, where he remained for the next five years. Throughout these years he kept up a regular, lengthy correspondence with Lord Fitzwalter in which he not only gave his analysis of the fine points of his commission work, but also lively descriptions of many aspects of Parisian social, economic, and political life; all of it chosen to show Fitzwalter that although Mildmay was most conscientious in fulfilling his government mandate, at the same time he did not overlook the well-being of his elderly patron, or neglect Fitzwalter's need for informative diversion.[52] This series of letters to Lord Fitzwalter forms the basis of Mildmay's extensive information on mid-eighteenth–century France: its economy, its legal and policing system, its lending and investment policies, and the religious and constitutional debate taking place between the Louis XV and his Jansenist subjects.

It is now impossible to discover what William Mildmay looked like. He had his portrait painted in 1768—the year in which he was created a knight and became Sheriff of Essex—and had it hung in Moulsham Hall. He died in August 1771, and Moulsham Hall and the Chelmsford estates were inherited by his wife Anne, Lady Mildmay, who on her death in 1796 left them to her eldest niece, Jane. Jane Mildmay had married Sir Henry Paulet St. John in 1786,[53] but Sir Henry St. John took the added surname of Mildmay and he and his wife lived at Moulsham Hall for three months out of every year until the outbreak of the Napoleonic War. During the war a regiment of soldiers was billeted in the Moulsham Park, causing extensive damage to the grounds, and in February 1806 the Chelmsford *Chronicle* recorded the sale of the contents of Moulsham Hall, prior to its demolition, and two months later all the trees on the property were felled.[54] Sir William's portrait, together with his papers, was then taken to Jane St. John Mildmay's Hampshire estate of Dogmersfield Park, near Winchester, where it survived until its tragic destruction in a fire in 1987 that severely damaged the interior of the house.[55] Thankfully, the purchase by the William L. Clements Library of a major part of Sir William's papers in 1934, and the gift of the balance to the Essex Record Office in 1957 and 1970, prevented the only record of Sir William Mildmay's observations, interests, and diplomatic work from becoming yet another casualty of the fire.

# 2.
# THE ANGLO-FRENCH COMMISSION: SETTING THE STAGE

IN JANUARY 1750 WILLIAM MILDMAY was appointed to be one of the two British members serving on an Anglo-French government commission in Paris, and for the following five years he was involved in one of the most fateful assignments given to British diplomats in the mid-eighteenth century. The purpose of this commission was to ratify certain clauses in the 1748 peace treaty of Aix-la-Chapelle, and its failure to do so precipitated a war that would ultimately determine both the future magnitude of the British Empire and the subsequent history of North America. During the Seven Years' War (1756–63) that resulted from this diplomatic failure, the British were able to establish the basis of their empire in India and to conquer Canada. As a consequence of the expulsion of the French from the St. Lawrence valley, Acadia, and the land around the Ohio River, the colonial governments of New England and Virginia were not only able to extend their boundaries, but to enjoy a confident sense of territorial security that, within a decade, had created a desire for independence.

In 1756, Mildmay inherited a large estate and became an influential member of the Essex gentry, but if he had been asked what he considered to have been the most important period of his life he would surely have named his diplomatic activities in Paris between 1750 and 1755. It is certainly that part of his life for which he was best known by his contemporaries, for during these years as a junior diplomat he came to know and, in some cases, become friends with, British and French government ministers and diplomats, magistrates of the *Parlement* of Paris, and directors and merchant members of the French East India Company. As with most people who are participants in a significant turning point of history, when Mildmay began his work he was unaware both of the immensity of his assignment and of its potential consequences. When he arrived in Paris on 1 May 1750, he was pleased that he had an interesting, prestigious appointment and believed that a successful ratification agreement was possible within a year or two. He was subsequently to discover otherwise. In the journal he kept on each commission meeting, in the official reports that he sent to three subsequent secretaries of state for the Southern Department (the duke of Bedford, Lord Holdernesse, and Sir Thomas Robinson), and in his private letters to Lord Holdernesse and his relative, Lord Fitzwalter, Mildmay has given a new and valuable insight on the five-year life of this commission and some of the reasons for its eventual failure.[1]

On 30 April 1748 government ministers representing George II of Britain, Louis XV of France, and Van Helm, grand pensionary and political leader of the Dutch United Provinces, signed a preliminary agreement to the treaty of Aix-la-Chapelle, thus ending the War of the Austrian Succession (1740–1748).[2] The negotiations to conclude this treaty had taken months of intense diplomatic activity and in order to reach an initial settlement the governments of Britain, Holland, and France agreed to allow negotiations on the ratification of certain contentious and unresolved issues to take place at a later date. It was therefore proposed that Anglo-French negotiators would meet in St. Malo to settle the disputed boundaries of Nova Scotia and Acadia, to resolve the ownership of the islands of St. Lucia, Tobago, St. Vincent, and Dominica and to decide both the appropriate division of costs for the repatriation of military prisoners of war and the compensation due to those French and British ship owners whose vessels had been captured as prizes.[3]

Throughout 1749 the British representatives, Messrs. Allix and Hinde, held a series of meetings in St. Malo with the French nominee, M. Guillot, commissioner general of the Marine,[4] in an attempt to resolve the disputes on the identification and value of the prize ships, and to establish an agreed convention for such repatriation costs. Their efforts broke down, however, over disagreements about the directions and agenda given them in their respective government instructions. The British ministry, in concert with the Dutch government, maintained that the wording of the peace treaty only covered those prizes taken since the end of hostilities in 1748; the French government insisted—notwithstanding these treaty provisions—that ships that had been taken both before and during the war should also be included.

In order to reach an agreement on these prize ships it was also imperative for the negotiators to agree on boundary limits for the Channel and the North Sea, as the peace treaty had declared that they could only consider compensation for prizes taken in these waters. Here again there was equal dispute. Guillot stated that according to his instructions, the western limit of the Channel ended at a line drawn from the Scilly Islands to Ushant, on the extreme point of north west France; Allix and Hinde maintained that this boundary line was from Cape St. Vincent, in the south of Portugal, to the southern tip of Ireland, thus incorporating both the Bay of Biscay and the Irish Sea. So far as the North Sea was concerned, the French government set its outer limit at a line from the Naise Point, at the mouth of the Narvik fjord in northern Norway, to the east coast of the Shetland Islands, while the British stated that the "British Seas" extended around the Shetlands and the Orkneys and took in the entire coast of Scotland.[5]

Given these conflicting instructions, by the end of 1749 the French and the British governments had realized that nothing useful was likely to be achieved at St. Malo and it was thus decided to establish a formal commission in Paris which would be under the direct guidance of Lord Albemarle, British ambassador to France, and the French foreign minister, the marquis de Puysieulx.[6] The British commissioners received their official appointment in January 1750; they were given their "full powers," or their official diplomatic status as the king's representatives, in April; and the full commission held its first meeting on 31 August 1750.[7] The two British commissioners were William Shirley, governor of Massachusetts, and William Mildmay.[8] Acting for France were Roland-Michel Barrin, marquis de la Galissonière, who had been the governor of Canada during the War of the Austrian Succession, [9] and the marquis Etienne de Silhouette. Over the following five years the commissioners for both governments attempted— without success—to negotiate a settlement of the disputed clauses. The commission was dissolved in July 1755 and on 17 May 1756 Britain declared war on France.[10]

Several causes have been suggested for the outbreak of the Seven Years' War in 1756, a conflict that is also known in American history as the second of the French and Indian Wars and dated from 1754 to 1759 or 1760. The documents that I have used in this analysis of the work of commission and its diplomatic background tend to confirm the views of Guy Fregault, who described a complex series of interlocking difficulties, national suspicions, misunderstandings, and political blunders, not the least of which was the inability of the governments of Britain and France to understand and take account of the territorial and economic imperatives which were driving the actions of their respective colonial subjects.[11]

The prevailing view of the diplomatic work of the Anglo-French Commission of 1750–55 is that it was an ineffectual and largely irrelevant exercise, since by 1754 large-scale warfare for the possession of North America was inevitable and no settlement negotiated between the governments of Britain and France could have prevented the war's outbreak.[12] In his particular examination of the commission's history, Max Savelle went a great deal further; in his opinion, the entire five-year negotiation process was not only futile, but was designed by both sides to be a deliberate exercise in delay. He has argued that both governments intended that these negotiations would be nothing but a cynical diplomatic maneuver, calculated to buy time for a future war.[13] Although he did not quite go this far, in 1870 Samuel Drake stated: "although the treaty of Aix is a noted epoch, it proved to be nothing but a kind of armistice, a hasty and ill-digested affair, determining none of the points in dispute."[14]

These scholarly opinions on the purpose of this commission, based as they are on hindsight of its eventual failure, do not seem to have been the views held by British politicians at the time that it was established. On 21 March 1749 Horatio Walpole, who had been British ambassador to France before the War of the Austrian Succession, spoke in the House of Commons during the debate on supply that followed the King's Address at the opening of the parliamentary session. In his address, George II had mentioned the permanent benefits to be expected from the treaty of Aix-la-Chapelle, and Walpole stated: "I am under no apprehension that the peace of Aix-la-Chapelle will be disturbed. As long as the same principles and motives that brought it about subsist, the peace will subsist too."[15]

In a speech to the Commons on 16 November 1749, Henry Pelham, first lord of the treasury and government leader, replied to Lord Egremont's bitter criticism that the preliminary treaty had left important issues undecided, and he strongly defended the course his government had taken. Egremont, who was chief of the supporters of Frederick, Prince of Wales, and thus in opposition to Pelham's ministry, not only disputed the government's assertion that a permanent peace with France had now been achieved, but challenged Pelham's reliance on a negotiating commission to obtain for Britain what the treaty, apparently, had not. In his reply, Henry Pelham reminded Lord Egremont: "In all general treaties of peace, such disputes are left to be adjusted afterwards by commissaries (commissioners), yet no one ever imagined that peace was not completely re-established as soon as the general treaty is signed and ratified by all parties concerned."[16] From Pelham's words it seems that in late 1749, the British government expected a successful outcome to the negotiations that the commissioners were about to undertake in the summer of 1750.

Six weeks before the commission began its work, British diplomatic opinion on the importance of concluding successful negotiations with France was stated by Joseph Yorke, first secretary at the British embassy in Paris.[17] On 8 July 1750 Yorke wrote to the duke of Newcastle, secretary of state for the Northern Department, that France "is a neighbour one should not wantonly provoke, and [we] should always be guarding against this [kind of provocation] by every possible method. This, they do us the justice to think is our system."[18]

Despite its obvious importance to studies of European eighteenth-century diplomacy and to North American colonial history, there has been no recent scholarly investigation of the Anglo-French negotiations that took place in Paris during the first five years of the 1750s. This apparent lack of interest is unfortunate, for the scope and importance of William Mildmay's contribution to the commission was seriously minimized, and even distorted, by the two historians who last investigated its work: the first in 1940 and the other in 1961.[19] This book proposes quite a different interpretation, both of the history of this joint commission and of Mildmay's work on it. I will be discussing the conduct and the motives of the two British commissioners from evidence given in Mildmay's commission journal, his official reports, his correspondence, and from the content of letters written by members of the British cabinet and by British diplomats.

The most detailed examination of the commission was made by Max Savelle in 1940, and for almost sixty years Savelle's book, *The Diplomatic History of the Canadian Boundary*, has remained the definitive authority on this subject. In 1967, Savelle wrote *The Origins of American Diplomacy* as a general survey of American diplomatic history from the sixteenth to the eighteenth century,[20] but in Chapter XVIII, which he calls "The Cold War of 1748–1755," Savelle repeats the judgments and conclusions on the commission that he had made twenty-seven years earlier, despite the new evidence that had become available during these intervening years and to which he makes no reference.[21] *The Diplomatic History of the Canadian Boundary* is still being cited by historians who have an interest in eighteenth-century European and North American diplomacy and who use its information and opinions as their major, and in some cases their only, source for the activities of the commission, but without any critical reappraisal of its documentary evidence.[22]

The first study of the work of this commission was made in 1936 by Theodore Pease, who used the State Papers exclusively as the source of his documents and who was, apparently, unaware of further extensive material on the commission in the Leeds and the Newcastle Papers in the British Library.[23] When Pease was carrying out his research in 1935 and 1936, the Leeds and Newcastle Papers were the only other sources of evidence available to him, the William L. Clements Library at Ann Arbor had not yet fully catalogued the part of William Mildmay's documents that they bought in 1934, and the first of the collection of Mildmay's papers that are now in the Essex Record Office at Chelmsford would not arrive there until 1955 (to be followed by a further group in 1970).[24]

Savelle worked with the Mildmay Papers in the William L. Clements Library at Ann Arbor, but his many citations from this collection present a problem. In 1939, the William L. Clements Library had not yet catalogued this collection into its present seven volumes; after they were acquired in 1934, all of the Mildmay Papers were initially placed into four volumes. Even in their present seven-volume form, these documents are still not foliated but are only bound in date order, and since Savelle rarely included any identifying dates for his cited letters and memoranda, it is very difficult to find any of these documents from his given reference to the names of the four original categories into which the documents were placed.

It is understandable that when Savelle worked on this subject in 1939 and 1940, the outbreak of the Second World War in Europe made it impossible for him to visit London to investigate other important areas of documentary research in the British Library, namely the collection of letters on the work of the commission by Lord Holdernesse, Lord Albemarle, the duke of Bedford, the duke of Newcastle, Joseph Yorke, Sir Thomas Robinson, and William Mildmay, which are in the Leeds and Newcastle Papers.

The unfortunate chain of omissions in the manuscript evidence that began with the work of Theodore Pease in 1936, and was followed by that of Max

Savelle in 1940, makes a study of this new evidence vital to a reexamination of the work of the Anglo-French Commission from 1750 to 1755. In this reassessment, I will be discussing what I find to be errors of fact in Savelle's report of the commission's five-year history, my disagreements with some of the conclusions that Savelle drew from his research, and the even greater errors of supposition, unsupported by any cited evidence, in the report on the commission by John Schutz in his biography of William Shirley.[25]

John Schutz wrote the most recent biography of William Shirley in 1961, and in his analysis of Shirley's commission work he gave his perception of the relationship Mildmay had with Shirley over the two years during which they were colleagues. In this analysis, for which Schutz cited Savelle as his only evidentiary source on the commission and its participants, he described Mildmay as "a middle aged barrister . . . a cousin of the Earl of Fitzwalter. Mildmay was a poor relation who had won the Earl's patronage by cultivating tastes of the theatre, the opera, the punch bowl and the chase. He was clever, intemperate and abusive."[26] Schutz's evidence for all of this is unclear, especially as Savelle mentioned nothing in his book about Mildmay's alleged bad temper, his immoderate drinking habits, or his sycophantic pandering to Fitzwalter's tastes, nor did he make the mistake of stating that Lord Fitzwalter was Mildmay's cousin.

It should be noted that a major intent of Savelle's history of this commission, and of Schutz's biography of Shirley, appears to be to establish William Shirley, the governor of Massachusetts, as its prime mover on the British side; in order to emphasize his view of Shirley's importance, Savelle seriously diminished Mildmay's contribution as a commissioner. His detailed reports of each of the commission meetings ended abruptly with May 1752, the point at which Shirley was dismissed from the post of senior British commissioner and was replaced by William Mildmay, the new negotiation leader. Savelle did not mention that this change of personnel had taken place, however, and he covered all the complicated negotiations that took place between May 1752 and May 1755 in the final page and a half of his chapter on the commission's history.[27] To this misreading of William Mildmay's influence as a commissioner by Savelle, Schutz added his own mistaken description of William Mildmay as unpleasant and acerbic.

Independent contemporary evidence certainly does not support Savelle and Schutz's estimation of Mildmay's abilities, his character, or of his value to the commission. In September 1751 Joseph Yorke, as first secretary, was acting as the British ambassador during the temporary absence of Lord Albemarle. In a cordial letter that Yorke wrote to Mildmay, on 22 September 1751, he asked whether Mildmay, who was at that time in Essex, would be returning to Paris with the diplomatic instructions that Yorke needed to conduct his discussions with the French court. After talking about his hopes for a successful outcome of the negotiations, Yorke told Mildmay: "I have, besides the National Interest and the Peace of Europe, another reason for wishing a speedy and Honourable end to these affairs which is wholly personal to yourself for, without flattering your modesty, I know nobody who has the welfare of the Public more at heart than you have, nor would go further to serve it than you would."[28]

Even after Joseph Yorke became the British ambassador at The Hague, his friendship with Mildmay continued. By February 1756 the commission had been disbanded for over seven months, but on 3 February 1756 Yorke wrote Mildmay a most complimentary letter of thanks for some copies of the published version of a memorial that Mildmay had recently written, and had sent to The Hague. In this treatise Mildmay had supplied many historical proofs of the right of George II to the territories in North America claimed by Britain, and had also given a long and detailed account of the history of the commission that could be used by the British government to justify the breakdown of negotiations. Yorke told Mildmay that he had already felt the need for such a document in his conversations with the Dutch government, and "what you have given us [in this memorial] is done in a masterly way. . . . I shall make good use of your work and in some shape or otherwise give it to the Foreign Worlds (distribute it to the European Courts)."[29]

This contemporary evidence demonstrates the obvious mistake that is made by ignoring the value of Mildmay's work to the commission; however, the effect of this error is still somewhat minor. Far more serious for future studies of mid-eighteenth century diplomacy is Savelle's judgment on the devious intent of all of the commission participants: French and British government ministers, diplomats, and commissioners. The result of this commission's failure to achieve its objective became so far-reaching, both for the future history of Britain and of North America, that a reexamination of its history is essential in the light of evidence that appears to refute Savelle's view of the Anglo-French Commission of 1750–55 as nothing but a futile diplomatic exercise: one that was designed to fail, staffed by cynical men, and used simply as a device to prepare for war.

I have designed this reassessment largely as a chronological narrative in order that the subtle ebbs and flows in the diplomatic efforts—changing from year to year in response to each shift of the political and military climate—can be kept as clear and understandable as they were to Mildmay and his diplomatic colleagues. This narrative method also presents the opinions of the participants on the basis of what they could or, conversely, could not have known on the day on which they wrote their letters. It appears to me that this discipline on the flow of information, based on a strict timeline, is essential in order to avoid any distortion caused by my own hindsight knowledge of the outcome of this five-year negotiation.

# 3.
# MILITARY, TRADE, AND POLITICAL INTELLIGENCE

❀

IN EARLY JANUARY OF 1750, William Shirley and William Mildmay discovered that they were to become diplomatic colleagues in Paris; other than their English birth and their legal training, however, Shirley and Mildmay had little in common. Shirley was atypical of eighteenth-century British governors who were sent out from Whitehall to administer a colony since he himself was an immigrant to British North America. In 1731, he had brought his family to Boston. He initially worked as a government lawyer, and by 1750, having lived there for nineteen years, he identified completely with the colonists of Massachusetts and saw himself as a representative of their interests. When Shirley arrived in Paris in August 1750 he was visiting France for the first time, but Mildmay already had a considerable first-hand knowledge of France and the French. Before becoming a commissioner, Mildmay had spent just over a year in France (from August 1748 to September 1749). From the content of the letters that he sent to his relative, Lord Fitzwalter, between 1748 and 1755, it is obvious that he had a considerable interest in and understanding of the French economy and society, had many French friends, and spoke the language fluently.[1]

In any competition to become a negotiating commissioner, William Shirley had several advantages over William Mildmay's claim. Shirley already held a prominent administrative position as the British governor of Massachusetts, with many years of experience and a first-hand knowledge both of the contested Acadian terrain and of the crucial nature of any military or territorial negotiated decisions. Moreover, he was a military hero: he was responsible for organizing and carrying out the successful campaign against the French fort of Louisbourg, taken in 1745, and, in consequence, he was seen as a trustworthy spokesperson by his fellow colonists in Massachusetts and New York. Against these formidable talents, William Mildmay could count on the strong patronage of his relative, Lord Fitzwalter, treasurer to the royal household, and, even more crucial, his ability to mobilize the "interest" and support of Lord Holderness, British ambassador to The Hague, who was Fitzwalter's son-in law and Mildmay's long-time friend. Such patronage could only go so far, however, and it was up to Mildmay to demonstrate that he had other useful talents that could offset the undeniable abilities of William Shirley.

Mildmay's principal advantage was his long-term enthusiasm and considerable talent for collecting detailed, accurate information, both economic and political, together with the ability to precisely analyze his data and an innate capacity to appreciate the future economic and military value of his material. He also moved easily in many levels of French society, and over the years he had built up a wide circle of well-placed friends from whom he could collect his information. Unlike Shirley, whose letters reveal little enthusiasm for anything outside his commission work, diplomacy was certainly not Mildmay's only interest, and in his avid collection of information he assembled data on a considerable variety of subjects. By 1750, some intelligent and timely reports that he had submitted to Lord Holdernesse and, in particular, another economic and political commentary sent to Henry Pelham in 1748, seem to have gone a long way to persuade the duke of Bedford to recommend William Mildmay to George II, albeit as the junior commissioner under William Shirley's direction.

Mildmay's collection of information was wide ranging, as his data covered the details and explanations of the figures given for the French import and export trade, the effect of the recent instructions and regulations issued by the French government to its merchants, the total revenue collected by the Crown from the provinces in the midi, the immediate prospect for the French grain harvest, the present state of the French marine dockyards, and the numbers and size of vessels in the French fishing fleets. In this gathering of data, Mildmay had two specific and overriding purposes: the promotion of the British export trade and the collection of military intelligence for the British government.

From August 1748 to November 1749, Mildmay lived in the provinces of Languedoc and Provence, where he examined their methods of government, their internal and external trading patterns, and the economic distress that British military action had inflicted on them during the recently concluded

War of the Austrian Succession (1741–48). This type of investigation was typical of all his later efforts; he considered that his observations had considerable value to the British government, both as military intelligence for use in a future war and as information on the state and vulnerabilities of the French economy, knowledge of which he considered vital for the successful development of the British export trade.

The sole use that contemporary scholars have made of Mildmay's information on France comes from his book *The Police of France*, but this description of the system used by the French government to maintain law and order in the mid-eighteenth century was only the second of four books that he published in the late 1750s and early 1760s. He published a rebuttal to the claims the French government was making to territory in Acadia in 1756, a review of the French police system in 1763, an analysis of the political economy of southern France in 1764, and in 1763 he published a detailed comparison of the British export trade with the trading practices of other countries and suggested improvements based on these practices.[2]

Mildmay stated his objectives clearly in the book that he wrote both before and during the Seven Years' War, but did not publish until after the 1762 Peace of Paris. In *An Account of the Southern Maritime Provinces of France*, he said he hoped his information would assist the British government in producing such economic distress in France that the French government would sue for a peace that would be ". . . advantageous to the landed and trading interests of Great Britain," since "to know the weak side of our enemy, or on what side the power of our enemy might be weakened, are equally very great advantages."[3] All his books were issued after he returned to England in 1755, but although his 1756 analysis of the Canadian boundary disputes was timely, and his detailed description of the French system of police in 1763 was still important knowledge for the London authorities, by 1764 the conclusion of the Seven Years' War had somewhat reduced the usefulness of his military data on southern France.

Mildmay transmitted the information he felt the British government should know immediately in his letters and memoranda, and at the same time he also demonstrated how valuable he could be to the government as a diplomatic negotiator. His insight into the Byzantine political activities of the French court and its ministries was based on his contacts with a large circle of influential friends, and since Mildmay was sending this data both to a British government minister and to an official in the royal household, he attempted to make sure that his reports were as accurate and up to date as possible. During his five-year residence in Paris, he gained his political intelligence from discussions with his many friends among the magistrates in the *Parlements* of Paris and Aix-en Provence, from his acquaintance with one of the *intendants* of finance and later councilor of state, Daniel-Charles Trudaine, and from his conversations in the Paris salons. His economic information came from his own observations on his travels to and from Aix-en-Provence and round the *île de France*, from senior members of the French East India Company, from French bankers, financiers, and merchants, from contacts he had at the naval ports of Brest, Toulon, and Rochefort, and from his journeys in the districts of Brie and Champagne. He also collected unofficial broadsheets and the official publications of the *Parlement* of Paris and the *Conseil d'Etat*, and sent these to Lord Holdernesse and Lord Fitzwalter.[4]

Part of the important work of all British diplomatic staff abroad was to collect specific information that could be of benefit to the government, and when Mildmay was appointed a royal commissioner he became an official member of the British embassy staff in Paris.[5] Accordingly, he responded to requests for such information with enthusiasm and sent lengthy reports to Lord Holdernesse on subjects in which Holdernesse had expressed an interest. Mildmay was not paid to do this work, however, nor was he reimbursed for any collection expenses. In a letter to Lord Fitzwalter, on 22 March 1752, Mildmay asked him to discover from Lord Holdernesse whether his expenses for the information he obtained on the French police system could be paid from the embassy "Secret Service" fund. On 3 May 1752, Mildmay acknowledged Fitzwalter's reply that although Holdernesse had asked for the information, he had refused to pay this expense money, and in the rest of his correspondence with Fitzwalter Mildmay did not make this kind of request again.[6] On 14 February 1753, Mildmay gave Fitzwalter some details about how he spent his commission salary, and in emphasizing how frugally he lived in Paris, he remarked: "My only extravagance, and it is a liberality which I am proud of, consists in several sums of money I have employed out of my private purse, for intelligence concerning the commercial state of this Kingdom, all of which . . . [information] I esteem as a treasure lying by me, in order to be able to lay it before your Lordship on my return."[7]

Mildmay's interest in the promotion of the British export trade did not begin with his travels in France. Ten years earlier, on 24 May 1738, he wrote

a letter to Lord Fitzwalter, who had just left his position of chief commissioner at the Board of Trade and had then been appointed treasurer to the
royal household.[8] Mildmay said the letter's purpose was to send Fitzwalter an
enclosed document in which he had examined the laws and policies that governed the British export trade, and he said this material was the outcome of a
study of "all the laws relating to this subject" on which he had been working
for some time. His papers do not contain a copy of his 1738 treatise to Lord
Fitzwalter on the British trade laws, but his continuing interest in the subject
led him, in 1746, to write another on "Reasons for admitting the Importation
of Cattle from Ireland upon account of the present distemper of the Horned
Cattle in England."[9] In the first treatise he discussed the benefits of employ-
ing more farm workers, of encouraging the growth of foreign trade, and of
increasing the circulation of money and credit. In the second, he gave the reasons why he felt that the statute that banned the import of cattle from Ireland,
first enacted in the reign of Charles II, had long passed its usefulness.

From two further documents in his papers it appears that in August 1748
Mildmay had already begun to consider the possible economic problems that
might negatively affect British trade by the end of the War of the Austrian
Succession. The preliminary agreement to the peace treaty of
Aix-la-Chapelle had been signed four months earlier, in April 1748, and he
was concerned about its effects on the British export market because of
renewed competition from French and Italian merchants. He kept his copies
of two memoranda on this subject that he sent from his chambers in the
Middle Temple: the first written on 3 August 1748 to Lord Fitzwalter, and a
second to Henry Pelham, first lord of the treasury and a government leader.
It seems that these documents might subsequently have had a considerable
effect on Mildmay's future, for Pelham may have been impressed by William
Mildmay's ability to anticipate the future economic trends and peacetime
influences on British trade.

In both memoranda he proposed that a government agent should be sent
to France and Italy as soon as possible to collect immediate information on
foreign trade. He said he feared that once peace was declared, both counties
would attempt to recapture the markets they had lost to the British, and that
the French would: "at the same time, enter into new measures to rectify
those defects, particularly with regard to their Marine, in which they have
discovered the ill consequences of their former neglect."[10] In his document
to Pelham, headed "A Memorial showing the Advantages that may be

obtained by sending an agent at this juncture into France and Italy to discover the present state of their Trade and Commerce. Most humbly submitted by William Mildmay to the Right Honourable Henry Pelham Esq.,"[11] he
emphasized his thought that British merchants and the British government
lacked accurate and immediate information about the trade and commerce of
France and Italy. This ignorance, he wrote, covered both their trading practices and any changes that France, in particular, was making in her ship
design and in her government decisions to open up new markets.

In contrast to the long-standing French government policies of establishing councils of commerce in their major cities to coordinate the flow of
information, and of appointing royal *intendants* of commerce to receive trading propositions and encourage commercial innovations from entrepreneurs, Mildmay pointed out to Pelham that those British trading policies
designed to be countermeasures to the French competition often were made
on entirely speculative information. He thus proposed that the British
should consider appointing "trade agents," whose job would be to travel
throughout France, but especially to the major ports, collecting information
on the state of the crops, the labor costs, and the prospects for any new products that might be under development in that district."[12]

As a final note, Mildmay also suggested that such a trade agent could, at
the same time, act as a "commissary" (commissioner), with whichever ministry Pelham's government appointed to negotiate a commercial or other,
related kind of treaty, but he cautioned: "As this service must be performed
with great exactness (competence in observation) and secrecy (because such
an activity would be regarded as spying), so it will be attended with experience and Hazard." He therefore advised: "so that . . . [the] person employed
in it may be supported in the one (the collection of information) and protected against the other (arrest by the authorities as a spy)," it should be an
official post and covered "by a suitable appointment and His Majesty's
Commission (which would carry diplomatic immunity)."[13] Mildmay's
papers do not contain any replies to this proposal, but at the end of August
1748 he traveled to the south of France where he collected and recorded any
trade and commercial information that he felt would be useful for the government to know. In the spring of 1750, he was appointed a British commissioner in Paris, where, over the following five years, he spent a great deal of
his time collecting the kind of data that he had proposed in his 1748 memorial to Henry Pelham.

Central to a precise knowledge of the true state of the French economy was accurate information on the revenue of the French Crown. A typical example of Mildmay's attempts to secure such information is a ten-page document he entitled "An Account of the Revenue of France, consisting of the Domaine, Aydes, Gabelles, as they are called, extracted from the Accounts of Monsieur Forceville (Jacques Forceville), one of the Forty Farmers General."[14] Mildmay stated that the revenue calculations of this general farm account were taken: "from 1738, the year in which it was let."[15] From this data, Mildmay gave a tabulated list of the various sums raised from licenses for the export of tobacco, wines, and other commodities by the Farmers General throughout the *généralités* of France.

In the same collection of information, he wrote a two-page analysis of the commodity prices in Languedoc in 1748, another on the state of the French army in 1748 (with details of the numbers of men in the "regiments of Foot," the cavalry, the dragoons, the royal grenadiers and the *milice* [militia]), a list of the provincial debts "since 1740, for corn," and information on the extent of the French fishery (the numbers of ships and men who were engaged in the domestic "Mud Fishery," or coastal fishing, and those in the fishing fleets sent to Cape Breton, Labrador, and the Gaspé each year from Normandy, Brittany, and the ports of Bayonne and La Rochelle). He also gave detailed estimates on sugar and coffee exports from various French colonies in the West Indies, together with a comparison of similar exports from the British West Indies. In a letter that Mildmay sent to Lord Holdernesse from Paris on 3 August 1751, he asked whether he should send this information on to Holdernesse, but there is no existing record of a reply to this query.[16]

Mildmay also bought books and pamphlets in Paris that provided the background to his information, and sent these over to Lord Fitzwalter and Lord Holdernesse. On 23 February 1752, he sent to Fitzwalter: "a few copies of the *Gazette à la Main* (a handwritten, unauthorized and anonymous broadsheet) which is brought to me twice a week, containing articles of secret news," and said that if Lord Holdernesse indicated he was interested in this bi-weekly pamphlet, he could arrange to obtain further editions.[17] He also sent over books that had been requested by both Fitzwalter and Holdernesse: memoirs of the Abbé de Montgon to Fitzwalter, and the letters of Madame de Maintenon to Holdernesse.[18] At the beginning of 1753, Holdernesse also received his copy of: "Monsieur d'Anville's map of the

Coasts of Coromandel, which having received its sanction from the . . . [French] East India Company, was yesterday (1 January 1753) presented to the King."[19] There were some books and pamphlets available in Paris that were officially banned, but the French government censors would sometimes allow a very limited edition to be sold so long as the sale was restricted and did not appear to cause an open scandal.[20] Mildmay gives an example of his purchase of such a book when he told Lord Fitzwalter that he had managed to obtain for him a copy of Voltaire's *l'Histoire Universelle:* "lately printed here by stealth and sold as a prohibited book, consequently bought and perused with great eagerness."[21] Presumably Mildmay used the safety of the British embassy's messenger service to carry Voltaire's *l'Histoire Universelle* to Lord Fitzwalter.

Mildmay arrived in France in the company of his friends, Sir Richard and Lady Hoare. Their destination was Aix-en-Provence, as Sir Richard had been advised to take the cure at that spa for his health. They reached Aix on 6 October 1748, remaining there over the winter while Sir Richard's health slowly improved.[22] This visit was not Mildmay's first to the south, however, and the real value of his military and trade information lay in the comparisons he was able to make between its prewar and its postwar economy. In a letter he wrote from Aix-en-Provence on 10 November 1748 he said that: "having traveled through this Province (Provence) before the commencement of this War, I was struck by the alterations (to its economy)."[23] In the opening paragraph, Mildmay said he had been told by Sir Richard that since the person to whom Mildmay was writing wanted to receive some information on conditions in the southern ports, he would shortly be visiting Marseille and Toulon in order to report on their state: "as soon as I can find an opportunity of sending a letter, as I do this, by private hand."[24] The receiver of his information, however, cannot be identified for certain. Unfortunately, this 10 November 1748 letter is the only one in which Mildmay did not follow his usual practice of writing the name of his correspondent at the bottom of each page. As the opening address is to "Sir" it could not have been intended either for Lord Fitzwalter or Lord Holdernesse, both of whom Mildmay never failed to address as "My Lord," but the contents of the letter gives no clue as to whom this "Sir" might be. It is possible that Mildmay was now sending to Henry Pelham the kind of information he had proposed in his memorial in August, but in the wording of the letter there is no direct evidence that Pelham was its recipient.

Mildmay made his aim very clear, however, when he told his unnamed cor-respondent: "It being uncertain some time ago how far, and in what parts, this Kingdom had been reduced to the want of men and provisions by the late War, I . . . [have] made that point the chief object of my enquiries."[25]

Typical of this kind of intelligence is his information on Lyon, through which he passed on his way to the south. He made a point of studying any damaging effects that the war had on its principle industry—the manufac-ture of various fabrics made from silk—and he reported that while its domestic production did not seem to have been affected, its oversees market had indeed been influenced. Since Lyon silk was a luxury product, with a large and profitable export trade, it was particularly vulnerable to wartime interruptions. Mildmay recounted that on his visit to the factories, the silk manufacturers had told him their trade with Spain had been severely reduced from the effect of the British blockade of Cadiz during the War of the Austrian Succession.[26] Cadiz was a major port for the export of goods to Spain's West Indian and American colonies and, as a consequence of this British blockade, he said he had been told that spinners on the Lyon silk looms who had been: "employed for many years before in working on gold and silver brocade to be sent by way of Cadiz to the Spanish West Indies," had also been discharged. He therefore suggested that if Britain wanted to damage the French export economy during a future war she should attempt: "an interruption to Spanish commerce . . . [as] although the French are not (or might not be) engaged in the quarrel, this . . . [interruption] will never-theless greatly affect their trade and manufactured trade."[27]

The ability to produce such an artificial depression of an important French industry was the kind of information that Mildmay considered would be most valuable to the British government, since any sustained interruption to the silk trade of Lyon would have a particularly bad effect not only on the town, but on the considerable revenue the French government gained from its economy. Lyon was a large and prosperous city, with a population of approximately 126,000, and in the mid-eighteenth century was unique among French towns in having a heavy concentration of employment in one industry. Over 60 percent of its workers worked in the manufacture of items made of silk: woven fabric, hats, stockings, embroidery, lace, and silver and gold braid.[28]

Once he reached Aix-en-Provence, Mildmay began his regular reports on the comparison between the economic conditions he had found in 1740 and

those of 1748. The provinces of Languedoc and Provence had experienced
serious wartime economic and social problems as a result of the British
blockade of the port of Marseille, which had cut off the supply of wheat from
North Africa on which these southern provinces depended for nine out of
every twelve months each year. By the autumn of 1748, Mildmay reported
that this shortage, made worse by the recent bad harvest, had caused the
price of wheat to double from its 1740 level.[29] There had been a widespread
dearth of grain across the south during the winter of 1747–48, and one of
Mildmay's interesting, and hitherto unknown pieces of information concerned the grain supply at Arles.

Arles was an important military center on the lower Rhone. In order to
ensure a grain supply to his troops in the large military barracks outside the
walls, Louis XV had ordered the city to build and stock a grain magazine at
the barracks for the exclusive use of his army. As a result of a poor harvest,
and compounded by the effects of the blockade, in the fall of 1747 there was
an acute shortage of bread grains (wheat, barley, and rye) in the city of
Arles, and during the winter of 1747–48 the Arles magistrates had appealed
to the ministry of war to have a portion of this military stock released to
their starving citizens. Mildmay said that the king's commissioners had
reported to him that if this were done, his troops would starve, and he commented: "this was a terrible dilemma for the King to be driven to, but he
cleared himself of it by ordering his Ministers, just at that crisis of time, to
sign the preliminaries of peace, which were accordingly signed at Aix-la-
Chapelle on 30 April 1748." Here, Mildmay was stating his firm belief, subsequently repeated, that the prospect of social disorder in southern France
during this winter was the direct incentive that brought the French government to the peace negotiation in 1747–48. He pointed out that such military
activity could produce the same result in any future war: "as the news of
peace was very welcome in these parts . . . [and] I was assured by several
people of different ranks of life that had it been postponed a month longer,
there would have been a serious danger of insurrection in all their maritime
provinces."[30]

Mildmay was alert to the consequences that a rise in the price of basic
foodstuffs had on the local living standards. He reported that in 1740, the
consuls of Marseille had concluded with the meat suppliers a fixed-price
contract for beef and mutton at the city markets, to run for the next six years.
By the spring of 1744, however, the passage of French and Spanish troops

across the midi to meet a British and Piedmontese invasion on the Savoy border had doubled the price that had to be paid by the suppliers to the farmers, resulting not only in the loss of all their anticipated profits, but putting them in considerable debt. To give a clear idea of the extent of the economic suffering experienced in the south during the 1740s, Mildmay gave a table showing the comparative breakdown in food prices between 1740 and 1749, and this table showed that the price of wheat, oats, and rye had doubled during these years.[31] He was happy to report that even the relief of this distress by British grain traders had its useful economic aspects. Somewhat cynically, he remarked that Britain had secured a double advantage: "first as we caused the distress, next as we relieved it, being happily enabled to supply the want on the conclusion of peace, which we had, ourselves, occasioned during the war."[32]

From a letter that Mildmay wrote to Lord Fitzwalter in the spring of 1748, it appears that some of the after effects of these blockades might not be entirely beneficial to the British government. The dramatic price increase had given British corn factors, or middlemen suppliers, the chance to make considerable profits by sending their grain to the south of France. In a letter to Lord Fitzwalter from Aix, on 1 January 1749, Mildmay said that English merchants now found it profitable to dispatch grain ships to Marseille, and a group of English ships had arrived at that port. It appears that these merchants were not content take their large profits simply from the sale of grain, however, and Mildmay asked Fitzwalter to pass along a packet of information enclosed with his letter: "to the person to whom it is addressed (presumably the previous, unnamed recipient)."[33] He informed his Lordship that some of the ship owners in this English fleet had sold not only the cargo, but their ships as well,[34] and they had then discharged their English crews at Marseille with, in some cases, less than one hour's notice and without the legally required two months compensation pay. He said this action had resulted in many English seamen: "being set adrift in a foreign country, and unable to get a passage by sea from Marseilles (*sic*), . . . [they] have procured passes from the Commandant of the town to go by land to other ports." As some of these British sailors had now arrived in Aix and were threatening to enlist in the French navy if they could not get compensation pay, he therefore asked Fitzwalter to bring this scandal to the attention of those "who have the superintending of His Majesty's navy," so that British ship owners would be forced to pay off their crews according to law.[35]

When Mildmay wrote a part of his book on the maritime provinces in the early 1750s there was still an uneasy peace between Britain and France, but he recommended that in any future war the British government should consider not only blockading the port of Marseille, but also intercepting any ships coming from the "Western Sugar Islands of America." To police this activity he suggested extending the naval embargo to cover the straights of Gibraltar, and he also pointed out that Marseille was the base for the extremely profitable "Levant trade" in the eastern Mediterranean. As the ports of Messina, Naples, and Genoa were used by the Levant fleets as staging points in their voyages to Marseille, he suggested the blockading of these ports as well. By the time he came to edit the finished manuscript, Britain was in the midst of the Seven Years' War and he therefore added a paragraph on the strategic importance of the capital of Minorca, Port Mahon, which had been captured by the French in 1756. He pointed out that this port could be used not only as a victualing base for the British fleet, but ships sent out from there could divide the naval forces of Spain and France and prevent troops from either country being transported to Italy by sea. He pleaded: "let us not conclude this war without retaking [Port Mahon], or having it restored upon the restoration of peace."[36]

Before leaving the south, Mildmay made the visits to Marseille and Toulon that he had promised his correspondent in 1748. His observations of these two ports were made from the point of view of the commander of a potential invasion force. He reported that he believed Marseille would not be too difficult to capture since all its defenses were facing the sea, leaving its landward side virtually unprotected. He suggested that an invasion force could be put ashore in the nearby "bays" (the *calanques* around Cassis), and by marching through the narrow defiles in the coastal mountains it could make a successful attack on Marseille from the rear.

Toulon, on the other hand, was a very different matter. This main base for the French Mediterranean fleet was almost impossible to invade from the sea: "both on account of its natural strength and its artificial fortifications." Moreover, he reported, the only access to the city was by two narrow roads, one from Nice and the other from Marseille, which had been cut through steep mountain passes and were thus ideal sites for an ambush. He described the massive walls that surrounded the port, pierced by only two, heavily fortified gates, and he noted that a secondary bastion had been built on the eastward side of the port, with the land between it and the walls cleared to provide an unobstructed line of fire "for the space of half a mile." Nevertheless, and despite the apparent impregnability of Toulon, Mildmay was resourceful and he obtained a detailed and elegantly engraved map of "the Dockyard, Bason (sic) and Harbour of Toulon," which he subsequently published in the final section of *An Account of the Southern Maritime Provinces.*[37]

Mildmay returned to England on 14 September 1749. His appointment to the Anglo-French Commission was made in April 1750 and on 1 May 1750 he arrived in Paris, where he continued his observations on the French economy.[38] This task was certainly safer than it had been while he was a private traveler, for as a commissioner he now had the protection of diplomatic immunity and no longer had to fear the "hazard" of being arrested as a spy, which he had expressed to Henry Pelham in 1748. The transmission of his information was also easier because he no longer had to rely on the services of other returning English travelers to carry his letters, but was able to use the royal messenger service at the embassy. On the other hand, Mildmay could now expect his activities to be more closely watched, for as a British diplomat he would be seen by the French government as someone with an official responsibility to collect whatever sensitive information the British ministers might find useful on any aspect of French society.

Mildmay's diplomatic status allowed him to gain entry to a level of Parisian society where he could acquire information on a wide variety of both economical and political subjects, and in his letters to Lord Fitzwalter he made several references to the methods he used to do so. As a diplomat Mildmay was expected to help the embassy staff in the entertainment of prominent English visitors to Paris, such as David Garrick,[39] but he also wined and dined his own French friends on a regular basis. On 19 December Mildmay told Fitzwalter that since his arrival in May, he had spent a substantial part of his expense allowance on giving frequent dinner parties, where the high quality of the food and the table decorations had been commented upon most favorably.[40] In a letter on 7 June 1752 he complained about the excessive visiting and entertaining he had to undertake for the many English visitors who were in Paris that summer, "as it is a disagreeable circumstance to me, in my publick character, to be obliged to visit so many new acquaintances that must be dropped as soon as they go away. If I do not visit them it is construed as a neglect of my countrymen." He did not resent the time he spent visiting his French acquaintances, however, for "The French I go to see to improve myself with observations as may be hereafter useful."[41]

The Paris embassy was regarded by the British government as one of the most important European diplomatic postings, both for the ambassador's ability to influence French foreign policy on behalf of the British king and for the political and economic information that he and his staff could acquire at the French court. All diplomats and embassy staff sent to the French capital were expected be sophisticated and genial with their hosts and to expand their contacts not only by their own entertainments, but also in their ability to move easily in upper French society.[42] At the dinners and soirées that Mildmay gave, and attended, he met many prominent people. One of his important contacts at the French court was Daniel-Charles Trudaine (1703–69), who was appointed a controller of finance in the Department of the Controller General, M. de Machault, in November 1751. Trudaine subsequently became an *intendant* of finance in June 1752, and was named a minister of state in April 1754.[43]

Mildmay appears to have met Trudaine sometime in 1751, for on 15 December 1751, one month after Trudaine had become a controller of finance, Mildmay mentioned to Lord Fitzwalter that "Monsr. Trudaine, an acquaintance of mine and who being at present charged with the details of *Ponts* and *Chaussées* (the royal administration of bridges and roads)" had asked Mildmay to get him a copy of "the little book of Ogilby on Roads, which your Lordship has, with the Counties distinct and Coloured."[44] By the beginning of the following year Mildmay had established himself as an even more useful friend to Daniel-Charles Trudaine. In January 1752 he transmitted a request to Lord Holdernesse from Trudaine that one of the latter's relatives in London might be introduced to George II, and on 2 February 1752 Mildmay reported Trudaine's thanks to Holdernesse "for the honour you have done him" in this respect.[45] On 6 March 1754, Mildmay announced to Lord Fitzwalter that his useful acquaintance "Monsr. Trudaine . . . will soon be one of the Ministers of State"[46] and he asked Fitzwalter to be kind enough to send over some Scotch fir seeds that Trudaine had asked Mildmay to obtain for him.[47]

Mildmay also had contacts within the directorate of the French East India Company. On 17 January 1753 he gave Lord Fitzwalter information on the recent financial distress caused to "the nabobs" of this company by the defeat and death of the Indian Carnatic prince who had ruled the territory around their trading factory at Pondicherry."[48] On 11 April 1753, he also warned Fitzwalter that the French East India Company was trying to acquire secret information at the highest level. He reported that a recent conversation he had with "one, who belonging to the East India company established here," had told him that the senior director of the company, M. Duvalear, was, ostensibly, on his way to London for a private visit, but Mildmay said his informant had admitted that Duvalear had actually come to find out intelligence about the state of the British East India Company.[49] Mildmay's information about the affairs of the *Parlement* of Paris was equally well informed and had been received first hand. From 1751 to 1755 he kept Lord Fitzwalter informed, on a regular basis, about the contents of the discussions and of the decisions taken by the various Chambers of the *Parlement*, and Mildmay said that the source of the verbatim details in his reports was one of the lawyer magistrates of that body.[50]

From the point of view of the British government, perhaps Mildmay's most useful contacts were the sources he had in the important military ports of the French Marine at Toulon, Rochefort, and Brest. On 31 August 1752, Mildmay replied to a letter from Lord Holdernesse in which he had been asked to assist a Mr. Boyd, whom Holdernesse and Admiral George Anson, First Lord of the Admiralty, had sent to Toulon to obtain information about the state of the French Fleet presently moored in the harbor. In his reply Mildmay informed Lord Holdernesse that he had: "a correspondent in those parts (Toulon and Marseille) who in June last year gave me an intimation of four ships of war being fitted out and that 100 workmen had been sent to Marseille to expedite their equipment. Two were 72 guns and two of 60 guns . . . I believe I transmitted this over to England."[51] On 24 February 1753, as the constitutional crisis between the *Parlement* of Paris and the king was reaching a head, Mildmay informed Lord Fitzwalter his informants in Brest and Rochefort had told him that as a consequence of the breakdown of government financial administration, in these royal dockyards "Their finances . . . [are] deranged, a Stop . . . [is] put to their Marine, Ships . . . [are] left half built, deserted upon the Stocks by the workmen for want of money to pay them."[52]

In several letters that he wrote to Lord Fitzwalter in 1754, and in early 1755, Mildmay again mentioned reports he had obtained from his informants at these ports on the depressed state of ship construction at the royal dockyards.[53] In a letter to Fitzwalter on 16 January 1754, in which Mildmay was able to supply him with details about the depleted labor force at the Toulon and Rochefort royal dockyards and the lack of any effective construction work being done in either place, he told Fitzwalter that he had obtained this information "by a letter which I myself received the other day from Toulon that no more works are carried on in that Quarter, and by another letter which a French gentleman of my acquaintance imprudently showed me (which had been sent to this French friend) from Rochefort."[54]

An example of data that had important military implications for the British government is found in the intelligence that Mildmay was able to pass to Lord Holdernesse, through Lord Fitzwalter, in January 1755. In his letter, Mildmay told Lord Fitzwalter he had been informed that large supplies of ships' biscuit had been ordered to be sent to Rochefort. He commented that he had been told of the order to bake: "six thousand *quintals* of biscuit, which will be sufficient of that sort of provisions for the sustenance of four thousand men for six months." Mildmay also reminded Fitzwalter that the French government had "the art of keeping the destination of their Fleet so secret that it cannot be guessed at but from the time for which they are victualled."[55]

This kind of information was invaluable military intelligence. With this advance knowledge on French naval victualing supplies the British government could calculate how long a fleet would be able to remain at sea: this was a vital matter in January 1755, as the threat of war between Britain and France increased. The continuing data that Mildmay collected on the French royal dockyards also gave the British government important information on the current state of the French navy. It was from such dockyard information that one year before the outbreak of the Seven Years' War, Mildmay was able to give the British government vital intelligence on the content of a French fleet that sailed from Brest with troops bound for Louisbourg and the defense of Quebec in the spring of 1755.[56]

Mildmay was equally concerned to keep the British government abreast of what he considered to be important commercial information. In his collection of data on French commerce and finances, Mildmay gave a table of figures on the value to France and Britain of the trade in sugar and cotton from their West Indian colonies in the late 1740s. He compared the quantities and monetary value of the various exports from the British and the French colonies and he estimated that the sugar exported from Jamaica, Barbados, Antigua, Nevis, and Montserrat came to 120,000 hogsheads of one hundredweight each, or a total of 6,000 tons, with a value to Britain of £2,880,000. From the French islands of Guadeloupe, Saint-Domingue (Haïti), and Grenada he estimated there was an export of 126,000 hogsheads of sugar and 40,000 of coffee, with a total value to the French economy of £2,640,000.[57]

Mildmay wrote a part of *An Account of the Southern Maritime Provinces* while the Seven Years' War was taking place,[58] and in it he emphasized the importance of not only capturing the French sugar islands in the West Indies, but of retaining permanent possession of them. He explained this importance by the fact that from their sugar trade: "the French navigation has been increased to such a degree as ought to alarm us much more than any encroachments their settlers have made on the continent of North America." He reported that the numbers of ships sent from "St. Dominique" (*sic*) had increased from 207 ships, with a total of 40,000 tons and 5,175 men in 1730, to 336 ships, with a tonnage of 70,000 and carrying crews of 9,050 by 1756. As the sugar exports from Martinique and Guadeloupe had grown in a similar way, he commented: "judge from hence how necessary it may be to stop the progress of that power.[59]

In his enthusiasm to assist in the promotion of British exports Mildmay felt it was important to inform Fitzwalter, and through him the British government, about any potential problems which might damage any aspect of English trade or manufacturing. In February 1752 he therefore told Fitzwalter of an attempt now being made to compete with British cloth manufacturers, reporting that a group of weavers from Manchester had emigrated to France who: "having escaped the punishment due to them (as Jacobites), are proving themselves to be Rebels and enemies to their Country by offering to set up the fustian manufacture at Rouen."[60] Mildmay said that the leader of the Manchester group was a cotton manufacturer called John Holker, who had been captured at Carlisle in 1745 as a Jacobite, but had escaped from prison in 1748 and had fled to France. In 1751 Holker had been refused a British pardon and by the beginning of 1752 he had arrived in Rouen, where he was granted a French government patent to promote his method of weaving a course cotton twill, or velveteen cloth, called fustian.[61]

Mildmay reported that Holker was now proposing to bring over a further number of skilled weavers from Manchester in order to establish a cotton factory in Rouen, and had been assured that many more such British tradesmen were anxious to join him. He was skeptical that Holker's true ambition was to become a textile manufacturer, however, as he told Fitzwalter Holker had indicated to him that: "if he could obtain his pardon, he would come back to England and break off all agreements." Mildmay also stated to Fitzwalter that he had duly reported this new development to Lord Holdernesse, for if Holker and his skilled artisans could set up a fustian factory in Rouen that was able to produce a similar and competitively priced product, they could undercut British foreign sales and weaken the Lancashire fustian industry. He told Fitzwalter that he was now waiting for Holdernesse's further instructions.

Holker's pardon was again refused, but the fact that he had approached Mildmay to act as his conduit to the British government is an indication Paris society acknowledged that, as a personal friend of Lord Holdernesse, Mildmay had privileged access to a Cabinet minister. Unfortunately, Mildmay's information on the potential damage that John Holker could cause to the fustian manufacturers of Manchester was ignored both by Lord Holderness and by the British government. With his skilled tradesmen and his manufacturing expertise, John Holker established a large and profitable weaving mill in Rouen, becoming one of the town's prominent merchants.[62]

In the same letter in which Mildmay warned about this threat to British cloth manufacture, he also passed along some information to Lord Fitzwalter about a French project to import English sheep "to be fed in the Province of Berry, where the soil being near the same as England, by having our brand of sheep they are in hopes of having our wool."[63] Mildmay pointed out that there were several British statutes, dating back to the third year of the reign of Henry VI, which prohibited the export of sheep from England. He suggested that the British government should ensure that the southern ports should be watched to prevent this illegal export, since he had been told that French agents at Boulogne and Dunkirk were awaiting the arrival of ships carrying these sheep."[64]

In the postscript to a letter that Mildmay wrote to Lord Fitzwalter on 30 May 1753 is an enigmatic reference that indicates that in 1753, he also had some contact with John Kay, the British inventor of the "flying shuttle." John Kay was in France in the spring of 1753 because a mob of artisan weavers had broken into his house in Bury, Lancashire, and had destroyed his weaving machines. Once in France he approached John Holker about the prospects of opening a spinning school in Rouen. From Mildmay's comments to Fitzwalter in May 1753 it appears that at some point John Kay had also approached Mildmay to ask him to intercede for a pardon in smuggling trade secrets out of England: namely the drawings of his new shuttle. It also seems that Mildmay's attempt on Kay's behalf had, this time, been success-ful, and the subsequent pardon had allowed Kay to return to England. On 30 May, however, an exasperated William Mildmay told Fitzwalter: "That ras-cal John Kay, whom I sent to London, is come back again (to join Holker in Rouen). I wish, instead of having solicited for his pardon, I had recom-mended him to have been hanged!"[65]

Mildmay not only transmitted any information he obtained on French initiatives against British trade, he also informed Lord Fitzwalter of some French trade secrets that had been offered to him which might be of bene-fit to Britain, if the government was prepared to pay for them. It appears that knowledge of Mildmay's close connection to a British government minister encouraged French inventors to ask for his help in promoting their cause in Britain. He seemed to be a veritable clearing house for such inven-tions, as on 20 February 1754 he told Fitzwalter: "it is inconceivable what numbers of projects are offered to me towards the payment of our National Debts, the better building of our ships and the greater advancement of our trade and commerce." He also gave his opinion, however, that as most of these inventions had already been rejected by the French Ministry, one should be wary of them.[66]

Despite his suspicions, there were some proposals that Mildmay regarded with enough interest to send them to the British government for its inspec-tion. On 31 August 1752, Mildmay commented to Lord Holdernesse that he had "taken the liberty of sending . . . a scheme of a Bank Lottery, which I think a very ingenious one and, accordingly, I have presumed to address to Mr. Pelham (first lord of the treasury) as the only consideration of such busi-ness comes more immediately under his sphere."[67] Unfortunately, there was a price to be paid for acting as a messenger for French promoters. On 6 December 1752 Mildmay was forced to ask Lord Fitzwalter what had become of this idea for a bank lottery, as he said that its promoter, a clerk in a gov-ernment bureau in Paris, was pestering him for an answer. He told Fitzwalter that he had already sent a second letter to Pelham, but without a response, and asked if Fitzwalter could discover whether the scheme had been approved when he visited Pelham's house in Arlington Street on Privy Council busi-ness. Mildmay said that the clerk "like all hungry ones, is extremely impa-tient" and even if this particular scheme were to be rejected, "I could wish I might be empowered to give him some gratification for his offer in order to encourage similar offers from this quarter in the future."[68]

The bank lottery scheme was, in fact, rejected by Pelham. In a letter sent to Mildmay on 26 December 1752 by Lord Ancram, and written on Fitzwalter's behalf, Ancram said that Pelham had asked Fitzwalter to make his apologies for not replying to Mildmay's two letters, but: "he has no occasion for Schemes of that sort this year and desires you would let him know if your Projector (promoter) wants to have his papers returned to him again. If he does, they shall be carefully returned to him."[69] Ancram made no mention of any "gratification" to be offered by Henry Pelham to the promoter for any future considerations. Nevertheless, despite this setback, Mildmay continued to pass along what he thought to be useful ideas and in February 1754 he seemed most impressed by a memorial on one such scheme. This he described to Lord Fitzwalter as "giving an account of a new invention to grind Sugar Cane, whereby there will be a vast saving to our Plantations in America, English as well as French, in the expense of building Windmills, Watermills and Mills worked by mules and oxen, as the grinding will be performed without the use of either." Mildmay told Fitzwalter that he proposed to send this invention to a Mr. John Pownall for his opinion on the merit both of the design and its possible application."[70]

John Pownall was an old friend and distant relative of William Mildmay. When Pownall was still a copy clerk at the Board of Trade, on two occasions he had given Mildmay considerable assistance in his commission work by sending him some confidential information that Pownall had learned through his employment at the board.[71] Mildmay had therefore sent the proposed sugar mill scheme directly to Pownall (now chief clerk and senior assistant to the president of the Board of Trade and Plantations, Lord Halifax) because Mildmay was concerned that this idea should be taken seriously by the Board.[72] He informed Lord Fitzwalter that the French Ministry had approved its use in the French West Indian Islands and "if the French therefore use it, it may give them a further advantage over us in the cheapness of their Sugars."[73]

There is no record of a reply by John Pownall to Mildmay's report on this new technology for powering grinding mills, but M. Robert, the agent for its inventor, a M. Graffon, told Mildmay that he had already sent a letter about it to "Milord Beckford."[74] William Beckford (father of the author William Beckford of Fonthill) was a wealthy and influential member of Parliament and city alderman, who owned large sugar plantations in Jamaica, but from Mildmay's papers there is, again, no evidence that Beckford responded to

Robert's description of this potential ability to grind sugarcane without the use of mule power.[75]

Given Mildmay's concern for the best interests of the British planters in the West Indies it is not surprising that on 3 August 1751 he wrote an anxious letter to Lord Holderness about a serious threat to this sugar trade. He referred Holderness to an enclosed report: "written to me at my desire by a native of this country" about the condition of the economy of the prosperous island of St. Dominique. He pointed out that since the planters in the British West Indies were in competition with those of France for the export trade in sugar: "it must be a surprise that it is only with our assistance that they (the French) are able to vie with us."[76] He said that his French friend had told him that British slaving merchants in Bristol and Liverpool were running an illegal trade from the Guinea coast into St. Dominique, and were supplying the French planters there with slaves at prices far below that charged by the French slavers from Nantes. He concluded: "Your Lordship is to be the best judge how far this [French] memorial is worthy of being communicated to the Board of Trade" for their ideas on how to prohibit this benefit to a trading rival.

Apart from his military and trade intelligence, there was one other subject on which Mildmay felt the British government should have immediate information. Between 1749 and 1756 the magistrates in the *Parlement* of Paris (the most senior of the French law courts) mounted a serious constitutional challenge to the legal authority of Louis XV, and in 1753 their fierce disagreement with the king culminated in an eighteen-month exile and a complete collapse of the French appellate court system. The initial cause of the dispute between the king and these judges was their refusal to allow the higher clergy of the French church, led by the archbishop of Paris, to annul a legal power that the *Parlement* of Paris maintained was its constitutional right; namely, the jurisdiction to hear and decide cases in which members of the clergy were accused of a gross abuse of the secular law—especially of any act that might cause a public scandal. In this instance priests were being accused of denying the sacraments to members of the Jansenists sect and, primarily, of refusing to hear their deathbed confessions.[77]

*Parlement* began investigating several of these complaints only to find that the cases were then "evoked" (transferred) to the King's Council, where no action was taken, and by 1750 what had started as a series of acerbic debates on the competing legal jurisdictions of the *Parlement* of Paris and the

Galican Church was rapidly becoming a constitutional crisis, in which the *parlementaires* were challenging the king's authority. Louis XV, urged on by his Jesuits confessors and by Christophe Beaumont du Répaire, archbishop of Paris, chose first to try and deflect the issue, then to procrastinate, and, finally, to forbid any further discussion and insist that *Parlement* comply with his orders to register his edicts immediately. At this point the *parlementaires* invoked their ancient privileges and refused to obey what they saw as an illegal process, whereupon the king and his ministers, responding to a perceived threat to the king's absolute power to govern, in May 1753 sent the entire *Parlement* of Paris into an eighteen-month exile.

From November 1750 to May 1755 Mildmay sent regular reports to Lord Fitzwalter and Lord Holdernesse on this religious and political conflict in the French State, and gave his views on the possible consequences the dispute might have for British foreign policy. Other than his own observations, he got most of his information on the proceedings and deliberations of *Parlement* from the magistrates within that body, one of whom, he told Fitzwalter, was his especial friend.[78] Invaluable first-hand information also came from Daniel-Charles Trudaine, who as a councilor of state had intimate knowledge of the deliberations of king and his ministers in the council. On 17 May 1752, Mildmay told Lord Fitzwalter that Louis XV had recently appointed Trudaine to the seven-man royal commission charged with investigating the refusal of priests to administer the sacraments to dying Jansenists.[79] With these excellent sources Mildmay was thus able to secure accurate information from both sides of the dispute and, indeed, his information was so precise and well informed that on at least one occasion the British ambassador to France, Lord Albemarle, in his report on the political dispute to Lord Holderness, used, verbatim, the text of part of a letter that Mildmay had sent, ten days earlier, to Lord Fitzwalter.[80]

The struggle for constitutional power between the *Parlement* of Paris and the king and his ministers was particularly interesting to observers at the time, and has also been studied extensively by later historians, but William Mildmay's commentary on this State crisis had a focus that was quite different from that of the French diarists.[81] The result of this suspension of the *Parlement* of Paris was a total breakdown of the necessary, indeed crucial, cooperation between the king's ministers and the only legal body that had exclusive power to "register," or agree to sign into law, the king's governing decisions. By the mid-summer of 1753 the inability of the government to pass royal legislation, and the absence of any supreme court of appeal, had brought both the French legal system and the tax collection process to a state of chaos.[82] Mildmay was acutely aware, as was the British government, that although such a legal and financial vacuum in the affairs of France might be an interesting spectacle to observe, given the present strained diplomatic relation it also had potential dangers for Britain. In his remarks to Fitzwalter and Holderness Mildmay was thus describing these events not only from the point of view of an informed British observer, but was transmitting sensitive, confidential information that might have considerable political implications for the British government.

His concerns were in four general areas: his anxiety that the French government might decide that a war with Britain could silence its internal critics; his speculation that, conversely, the refusal of *Parlement* to register any of the king's proposed laws, and the French government's consequent incapacity to collect any taxes, might make such a war impossible to wage; his hope that this crisis would divert the French government's attention into solving its domestic problems, and away from a growing belligerence over the disputed North American boundaries; and, finally, his apprehension that Louis XV might be forced to impose martial law, with all of its unpredictable consequences, in order to be able to govern at all.

In May 1753 the British government was extremely interested in the legal impasse caused by the king's exile of *Parlement*, but Mildmay advised Lord Fitzwalter that there should not be universal rejoicing in Whitehall. In a letter on 30 May 1753 he told Fitzwalter that even though the ministers were divided and the population was discontented, there was always a danger that in order to resolve their internal dilemma, which was rapidly getting out of hand, the French government might resort to an external enemy, or: "[to] push matters so far as to find no other method of healing their divisions at home, than by declaring war abroad." He also pointed out the danger that the political and religious arguments now raging might well ignite a general reformation in France, with unknown consequences. He told Fitzwalter he felt that if *Parlement* persisted in its challenge to the authority of the Crown, this might result in a political reformation (or the replacement of absolutism with a constitutional monarchy), but he also said: "If there is a likelihood of a reformation in the State, we should not be without our apprehensions that there may be one in the Church, and this from the indolence of the Clergy, the same cause that brought about the other Reformations."[83]

For Mildmay's generation of mid-century Anglican gentlemen, the word "reformation" brought with it uneasy memories of the excesses of the seventeenth-century religious wars. A year earlier, when describing the bitter arguments between the Jansenists and the hierarchy of the Galican Church on the denial of the sacraments, Mildmay had told Lord Fitzwalter: "it brings on violent disputes on all sides between the High Church and the Low, as in the times of Dr Sacheverelle (*sic*) with us": a prospect he found troubling.[84] Even while he worried about the possibility of a political and religious upheaval in France, however, Mildmay was still more concerned about how this political and religious dispute would affect British interests than he was in the stability of either the French government or its church. In his concluding paragraph in this letter he remarked to Fitzwalter: "Let us draw some comfort to ourselves, since by having such disturbances amongst themselves, they will have less leisure to disturb us."[85]

By the winter of 1753 these "disturbances" had become an acute financial problem for the Crown. To try and get his legislation passed into law, Louis XV had set up an alternative senior appeal court: the *Chambre Royale* at the Louvre, with the same powers as the exiled *Parlement* to register royal edicts. Unfortunately for this attempt, the legal status of this new court was being questioned by many of the lower courts, in particular by the court of the *Châtelet* in Paris, whose jurisdiction covered not only the city of Paris and its hinterland, but any court in the country where a warrant had been issued by this court for a suspected offense. The *Parlement* of Paris was the only superior appeal court legally recognized by *Châtelet* courts, and for several months these court judges refused to register the royal Letters Patent establishing the *Chambre Royale*. Even after they had finally done so, under the extreme pressure of several of their number being imprisoned in the Bastille, Mildmay commented to Lord Fitzwalter: "In vain was such a jurisdiction erected, when not a Procurator (prosecutor) would carry his client's case to be tried before it," and, in many cases: "the clients themselves have withdrawn their suits."[86]

With this kind of general distrust in the legality of the *Chambre Royale* it is not surprising that on 19 December 1753 Mildmay reported to Lord Fitzwalter that a royal taxation edict that had recently been registered by this court was regarded as suspect, and without legal force. He surmised to Fitzwalter: "If any scruple be made in the payment [by the taxpayer], the Impost (tax) must be levied by military force, which will be reducing the

People to the utmost extremity of oppression."[87] Mistrust in the financial stability of the Crown had appeared among the investors in government bonds at the outset of the crisis. Mildmay had many friends in the merchant community, and within two months of the exile of Parlement he reported to Fitzwalter they had told him that lenders were now withholding their money in the current legal uncertainty, and the Treasury was having great difficulty in raising a royal loan of three million *livres* from the "rentes," or government bonds.[88]

The king and *Parlement* finally came to terms a year later. On 1 July 1754 Louis XV met the First President of the *Parlement* and his colleagues at a private audience at the Louvre, and on 2 September 1754 the *Parlement* of Paris reassembled, but the peace was only temporary. On 23 April 1755 Mildmay told Lord Fitzwalter that *Parlement* was again protesting to the king, and on the receipt of another "severe reprimand," the *parlementaires* had again threatened to "resign their functions." He speculated: " If there be no *Parlement,* then there can be no *Imposts* (taxes) to be levied. How then is He (the King) to carry on a war against his neighbours? Surely this will bring Him to offer terms to us and surely our Ministers will not fail of the opportunity to take advantage of it?"[89] Unfortunately for Mildmay's hopes, the time was long past when either George II or Louis XV could determine their foreign policies on such domestic practicalities, for by the spring of 1755 their respective colonial subjects were directing military events on the other side of the Atlantic in their own interests.

Throughout his five-year term as a British commissioner and despite the pace of the negotiations, the contents of Mildmay's frequent letters to the Lords Fitzwalter and Holdernesse covered a variety such subjects. In them he demonstrated his talent for recognizing useful information, and his clear, analytical grasp of items that would be of political, military, and economic use to both the British government and to English trade entrepreneurs and exporters. Although his position in Paris was limited to that of a commission negotiator, Mildmay was acting in a far more significant capacity; he was, in fact, carrying out all of the intelligence gathering and analytical functions of a modern trade consul, but unpaid, and in some cases unasked, working without the benefits of either an expense account or a staff of assistants. In his writings he showed a lively understanding of the economic and military value of accurate trade and financial information and, although he worked efficiently on the commission for five years, in his correspondence with

Lord Holdernesse he gave only one brief indication of what he would have liked to become if circumstances had made it possible.

On 3 August 1751, three months after Holdernesse had been appointed the secretary of state for the Southern Department, Mildmay wrote him a long letter. In it he confirmed that, as requested, he would keep Holdernesse informed on the subject of the trade and revenue of France in a series of papers on the state of the French economy, some of which he had already prepared.[90] In his final paragraph, however, Mildmay talked about the insights he had gained from his travels and observations in France, and told Holdernesse he felt he could make a similar useful contribution if he were posted to Italy. He commented: "I should be ambitious in serving His Majesty in that part of the world (Italy) as soon as my commission is finished in Paris," and to promote this request he continued: "I beg leave to observe to your Lordship that we have at present, neither Minister nor Consul established at Naples, where a person in both these capacities might be useful; considering that whenever the event of the King of Spain's death may happen, there will certainly be motions in that State for which it will be necessary for our Court to be appraised."[91] Unfortunately for Mildmay's hopes, in 1751 his Paris commission was to wander on without a conclusion for the next four years, and when he was recalled to London, in May 1755, with the existing bellicose climate in Europe the last thing that the British government would wish to consider would be the establishment a new diplomatic post at Naples.

# 4·
# THE OPENING YEAR: APRIL
# 1750 TO DECEMBER 1750

THE DIPLOMATIC COMMISSION THAT HENRY PELHAM had assured the Commons in 1749 would achieve its desired result was officially established in April 1750, when William Shirley and William Mildmay received from George II the document that gave them "full powers" to act as his diplomatic representatives to the French Court.[1] This royal appointment in April was not Mildmay's first indication, however, that he was to be given this position. In the "Memorandum" with which he opened his journal on the commission conferences, Mildmay noted that on 16 January 1750 he and Shirley had been named as: "His Majesty's Commissaries" on a per diem salary of: "three pounds for each, with a further allowance of twenty shillings a day, to be divided between us, towards defraying the expenses we might be at in maintaining a secretary."[2] Among his papers Mildmay also kept an account of the money he had received from the Exchequer between January and April 1750 and he recorded that he had been given £300: "for his equipage (coach and horses)," and another £300: "as my second ordinary (his daily salary) by way of an advance, from 16 January 1750 to 17 April 1750, being 91 days."[3]

If the British government wanted a diplomat to be in place in a foreign capital by a certain date it was always necessary to give him sufficient advance preparation time and some money with which to prepare. Mildmay's "equipage" grant and the 91-day advance on his salary was the standard allowance given to diplomats at the beginning of a foreign posting, and his daily salary, of three pounds, indicated that he was classed on the same level as a British "Resident," or representative of the British Crown where there was no embassy.[4] Mildmay spent from 16 January to 17 April learning his future responsibilities, and getting ready for a long stay in Paris.

In a letter that Sir Benjamin Keene wrote in 1745 to his friend Abraham Castres, the British consul in Lisbon, Sir Benjamin described the reasons for the length of time that it was taking him to be able to leave for his appointment as British ambassador to Court of Portugal.[5] From Sir Benjamin's comments it seems that even in cities as sophisticated as Lisbon or Paris, it was still necessary for a diplomat who would be spending some time abroad to equip himself with domestic linen, fine tableware, and other household goods, and to arrange for their shipment. He would also have to make advance arrangements to rent a dwelling and a carriage, and to engage some servants; not the least important of whom would be an English private secretary, a French *valet de chambre*, and a reliable coachman.[6] Given Sir Benjamin's preparation time of over a year, it seems that Mildmay was remarkably swift in being ready to leave in the three months between his appointment in mid-January and his arrival in Paris on 1 May, but organization was always his strong point.

From evidence in letters between the duke of Bedford and Lord Albemarle, however, it also appears that Mildmay was under some considerable pressure from Bedford to begin his work. Far from looking on the commission as a futile diplomatic exercise, both the British government and George II were anxious that Mildmay should begin the negotiations in Paris as quickly as possible. On 12 February 1750 (OS) the duke of Bedford informed Lord Albemarle that: "the Commissaries for settling the Limits, Prizes etc. (the boundary limits of Nova Scotia, Acadia, the Channel and the North Sea, and the compensation to be paid for prize ships taken after the war had ended) will be ready to set out for Paris as soon as Governor Shirley has finished some affairs now depending with the Board of Trade, and in the meantime Mr. Mildmay, whom the King has appointed . . . for settling the accounts of the Prisoners of War, may set out immediately for Paris in order to finish that affair before Mr. Shirley's arrival."[7]

The Duke of Bedford might originally have intended that Mildmay would be in place this swiftly, but on 29 March (OS), six weeks later, he wrote again to Albemarle, telling him that Mildmay would be arriving in Paris shortly, as the king had now signed the negotiation instructions that were to be given to the two commissioners.[8] Even this timetable still appears to have been somewhat optimistic, however, since it was not until 16 April (OS), or 27 April (NS), that Bedford was able to assure Albemarle: "Mr. Shirley and Mr. Mildmay, or at least one of them, will, I hope, be at Paris very near as soon as this letter. The first thing they will do will be, of course, to wait on Your Excellency to receive your directions for their conduct on their arrival, as the King is extremely desirous that they should begin their business as soon as possible." Bedford also instructed Albemarle to ask the French foreign minister, the Marquis de Puysieulx, to meet with Shirley and Mildmay as soon as possible so they could present their credentials.[9]

Mildmay actually landed at Calais on 22 April 1750 (NS). This date is established from a letter that he wrote two years later to Lord Fitzwalter, when, on 22 April 1752, Mildmay noted: "this day completed my second year of being abroad."[10] As Mildmay's letter to the duke of Bedford of 6 May 1750 (NS) stated that he had arrived in Paris on 1 May (NS),[11] he thus took a further ten days to reach Paris. It appears that he had been encouraged to leave London so hurriedly, however, that on the same day on which Bedford had informed Albemarle of Mildmay's imminent arrival he was forced to write a second letter, telling the ambassador that by accident, Mildmay had set out for Paris without his royal warrant. Bedford asked Albemarle to assure Mildmay that as this document would be following in the pouch of the next embassy messenger, he should not delay in beginning his work on that account.[12]

On 5 June 1750 Mildmay wrote to Lord Holdernesse that he had taken up his appointment in Paris, included some details of his commission responsibilities, and said that he was still waiting for his colleague, William Shirley, who was now expected to arrive in about two weeks. He told Holdernesse that he had been given two separate responsibilities: the first was to settle the accounts for the ransom of military prisoners, which he was to carry out singly, and the second was to be a joint commissioner with Shirley: "to adjust the disputes between the two Crowns of England and France concerning their rights in America and also concerning the prizes taken at sea after the time when hostilities should have ceased."[13]

Mildmay continued that in his single commission on the ransoms he had already begun to make some progress, but the question of the prize ships involved a determination of the limits of the seas in which these ships had been taken and the Dutch government was keenly interested in any discussions which would decide the precise boundaries of the Channel and the North Sea. He said he appreciated that since the Dutch had been allies of Britain in the late war they must be treated with care, and he had already been to see the Dutch Ambassador and "Minister Larrey," one of the Dutch commissioners appointed to monitor these negotiations, "in order to assure them of my friendly assistance, according to my instructions."[14]

In a second letter, written on 31 July 1750, Mildmay told Lord Holdernesse that although he continued to make steady progress with the ransoms, William Shirley had still not arrived in Paris and his continued absence was now causing a delay to the beginning of negotiations on the sea limits. Mildmay said was concerned about the security of their correspondence and he asked Holdernesse to tell him whether "a secret method could be contrived (for the delivery of letters), as I have many things to communicate."[15] He also congratulated Holdernesse on the recent birth of his son, followed this with information on a riot which had taken place in Paris in the previous month, and concluded by saying he would continue to keep Holdernesse informed of any entertaining occurrences in the French capital. This letter is typical of much of the correspondence that Mildmay was to have with Lord Holdernesse while he was secretary of state for the Southern Department, but the interest in these letters is that in 1750, Holdernesse had not yet been appointed to this position.

In 1750, Lord Holdernesse was still the British ambassador to the States General at The Hague, having been sent there in May 1749, and he did not become the southern secretary until 18 June 1751.[16] Mildmay's correspondence with Holdernesse during 1750, however, was an outcome of the long-standing friendship he had established with Lord Fitzwalters's stepson following the marriage of his mother, Frederica, dowager countess of Holdernesse, to Fitzwalter in 1724.[17] Now that both Mildmay and Holdernesse were in the diplomatic service, it appears they considered it appropriate to exchange diplomatic as well as personal information. When Holdernesse was appointed to the Southern Department their diplomatic correspondence, understandably, increased, but Mildmay's family connection with Holdernesse continued to give him a special, private relationship that was over and above his official post.

At the same time that he was writing to Lord Holdernesse, Mildmay also kept in constant touch with Lord Fitzwalter, who had been his friend and patron for the past thirty-four years.[18] Between May and December 1750 Mildmay wrote to Fitzwalter on a regular monthly basis, and in these seven letters he discussed, at length, the demands of the French commissioners on the ransom of prisoners, their disputes over the sea limits, their position concerning the boundaries of Acadia, and his own opinions about proper negotiating methods and the transmittal of orders to the commission from London. In a letter to Fitzwalter on 2 December 1750 Mildmay also gave his unflattering opinion of William Shirley, whom he described as: "the slow mule with whom I am coupled," and said he felt that: "if left alone I flatter myself I should have been able to have given some satisfactory account of my other commissions."[19]

From this series of letters to Lord Fitzwalter in 1750 it is evident that Mildmay intended to keep in regular communication with his influential relative. He made his reasons very clear to Fitzwalter in his letter of 2 July 1750 when he said: "I have ventured to give your Lordship this information on my progress [in his negotiations] before I have made my papers sufficiently complete to be sent to Whitehall. I know I can safely repose myself in your secrecy, but it is your Lordship's advice that I want and your approbation that I am ambitious of."[20] Even at this early stage in the five-year history of this commission it seems that Mildmay had already appreciated that there were going to be difficulties with the conduct of the negotiations, and in this position he might well need the good offices and advice of his patron as a friend and protector with whom he could exchange vital and confidential information. Moreover, Lord Fitzwalter could, if necessary, transmit this information to the highest possible levels in the British government and the court.

In 1750 Lord Fitzwalter was seventy-nine, but he still had considerable influence at the Court of George II. He had served as chief commissioner of the Board of Trade from 1735 to 1737, and in 1750 he was the treasurer to the royal household,[21] but he had a somewhat closer and more intimate connection to George II than this court office. Fitzwalter's wife, Lady Frederica, was the eldest daughter of the second duke of Schomberg, but her mother, Charlotte, had been the daughter of Charles-Lewis, the Elector of the Rhine Palatinate and brother of Sophia, Electress of Hanover. As her grandfather, Charles-Lewis, was thus the uncle of George I, Frederica, Countess Fitzwalter, and George II were second cousins.[22]

Because of Lord Fitzwalter's prominent and influential position, Mildmay also saw him as a useful ally to assist in any financial problems that the commissioners might be having with the Treasury. In his last letter to Fitzwalter in 1750, on 30 December, he reported that both commissioners had recently written to Henry Pelham, pointing out to him that although the year was now ending, they had not received any salary since May. To emphasize the

difficulties this delay was causing, he gave Fitzwalter a detailed account of
the expense of living in Paris, however modestly, and stated that he could
only manage to save a proportion of his salary because he was: "too old and
past the temptation of falling into the follies and vices by which too many are
led into extravagancy."[23]

Max Savelle stated that although the commissioners had been appointed in
April of 1750, the first meeting of the Anglo-French commission did not take
place until 31 August and that, as a consequence of this delayed start to the
negotiations, nothing very much happened during the intervening four
months. Savelle put this four-month inaction down to a lack of enthusiasm to
negotiate on the part of both governments, and to the vague and conflicting
instructions which had been issued to the British commissioners on their
appointment: both from the duke of Bedford and from the president of the
Board of Trade, Lord Halifax.[24] Savelle's interest in the commission was
entirely in its negotiations on the North American boundaries, however, and
in his judgment on the apparent lack of progress in this area he overlooked the
attempts to resolve the other three issues under dispute: the ownership of St.
Lucia, the compensation for the prize ships, and the costs for the ransom of
prisoners. Mildmay was, in fact, far from inactive in that part of his commission for which he was solely responsible, and on which he had been instructed to proceed: "without any unnecessary delay."[25] He had been meeting with
Martin Seigneur, the French commissioner nominated to negotiate the ransom
of prisoners, since his arrival in Paris in May, and he described his progress in
an initial report that he submitted to the duke of Bedford on 3 June 1750.[26]

The first issue Mildmay said he had to establish was a complete description of the French and British prisoners covered by these negotiations, and
this information had to include not only their names, but also their regiments
and military ranks, the date and place of their capture, whether they were
still alive, in which prison they had been held, or, if they had been wounded,
the hospital in which they been kept, and for how long. All of this data took
time to assemble, and between May and August 1750 Mildmay sent a number of letters of inquiry to the superintendents of British prisons and hospitals, and to Arthur Villette, British Resident at Berne, who had been responsible for paying the subsistence for French and Spanish prisoners captured
during the British campaign in Provence in 1744 during the War of the
Austrian Succession.[27] He also told the duke of Bedford that he had been able
to call on Lord Albemarle, (the British ambassador to Paris), and Joseph

Yorke (first secretary at the embassy), for their assistance in his inquires on the original regiments of some the French prisoners: a point difficult to establish after this elapsed time.

In this first report to Bedford, Mildmay gave a total of 50,220 *livres* demanded by the French for their British prisoners; of this sum, however, 19,432 *livres* were owed on behalf of Hanovarian troops captured in Flanders and a further 10,642 *livres* for some Hessians. He therefore asked was it the king's wish that these particular soldiers should also be paid for.[28] In a letter he wrote to the duke of Newcastle on 10 August, and sent to Hanover, he confirmed Newcastle's previous instructions from George I that the Hanoverians and Hessians were to be treated in exactly the same manner as the British soldiers. Accordingly, he informed Newcastle that, having taken these calculations into account: "it is some satisfaction to me to find all these together fall very short of the demands we make on account of the French prisoners . . . [as] the sum due to His Majesty amounts in French money to 407,290 (*livres*)," a difference of 357,070 *livres*.[29] On the following day (11 August) Mildmay wrote to the duke of Bedford, informing him that as William Shirley had just arrived in Paris, he expected that they would shortly be starting the important business of their joint commission, and he would thus take care: "to regulate my business that my duty in one Employment [the boundaries and the prize ships] may not be interrupted by the execution of the other [the ransoms]."[30]

So far as the territorial negotiations were concerned, in his two letters to Lord Holdernesse in June and July Mildmay certainly did not complain that he felt hampered by any lack of government instructions. To the contrary, in a letter that he wrote to Lord Fitzwalter on 22 August 1750 he said: "we have received our instructions from His Majesty at Hanover, which being drawn up by the Board of Trade are so full and clear that I don't fear demonstrating His Majesty's just right to the claims he makes if the principles of reason and justice are the rules by which this [French] Court is to be determined (governed)."[31] Mildmay's activities in the early summer were also not confined solely to the ransom question, for on 2 July 1750 he reported to Fitzwalter that, despite Shirley's tardiness in his arrival, he had already been informed of the French government's position on the "late proceedings [the continuing military skirmishes] in Nova Scotia."[32]

Mildmay's statement to Lord Fitzwalter on the clarity of his mandate is perfectly accurate; far from being in the least "vague," the instructions that were given to Mildmay and Shirley by George II were both long and explicit. They contained the precise boundary limits of the territory of Acadia ceded to Britain in the Treaty of Utrecht (1713), a lengthy description of the boundary limits of the areas off the coasts of Acadia and Nova Scotia in which the British would allow the French to catch fish, and full details of the British claim to the islands of St. Lucia, St. Vincent, Dominica, and Tobago. All of these points were also covered under the Treaty of Utrecht. In order that they would be able to uphold these rights during the negotiations, the commissioners were told that they would be given "all papers necessary to prove the facts therein," they were to be shown two memorials that had been sent by the British government to Lord Albemarle, and they could call for any further papers or documents they might feel they needed. They were also not left without support, either in Paris or from London, as they were instructed to keep Lord Albemarle informed of all the details of their commission meetings, calling on him for any advice and assistance they needed during their negotiations, and to send regular reports on their progress to the duke of Bedford, with copies to the commissioners of the Board of Trade: "so far as the same may relate to their cognizance."[33]

Mildmay and Shirley had also received further directions on the subject of the prize ships in a document headed "Sketch of Instructions for William Shirley and William Mildmay, Esquires, Commissaries appointed by His Britannic Majesty to the Court of France."[34] This paper told them that the negotiation problems at St. Malo had largely been caused by disputes over the limits of the Channel and the North Sea, by questions on whether prewar prizes could be included in the list of claims, and by debates on whether the indemnity disputes could be settled by the two governments or must be achieved by litigation between the aggrieved parties. They were therefore informed that Lord Albemarle had been instructed that, with the exception of the prewar prize issue, he should attempt to secure a prior agreement with the French government on the other matters in a way that would not prejudice the British position (the details of which were laid out in point form). Accordingly, both sides exchanged memorials with each other on the subjects of the sea limits and the legitimacy of prizes, but although the wording of each memorial was careful to emphasize the respective government's belief that it was acting in good faith in its desire to achieve harmonious success, it appears that the fundamental disagreements that had been present at St. Malo still existed in Paris in May 1750.

The acerbic debate that had begun at the meetings at St. Malo in 1748, and continued unresolved, throughout the entire five-year negotiations, centered on the definition of what constituted a lawful prize ship and stemmed from the specific character of eighteenth-century naval warfare. The royal navies of both Britain and France were somewhat in the nature of part-time forces; many of the warships were laid up in peacetime and, until war seemed imminent, many of their officers were also put on half-pay. Once a war had actually been declared, French and British naval captains were legally permitted to take any ship they had captured as a prize of war and the captain and crew that took it were entitled either to a ransom from the owner on its return, or to the value of the ship when sold. The majority of the ships that carried out aggressive activities against foreign craft, however, were private merchant vessels. These were called "pirates" when governments were not at war with each other, or "privateers," acting under government "letters of marque," when their wartime services were required.

The private mercenary armies that had dominated and decimated Europe from the Middle Ages until the religious wars of the seventeenth century had been suppressed by eighteenth-century French and English monarchs as a universal menace. The mercenary privateers were still active at sea, however, and the illegality of prizes taken by these privateers was the cause of endless arguments in every peace treaty. At the signing of the Treaty of Aix-la-Chapelle in 1748, the French government had bitterly protested the large number of French merchant ships that had been captured immediately before the outbreak of the war by British privateers—who were ostensibly acting under such letters of marque. Even if the British government had wished to satisfy such protests, however, the difficulty lay in how to compel these private captains to disgorge their prize money, even supposing such men could be found in the first place. Thus to allow this subject of illegal prizes that were taken before the war had been declared to be discussed as a government responsibility—one that could be negotiated at a "Court to Court," or a British and French government minister level—was to lay the British Crown open to massive damage claims, with no possibility of recovering the money.

In a letter Mildmay wrote to Fitzwalter on 31 January 1753, he clearly illustrated the dangers he saw in these financial debates. He said he feared, given the tone of the arguments being used by the French commissioners, that this issue of the pre-war prizes might cause the outbreak of another war and, if such a disaster were to happen, he felt it would be due entirely to: "the late behaviour of our Privateers, as adhering more to their *own* (*sic*) Interests than to the Laws of Nations. Tis' hard that our Government should be called upon to pay the whole load of the Damages."[35] Nevertheless, however much the British government declared it to be outside the commission mandate, the French commissioners were instructed to insist that such prewar claims must be discussed and the British commissioners were told to resist this attempt at every conference at which it was raised.

Lord Albemarle's ongoing support to Shirley and Mildmay on this issue was carried out in agreement with his instructions from Whitehall. The British memorial on prizes that was sent by Albemarle to M. de Puysieulx, and to which the British commissioners were directed in their own instructions, was based on a report written on 16 April 1750 by the duke of Bedford to the duke of Newcastle.[36] In this document Bedford outlined precisely what Shirley and Mildmay were expected to achieve and how the British government intended that they should negotiate on the subject of the prize ships. He reviewed with Newcastle the present state of the French claims for these ships that were contained in Puysieulx's memorial to Albemarle, and in a point-by-point analysis Bedford answered each French government position.

In order to establish the legality of the taking of a prize ship, the boundary of the area in which it was taken was of paramount importance. Allowing for the length of time it would take the captain of a sailing ship to be contacted and informed that a state of war, or a treaty of peace, now existed, the rules of naval warfare stated the notification period for ships at sea within boundaries of the Channel and the North Sea would extend to two weeks, and the grace period for ships "beyond the line," or ships outside these waters, was six weeks. All ships that were attacked and taken outside these agreed time limits were deemed to be illegal seizures, so in the present dispute the status of prizes thus depended on where the limits of the Channel and the North Sea were set. In his 16 April report Bedford covered the problem of the disputed Channel boundaries by referring Newcastle to the exact wording of the Treaty of Utrecht, cited in Puysieulx's memorial, in which it was stated that Cape St. Vincent, on the southern tip of Portugal, and not the Lizard Point of Cornwall, was expressly mentioned as one of the western boundaries limits of the Channel.

In a British government document entitled "Memorial in Reply to the Objections of the French Court to the Instructions for the Commissaries to the Limits and Prizes," this reference to the Lizard Point is more fully explained. The text commented that "The French Court is pleased to set out with a pretty extraordinary observation on this Head, that as the Lizard Point is the last land seen in going out of the Channel, all Seamen look to Themselves to be out of the Channel as soon as they have doubled that point, whereas from the most authentic Accounts it appears clear to us that the Channel has been reputed to extend to Cape Finisterre, and often as far as [Cape] St. Vincent, and that in the opinion of the Seamen of most Nations in Europe."[37]

In his report to Newcastle, Bedford also pointed out that at no time had the British memorial suggested that the British commissioners, alone, should have full powers to determine these limits. Indeed, he said it was expressly stated in this memorial that the commissioners would abide by the decisions of Lord Albemarle, and any other construction read into the memorial must be put down to a fault in the French translation. In particular, Bedford emphasized to Newcastle that: "the powers given to the Commissaries do not extend to prizes taken in general before the War . . . [as] this was an entirely new matter, and so totally foreign to the commission . . ." He said he felt that "the only consequence of such an Enquiry [on prewar claims] would be to endanger discussions, and a ripping up of old quarrels and disputes, which in the interests of both Crowns should be left as dormant as possible."

In contrast to the duke of Bedford's emphasis on the difficulty of an agreement on the prewar prize ships, it seems that in April 1750 the British government saw the securing of a settlement of the boundaries of Acadia, and the ownership of St. Lucia, Tobago, St. Vincent, and Dominica as somewhat less of a problem. On these territorial issues, the document prepared in reply to the French objections stated: "The Greatest Care will be taken to give the Commissaries proper Powers and instructions on these Heads, that the whole may be brought to an amicable Determination as soon as possible, and a Basis laid for a Solid Friendship between the two Crowns by the adjusting of those Difficulties which, if not settled, may otherwise interrupt that friendship thereafter."[38] Although Bedford was anxious to have these territorial negotiations underway, it appeared that Shirley would be unable to reach Paris for some time and he therefore recommended to Newcastle: "the want of a definitive discussion on those Heads [disputes about Acadia and the islands in the West Indies] is no reason why the Commissaries [Mildmay and his two French counterparts] should not immediately treat upon the . . . [other] points which the Treaty of Aix has left to their discussion [the ransoms, the prizes, and the sea limits] and which afterwards, by the consent of both Courts, . . . [were] agreed to be comprehended under the same commission."[39]

Although, in retrospect, Bedford's assessment of the potential ease with which the territorial issues could be resolved appears overly optimistic, from the evidence of this document he certainly seemed to believe that with the clear position taken in the British memorial and the British reply to the French objections on the prize issue, both Lord Albemarle and Mildmay now had instructions that were full and broad enough to allow them to proceed with confidence. On 14 April 1750 Bedford told Albemarle: "I flatter myself that upon an impartial comparison of the one with the other [the French and the British memorials] the French Ministers will consent to such a previous and joint-concerted plan between the Two Courts as may bring this part of the Commission [the resolution of the disputes on ransoms, prizes, and sea limits] to a speedy, as well as an equitable issue and, by so doing, prove at least a desire to a disposition on both sides to remove every difficulty whatsoever [on the territorial disputes]."[40]

It is true, as Savelle pointed out, that although Shirley and Mildmay had received their royal warrants in mid-April 1750, and Mildmay had arrived in Paris on 1 May, the full British commission did not meet with its French counterpart until the end of August, but this apparent procrastination was not caused by a reluctance to begin negotiations on the part of either the British or the French government. The unavoidable four-month delay in starting the conferences on the territorial disputes in North America was caused entirely by William Shirley's absence from Paris. Shirley's appointment to the commission had initially been made in January 1750 but, as the duke of Bedford had told Lord Albemarle in February 1750, it was his "affairs now depending with the Board of Trade," and which actually involved a serious investigation by the Board on the proper accounting of Governor Shirley's military budget during the War of the Austrian Succession, that had prevented his arrival in Paris until the latter part of August. In his letter of 22 August Mildmay confirmed to Lord Fitzwalter that Shirley had at last arrived but, as evidence of the obvious difficulties that lay ahead, he said the French commissioners continued to repeat to him their demand that compensation for ships taken before war was declared must also be included in any conference discussions on prizes.[41]

The first time that this requirement had been put forward was at the joint meetings at St. Malo. On his appointment in January 1750 Mildmay had filed a British memorandum entitled "Sketch of a Plan of Instructions sent in December 1749,"[42] and this document, given to Messrs. Allix and Hind at St. Malo, had stated that the French government had not only insisted on the inclusion of the prize ships on the agenda, but had also refused to agree with the British position that the Admiralty courts of each country should arbitrate between the owners and the captors of each ship, based on the merits of each incident. On the contrary, the French government had demanded that such negotiation take place *de Cour à Cour,* or between the ministers of both governments. There were also considerable differences noted in this document concerning the boundaries of "the Channel and the Northern Seas," although there was some joint agreement on the time limits to be allowed for the notification of any ship's captain that war had been declared, or that a peace agreement had been signed.[43] The report by the duke of Bedford to the duke of Newcastle on 16 April 1750 indicated that, despite this agreed flexibility on such time limits for notification, the present views of the British government on the French demand for a discussion of the prewar prizes had not changed substantially from those outlined in the "Sketch of Instructions," issued in December 1749. Mildmay's responsibilities as a commissioner were to negotiate the ransom of prisoners and the negotiations on prizes, on sea limits, on the boundaries of Acadia and Nova Scotia, and on the ownership of St. Lucia. These were all part of his joint commission mandate with William Shirley. In a letter that Mildmay sent to the duke of Bedford on 6 May, however, he said that on his first visit to Lord Albemarle, the British ambassador: "was also pleased to discourse with me upon that material point relating to the Limits of the British Seas [the boundaries of the North Sea and the Channel]."[44] From the evidence of Mildmay's letter of 22 August to Fitzwalter it appears that following this meeting with Albemarle, and taking into account Bedford's opinion of 16 May that negotiations on the prize ships and the sea limits need not necessarily wait for discussions on the territorial disputes, Mildmay had decided that Shirley's protracted arrival allowed him to begin some preliminary discussions on these two subjects with the French commissioners. Beyond these explorations of the disputes over prizes and sea limits, from his remarks to Fitzwalter on 2 July it also appears that Mildmay felt that he could hold introductory talks on "the late proceedings in Nova Scotia." When Shirley finally appeared in Paris he may have felt otherwise, of course, and from what took place between Mildmay and Shirley during the year that followed, it seems that he did.

The purpose of the first official meeting of the commission, held at the apartment of M. de la Galissonière, the senior French commissioner, on 31 August 1750, was to establish the groundwork for future negotiations. Mildmay kept a journal in which he recorded the content of each commission conference, and in his entry for 31 August he stated that, as expected, the French commissioners opened the discussion with the contentious issue of compensation for the prewar prizes. To this, Mildmay wrote that he and Shirley replied that they were bound by the terms of the Treaty of Aix-la-Chapelle, which referred exclusively: "to those [ships] who were, or might have been taken after hostilities had ceased [in 1748]." Beyond the date of their capture, however, the question of the legitimacy of these prizes was also based whether they had been taken within the western limit of the Channel and the northern boundary of the North Sea. On this point, Mildmay said the French commissioners were told that as the governments of Britain and France had already agreed that Lord Albemarle and M. de Puysieulx would negotiate the precise limits of these waters, nothing further could be decided on individual claims until the sea boundaries had been determined. He said that he and Shirley then stated they were fully prepared to discuss any prizes that had been taken outside these limits, and suggested that each side prepare a specific list of these instances.[45]

When the discussion moved to the disputed boundaries of Acadia and Nova Scotia, the French commissioners now raised a new issue. Mildmay reported Galissonière and Etienne de Silhouette (the second French commissioner) had said that that in order for them to agree with British proposals to begin negotiations on the limits of Acadia, they needed an assurance that the ownership of the island of St. Lucia would also be negotiated, in alternate discussions with that of Acadia. As this demand was novel and completely unexpected, Mildmay said he and Shirley countered with the statement that in the interests of curtailing the present danger of armed warfare in North America: "the necessity of making Acadie (*sic*) the object of our immediate discussions" was the most important consideration for the British government. Mildmay explained that the problem the British side saw in holding discussions on St. Lucia concerned the fact that although the terms of the peace treaty had stated that St. Lucia was to be a "neutral" island—inhabited by neither side—the French soldiers and settlers there had not yet been evacuated. He said he and Shirley had thus told the French commissioners that until some evidence was produced that this evacuation had been carried out, they were instructed that no such negotiation could be agreed to. Galissonière and Silhouette answered that they would ask their Court for further directions on this point.[46]

Nevertheless, in further discussion between the four commissioners it appeared that the French demand for an immediate negotiation on St. Lucia had raised the possibility that there could be some kind of accommodation over the disputed territories in North America and the West Indies. In the official report on this conference that Shirley and Mildmay sent to the duke of Bedford, they said the French commissioners had requested their proposition that: "the King [Louis XV] would make a sacrifice of some parts of His Right [to Acadia] in order to maintain it [in St. Lucia]" should be sent to Whitehall. In light of its potential importance to the future of the negotiations, Mildmay and Shirley said they asked the French commissioners to give them this statement in writing, and Bedford's verbatim copy reported: "*Le principe sur Lequel les Commissaires du Roy de France ont fait connaitre qu'il seroit à desirer qu'on tout ce qui pourrent donner de trops grandes facilites aux deux Nations pour y'on commoder, et s'envalier, meme en temps de Guerre (sic).*"[47] In his conference journal Mildmay reported that since the French commissioners had also declared that their instructions were to proceed on the principle that in order to reach a general agreement on all these points, some compromise would be required by the governments of both sides, in his summation of the sense of this first meeting he concluded: "The French Court . . . [wishes] to discover our Disposition to allow as what they look on as our favourite points in one part of America [Acadia] in order to obtain their end in another [St. Lucia]."[48] This appraisal was also repeated by Mildmay and Shirley in their official report to Bedford.

This first conference had thus established the three main problems with which the commission had to grapple: whether prewar prizes would be allowed, what were the boundaries of the Channel and the North Sea, and whether the commission agenda would include immediate, and alternate discussions on the ownership of St. Lucia. The next meeting took place at William Shirley's apartment a week later, on 7 September 1750, and was entirely concerned with the French demand to discuss St. Lucia.

In his journal Mildmay said that in order to answer the British complaint of the continued presence of French troops and settlers on St. Lucia,

Galissonière and Silhouette began by producing an official document of instruction from their government. This stated that so far as the prior evacuation of St. Lucia was concerned, the actual wording of the treaty had said only that in order to begin negotiations, instructions for such an evacuation must be sent to the French governor within fifteen days of the appointment of commissioners for both sides, or at the end of April 1750. In the ensuing discussion, Galissonière and Silhouette pointed out that there was nothing in the treaty which stipulated that an actual evacuation of St. Lucia had to have taken place before its status could be discussed by the commission, and Mildmay reported that he and Shirley were now assured that instructions to vacate this island had, in fact, been sent in April; the four-month delay in their implementation had been entirely caused by the subsequent death of the governor of Martinique, M. Caylus. Now that a new governor, a M. Bompar, was on his way to the Caribbean, Mildmay said that Galissonière and Silhouette thus insisted that the negotiation of St. Lucia should now proceed in tandem with that of the disputed boundaries of Nova Scotia and Acadia: "since the settling of the Right to St. Lucia was as interesting a Point to Them, as settling the Limits to Acadia was to the Crown of Great Britain." Even more germane to this topic, he noted that positive evidence of this interest was revealed in their repeated statement that: "The French King was disposed to make a Sacrifice of part of His Right to us [on Acadia], for the sake of establishing Harmony between the two Crowns [over St. Lucia]."[49]

As if this sudden demand for a territorial linkage in the discussions were not enough of a problem, in his journal Mildmay noted that Galissonière and Silhouette had at first appeared to indicate that all of the issues under dispute must also be included in any agreed settlement of the territorial claims: "in order to form a Convention on the whole," or, in other words, that none of the subjects under negotiation, including the prizes and the ransoms, could be determined by a single agreement on any one issue. After further questioning, however, he said the French commissioners had made it plain that although it was only the territorial issues that were interdependent, this dependency was, in fact, absolute: even if a joint agreement on the boundaries of Acadia was reached, a British refusal to accept the French right to St. Lucia, and to the other islands claimed by France, would prevent a final settlement of all territorial disputes. Mildmay and Shirley's reply to this demand was that the settlement of the contested boundaries of Nova Scotia, where both countries already had inhabitants, was too urgent to wait for a decision on the right to any neutral islands, which: "were, or ought to be evacuated." However in the interests of trying to discover some kind of compromise that would prevent a possible rupture, or, as Mildmay put it: "not to dispute upon methods of concluding when we were just beginning," the British side asked to postpone further discussion until they had received their instruction on the French request for alternate conferences on Acadia and St. Lucia.[50]

These new French demands to negotiate the ownership of St. Lucia were noted by Joseph Yorke. In a letter that he sent from Paris on 14 September 1750 to Sir Benjamin Keene—now the British ambassador in Madrid—Yorke told him of this French insistence that the boundaries of Acadia and of Nova Scotia and the ownership of St. Lucia must now be treated as equally important issues and outcomes, and discussed alternately. Yorke told Sir Benjamin that before the British commissioners could agree to this demand they would require fresh instruction from London: "which they now wait for, and you will easily believe that tho' this is the first, it will not be the last difficulty attending this negotiation."[51]

In his journal Mildmay noted that following the second meeting he developed a fever, and the third conference thus had to be postponed for two weeks. Upon his recovery the commission assembled in his apartment on 21 September, where both sides exchanged formal memorials with each other concerning their official positions on the boundaries of Acadia and Nova Scotia.[52] The French commissioners had agreed to prepare this document on the British "favourite point," or the North American boundary disputes, because Shirley and Mildmay were forced to admit that they had not yet received their instructions on whether they could negotiate on the question of St. Lucia. Mildmay said that although they had sent their request for such directions to Whitehall on 8 September, the duke of Bedford had told them that the French demand to have discussions on St. Lucia must now be sent to Hanover, where George II, who was on his summer visit to his Electorate, would make the final decision.

The British memorial on the limits of Nova Scotia had been prepared by the Board of Trade, and in his journal Mildmay said that it described a territory bounded:

On the West towards New England by the River Pentagoet [Penobscot], that is to say beginning at its Mouth, and from thence drawing a Straight Line towards the north to the River St. Laurent [*sic*], or the great River of Canada; on the south of that River all along for as far as Cape Rosiers [Cape Gaspé], situated at its entrance; on the east by the great Gulf of St. Laurent, from the Cape Rosiers to the South East by the Island called Cape Breton, leaving the Islands [the Îles de la Madeleine and the Île St. Jean] and the Gulf on the right [or within its territory], and Newfoundland and the Islands [St. Pierre and Miquelon] belonging to it on the left [or outside the boundary], unto the Cape, or Promentory called Cape Breton; for the south by the great Atlantic Ocean, going south west from Cape Breton by Cape Sable; taking in the Island of that name, down to the Bay of Fundy, which reaches to the east of the Country, as far as the mouth of the River Penobscot, or Pentagoet.[53]

Having been so precise in their own geographic description, Mildmay reported that he and Shirley were astonished to find that the French memorial setting out the boundaries of Acadia was "extremely vague," or nothing but a description of what this territory did *not* contain. He said it stated that as Port Royal (later Annapolis Royal), facing the Bay of Fundy, was not within the ancient boundaries of Acadia, but formed an enclosed British enclave the French territory of Acadia thus occupied only "a part of the Peninsular which goes by that name." He continued that the island of "*Canceau*" (Canso) was similarly excluded from the French claim and, as the present boundaries between Acadia and Nova Scotia corresponded to those laid down in the Treaty of Utrecht, the French memorial stated that "these limits therefore ought to remain as they were before [or on the same boundary lines that had been established by this Treaty in 1713]."[54] When asked to give a more exact description of their proposed boundaries, Mildmay said the French commissioners replied that as the "demanders" it was up to the British to prove their right. What could not be proved then became the undisputed possession of France, as owner of the territory, or as Mildmay and Shirley's official report puts it, "they being in possession."[55] In this report they also told the duke of Bedford that Galissonière and Silhouette had requested the British government to supply copies of the entire list of documents it was citing in proof of its claim to the territory of Nova Scotia and, moreover, that all future arguments the respective sides intended to make in support of their territorial demands should be put into written form.

In his examination of the Anglo-French commission, Savelle states that as early as the end of September 1750 the differences of opinion shown in the conferences on the North American boundary disputes demonstrated that this commission had already become nothing but a futile exercise: one destined to wander on for another five years.[56] After only a month of diplomatic activity, and with four separate areas of disagreement to negotiate, such a hindsight conclusion might have seemed a little premature to four commissioners who had, as yet, held only three conferences on the boundaries of Acadia and Nova Scotia. If the history of these conferences concentrates entirely on the disputed territories in North America, then it is accurate to describe them as series of torturous discussions that became less and less relevant and ended in failure. The military skirmishes that took place in the Ohio valley and Acadia in 1754 did, indeed, become a major cause of the outbreak of the Seven Years' War, but in 1750 the crucial importance of settling the limits of these Nova Scotia and Acadia boundaries would not necessarily have been quite so obvious to the four commissioners.

The interest of both governments in deciding the ownership of territories was not limited solely to those in North America. The British certainly regarded such a settlement in Nova Scotia as their "favourite point" in these negotiations, but although the French had an interest in protecting the strategic fortress of Louisbourg and in securing its access to Canada across what is now northwestern Nova Scotia, their main objective was to obtain possession of the potentially lucrative sugar island of St. Lucia. Taking account of the other contentious issue, however, a major reason given by Louis XV for his decision to declare war on Britain in May 1744 concerned both the French prize ships that had earlier been captured by British privateers who were operating under royal letters of marque, and the blockade of the harbor of Toulon by the Royal Navy in the spring of 1744.[57] In 1750, given these considerations, perhaps the four commissioners could be forgiven for concluding that a settlement of what had been such a key irritant during the previous war might be an important contribution to prevent the outbreak of another.

In any event, if all his efforts had now become futile, Mildmay certainly did not appear to know this; but at this stage in the series of conferences, the mutual suspicion that the British and French commissioners had toward each other's intentions became the main obstacle in moving negotiations forward. This obstacle, in retrospect, was to have distressing results. In his journal for 25 September 1750 Mildmay reported on a conference, held in Silhouette's apartment, at which three of the major points in contention were on the agenda: the offer of the French commissioners to negotiate an immediate settlement of the limits of the North Sea and the Channel in order to obtain compensation for those ships' owners whose prize claims were uncontested (or within the commission mandate); their views on the compensation that should be due for the cargo of these prize ships; and their announcement that they were now prepared to discuss the boundaries of Nova Scotia and Acadia without also insisting on the prior negotiation of the ownership of St. Lucia.[58] Galissonière and Silhouette said they wanted their proposal for a prompt settlement of the sea limits to be given Lord Albemarle for his immediate decision, as: "the Damages to the claimants [the ship owners] would be increased by its being delayed."

Unfortunately for this promising beginning to what appeared to be a breakthrough in the negotiations, Mildmay and Shirley reported to the duke of Bedford they felt this French proposal might be an "ensnarement" that was calculated to lay the groundwork for "any future dispute concerning the extent and limit of these seas," and said this was also the opinion of Lord Albemarle when they consulted him on it later.[59] In his journal, Mildmay said that Galissonière and Silhouette were told, once again, that any immediate decision on the sea boundaries was out of the hands of this commission; they were reminded that since it had been already been decided that this subject was of too great importance to be negotiated by the commissioners, it had been referred to Lord Albemarle to discuss with M. de Puysieulx.

Mildmay said the problem he and Shirley saw with the second point concerned a difference of opinion on whether a ship's cargo was to be estimated on its value at the time of its capture, or on its value at the current market prices: the British government maintaining that it should be the former, and the French government insisting on the latter. He also reported that the offer to have immediate negotiations on the boundary disputes in Acadia and Nova Scotia had caught him and his colleague by surprise. As at a previous conference the French commissioners had insisted that any further discussion on this subject would require a prior agreement to hold alternate negotiations on the disputed claims to St. Lucia and Acadia, he said that the British side was thus unprepared for this matter to be raised. Mildmay attributed this apparent reversal of the French position to a meeting that Lord Albemarle had held with M. de Puysieulx on an earlier French threat to withdraw from the conferences, but as this concession on the protocol of the boundary negotiations had only been brought forward at the end of a long meeting, he reported that both sides had agreed to postpone this discussion until another conference. The French commissioners sent their own synopsis of the conference to the Marquis de Puysieulx on 1 October, and in it they asked him to pass to M. Rouillé (the French minister of the Marine) their report on what had taken place. On the question of St. Lucia, they told Puysieulx that they had assured the British commissioners that the king's sincere intention to establish a secure base for negotiations had been the reason for the French concession to allow the negotiations on the limits of Acadia to precede that of St. Lucia, and they also asked that they might be given a more precise geographical definition of the limits of the Acadia boundaries as soon as possible.[60]

At the next meeting, held on 5 October in Mildmay's apartment, it seems that Mildmay and Shirley were so encouraged by the apparent retreat of the French government on St. Lucia that, armed with some recent dispatches from Hanover containing further proofs of the British claim, and despite their lack of any government instructions on the position they were to take they decided, quite unwisely, as it turned out, to hold a thorough exploration of the North American boundary issue. In his journal, and in the report to the duke of Bedford, Mildmay said that at the outset of this 5 October conference the French commissioners took strong exception to the extensive amount of land that the British memorial had claimed for Nova Scotia, pointing out that this British assertion covered most of the territory that historically had been known as Acadia.

Mildmay and Shirley defended the justification for this claim by referring Galissonière and Silhouette to the terms of Treaty of Utrecht, which the French government had itself put forward as a settlement basis in its own memorial. They pointed out that in the preamble to this treaty, signed by Louis XIV in 1713, the land awarded to Britain was called "*Novelle Ecosse autrement dite L'Acadie en son entire* [sic]," and this description "necessarily took in Nova Scotia as well as Acadia." The French commissioners countered with the full quotation from the treaty which, they said, continued ". . . *en son entier conformement à ses Ancienne Limites,*" and as Nova Scotia had not been founded until 1621, while Acadia dated from its first discovery by Samuel de Champlain, these "ancient limits" stated in the Treaty of Utrecht thus described the territory ceded by Louis XIV as one in which Nova Scotia was an integral and indivisible part of Acadia. Shirley and Mildmay also told Bedford that the French commissioners had described the British version of the limits of Nova Scotia as "*Un Mot en Air* [*sic*], and did not comprehend any territory that they acknowledged by that name."[61]

It was at this point that Mildmay and Shirley's imprudent decision to proceed without some carefully considered instructions became evident; these joint exchanges quickly deteriorated into an semantic and acerbic argument over the meaning of the Latin text of the Treaty of Utrecht, and specifically on the words *sive* (or) and *et* (as well as, or both). Contrary to the preceding argument made by the French commissioners on the indivisible nature of this tract of land, Mildmay and Shirley told Bedford that Galissonière and Silhouette now maintained that the words "*Novam Scotiam sive Acadiam*" in the body of this treaty meant that these were two separate territories (Nova Scotia, *or* Acadia)—one to be owned by Britain and the other by France—and this phrase had never been intended to describe a single place. Against this French government interpretation, Mildmay and Shirley argued that as *sive*, in one of its meanings, had always been construed to be the equivalent of *et*, the sense of this description was "Nova Scotia, as well as Acadia;" in other words, in 1713 Britain had been given both Nova Scotia and Acadia under the Treaty of Utrecht. Further, Mildmay said Galissonière and Silhouette were told that to say Nova Scotia was "*un mot en air* was denying that there was such a country. That this was, as the logicians term it '*tollere Subjectuum Questioni*'. . . and that we could, by the like argument, prove that Canada was not in New France."[62] As Mildmay in retrospect said he felt that this kind of debate was abrasive and unproductive, he reported that when, "after many altercations of this nature, the meeting broke up," he and Shirley had mutually agreed it would be better to exchange written memorials in all future negotiations. They took the precaution, however, of sending further copies of their report to Bedford, to the duke of Newcastle in Hanover, and the Board of Trade in London.[63]

The proposal to have all future negotiations conducted in a written form produced an immediate response from the French government. On 16 October a draft of a project to define the French claim to the boundaries of Acadia was sent by M. Rouillé to Galissonière and Silhouette, and in the margin at the end was the notation, "this project has been submitted because Mildmay and Shirley persist in demanding this declaration of the French claim, which sets out the limits of "*Nouvelle France et la Nouvelle Angleterre*" [*sic*], as laid down in the Treaty of Utrecht. Attached to this draft was a signed copy of the treaty itself, in Latin, that had been given to the French commissioners by Mildmay and Shirley, in the side margin of which the clerk had noted: "And the commissaries say, on behalf of the King of Great Britain, they demand that the necessary orders are sent for the complete execution of the above mention Treaty of Utrecht, following the true intent and spirit of the Treaty, for the removal of settlements made by the subjects of the Most Christian King [of France]."[64]

As a result of this decision to reduce all further proposals to a written form, on 28 October Mildmay discussed with Fitzwalter his ideas on this new negotiation method that he and Shirley had now been instructed to adopt.[65] Max Savelle states that the decision, made in October 1750, to change this process from oral discussions to written reports—now to be made in the form of an exchange of memorials—was caused by the sense of futility in the present arrangement felt by the commissioners on both sides, and as his evidence for this conclusion he cites this letter of 28 October from Mildmay to Lord Fitzwalter.[66] A further reading of Mildmay's letter to Fitzwalter, however, taken together with an earlier entry in his commission journal, puts a somewhat different perspective on the reason for the alteration.

From the evidence of Mildmay's conference report of 5 October it seems that the change took place not so much from a sense of futility but from an alarm that the discussions appeared, suddenly, to have gotten out of hand. By Mildmay's own earlier admission, it seems that he and Shirley certainly should have waited for their instructions from Whitehall, for in his journal entry for 21 September Mildmay had already stated that since the list of justifications and proofs that must now be attached to the British and French memorials were both long and complex, the French commissioners had therefore suggested that each side should now: "reduce into Writing the arguments we should respectively make use of in our negotiation, in support of our demands; and also give copies of all Papers and instructions in Writing, which we should produce in proof of the claims we set up." Accordingly, Mildmay stated that on 23 September he and Shirley had written to the duke of Bedford, pointing out that this procedure of negotiating from written instructions seemed to be acceptable, given: "on our part no mistrust of the validity of our Arguments. . . ."[67]

Since Mildmay and Shirley had initially caused the problem by their decision to negotiate the boundary issue without first obtaining Bedford's instructions, Mildmay's version of these events seems somewhat disingenuous. In this letter, cited by Savelle, Fitzwalter was told that this change in method was

adopted because the previous negotiation process that relied on verbal presentations had become rather chaotic. Without any written record of the discussions, Mildmay said the meetings "generally broke up without coming to
any conclusion and as it was left to each of us to give such an account of our
debates as might be suggested by memory, whereupon our respective Masters
[the British and French governments] have given us orders to reduce our
demands to the reasons and evidence in support of them in writing, that there
might be some record." This was certainly putting the best face on what had
now become an abrasive and unproductive situation, and Mildmay was also
forced to admit that the time needed for each side to prepare their memorials
delayed the process. He told Fitzwalter, however, that he was now busy writing and correcting these memorial documents.[68] This remark certainly seems
to challenge Savelle's conclusion that from then onward "the preparation of
the British Memorials were in large measure taken out of the hands of
Mildmay and Shirley by the Board of Trade,"[69] implying, as it does, that they
had now become mere messengers in the transmittal of documents.

The 5 October negotiations on the territorial issues having proved so
troublesome, the subject of the next conference, held on 12 October at the
apartment of Galissonière, was exclusively concerned with the prize ships.
In his journal Mildmay said that, once again, the French commissioners
raised their concerns that under the law of Equity, merchants who had sustained subsequent losses arising from the unlawful seizure of their vessels
after the "cessation of hostilities" should be able to claim any future damages
suffered as a consequence of the seizure (or any losses caused by an increase
in the current market price).[70] Mildmay and Shirley countered with the argument that the commission was bound by its mandate in Article 4 of the
Treaty of Aix-la-Chapelle on the money to be paid for taking an unlawful
prize, the clear wording of which mentioned nothing about any subsequent
losses, but was restricted entirely to compensation for the value of the ship,
its gear, and its cargo at the time when it was taken.

In the commission report to the duke of Bedford, Mildmay and Shirley
said that in order to end any more argument about the eligibility of prewar
ships they read this fourth article to Galissonière and Silhouette, which stated: "*Et tous les Vaisseaux tant de Guerre, que Marchands, qui auront ete pris
depuis l'expiration des Terms convenus pour la Cessation des Hostilités en Mer,
seront pareillement rendu de bonne foi, avec tous leur Equipage et cargaisons*
[*sic*]."[71] Despite this clear description of "all ships of war, that are merchant

ships, . . . [and] which have been taken since the expiration of the terms [time limits] agreed to for the end of hostilities at sea . . . ," together with the lack of any mention of subsequent damages in the reference to payment for their "equipment [gear] and cargoes," they said the French commissioners then: "declaimed, in a loose manner, on the rules and principles of Equity, which took in all circumstances, and ought never to be limited by Time, or particular agreements." To this, Mildmay and Shirley said they replied that this principle should have been considered at the time the treaty was written and the commission could not make such an arbitrary adjustment two years later. In order to begin a serious consideration of the prize issue, however, Mildmay said they suggested that both sides should now prepare a general account, laid out in columns, and specifying the name of the ship and its captain, when and where it was taken, and the value both of the ship and of its gear and cargo. The French commissioners agreed to this proposal, but not before declaring they would also include a column headed "general damages," to which remark Mildmay and Shirley said they replied that: "they might indeed . . . [so] add, but we would strike out whatever they charged on that account."

On 21 October 1750 Mildmay and Shirley sent a letter to the Board of Trade asking for directions on what they were to do about St. Lucia.[72] It appears the British government then decided that as a result of the previous, unsatisfactory exchanges on Acadia and Nova Scotia, it was time for Britain to make a concession. The commissioners' correspondence contains two letters: one to the duke of Bedford and the other to the Board of Trade, acknowledging that they had now given been given permission to discuss the ownership of St. Lucia. In his journal for 19 October Mildmay noted that at this conference, held at Shirley's apartment, they were able to report to the French commissioners that in order to assist in the success of these negotiation George II (or rather the duke of Bedford) had directed them to agree with the French proposal to have alternate discussions on the disputes in Nova Scotia and in St. Lucia.[73]

This agreement was not entirely open-ended, however, as in exchange for this concession the British government said that once these two issues had been settled, it expected that immediate instructions to evacuate these neutral islands, and to end the military incursions in North America, would then be sent by each court to its colonies, and without waiting for any similar settlement of the disputes about either the prize ships or the ransom of prisoners. The French commissioners replied that they would communicate this demand to the foreign minister, but as the court was now at the palace of Fontainebleau for the autumn hunt, no reply could be expected for at least five weeks and, accordingly, the next conference would have to be postponed until 9 November.

Mildmay said the conversation then returned to subject of the previous meeting, but that Galissonière and Silhouette again restated their previous demand that prizes taken before the late war should also be included in the proposed general list of prizes. Mildmay and Shirley once more responded that they could not receive memorials about subjects that George II and the British government had already declared they would not discuss. To this, Galissonière and Silhouette answered that they did not expect the British commissioners actually to discuss these memorials, but to pass them on to Whitehall, at which point Mildmay reported that he and Shirley asked why the French government ministers did not send these documents to their British counterparts in the first place, and instead wasted the time of the commission by expecting it to act as a messenger. Before this conference broke up, once again the proceedings seemed to have become more than a little heated, for Mildmay reported that he also asked why the French king expected to be able to open such a discussion, as: "it was on account of these pretended unlawful captures made by the English before the War that the French King founded his declaration of War, which War then continued for some years and then was happily determined by this Treaty of Peace; and must not a Treaty of Peace be supposed to bury all those injuries in oblivion which occasioned the War to which this Treaty puts an end?"

The proposed conference on 9 November did not take place, as Mildmay said that the French government still had not produced its promised memorial on the French claim to St. Lucia,[74] and it was not until 18 November that the commission again convened. It seems that despite the previous, somewhat charged atmosphere, the commissioners were still able to meet socially. In a letter to the marquis de Puysieulx, written on 9 November, Galissonière informed him: "Sir, we have met today, not to confer, but to dine with the commissaries of Great Britain." The reason he gave for the delay was not the absence of their memorial on St. Lucia, as Mildmay had stated in his journal, but rather that: "these gentlemen have not yet put into a [proper] form their memorial on the Limits of Acadia."[75]

Despite their public, social lives, by this point it also appears that Mildmay and Shirley were not in the close and harmonious agreement with each other that Mildmay's journal implied. Ten days after the somewhat pointed meeting with the French commissioners on the prize ships, in his 28 October letter Mildmay told Lord Fitzwalter that his main problem, as he saw it, centered around William Shirley, whom he now described as a "slow mule . . . and as yet obstinate in his way. But the worst part of his character is his secret and reserved manner of sending private accounts to the Ministers upon points relating to our joint commission. This has been observed by other great personages here [Lord Albemarle and the senior diplomats] with proper indignity."[76] In his study of the work of this commission Savelle cites this letter as his evidence that "these commissioners themselves fell to quarrelling," but at no point does he state why. Savelle ends his quotation from this letter with Mildmay's description of Shirley as a "slow mule," but he does not give the text of Mildmay's next sentence about Shirley's secretive behavior and its divisive implications.[77]

Shirley was eleven years older than Mildmay, but the circumstances of their lives have a curious similarity. They were both the only sons of businessmen; Shirley was born in Preston, Sussex, in 1694 to a prosperous London merchant, and when Mildmay was born in Surat, in 1705, his father was the president of the East India Company's factory. Both of them became orphans at a young age and neither of them inherited great wealth; Shirley's parents had both died by the time that he was six and as his father's business had also failed, he inherited a very small annual income. As children, however, they were both aided by men who later became their patrons. Mildmay, who became an orphan at the age of eleven, was helped financially by Lord Fitzwalter, and Shirley received some assistance from a family friend, the duke of Newcastle. Shirley was sent to the Merchant Taylors School in London and in 1712 he also went up to Cambridge, but to Pembroke College rather than to Mildmay's destination of Emmanuel College (which he entered in 1723). When Shirley matriculated from Pembroke College in 1715 he then enrolled as a student at the Inner Temple, whereas Mildmay's Inn was the Middle Temple. Shirley was called to the Bar in 1720. He married a Frances Barker in the same year and, again like Mildmay, until 1731 he earned his living as a London lawyer.[78] This similarity in the circumstances of their lives extended even to the year of their deaths. William Shirley died in Roxbury, Massachusetts, in March 1771 at the age of 77,[79] and Sir William Mildmay died in Bath in August of the same year, aged 66.[80]

From 1731 until 1750, however, these circumstances completely diverged. In 1731, Shirley immigrated to Boston with his wife and nine children where, with a letter of introduction from the duke of Newcastle to Governor Belcher of Massachusetts, he was able to become a clerk in the Massachusetts courts. He moved steadily upward in Boston's bureaucratic and political circles and in 1741 he was appointed governor of Massachusetts. During the War of the Austrian Succession, Shirley distinguished himself by raising and organizing a militia force from New England that captured the French port of Louisbourg in 1745.[81] Much to Shirley's profound disgust, under the terms of the Treaty of Aix-la-Chapelle Louisbourg was handed back to France in 1748 in exchange for the withdrawal of the French from the Netherlands and the grant to Britain of the French East India Company port of Madras.[82]

Shirley's life began to intersect with that of Mildmay in 1749, when Shirley's political opponents in Boston persuaded the British government to hold an investigation into his possible misuse of military expenditures during the recent war. In the early autumn of 1749 Shirley received permission from the Board of Trade, and from the duke of Bedford, to have a temporary, acting governor sent to Boston in his absence; in late 1749 he returned to London to ask for the help of Bedford and Lord Halifax, president of the Board, in defending himself from these charges.[83] The inquiry was to drag on for two years, and until August 1750 Shirley was forced to remain in London. As he had considerable experience of the conditions in New England and held strong views on the problem of the boundary disputes, in December 1749 Bedford proposed to the duke of Newcastle that Shirley should become the senior British commissioner on the Anglo-French commission in Paris. After some initial resistance on Newcastle's part, as Bedford and Newcastle were on anything but good terms, Shirley's appeals to his patron were answered and in January 1750 he and Mildmay were appointed joint commissioners.[84]

Their early lives may have been somewhat similar but their personalities were very different. Shirley was a tall, imposing man whose character was somewhat closer to a part of the description that John Schutz has given to Mildmay: that of being "clever [and] intemperate," although there is no evidence from the letters of either man that Shirley was also "abusive." It was in their objectives for the outcome of the negotiations that Mildmay and Shirley had the sharpest differences, however, for Shirley had lived in Massachusetts for a large part of his adult life and he not only represented this colony as its British governor, but identified completely with the aims and fears of his fellow countrymen in New England. He was also the only person from the entire British side who had actually been to Nova Scotia and Acadia. In the Paris negotiations, therefore, he was not discussing a specific territory in the abstract, nor was he describing the region from vague and somewhat inaccurate maps, but in his advice on the strategic importance of a piece of land he was using his firsthand knowledge of its actual typography. In this respect Shirley must have found the unavoidable ignorance of both his colleague and his political masters in Whitehall to be very frustrating.

Shirley came to Paris, by his own admission, with three aims. The first was to defend both the territory of the New England colonists and their fishing fleets from any further military aggression by the French from Canada and Acadia, particularly by attack from the port of Louisbourg. The second was to secure for Virginia and Maryland the right to expand into the Ohio Valley from their present constricting boundaries. If it were possible, his ultimate aim was to remove the French from the continent of North America entirely, using any method by which this could be achieved and certainly not excluding warfare.[85] Shirley had already demonstrated, both in his administration of Massachusetts and in his military campaigns, that he was a forceful, determined man who did not suffer setbacks with much patience. He was also a clever and thorough bureaucrat whose letters were so dense with arguments and supporting evidential material that, in his strong efforts at persuasion, they frequently ran to six to eight pages per letter.[86] The notorious length of Shirley's letters was the subject of an amused exchange at the end of 1751 between Lord Albemarle and Lord Holdernesse, who was now the secretary of state for the Southern Department. In a letter written to Albemarle on 28 November (OS), Holdernesse backed Lord Duplin as the most voluminous of his correspondents but in his reply, on 22 December (NS), 11 December (OS), Albemarle countered with the remark: "If you boast of our friend Duplin for a long winded writer I think I can match him *dans le personne de Mr. Shirley.*"[87]

Shirley's major weakness, however, lay in the area that was Mildmay's strength: that of patient flexibility. Shirley was no diplomat, while Mildmay had all the characteristics of a very good one, along with some considerable advantages as a negotiator. He knew a great deal about France and the French, a subject on which Shirley did not seem to have much interest, and he also spoke and wrote fluent French, had traveled extensively in France before 1750, and continued to do so while he was a commissioner. It appears that Shirley may not have been as fluent in French as most of his embassy colleagues, and Mildmay did not bother to hide his contempt for Shirley's ignorance when—in his letter to Lord Fitzwalter of 28 October 1750—he gave a description of his colleague as "a slow mule that understands neither French nor English."[88] Mildmay exaggerated considerably here, however, for in his journal he stated that many of the conference negotiations were conducted in French,[89] and while Shirley may not have had such a good command of written French, in his ability to express himself in English he was certainly Mildmay's equal.

An essential part of Mildmay's negotiating ability was his familiarity with the nuances of French social and diplomatic behavior and his obvious enjoyment of life in Paris. Certain aspects of the Byzantine political and diplomatic activities of the French court irritated Mildmay as much as they did Shirley, but Mildmay was far too urbane to allow his irritation to become apparent and thus disturb the sensibilities of his French hosts. Consequently, he was popular in French society and had many friends and contacts—both in Paris and in the south of France—from whom he was able to acquire useful information. This kind of social interaction with important people in the host country was the required conduct for a successful diplomat,[90] and Mildmay practiced it thoroughly during his four and a half years in Paris.

Whatever Mildmay's reservations about Shirley's secretive behavior, there was an urgent need to move the negotiations forward. On 8 November another conference took place, but it proved to be as frustrating as the preceding meeting in mid-October. In his journal Mildmay stated that although he and Shirley had understood that its purpose was to receive the French memorial on the claim to St. Lucia, the French commissioners had insisted on returning to the prewar prizes, but only to state that without an agreement on the principles of negotiation they could see no point in any further conferences on the whole subject. He wrote that Galissonière and Silhouette gave their main areas of concern on these disagreements of principle; that the limits of the Channel and the North Sea had not yet been decided; that the question of any subsequent damages for prizes was still unresolved; and that there was a complete refusal by Britain to discuss any prizes that were taken before the war began.

On the second point, Mildmay said he and Shirley again repeated that their commission was limited to the bounds of the valuation of these ships, or their immediate value when captured, as laid down in the peace treaty. He then reported that the French commissioners had countered with the proposal that in order to reexamine the terms of this mandate: "the Plenipotentiaries that made the Peace (the British and French negotiators) are still in being, and could be resorted to." At this point Mildmay said they had told the French commissioners that it would only be "beating the air" to attempt reopen this agreement, particularly on damages for ships captured before 1744 as the British government had already stated its absolute refusal to entertain any such prewar prize claims.[91]

By the end of this conference Mildmay had concluded that this: "affected manner of talking upon matters that they well knew had been absolutely refused by our Court" had been to produce one of two objectives: either to stall on issuing their St. Lucia document until the British government produced its reply to their earlier position on Acadia, or else to disguise the fact that the French court had still not agreed on the contents of their St. Lucia memorial. Either way the ruse did not succeed, as the French commissioners were reminded that they had promised to give a full geographic description of their Acadia claim before they could expect the British reply. In a note in his journal Mildmay stated that on the following day, 19 November, the long-promised memorial on the limits of Acadia, signed by Galissonière and Silhouette, was delivered and sent to Whitehall for a detailed inspection.

These issues of the prize ships, the Channel limits, the North American boundary disputes, and the ownership of the West Indian islands were proving to be far more contentious than Mildmay had believed them to be in May 1750. It also appears that his initial optimism on the prospects for a speedy success in his other responsibility—the ransom negotiations—had begun to erode as early as August. As requested in May, Mildmay had compiled the full details of the indemnities required for the French prisoners of war and had handed over his list, and on 23 August 1750 he gave the duke of Bedford the full details of information that he was later to repeat to Lord Fitzwalter on 22 September. In this letter he told Bedford that in early August, commissioner Seigneur had sent him a memorandum which stated that that the French government was both contesting the payments listed for French sailors taken as prisoners on the prize ships and objecting to the amounts claimed for subsistence for all of the prisoners.

Mildmay explained that the dispute over the payment for the French sailors was based on the grounds that the French Ministry of War did not regard such men as combatants but simply as sailors, who were under the direction of the Ministry of Marine. As such they were not covered by the description in articles IV to XXXII in the Cartel of Frankfurt (signed on 18 July 1743) on the types of military prisoners for whom indemnity payment was required.[92] Mildmay told Bedford that from his previous inquiries to the superintendents of British prisons and hospitals, he had discovered that these sailors had been kept together with the French soldiers in the hospitals and prisons, had been looked after in an identical fashion to the soldiers, and had all been accepted as legitimate prisoners of war when they were handed over to the French commissioner for War at Calais in 1748. This official had given a receipt for the future indemnity of all these prisoners—both soldiers and sailors—under the Cartel of Frankfurt, and he thus observed: "If the objection should have been made at all, it ought to have been urged at the time they were offered to be exchanged as soldiers."

As for the objection to the subsistence payments, he pointed out to Bedford that although the Cartel of Frankfurt had only specified that a daily allowance of bread and straw would be given to each prisoner, at the time this agreement had been signed in 1743 it was assumed that these prisoners: "would be taken on the Continent, who might be mutually exchanged in 2 or 3 days, and therefore no other provision would be necessary, but it was not foreseen that an invasion would be made on England [in 1745, in support of the forces of Prince Charles Edward Stuart], and entire regiments at once be taken Prisoners of War, without the possibility of sending them back under several months." He said he felt it was thus completely unreasonable: "that such a just and humane gesture should be disputed by a Court that claims to be governed by these same principles," and he asked Bedford for further instructions on how to deal with these two objections.

In a letter he wrote to Lord Fitzwalter a month later, on 22 September, Mildmay gave a synopsis of Seigneur's objections in point form.[93] He noted the objections that the sailors and soldiers had been "blended together" in his accounts (since the French custom was to was to keep them under separate ministries, which required separate commissions), that full details of the maintenance receipts for the prisoners were lacking, and transportation costs were included that were far above the French limit of five shillings per head. Mildmay repeated to Fitzwalter his view that throughout their captivity these prisoners had described themselves as "land soldiers," they had been received as such by the French commissioners at Calais, and that such an objections should have been made at that time, and not two years later. So far as the receipts were concerned, he recounted that he told Seigneur that part of the overall costs was for the weekly maintenance of these men in the hospitals, and said he felt that the accuracy of the certificates supplied by the "Commissioners of the Sick and Wounded" as a record should be accepted without question. Nevertheless, in an effort to show he was willing to make a compromise on this matter, he told Fitzwalter that on 23 August he had sent Seigneur's objections to the duke of Bedford for his direction on whether Mildmay should now make a formal insistence, in writing, or whether Bedford preferred that Lord Albemarle should to take this up at a higher level.

In his letter to Fitzwalter, written one month later, he said that from his several exchanges with the French commissioner over the past few months he now had the impression that the French Ministry intended to refuse to pay their share of any of these ransoms. On the question of the prize ships he said he felt that from their insistence on discussing incidents that took place before the war began the French government was only trying: "to set up a claim for pretended [or so-called] unlawful captures,"[94] and he therefore told Fitzwalter that his advice to the duke of Bedford was that if no compromise was offered, the government should "stand firm" and on both of these issues. Further, he went on to say he felt this was the method of pressure for a compromise that should be used for all of the subjects under dispute, and he was comforted that this also seemed to be Bedford's position in the last letter he had sent to the commission.

He expanded on his information to Fitzwalter in a letter he sent on 24 November to Richard Neville Aldworth, private secretary to the duke of Bedford. There was now some urgency in this message; he asked Aldworth to tell Bedford that at their last meeting, Seigneur had threatened that if the French demands on the issue of the prewar prizes, the limits of the Channel and the North Sea, and the subsequent damages for ships' cargoes were not met, the French government would break off all negotiations on the subject of the prisoner ransoms: "and reserve their demands as a Standing Debt against us at some future occasion." He noted to Aldworth the new linkage that now appeared to have been set up between his sole responsibility for the prisoners and his joint commission with Shirley on the prizes and the sea limits, and repeated to Aldworth the opinion he had given Fitzwalter, ask-ing: "will it not be better, if, a debt is to remain, that it remain to the full extent of our demands in order to be hereafter set up against a debt which the Crown of France may demand on Us on account of unlawful Captures at Sea."[95]

The final commission conference of the year, held on 23 November at the apartment of Galissonière, was equally unproductive so far as the St. Lucia memorial was concerned. Despite the insistence of the French government at the outset of the negotiations that this subject was "their favourite point" for discussion, in his journal Mildmay reported they were surprised when the French commissioners stated that the document had not yet been drawn up and they could not say exactly when it would be ready. He said he again concluded that this delay was deliberate. In a report sent by both commissioners, the duke of Bedford was told that Galissonière and Silhouette had said: "they should not be ready with this memorial concerning their right to St. Lucia until we should deliver ours [the British response to the recent French memorial] to maintain our claim, which we insisted to be the Ancient Limit of Acadia." In order not to give the French government any opportunity for further delay, Shirley and Mildmay asked that the proposed British memorial on this subject be sent to them as soon as possible.[96]

It seems that from their previous unhappy experience in attempting to conduct negotiations without prior government direction, Mildmay and Shirley had also become far more cautious. In his journal for 23 November Mildmay said they also declined the French commissioners' suggestion that, in the absence of this British memorial, the commission could proceed to negotiate the limits of the Channel without prejudice to any other sea claims made by Britain, replying that even to enter into verbal discussions on such an issue they would need clear instructions from their government. The conference ended with an agreement to postpone the next meeting for ten days, during which time Galissonière and Silhouette said they would consult with their court at Versailles, but this consultation did not seem to produce any enthusiasm to continue. In a letter to the duke of Bedford on 2 December, Mildmay and Shirley said they had told the French commissioners they were ready to meet with them at any time, but until the British memorial had been delivered to them Galissonière and Silhouette had declined. They also said they were almost ready to present the memorial on the French "Right to St. Lucia."[97] This climate of stalemate was confirmed on 7 December by Silhouette, when in a letter headed "10th conference" he noted to the marquis de Puysieulx: "the conference [held] today was as sterile as its predecessors."[98]

What Mildmay saw as a deliberate delay in the negotiations on St. Lucia, coupled with the French refusal to settle the ransom, sea limits, and prize issues, was worrying enough, but throughout November and December 1750 he had another concern that he regarded as even more serious. In the negotiations to do with territorial claims, Shirley had been given the primary responsibility for the boundary disputes in North America, and Mildmay was given the task of upholding the British claim to St. Lucia. When the French commissioners delivered their memorial on the limits of Acadia on 19 November, Mildmay and Shirley promptly dispatched it to the British government and Shirley began to draft a preliminary reply that Lord Albemarle would send to London for examination and approval. As the memorial that the French commissioners had promised to deliver on St. Lucia was also expected to arrive shortly, Mildmay began his preparation of a position paper on the British claim to that island also. On 22 November Mildmay wrote to Lord Fitzwalter with his second complaint about Shirley as "a slow mule," explaining that when his own document on St. Lucia was ready he discovered that Shirley had done little about his draft on Acadia, except to produce a document on the day it was to be presented and which, in Mildmay's opinion: "I found dressed in so poor a stile [sic], in so confused an order, and with so many improper observations, that I was forced immediately to take pen in hand and draw up one in a different form, which I finished in five days. . . ."[99]

Mildmay told Lord Fitzwalter that he presented this recast draft of the Acadia reply to Joseph Yorke and to Lord Albemarle—both of whom approved it—but at this point Shirley refused to allow his work, for which he had been given the sole responsibility, to be dismissed in so casual and arbitrary a manner. He thus insisted that both of these drafts on Acadia must be sent to the duke of Bedford for his decision on which of them should be presented to the French, or whether yet a third should be drawn up. As a consequence of this dispute between himself and Shirley Mildmay reported that the Board of Trade had now been asked to draft the British statement, while the French commissioners continued to refuse to resume negotiations on the disputed boundary of Acadia and Nova Scotia until their latest memorial was answered.

In this letter of 22 November Mildmay also gave the reason why he and Shirley were on bad terms at the end of 1750. He explained to Fitzwalter that even more disturbing than this dispute over the wording of drafts, he had received proof of the information he had given to Lord Fitzwalter in October on Shirley's covert activities through a letter from his friend John Pownall, a senior clerk in the Board of Trade whose job was to copy the letters of its president (Lord Halifax). He said Pownall's letter confirmed that Shirley had, indeed, been sending private letters to Lord Halifax that contained copies of the correspondence between the commission and the duke of Bedford.[100] Mildmay did not reveal Pownall as his source, but rather said that "his informant" had told him that in a letter Shirley had written to Lord Halifax on 21 October, he had even gone so far as to tell Halifax he feared: "ill consequences from the instructions received from His Grace [Bedford] and intimating to His Lordship whether it would be proper to hint the same to "Lord C" [Lord John Cartaret, president of the Privy Council] and "Mr. P" [Henry Pelham].[101]

The "instructions" to which Shirley referred were, presumably, those that the duke of Bedford had issued to the commission in early October, in which he had agreed that the British commissioners could now concede to the French the right to hold alternate conferences on the ownership of St. Lucia. The French had stated at the outset that since the determination of this island was as important to them as the boundary of Nova Scotia was to Britain, they might be willing to make territorial concessions in North America in exchange for the secure possession of St. Lucia. Shirley, as governor of Massachusetts, was greatly concerned with the defense of colonial interests on the frontiers of that colony and, given his experiences of French land encroachment over the preceding decade, he was also profoundly distrustful and skeptical about what he considered to be the true intentions of France: in particular, those of his old wartime adversary in Canada, the marquis de la Galissonière. Moreover, he also knew that Lord Halifax, the founder of the two-year-old settlement in Nova Scotia bearing his name, was equally determined to defend this valuable, but vulnerable colonial outpost.

It is possible that as Shirley's chief fear was for the future of New England, his distrust of French intentions had also caused him to distrust Mildmay's easy ability to move in French society, and even to suspect Mildmay's true motives. He certainly suspected that both the duke of Bedford, and later Lord Holdernesse, were not as determined in their defense of the interest of the British North American colonists as Shirley wished them to be. His letters to Lord Halifax, and through Halifax to the Board of Trade, were certainly designed to counter what Shirley saw as this weakness on the part of Bedford. Unfortunately, Shirley's lack of any previous diplomatic experience led him into the direct and somewhat naive method of stepping outside the chain of command.

Whatever Shirley intended by his correspondence with Lord Halifax, in his letter of 22 November Mildmay told Fitzwalter he was now seriously alarmed that when the duke of Bedford heard what had been taking place, he would assume that Mildmay was a party to this secretive, disloyal behavior and thus he, as well as Shirley, would be disgraced. On the other hand, he also feared that if he disclosed anything to Bedford, the working relationship he had with Shirley would be ended and so would the future of the commission. He said he had therefore decided his only present course was to continue as though he were unaware of Shirley's activities, while, at the same time, making this private protest to Fitzwalter as evidence that could be used for his future protection. One month later, on 19 December, Mildmay thanked Fitzwalter for his good advice on this issue and told him that the problem seemed to have been resolved by some new instructions that had been issued to the commission by the duke of Bedford. He was very discreet and did not intimate directly that Lord Fitzwalter had any hand in this solution, but he stated that "orders [the draft written by Shirley] which I had refused to sign are laid aside and. . . . we are to proceed under the sanction of orders [the draft statement issued by the Board of Trade] for which I am in no way accountable."[102]

On 6 January 1751 the memorial on Acadia that had been prepared by the Board of Trade on 10 December 1750 arrived in Paris. Mildmay and Shirley reported to the duke of Bedford that it would now be translated and, together with the English original, would be presented to the French commissioners as soon as Galissonière returned from a visit to Versailles.[103] This memorial contained a long and detailed argument on the historical justifications for British claims to ownership of the territory of Acadia, and it was finally printed in the collection of all the memorials that had been exchanged between the two sides, and which the British government published in 1756 as a justification for its actions.[104]

As this British memorial on Acadia was to become the ostensible cause of a long and disastrous delay in the negotiations, the report the commissioners sent to the duke of Bedford about its delivery is enlightening. On 13 January 1751, Shirley and Mildmay informed Bedford that when they handed over both the English original and the translation, they had emphasized that the English document was: "what we should appeal to in case of any dispute concerning the sense of the memorial, and that the other was to be considered only as our translation of it into French for their ease, but that we did not hold ourselves concluded by any defects which might be found in it." Mildmay and Shirley had, of course, no knowledge that their remark would lead to a delay of over two years in the territorial negotiations (from June 1752 to September 1754), but this claim that the English version of the memorial would prevail in all cases of dispute was later to be used by the French government to justify a demand that all memorials must first be submitted in French, as the predominate and official diplomatic language: a requirement that the British government found totally unacceptable and rejected.

Mildmay and Shirley continued in their report to Bedford that although at the conference of 23 November 1750 the French commissioners had promised to release their St. Lucia memorial as soon as they received that of the British on Acadia, seven weeks later, Galissonière and Silhouette had not only admitted that this memorial was still not ready, and could give no date when it would be, but that: "this declaration was made with an Air, which now plainly demonstrates an affected delay in their part, after a regular method of proceeding on ours." They said that all they could secure was a promise to meet again in ten days, after their memorial on Acadia had been examined in Versailles.[105]

It is true that the first four months of negotiations had decided nothing of substance and the distrust between the countries was deep, but certain progress had been made. Each government had laid out its positions, and had discovered the main sources of their disagreements. France had stated that she required serious discussions to take place on the ownership of St. Lucia—carried out in tandem with negotiations on the Nova Scotia and Acadia boundary lines—and had also indicated that in exchange for a confirmation of her ownership of St. Lucia, she might be prepared to make certain concessions on Acadia. Britain had conceded the diplomatic protocol to alternate discussions on these two claims, but she had also obtained a negotiating advantage: a beginning had been made on establishing the boundaries of Nova Scotia and Acadia in four memorials (two from each side), while the ownership of St. Lucia was yet to be dealt with.

So far as the prize ships were concerned, although Britain had also obtained an agreement, albeit qualified, to have a "general list" of such ships prepared for settlement, France still maintained the right to raise the contentious issues of the prewar prizes and the subsequent damages owed to ship owners for any prizes taken after April 1748, and continued to insist that a successful negotiation on the prisoner ransoms was dependent on the terms of these prize ships being met. The Channel and the North Sea limits were even further from an agreement, and the second year of negotiations would obviously be crucial in order to achieve a breakthrough on any of these issues. By December 1750 the impetus of the talks appeared to have stalled somewhat, however, and the tempo of next year's negotiations must obviously be increased if any of these disputes were to be settled.

# 5.
# THE TIME OF POSSIBILITY:
# JANUARY 1751 TO MAY 1752

❧

AT THE BEGINNING OF 1751 THE MOST urgent problem that the British government needed to settle was the boundary dispute in North America, but
during the first thirteen weeks of the year the joint commission held only
three conferences. These took place on 21 January, 15 February, and 8 April
and all were on the subject that France had declared to be her "favorite
point" in the autumn of 1750: namely the ownership of St. Lucia.[1] The 21
January conference in Mildmay's apartment was convened specifically to
receive the French government's memorial on St. Lucia, but when
Galissonière and Silhouette arrived they admitted that although they had
received the British memorial on Acadia on 13 January, their St. Lucia document still was not ready to be exchanged and said they hoped to be able to
present it in about two more weeks.[2]

After three months of such assurances Shirley and Mildmay had become
increasingly impatient with this procrastination, and as the French government had already stated that it was prepared to explore the possibility of a
territorial linkage between the French claim to St. Lucia and the disputed
boundaries in Acadia they were understandably concerned at any further
delay. From the evidence of letters that they sent to Whitehall between
January and March 1751 it seems that early in January they began their
efforts to accelerate the pace of negotiations on St. Lucia by suggesting that
the British might preempt the French claim with one of their own.

In a letter written on 17 January Shirley and Mildmay sent the duke of
Bedford two separate drafts of a memorial entitled "A State of His Majesty's
Right to that Island (St. Lucia) . . . according to the light of the Subject
Matter as it appears to each of Us." This, they said, had been drawn up from
various documents sent to them by the Board of Trade. They asked Bedford

if he found either the whole or any parts of these alternate versions to be satisfactory, did they then have his permission to recast the document and give
the approved memorial to the French commissioners before the promised
French memorial arrived. They said they felt this might be the only way to
bring the tactic of endless delay to an end, and they also noted that they had
sent over a copy of the French translation of the British Acadia memorial of
6 January, and asked for a speedy decision from the Board of Trade on their
proposed St. Lucia document in order that it could be similarly translated.[3]

These efforts to anticipate the French memorial on St. Lucia, however,
had not been well received in Whitehall, either in their intent or in their
presentation. The existence of these two versions of the same document
indicates that Mildmay and Shirley still had not resolved their private differences on the wording of these draft memorials, and from the text of a letter
written to them by the duke of Bedford on 11 February 1751 (OS), 22
February (NS), and delivered in Paris a few days later, it is clear that their
method of giving him their differing opinions in two separate versions of the
same subject did not please the southern secretary. Bedford stated his disapproval in a very blunt letter that told them: "your method of sending separate
States of your Memorials on some subjects has, with justice, given us great
displeasure, and the more so as you have not marked out in the margin, the
points in which you differ in your opinion, which was the more necessary to
do as they [the differences] are, in several places, too trivial and immaterial to
be otherwise observed."[4]

Bedford had obviously been informed of the strained relationship that had
been growing between Mildmay and Shirley throughout 1750, as he went on
to say: "The unnecessary trouble occasioned by this way of proceeding is not
the only objection to it. There is another, and that is the more material, which
is that it carries with it the appearance of some distrust or jealousy between
yourselves, than which (if true) nothing can be more detrimental to the
Services you are employed upon, and I hope, therefore, I shall have no further cause for any such suspicion." He instructed them that in the future they
should write a joint version of those things on which they both concurred:
restricting any views on which they differed to separate observations in the
margin of the joint document at the appropriate place.

Having dealt with his quarrelling commissioners, Bedford then explained
why the government did not want any British claim to St. Lucia to be presented before the French had submitted their own, and in this explanation it

is clear that the nebulous and inexact territorial description that the French government had produced in their 21 September 1750 memorial on the supposed limits of Acadia still rankled, both with the British government and with George II. Bedford told Mildmay and Shirley that no instructions had been sent concerning their 17 January draft memorials because: "the King did not think it proper that the French should be acquainted with the particulars of His Majesty's Rights to the Points in dispute before they had given, in any particular, their own Rights, which they cannot pretend to have done in their vague and loose description of the Limits of Nova Scotia, or Acadia, as contended by them." He said the Cabinet had therefore decided that the French must be the first to declare their terms, and that any discussion of British rights in the draft memorials that Shirley and Mildmay had put forward must wait until an informed analysis of the French claim could be made in Whitehall.

It was undoubtedly necessary to obtain the king's permission before proceeding to issue an official memorial, but the duke of Bedford did not appear to appreciate that there was an urgency to Mildmay and Shirley's present efforts in Paris. Although their innovative proposal to end the French procrastination on the ownership of St. Lucia had been sent to Bedford on 17 January his answer did not arrive in Paris until late February, and by the middle of that month any such permission had become academic. On Saturday, 17 February, Mildmay and Shirley informed Bedford that two days earlier they had been presented with a memorial on "the State of Pretensions of the Court of France to the Island of St. Lucia;" but as this massive document (which Mildmay's journal stated took them over three hours to read) now needed to be copied by their secretary, it was not until 21 February that they were able to confirm that the original was on its way to Whitehall by diplomatic courier.[5]

In order for the Board of Trade to make a careful examination of this French memorial on St. Lucia it was obviously necessary to have access to the entire collection of justification documents on which the French government was basing its claim, but on 17 March—over a month after this memorial had been presented to them—Mildmay and Shirley informed the duke of Bedford they were still without the majority of these French historical proofs. In this 17 March report they also said that although they had been pressing the French commissioners for the long-awaited French reply to the British Acadia memorial of 13 January, it had not yet arrived and, in fact, they had been told that the French government still needed some time to prepare its answer. Despite Bedford's previous instructions that nothing would be given to the French Court on any British claims to St. Lucia until all of these proof documents could be examined, once again Mildmay and Shirley attempted to end this deliberate stalling by asking whether the Board of Trade could issue a preliminary reply on the French claim to St. Lucia based on the what had already been sent to Whitehall in the French memorial, "as the most practicable method of forcing an answer from them to our memorial [on Acadia], and by breaking their affected delays."[6]

There is no record of a reply to this second request, either in the commission reports or in Mildmay's journal, but in his journal entry for the commission conference of 8 April Mildmay recorded that when the entire set of French justifications on St. Lucia was finally handed over there were so many of these documents that they were bound into a large folio volume complete with an index. In their letter to the duke of Bedford on 13 April, Shirley and Mildmay told him this volume was entitled: "*Les preuves des droits du Roy sur L'isle de St. Lucia*" and with the enclosed copy of the French memorial on St. Lucia, the book contained some 886 pages. They said they had been told they could make copies of the documents, but as the transcription of this large amount of proofs would take the embassy staff a considerable amount of time, they said that they had Galissonière and Silhouette's permission to send the book to Whitehall to be copied before returning it. At the same meeting (8 April) during which Galissonière had handed over the proof documents, they said he had also asked for the British answer to the French memorial on St. Lucia. Therefore, in their 13 April letter, they gave Bedford their initial, brief observations of these historical justifications.[7]

Since the British government was now fully occupied in reviewing a large number of French documents, and the French commissioners had already indicated that their answer to the Acadia boundary issue was far from ready, in mid-April Mildmay and Shirley received instructions that they were now to turn their attention from the territorial disputes to the subject of the prize ships. In his journal Mildmay said that the series of conferences that followed were initiated by a letter from the duke of Bedford that arrived in Paris in the second week of April. Bedford wrote to Mildmay and Shirley on 25 March (OS), 5 April (NS), telling them that he had just received a letter from the duke of Mirepoix, French ambassador to Britain. In this letter, he said that Mirepoix: "was proposing that Directions might be given to you and the

French Commissaries to proceed, without further loss of time upon that Part of your Commission which relates to the Prizes taken at Sea since the Term fixed for the Cessation of Hostilities. . . . If therefore you can agree with the French Commissaries to set aside one or two days a week for this Separate consideration . . . the sooner you enter upon it the better, that the Persons interested may not offer any delay that is not absolutely necessary."[8]

In his journal Mildmay reported that they accordingly asked the French commissioners to discuss this issue in a meeting that was held at Shirley's house on 22 April.[9] Assuming, from Bedford's letter, that Mirepoix's reference to "Prizes taken at Sea since the Term fixed for the Cessation of Hostilities" indicated his government's final acceptance of the British demand to consider only post-war claims, and given Bedford's inference that a speedy resolution of the dispute was now desired by both sides, Mildmay said that before the conference took place he and Shirley had prepared an itemized agenda of the other three questions that still remained to be negotiated with the French ministry. These he listed as: "1st, The manner of fixing the Limits of the Channel and the North Sea; 2ndly, Whether in determining the Quantum of the damages we were to allow only to allow the value of the ship and cargo at the time of capture, and not any subsequent damages; 3rdly, Whether the balance was to be struck on a general account [to be settled] between the two Crowns, or whether the Parties complaining were to seek for recovery against their respective Captors, according to the Decision that should be made on each case by the commissaries."

To Mildmay and Shirley's consternation, when the conference opened Galissonière and Silhouette stated that before anything could be determined on these prizes it must first be agreed that all decisions would be based on the principles of equity law and "natural justice." In his account of this meeting Mildmay said he then asked whether such a demand meant that they intended to use such "principles" in order to negotiate their claims for ships taken before the war had been declared, and, if so, whether this was also the instruction they had received from their Court. He reported that the French commissioners answered yes to both questions, and he then recounted: "It was indifferent [to them] what answer we should give, for if we refused it, and did not think fit to regard these general principles of Justice and Equity . . . the Court of France would know what part they had to act."

Shirley's immediate response was to ask for an official, written declaration of the French government's demand for this application of equity law but, in an effort to head off what suddenly appeared to have become a critical situation that could jeopardize the negotiations entirely, Mildmay said he urged that a memorial be prepared stating which points the commissioners felt they did not have the power to negotiate, leaving it to the government Ministers of both countries to judge whether these powers could now be expanded. Despite this attempt to moderate the tone of the discussion, however, Galissonière and Silhouette still replied that their written statement would contain their demand about the legal principles that must underlie the commission's work, and they would deliver such a memorial to the British commissioners at their next conference.

This memorial was handed over at a meeting at Silhouette's apartment on 29 April, and Mildmay recorded the five questions to which the French government now required that Britain give definitive and unequivocal answers. These were whether prizes taken before the war, and specifically from 1738 onward, were to be within the commission mandate; whether the commission had the legal power to determine damages claimed by the ship owners; whether all payments for these damages were to be guaranteed by the two governments and did not to have be recovered from the individual captors; whether the indemnities would include subsequent damages, beyond the value of the ship and its cargo; and lastly, whether the commission was to be given the sole authority to determine the limits of the Channel and the North Sea.[10] These were all questions that had already been addressed and answered in the British memorial on the prize ships, but given Shirley's confrontational response to the French commissioners' thinly disguised diplomatic blackmail, together with the additional threat that they intended to issue an official document that would state the French position, Mildmay had already decided he must now inform Lord Albemarle and seek his assistance.

He had easy access to Albemarle because, as a commissioner, Mildmay was one of the staff of diplomatic officials attached to the British embassy at Paris;[11] but beyond his official position, it appears that he was often in the ambassador's company on a social basis. On 7 June 1752 he told Lord Fitzwalter that "my chief time is taken up with Lord Albemarle's family, whose house and table are always open to me."[12] In his letters to Sir Horace Mann, Horace Walpole confirmed that Lord Albemarle was a very hospitable diplomat who "kept an immense table there, with sixteen people in his kitchen, his *aide-de-camps* invite everybody." When Albemarle died in December 1754 his debts were also immense.[13]

Mildmay's commission instructions required that he keep the ambassador informed, but he had also decided to consult Lord Albemarle because he knew that Albemarle was a skilled diplomat. Contrary to the low opinion of Horace Walpole, who stated in a letter to Sir Horace Mann that Albemarle's diplomatic appointment was entirely due to his long and close friendship with the king, Albemarle's position at the Paris embassy was not, as Walpole implied, simply a patronage sinecure. He was, indeed, a friend of both the duke of Newcastle and George II, but he was also seen by the British government as a valuable diplomatic representative whom the French Court regarded with favor. His urbane and gracious manner was well suited to the ceremonial etiquette of Versailles and he had a wide circle of influential friends.[14]

As Mildmay saw Lord Albemarle frequently a letter would normally have been unnecessary, but it seems Mildmay considered the present situation to be sufficiently serious that on 27 April—two days before the French memorial was officially received by the British commissioners—he gave Albemarle a private, written report on the latest conference of 22 April.[15] He said he knew that Albemarle would be meeting that day with M. de Puysieulx and, in order that he be well prepared, Mildmay felt it important to outline the main points that had been made by Galissonière and Silhouette. He informed Albemarle that although the March letter from the duke of Mirepoix to the duke of Bedford had stated that France wished only to negotiate the problem of prize ships taken after the end of the war, Galissonière and Silhouette had unexpectedly renewed the original demand to include those ships that had been taken since 1738. He also reported their implied threat to take unilateral action if this demand were not met, and of the announcement of a forthcoming, official, written statement on this issue.

On the latter point he said: "if the memorial of the French commissaries, which they threaten to deliver to us on the next Thursday should be written in the same stile [sic] in which Monsieur de Silhouette was pleased to declaim himself by word of mouth, it must necessarily produce an answer that may not be suitable to the harmony at present subsisting between the two Nations." Mildmay appreciated that Albemarle was an equable diplomat and therefore advised that while he felt the British government should stand firm on their position, in the interests of reaching some negotiated agreement on this issue he considered that Albemarle's customary, calm demeanor would be most effective in "preventing the consequences that may arise from too warm, or too presumptuous demands."[16]

This advice is typical of the style of negotiation that Mildmay not only advocated, but practiced. He was firm, but he also displayed a patient pragmatism, strongly believing that government ultimatums should, if possible, be avoided. In his remark to Albemarle about the "too warm, or too presumptuous demands" Mildmay was referring not only to the behavior of Galissonière and Silhouette; for in his aim to achieve a final and mutually acceptable peace agreement, rather than to gain satisfaction from a belligerent defense of national "rights," he feared he might be on a collision course with William Shirley, whose aims and behavior were the precise opposite. Mildmay's immediate problem was to prevent Shirley from endangering the future of the commission by any impetuous, undiplomatic behavior, and his approach to Lord Albemarle in April appears to have been successful, as the British commissioners were now given some guidance from the ambassador on how they should proceed.

On 5 May, a week after the 29 April conference at which they had received the French memorial that asked for a statement of British intent, they informed the duke of Bedford that they had now prepared an answer that contained several preliminary proposals for the successful negotiation of the disputes on the prize ships. Bearing in mind Bedford's earlier instructions on the required method for presenting such analyses and suggestions, they enclosed a copy of the French memorial and accompanied it with two drafts that were written on either side of this document: "the one proposed by Mr. Shirley in English, the other by Mr. Mildmay in French, written in columns, with the [French] memorial between, that your Grace may more easily perceive the reasons given in each in order to form such an answer as shall be thought proper to be returned." They also said they had noted the warning given to them by Bedford not to "enter into a mutual Agreement in writing" on the boundaries limits of the North Sea without careful consultation with the Board of the Admiralty, as the only body with the ultimate responsibility to determine these limits.[17]

Within three weeks they must have received their instructions from Bedford, as the correspondence files of the French Foreign Ministry contain a document, written and signed by Mildmay and Shirley on 26 May, entitled *Réponse aux observations des Commissaries de Se Majesté Tres Chrétien touchant les prises sur me.*[18] In this document Mildmay and Shirley stated they had been instructed to say that the British government had never intended to have any discussions on pre-war prizes. The only part of this issue they said had been agreed would be discussed between the two Courts concerned ships that were captured during the first six months after war had been declared (mid-March to mid-August 1744), since these seizures were covered by the nineteenth article of the Treaty of Utrecht. In the second part of the statement they said that all prizes that the British Admiralty Courts ruled had been taken illegally would receive compensation from those captains who had been responsible for seizing the ships, and payment would be made after all debts that were owed to the French and British Crowns had been settled. In their last observation, concerning the limits of the North Sea, they stated that in the view of the British Ministers: "the North Sea extended from the eastern end of the Straits of Dover to the islands of the Orkneys and the Shetlands, and the British Seas were those described as surrounding all the coasts and territories of the British King."

Three days after they had issued this statement, on 29 May, Mildmay and Shirley were forced to remind Bedford that they were still awaiting the return of the large volume containing the French justifications on St. Lucia, the French commissioners having requested that their documents be sent back as soon as possible. On 9 June they asked for Bedford's clarification on whether the statement in the British memorial that any claim made by the owner of a prize ship against an insolvent ship's captain, or his agent, could always be brought before the Admiralty Courts, would also take legal notice of the prior determination made by the commission on such claims for damages. They said they were apprehensive that they would be pressed by the French commissioners on this legal point, and urgently needed his instructions. In accordance with Bedford's caution on the issuing of any written agreements, on 16 June he was informed that Mildmay and Shirley had accepted the French commissioners' assertion that their respective governments must approve the final wording of any positions put forward by both sides on the limits of the Channel and the North Sea, and accordingly, each group had thus declined to commit themselves to specific, written proposals until this had been done: a process which they said they had been assured by the French commissioners would take some "three to four days."[19]

On 28 June, after a hiatus of two months, Mildmay and Shirley attended another conference at Galissonière's apartment at which they delivered a formal reply to the objections made by the French commissioners to the British position on prize ships and sea limits, and presented to Mildmay and Shirley on 29 April. Perhaps the meeting between Lord Albemarle and M. de

Puysieulx, and the length of time since the commissioners last met, had caused the French government to reconsider its stance on these issues, as Galissonière and Silhouette certainly seemed to be somewhat less belligerent in their responses than they had been at the end of April. In his journal entry Mildmay quoted from the content of this British memorial, and reported the details of a subsequent discussion that had been held on it. He said that in response to the British statement that: "No other answer can be given to this Article (Article 4, on the definition of a legitimate prize as a post-war capture) than what has been already made to the Court of France," the French commissioners had replied: "they should give us no further trouble thereon."[20] Mildmay reported, however, that Galissonière and Silhouette were less approving of the second article. In this the British government stated that it refused to allow ship owners to recover their losses directly from the respective governments, insisting that other than for those ships captured by: "Captains of Ships of War, since Dead or insolvent," owners of all other prizes could take their claims against a specific captain to the Admiralty Court. Mildmay told Bedford the French commissioners had complained that this method was of little help to such owners, since after so much time had elapsed it would now be impossible to find these individual captors, or their agents.

Similarly, on the questions of any allowable damages beyond the value of the ship and cargo at the time of their capture, Galissonière and Silhouette had said it was unclear the British statement that: "As Ships as well as their Cargoes are of a perishable Nature, justice demands that Indemnification required in this respect should be taken at the time they were made," actually answered the question of whether: "consequential damages should be taken into consideration." On the final issue, concerning the limits of the Channel, the French commissioners charged that the British definition that this area was bounded by: "the South Foreland at Calais to the Eastward, and from the Westermost part of Ireland, to the Westermost part of Ushant to the Westward" was a cynical attempt to protect those captures that had been made by British captains near the coasts of northern and north-western France by claiming that this entire body of water was owned by the British Crown. Mildmay said that this conference ended with a statement from the French commissioners that as they had found these last three clauses to be completely unsatisfactory, they would be presenting another memorial in due course.

In the margin of his journal entry for 28 June 1751 Mildmay also noted that on the following day, 29 June (NS), 18 June (OS), "His Majesty was pleased to appoint the Right Honourable the Earl of Holdernesse" to replace the duke of Bedford as Secretary of State for the Southern Department,[21] and as diplomatic relations with France were a part of the southern secretary's responsibilities, Holdernesse was now in charge of the commission in Paris. Lord Holdernesse's appointment was to have great importance for Mildmay. His long friendship with and patronage from Holdernesse's stepfather, Lord Fitzwalter, gave him a far greater influence with his new political master than he had under the duke of Bedford.

This influence is demonstrated in a letter that Lord Holdernesse sent him on 7 July 1751 (OS), addressed "To William Mildmay Esq. Private" on its cover page, in which he told Mildmay: "I cannot let this messenger go away without repeating the assurances of my steady friendship for you. Your publique letters will be acknowledged from my office. . . . These lines are for you *only* (*sic*)." Holdernesse was about to make an official, ministerial visit to the Princess Regent of Holland, but he promised Mildmay: "as soon as I return from Holland I shall very seriously attend to your Branch of Business," telling him that rather than entrusting any private correspondence to the ordinary mail, he was to give them to the First Secretary, Joseph Yorke, who: "will transmit them safely to me (via the King's Messenger service)."[22] Accordingly on 3 August Mildmay wrote Holdernesse a private letter that noted his Lordship's return to Whitehall at the end of July and, in keeping with his considerable interest in the state of French trade and commerce, Mildmay also enclosed some information on the present economic condition of the French-owned island of St. Dominique (later known as Haiti) that he had obtained from one of his useful French contacts.[23] His letter also discussed with Holdernesse the present state of the French economy in general and the possible trade advantage to British manufacturers in establishing a government trade consulate in Naples.[24]

The new secretary of state needed to become acquainted with the details of his portfolio and in order to give Holdernesse a knowledgeable overview of what had already taken place, on 7 July Mildmay and Shirley sent him their appreciation of the first eleven months of negotiations on the territorial and prize issues. They began their four-page report by referring Holdernesse to the numerous documents and letters they had exchanged with the duke of Bedford on the territorial disputes, and they emphasized that eleven months

had elapsed between the present date and the first exchanges on this issue in
1750. This apparent procrastination had, they said, been caused by the unexpected insistence of the French government that their claim to the ownership
of St. Lucia must receive an equal consideration with the disputed boundaries
of Acadia and Nova Scotia, and be discussed alternately: a demand which, as
Mildmay and Shirley said they had received no prior instructions, had apparently had taken Whitehall by surprise. The second, unavoidable, reason for
the slowness of negotiations was, they said, a function of the decision by both
governments to negotiate mainly through written memorials, and the final
delay had been caused both by the time it was taking for the French ministers
to reply to the British memorial on Acadia, and the reluctance of the French
Court to commit itself on the proof of its right to St. Lucia until April of this
year.[25]

From their comments to Lord Holdernesse it is obvious that these delays
were not entirely one-sided. The duke of Bedford's disinterest with the work
of his portfolio was notorious but in Claudius Amyand the Southern
Department had an able and experienced chief clerk and professional civil
servant, and neither the president of the Board of Trade, Lord Halifax, nor
one of its most active members, Charles Townshend, could be described as
either incompetent or unconcerned with the subject. The length of time that
it took for official documents to emerge from Whitehall during these ten
months was a serious setback to the early momentum of the negotiations,
however, and this unfortunate delay could, perhaps, have arisen either from
a failure to appreciate the importance of seizing the initiative, from an overly cautious attitude to decision making, from debate and disagreement, both
between and within the Cabinet and the Board of Trade, on the best course
to take, or from a combination of any of these reasons.

In their report Mildmay and Shirley made Holdernesse aware of the time
that had been taken by the Board of Trade and the Cabinet to produce the text
of the British memorial on the boundaries of Nova Scotia and Acadia;
although the king had ordered its preparation on 7 October 1750, it did not
arrive in Paris until 23 December of that year. After they had described their
many, fruitless attempts to obtain the French memorial on St. Lucia, they
referred Holdernesse to the proposed memorial they, themselves, had written
on the British claim to St. Lucia—designed specifically to preempt the
French claim—and had sent to the duke of Bedford on 17 January 1751.
Holdernesse was further informed that in their 17 January letter they had

asked Bedford: "how far it might be proper to deliver it in the first instance," but since they received no instructions from Bedford on this matter until his letter arrived at the end of February (written in London on 22 February [NS]), their efforts had been overtaken by the delivery of the French memorial in the second week of February.

They also reported that this French memorial on St. Lucia had been sent to Whitehall on 21 February (NS), 11 February (OS), but although they had been informed by Bedford on 13 April (OS), 24 April (NS), that: "the same is referred by His Majesty to the Board of Trade to draw up an answer," it was now the beginning of July and nothing, as yet, had arrived from the Board. This delay in the timely delivery of documents applied equally to the French Ministry, however. Shirley and Mildmay stated that despite the many requests they had made to the French commissioners, the promised reply to the British memorial on the boundaries of Acadia—first presented to Galissonière and Silhouette in the first week of January 1751—had also not materialized.

Three weeks after their first letter, on 1 August Mildmay and Shirley sent Lord Holdernesse their official report on the reaction of the French commissioners to the content of the British memorial on prizes and sea limits (presented to Galissonière and Silhouette at the 28 June conference and reported in Mildmay's journal entry on this meeting). They noted that at first glance, it appeared that Galissonière and Silhouette had now accepted that prizes taken before the outbreak of war would not be included in the list of damages, but when they had reexamined the agreement of these commissioners: "to observe nothing further on this point," Mildmay and Shirley said they had seen a potential problem. They pointed out that the French Court appeared to be under some misapprehension about the degree to which British government ministers would become involved in a discussion of time limits; the use of the phrase "*de Cour à Cour*" in the French reply seemed to assume a direct intervention by the ministers of both Crowns on this issue, whereas the British position had always been a constant refusal to hold any discussions about pre-war time limits.[26]

Mildmay and Shirley told Lord Holdernesse they agreed that the British memorial stated: "Justice should reciprocally be done between the two Crowns if any complaints should be subsisting there from," however they noted that this answer specifically named those prize ships that had been taken in the immediate six months that followed the declaration of war in

March 1744, and did not indicate any expansion of the time period to included prizes taken before this date. The latent problem they said they saw in this apparent misunderstanding by the French commissioners was based on the earlier French ultimatum given at the conference on 22 April, and they reminded Holdernesse that at this meeting Galissonière and Silhouette had said that: "upon our refusing to render then justice upon this point at present, they shall have an opportunity hereafter of taking their satisfaction of seizing upon all English vessels that shall be found in our ports upon any [future] declaration of war."

Beyond the problems caused by the late arrival of memorials from the Board of Trade, it appears that the change of secretaries at the Southern Department on 29 June 1751 had also caused a critical hiatus in their diplomatic instructions. Having received no response to their letter of 9 June to the duke of Bedford, in this letter of 1 August, Shirley and Mildmay now asked Lord Holdernesse for his immediate and specific direction on the answer they should give regarding the damage claim process. They said they needed to know, as a matter of urgency, whether the British government position continued to be that such indemnity should be sought from the individual captors "in the course of law," or if "His Majesty will [now] consent to the admitting of the Claims on each side, to be adjusted in a national manner between the two Crowns."

On the question of any reimbursement to ship owners for subsequent damages, Mildmay and Shirley referred Lord Holdernesse to the fourth article of the Treaty of Aix-la-Chapelle which, they said, stated clearly and precisely: "no other damages could be allowed than the bare restitution of the Ship and Cargo at the time it was taken." They therefore suggested that in order to prevent the establishment of a precedent, Lord Albemarle should repeat the text of this article to the French Foreign ministry, as the French commissioners had constantly attempted to begin discussions on items that were unrelated to this Treaty. So far as the British definition of the limits of the Channel and the North Sea were concerned, Shirley and Mildmay pointed out to Holdernesse that: "we have hitherto been Instructed to insist that the Intent of the Convention upon this point was to include all the British Seas washing the Coasts of any part of His Majesty's territories."

They concluded their report by asking whether the British government intended to issue a further memorial on these points raised by the French commissioners in June, and they also observed that as they expected both an imminent answer from Galissonière and Silhouette to the British memorial on the: "Ancient Limits of Nova Scotia, or Acadia," and the demand for an answer to the French claim to St. Lucia that the king had ordered the Board of Trade to draw up, it would be helpful to them to receive the latter as soon as possible so that both documents could be exchanged together. This request was followed by a letter to Holdernesse, on 9 August, in which they acknowledged they had been told by Lord Albemarle that they would be receiving further instructions, but pointed out to the secretary that it was now midsummer.[27] This was traditionally a time of government inaction in Paris; the senior French law court, the *Parlement* of Paris, recessed from the beginning of August until the end of October and Louis XV and many of his courtiers habitually spent from mid-summer to the early autumn hunting in the forest of Compiègne. In London the same inactivity took place; the Parliamentary session ended in late May, George II took the opportunity to visit his Electorate of Hanover until the end of October, and most of his ministers spent this period at their country estates. It was, therefore, the normal diplomatic practice in both countries to suspend any major activity until the autumn.

By August 1751 Mildmay had lived in France for over fifteen months without any home leave and in his journal he noted that on 20 August (NS) he received the king's permission to return to England "to settle some private affairs." He arrived in London on 24 August (OS). Since Lord Albemarle had also returned to England for a visit, the Paris embassy was left in charge of the first secretary, Joseph Yorke, and William Shirley became the sole commissioner representing the British side. No conferences were held during August and September, and the only event of note took place on 8 September 1751 (NS), 29 August (OS), when Yorke informed Lord Holdernesse that "Mr. Puyzieulx" (*sic*) had been replaced as the French Foreign Minister by M. St. Contest, whom Yorke estimated to be "under the strict direction of the *Garde des Sceaux* (Machault d'Arnouville), and those who placed him there."[28]

The business of the commission began to pick up again in early October. In a letter from Paris on 5 October 1751 (NS) Shirley told Lord Holdernesse he had received word from the French commissioners that the French government expected soon to receive: "our answer for their memorial upon H.M.C.M's. (His Most Christian Majesty's) pretensions to the island of St. Lucia . . . and that they desire a conference with me to discuss the limits of

Acadie and would then deliver to me their answer to our memorial on that subject." He also asked, once again, if Mildmay could bring back with him the volume of French justification documents on St. Lucia, as the French commissioners were pressing him for its return in order to prepare their claim to the island of Tobago.[29]

Over the past year Shirley had developed deep suspicions of the diplomatic "chicanery" he felt was being practiced by the French Court, and at this point the actions of the new minister of foreign affairs, M. St. Contest, did not make the efforts of Galissonière and Silhouette to dispel these suspicions any easier. In his journal Mildmay noted that although the French commissioners had informed Shirley on 5 October that before they could deliver their long-awaited answer on the boundaries of Acadia they would require a prior discussion on the content of the British memorial, when they finally presented this answer to him on 11 October, its date of 4 October clearly showed that the French Foreign Ministry had this document prepared and ready to hand over on the day before the two commissioners had spoken to Shirley.[30]

There were two reasons for Mildmay's return to England in late August 1751. One was domestic and the other had to do with his commission work. Behind his reference to the "private affairs" that required his presence in England lay a tragic event, for on 7 August (OS) 1751, 18 August (NS), Frederica, Countess Fitzwalter, and Lord Fitzwalter's much loved wife, died in Bath of the effects of chronic gout; her elderly husband was devastated by her death.[31] Other than his respect for the late Lady Frederica and his concern for the welfare of his frail relative, the second, significant reason for his return in late August was to brief Lord Holdernesse on the urgency of replying to the French claim to St. Lucia, and to discuss the precise position the British negotiators should take on the boundaries of Nova Scotia and Acadia before the arrival of the expected French memorial on this issue.

Lord Albemarle was almost certainly in London for the same purpose because he had lived permanently and openly in Paris with his Flemish mistress and their children since his appointment as British ambassador in 1749, and had been estranged from his English wife for years.[32] The status of his Paris family was acknowledged to the point where in their correspondence both Lord Holdernesse and Lord Albemarle referred to Albemarle's longtime companion as "*la belle Ambassatrice*,"[33] and, in fact, Albemarle was so adjusted to his life in France that many of his letters to Holdernesse were either written entirely in French, or else were in a complicated mixture of the two languages within the same letter.

Mildmay was to remain in England until the beginning of November. In a letter that the duke of Newcastle wrote to Lord Hardwicke on 6 September 1751 (OS) he told Hardwicke: "Mr. Mildmay, the commissary, who is now in England, has a notion that France would consent to a proper boundary to Nova Scotia and Acadia, which would secure to us the bay of Fundy and be sufficient for us, and even give us Tobago on our yielding to them St. Lucia in property, to be inhabited and possessed by them." Newcastle concluded to Hardwicke that if Britain wished to settle these boundary differences in America: "this can be done no way but by concessions on both sides."[34]

Mildmay laid out his "notion" in considerable detail in a long memorandum to Lord Holdernesse entitled "The State of the Contests between the Crowns of Great Britain and H.M.C.M. relating to the ancient limits of Nova Scotia and Acadia."[35] In the section he called "Observations," he gave his opinion on the best method to resolve these boundary disputes, stating that as the French: "are fearful of suffering any English colonies to be planted on the Island of St. Lucia," it might thus be possible to secure their agreement to remove all the French settlements on the Île St. Jean (now Prince Edward Island) and along the coasts of the Bay of Fundy. He said his remarks were predicated on: "whether it might be proper to conciliate these disputes by proposals of some accommodation" and he posed the question: "if the Court of France would agree to relinquish all of their forts and settlements in Nova Scotia, or Acadia, [whether] His Majesty might not, on that consideration, suspend his demands for the immediate evacuation of St. Lucia." Further, he suggested that in exchange for a French agreement to abandon its claim to the island of Tobago, the British might then reciprocate by giving up its entire claim to St. Lucia.[36]

This document, in Mildmay's handwriting and signed with his initials, "Wm.," has no date but it has been filed by the manuscript department of the British Library in volume 135 of the Leeds Papers and has been placed between a letter written by Lord Holdernesse on 4 July 1751 (OS) and another from him dated 4 September 1751 (OS). Mildmay probably wrote this document before he arrived in England on 24 August (OS), as this would allow enough time for its contents to be discussed with Holdernesse and the duke of Newcastle, and be reported by Newcastle to Lord Hardwicke on 6 September (OS). The content of the letter from the Newcastle to Hardwicke, and the suggestions in Mildmay's memorandum, clearly contradict the impression given by Max Savelle that William Mildmay made no serious contribution to the work of the commission and was generally regarded as a lightweight member of it. There is also no indication, either in Mildmay's report or in Newcastle's letter to Hardwicke, that William Shirley had contributed any part of the contents of this memorandum, and as it contained a strong plea for compromise on these territorial claims, Shirley would have hardly been likely to have agreed with it in any case.

Among Lord Holdernesse's papers is a copy of the draft notes made at a Cabinet meeting, held in late September, with the heading: "A Memoranda of a Conference at Lord Holdernesse's House, September 25th 1751 (OS)." It is an outline of the British government's instruction to Shirley and Mildmay on the answers they were to give the French commissioners concerning the boundaries of Acadia, the limits of the Channel and the North Sea, and the prize ships. They were instructed to say that the British memorial, prepared as a reply to the French claim to St. Lucia, was almost ready to be submitted but it would only be delivered on the condition that, at the same time, the commissioners received the French answer to the British statement of right on the limits of Acadia. The second paragraph noted that in the Treaty of Aix-la-Chapelle the French had already agreed that the only prizes to be recognized as illegal would be those taken after the six-month grace period for the ending of hostilities. On the determination of compensation to be paid, the document continued: "restitution shall be made of the same by the respective Crowns to each other, and not by the individual, to be settled and adjusted as an Article in the General Account, towards making a Balance of all debts and demands of money in the dispute between the two Crowns." In conclusion, their instructions stated that the British commissioners were to take their direction on the limits of the Channel and the North Sea only from the lords of the Admiralty, who would make this determination in a future report.[37]

As the French commissioners had been pressing for a swift resolution of the limits of the Channel and the North Sea, this Cabinet decision to remove the resolution of these limits from the British commissioners to the Board of the Admiralty was not something that they were likely to find agreeable. The decision that the validity of prizes, and their indemnity, would be determined and paid by the two monarchs, and not left to the individual owner's ability to pursue their captors in the courts, appears, however, to agree with the original French government position, as noted in the "Instruction" document that was issued to the commissioners by the British government in 1749, and subsequently sought by the French commissioners in their negotiations. It thus seems to represent at least some small foreword movement in this area of dispute.

At the Paris embassy there seemed to be a certain optimism on the progress of negotiations. On 22 September 1751 (NS) Joseph Yorke acknowledged a recent letter that Mildmay had sent him from London, and he expressed a cautious hope that the instructions Mildmay would bring back with him to Paris: "may tend to draw your commission to a conclusion. I know how tender the Points you have on Hand and how cautiously the Ministers proceed upon them."[38] Mildmay arrived in Paris on 11 November 1751 (NS) and he confirmed in his journal entry, and in a letter written to Lord Fitzwalter on the following day, that he had returned with the memorandum instructions for the conduct of the British commissioners that had been given to him by Lord Holdernesse.[39]

With this letter to Lord Fitzwalter announcing his arrival in Paris, Mildmay began a regular correspondence in which he and Fitzwalter replied to each other's letters several times a month. It seems that the sudden death of Fitzwalter's wife had changed Mildmay's long association with Fitzwalter as his mentor and patron into a new and more dependent relationship on Fitzwalter's part; almost into that of a elderly father and his middle-aged son. Mildmay was a formal man and he never ignored the social etiquette required in a letter between a gentleman and a peer, but from this point on he always apologized to Fitzwalter if one of his letters was delayed and he began to reassure Fitzwalter that he looked for official opportunities to be able to visit him at Moulsham Hall more regularly. By 1751 Fitzwalter had been Mildmay's patron for over thirty years and, even though he was now eighty-one, he had not lost his ability to give Mildmay sound political advice and active help; through his post of treasurer of the Royal Household Fitzwalter had direct access to the king and members of the Cabinet[40] and within a few months Mildmay was to find this access invaluable.

In late October the French commissioners had announced that they were now able to deliver their answer on the British claim to the limits of Acadia, and as it had been decided that there would be a reciprocal exchange of such documents, Mildmay arrived at the conference that was held on 17 November with the answer from the Board of Trade to the French claim to St. Lucia: a document which was translated into French and given to Galissonière and Silhouette at this 17 November meeting.[41] The British commissioners had been eagerly awaiting this promised British memorial; in his journal Mildmay stated that he had been instructed to deliver it as soon possible, and that it was immediately translated into French within the six days following his arrival on 11 November. Since the translation of this particular memorial was to develop into a major dispute in the following year, however, it is unfortunate that Mildmay did not also say by whom this swift translation was made.[42]

In the context of this later dispute it is also interesting to look at a letter from the British commissioners, dated 9 December. On that day they wrote to Claudius Amyand, the chief clerk to the Southern Department, advising him that in the enclosed copy of the British memorial on St. Lucia it should be noted that: "as we delivered this answer in French, the same is not strictly a translation of the English one [brought to Paris by Mildmay on 11 November] which was sent to Lord Holdernesse from the Board of Trade, and [is] returned herewith." Mildmay and Shirley suggested to Amyand: "it may be necessary, in case it be thought proper to have it in English, that a verbal translation be made from the [enclosed] French copy."[43] The chance of mistakes and misinterpretations in this process of translating the British memorial into French, followed by a re-translation of the French document back into English, was considerable, however, and this procedure was, indeed, to cause serious problems both to the joint commissioners and to the ministers of the two governments.

On 24 November 1751 the commissioners held a formal conference in Galissonière's apartment, where Mildmay and Shirley delivered the final answer of the British government on the prize ships.[44] Its first article dealt with the British insistence on certain time limits, and the apparent misunderstanding of the French government about the British proposal for the involvement of government ministers. In his journal Mildmay said Galissonière and Silhouette were told that on this question of time limits the document clearly stated that there would be no discussion of prize ships taken before the war began, and that any "*Cour à Cour*" references applied only to ministerial negotiations on ships captured within the six-month period following the signing of the peace treaty. He reported that the second article agreed with the French demand that any restitution should now be made under a general account, paid by the two Crowns, and not by the captains who actually captured the ships, and the third article reiterated that only the value of the ship and cargo "at the time of capture" would be considered. Finally, he said the boundary of the Channel was now declared to be from the eastern limit of the Strait of Dover to a line drawn from the southern tip of Ireland to Cape Finisterre (not Cape St. Vincent), while that of the North Sea was from the Strait of Dover to beyond the furthest extent of the Shetland Islands. This definition, which incorporated both the Irish Sea and the Bay of Biscay, thus covered all the seas surrounding the coasts of England and Wales, eastern Ireland, and western and northern Scotland, together with the entire length of the coasts of northern and western France.

Mildmay said the immediate reaction of the two French commissioners to these articles appeared to be one of either real, or feigned outrage. On the question of the pre-war prizes, Galissonière: "was very warm in his expressions; declaring that several of those [prize] captures taken [in or near British ports] were little less than Piracy," and pointing out that those British ships that had been in French ports when the war broke out were allowed to leave unmolested. He also stated that the "peremptory" refusal to discuss these illegal seizures would: "perhaps induce them [the French government] to turn this example to their own advantage upon all future occasions," or, in other words, to capture any British ships found in French ports at the first sign of any future war. Mildmay said he and Shirley replied that George II had already acknowledged that under the nineteenth Article of the Treaty of Utrecht all ships, either in ports or at sea, that were captured within the six-month period after war was declared were illegal captures, and that he would uphold this Article in law. It was the French claim for ships alleged to have been taken before March 1744 that the British government disputed.[45] They stated that as Louis XV had declared war on Britain in order to get satisfaction for these captures, his signature to a peace treaty that was made to bring a permanent end to such quarrels prevented him from trying to obtain it by other means. Mildmay said they concluded by pointing out that the decision of George II to have his ministers deal with those prizes taken in British ports between 17 March and 17 August 1744, together with those illegally taken after the appropriate notification had been given to the captains of British ships that the Treaty of Aix-la-Chapelle had been signed in April 1748, was evidence of his wish that "justice should be done for all," in accordance with the treaty.

Mildmay's journal noted that after these comments on the ship seizures, the French commissioners had then said they had no objection either to the second article—the settlement of damages by the ministers of the two Crowns—or to the third, which dealt with the value placed on the ship and cargo when it was captured, but they complained that in the fourth article the limits of the Channel and the North Sea had been: "carried too far on both sides" of internationally accepted sea boundaries, and if the British government insisted on these limits, they might well make moot any further discussions on prizes. Mildmay said the conference ended with an agreement from the French commissioners to deliver this British position on prizes and sea limits to their government ministers and to carry out a suggestion, previously proposed by himself and Shirley, to prepare a "general list" of all their prize claims.

As the French government now had two British memorials to study in December—the preliminary answer on the French claim to St. Lucia and the statement on prizes and sea limits—no further conferences were held in 1751, but in a letter that Mildmay wrote on 4 December 1751 he gave Fitzwalter the first hint that there was a serious renewal of the old problem of a lack of cooperation between himself and Shirley. Mildmay told Fitzwalter that Shirley was in the process of writing a reply to the French memorial of 11 October on the limits of Acadia, but had refused to show Mildmay his efforts: "though he has informed the French commissaries he is busy preparing another memorial for them, and that it has cost him vast pains to answer theirs." He continued: "I don't know if this method of proceeding with giving further memorials will be agreeable to our Superiors. If so, I shall be ready to add my endeavors in support of His Majesty's right by either correcting what my colleague offers, or offering one myself to his correction." Whether or not this process of exchanging memorial was found to be acceptable, he stated to Fitzwalter that he considered that anything that came from the commission must be reviewed by him, because he was jointly commissioned with Shirley and thus carried a joint responsibility for the conduct of the negotiations.[46]

The commissioners' report to Lord Holdernesse on 24 November had not mentioned that Shirley was preparing such a document on Acadia, but on 1 December, and three days before he informed Lord Fitzwalter, Mildmay wrote a private letter to Holdernesse, protesting Shirley's arbitrary behavior.[47] He pointed out that although the French memorial on Acadia had been given to Shirley on 11 October: "he has kept it in his hands till now in order to draw up a reply thereto, which nevertheless he does not communicate to

me, acting as if I were not jointly concerned with him on this commission."
He told Holdernesse that, in any case, he disagreed with these frequent
exchanges of memorials and believed that, at this stage: "it would be better to
rest on both sides without further replies and, laying the argument of right
aside, endeavour of some compromise by an acquiescence in such other's
claims."[48] Mildmay was thus restating to Holdernesse the same opinion that
the duke of Newcastle had given to Lord Hardwicke in September, and that
Mildmay had also proposed in his August memorandum, namely that compromise and a trade of territory, rather than these endless, formal reiteration
of "rights," were the only way in which such disputes were ever going to be
settled.

On 22 December Shirley sent Lord Holdernesse a draft of the first part of
his reply to the French memorial on Acadia, but still without any consultation with Mildmay, and the situation had now reached the point where
Mildmay decided he must seek Lord Fitzwalter's direct help and protection.
In a letter to Fitzwalter, also written on 22 December, Mildmay asked that if:
"a certain person mentioned more than once in my former letters, transmitted any writing to one of Your Lordship's friends [Lord Holdernesse, or any
other Cabinet member] I beg it may be known that it was entirely without my
knowledge and without acquainting me with any part of the contents."[49] It
appears that the arrival of Shirley's proposed reply to the French memorial
must have caused some disquiet in the Southern Department, however, for in
a letter to Lord Holdernesse, written on 29 December, the commissioners
acknowledged that they had just received instructions that the king had
referred the French memorial on Acadia to the Board of Trade Board, and
that nothing further should be done about any reply until the commissioners
were told the king's wishes on the matter.[50]

Despite these clear orders Shirley continued his writing activities and on
31 December Mildmay, as an experienced lawyer, decided that he needed an
independent deposition of the facts to use as evidence of Shirley's uncooperative, secretive, and potentially imprudent diplomatic activity. Mildmay kept
this deposition among his papers, and it was made, on 31 December 1751, by
the secretary to the commission, "Mr. J. Appy."[51] As he had earlier indicated
to Lord Fitzwalter, Mildmay distrusted Shirley's grasp of the subtleties of
written French, for John Appy stated that, to his knowledge, on Sunday, 14
November 1751: "Mr. Mildmay, being returned to Paris two days before,
[and] understanding that the copy of the answer of the French government to

the British memorial on the limits of Acadia [the copy that had been made by Shirley after this French answer had been presented on 11 October] had not been examined by the Original," asked Shirley to send him both documents so that he (Mildmay) could compare Shirley's copy with the original for any possible inaccuracies before the original document: "was sent to Whitehall, as it was intended to be." Appy testified that Shirley sent over the original memorial and its copy on the following Wednesday (17 November), at which point Mildmay and Appy examined "a part thereof . . . and he [Appy] and another person" checked the remainder on the same day. Appy continued that although Mildmay returned both documents on Tuesday, 18 November, Shirley only sent his copy to London, saying that he would keep the original French memorial: "in order to finish, as he said, a reply thereto which he was preparing." Appy then stated that: "a few days after, I applying [to Mr. Shirley] again, by Mr. Mildmay's order, that he might have the French Memorial again to reperuse and ponder, Mr. Shirley desired I would inform him that he, Mr. Shirley, had constant occasion for it for drawing up his reply, and could not part with it until he was finished."

Appy further reported that on Tuesday, 30 November, at ten o'clock in the morning, he delivered to Mildmay a part of: "Mr. Shirley's draft of a reply to the French commissaries' memorial concerning the limits of Acadia, for his perusal." Since Shirley had said that he would like it back as soon as possible, within two and a half hours he, Appy, returned this unfinished document to Shirley, at his house. Although on 30 November Mildmay had only been shown a partial draft, Appy stated that on this day (31 December) Shirley had delivered to the French commissioners his reply to their memorial on Acadia, but still without showing this official commission document to Mildmay in advance, for his approval. Appy stated: "Mr. Shirley, having sent an answer to the French commissaries to the Memorial concerning the limits of Acadia this morning [31 December], by a servant, Mr. Mildmay sent for me and showed it [the answer] to me, declaring that it was the first time that he had seen it since he sent it [the partial draft] back to Mr. Shirley, after having examined it on Tuesday the 30th of November." Apart from this deliberate exclusion of William Mildmay from the preparation of an official commission document, it appears that Shirley had also concealed from Mildmay the promised comments that George II, or rather the Cabinet and the Board of Trade, had sent to the commissioners concerning this proposed memorial on Acadia. In the last paragraph of his deposition Appy said that on 31

December Mildmay also showed him: "some sheets containing 48 pages, wrote upon a half margin, being part of the copy [of a reply] to the Commissaries, by the King of Great Britain, to a Memorial drawn up by Mr. Shirley."[52]

Appy's declaration makes it clear that Mildmay now felt he needed to keep a careful watch on William Shirley, but at this point in the negotiations Shirley's behavior, however disturbing, was not Mildmay's greatest problem. The 24 November 1751 conference, at which the British memorial on the prize ships and sea limits was discussed, had ended with a statement from Galissonière that he "would now deliver our Memorial to his Ministers and take their Orders," and the response was not long in coming. Instead of producing an internal commission document, to be exchanged between governments, at the beginning of December the French government decided to publish their answer, and since this memorial, written by M. Silhouette, contained both the details of the compensation that France felt was due to her for these ships and a long explanation of the French belief that this indemnity should cover all pre-war prizes, its publication caused consternation in Whitehall.[53]

In a private letter that Lord Holdernesse sent to Lord Albemarle on 28 November (OS), 8 December (NS), he commented that he had never considered M. St. Contest, the French foreign minister, to be: "*un grand Genie,* but as he seems to act with a continued reserve [secrecy]," Holdernesse therefore asked: "what can be the meaning of their printing their last long winded memorial? Is it a Manifesto?"[54] In his reply on 11 December 1751 (NS), 30 November (OS), Albemarle told Holdernesse this publication was part of the endless efforts made by the French government to establish their right to discuss compensation for the pre-war prize ships, and he described the frustration that this continued campaign was causing both to the British commissioners and to his own efforts to negotiate a settlement with St. Contest. Albemarle also said that St. Contest was no help in this matter, for: "the printing of their last Memorial, or Manifesto, is entirely owing to Noailles [Vicomté de Noailles, minister of state]. It was originally writ (*sic*) by Silhouette, his creature, and corrected by Machault, consequently I can't expect any assistance from him [St. Contest] to stop the publishing of it."[55]

Mildmay was as unhappy as Lord Holdernesse about the publication of the French memorial on the prize ships, and for good reason. On 8 March 1752 he told Fitzwalter, in what was, for him, uncharacteristically emotional language, about a recent article in the Dutch *Gazette* that had been placed in this paper by the French government. He said it gave a detailed explanation of the French reasons for demanding that prizes taken before the war began were legitimate subjects for negotiation, and, furthermore, it also charged that the British, by refusing to discuss this issue, were now responsible for the delay in settlement. Mildmay's alarm was caused not only by the fact that these negotiations were his commission responsibility, but also because articles placed in the Dutch *Gazette* were known to be one of the methods by which the French government distributed propaganda throughout the European Courts. British diplomats took such articles seriously and were afraid of their effectiveness in spreading false news.[56]

In his 8 March letter Mildmay pointed out to Fitzwalter that, in his opinion, the time was now long overdue for the British government to publish a rebuttal that gave the true reasons for their refusal to reopen an argument that had already been settled as a consequence of war. Restating to Fitzwalter the opinions he had expressed to the French commissioners at the 24 November 1751 conference, he said he felt the terms of the Treaty of Aix-la-Chapelle had declared: "an oblivion of all that went before" and the French king, by his original declaration of war on this issue, was thus precluded from raising a subject in the peace negotiations which he had been unable to obtain by warfare. He continued, forcefully: "The French King demanded satisfaction by the sword. He had it. Upon what pretence therefore can he demand another kind of satisfaction. Treaties of Peace are but waste paper if they are not to be a firm decision to the dispute that occasioned the War." Mildmay was sufficiently concerned to propose that if George II should find this demand of the French government to be unreasonable and unjust, the king could use it as grounds to recall the commission.[57]

As if public discussion of the pre-war prize issue was not upsetting enough, at a conference held at Shirley's house on 18 March 1752 the language used in the British answer on the French claim to St. Lucia now became a subject of considerable dispute. As this document concerned the territorial claim that was most important to the French government, Galissonière and Silhouette had been impatient to receive it. Mildmay and Shirley were equally unhappy about the length of time it was taking the Board of Trade to produce their St. Lucia answer, so when, in the previous November, Mildmay finally brought the memorial to Paris, it had therefore been translated at the unaccustomed speed of only six days. It now, however, emerged that this eager haste might have been a costly mistake.

In his journal Mildmay noted that after an interval of four months had elapsed since the document had first been presented, Galissonière and Silhouette had then issued a list of twelve unacceptable words and phrases they had found in the French translation of this British memorial, saying: "they seemed to be too harsh, and therefore prayed that we would change them to a milder form."[58] Mildmay said he reminded Galissonière that when this document had been delivered to him, on 17 November 1751, both he and Silhouette had read it and at that time they had not raised these objections about its language. Mildmay therefore said he felt that these complaints should have made long before the middle of March 1752, as after this length of time, during which the French government had, apparently, acquiesced to it, the British commissioners should not to be asked to amend: "what ought to be looked on as established."

Although Mildmay was disturbed that this matter had been raised, he said that in order not to have a dispute about a few words he and Shirley had agreed to take this list and send it to the British ministers for their decision on whether such amendments ought to be made, as: "we were sure [these ministers] had no intent to give any offence in the manner of the expressions." Mildmay reported that in addition to this request for an change of wording, the French commissioners also asked for the documentary proofs of some of the British claims to the prior ownership of St. Lucia, and Mildmay said they agreed to request that the Board of Trade supply such original documents: "if they be in our Custody."

The report on this conference that Galissonière and Silhouette submitted to the French Foreign Ministry on the same day (18 March) was surprisingly short and gave no indication that they were particularly outraged, or even unusually disturbed by certain terms in the British St. Lucia document. They said that they had asked for these changes as the words used had been found to be embarrassing, even impolite, but they seemed to indicate that they foresaw no difficulty in this request to the British government.[59] As the subsequent dispute over the language used in this document was to have such damaging and far-reaching consequences, the apparent lack of rancor in their report, made at the time, is illuminating. It raises the question whether, on later reflection, the French government decided to use what it had, initially, seen as a relatively minor argument about language as part of a larger, political agenda.

The sudden arrival of this potential danger to their mandate was not enough to unite the British commissioners. It was not until his 8 March letter to Lord Fitzwalter that Mildmay reopened the subject of his unhappiness with William Shirley, but in the interval the relationship between the two commissioners had obviously deteriorated. In this letter Mildmay speculated on Shirley's motives for his continuing behavior, and said: "My colleague is still trying to frame a Memorial concerning Nova Scotia [the second part of the memorial on the limits of Acadia that he had sent to Holdernesse in December] without in the least consulting me. What his design therein may be is equally a secret. If it be to print it, when all is over, by way of appeal or justification of his own private sentiments, it would be better he should be anticipated by a Memorial drawn up by authority; for bad and improper defense may do more harm than no defense at all. But as I understand that he has given orders for a fair copy of this memorial [to be made], it is possible he will ere long communicate to me his intentions thereon."[60]

By now Mildmay had begun to suspect that Shirley's increasingly arrogant behavior indicated that he was acting on the authority of those who disagreed with the policy of compromise advocated by the duke of Newcastle and Lord Holdernesse, and, specifically, with the encouragement of the president of the Board of Trade, Lord Halifax. On 9 April 1752 Mildmay was able to substantiate these charges in detail. In his letter of that date to Lord Fitzwalter he said that Shirley: "has been privately at work finishing the memorial that he sent some time ago, the first part, to my Lord Holdernesse, but without consulting me, or communicating it to me, until these three days past." When, at this point, Shirley showed him this revised document: "finished, as he says it is," Mildmay said it appeared to bear very little resemblance to the memorial that Lord Holdernesse had received in December. He told Fitzwalter he did not intend to review this present memorial until he had some idea what use Shirley intended to make of it, and continued: "I understand that he has also sent another copy of it by private hand to England, and it is probable that he has skipped over the only person [Holdernesse] to whom such an affair ought first to have been communicated, and that it is delivered into the hands of a certain Person at the Head of a Certain Board [Lord Halifax], but whether my suspicions be true or not may be discovered by the enquiry that may be made of it [the copy] in England."[61]

His relationship with Shirley had obviously become so difficult that in this 9 April letter Mildmay began to explore a possible solution. He referred Fitzwalter to a proposal he had enclosed with his letter, prefacing his remarks with the information that M. Silhouette had just been appointed chancellor to the duke of Orlèans and, with his new responsibilities, it seemed unlikely that Silhouette would be able to give much of his attention to the commission. This being the case, Mildmay speculated that as the French side had now been reduced to one person, perhaps there was no need for two British commissioners. Since he said he considered: "Mons. de la Galissonière, the other French Commissary, to be a person that would act in a fair and candid manner," he suggested that perhaps the joint commission might have more success if it were reduced to two men, each of whom: "may be more safely entrusted with the secret instructions of his own Court, and both may act with the more mutual confidence in each other." He was careful to add, however, that this suggestion was motivated entirely: "from my sense of public duty, in which neither private interests, nor inclination have any share," and said he felt unable to say whether: "my colleague, or myself, or any other person may be the most proper to be employed in bringing abut such an accommodation. [That decision] is entirely submitted to a superior direction." Mildmay was, of course, being entirely disingenuous, as in this case the "superior" would be Lord Holdernesse, to whom Mildmay was confident Lord Fitzwalter would both communicate and support his "proposal."

Meanwhile, and despite the British commission's difficult internal working climate, until Lord Holdernesse could be consulted the negotiations must continue. In his journal Mildmay said he and Shirley requested that a short conference might be held at Shirley's apartment on Saturday, 8 April, to hand over the justification documents that the French commissioners had requested the British produce in support of their claim to St. Lucia. He reported that at this 8 April meeting the only response of Galissonière and Silhouette was to question why some of these documents were only extracts, and said the reply they were given was: "an obvious one; that these entries were relative to other matters, and therefore it was foreign to the purpose to produce anything more than what was relative to the present situation."[62]

The next conference was scheduled to take place on 2 May, but the tenure of William Shirley as a commissioner was about to come to an end. On 19 April 1752 (NS), Shirley wrote Lord Holdernesse a terse letter, of two paragraphs, which acknowledged that on the previous day Lord Albemarle had notified him that the king had revoked his commission appointment, and said he hoped: "that this alteration has not proceeded from any displeasure of His Majesty at my conduct in this part of his service."[63] Shirley had good reason to fear displeasure, but not necessarily that of George II. In 1749 the duke of

Newcastle had agreed, somewhat reluctantly, to place Shirley on the commission at the request of the duke of Bedford and Lord Halifax. Shirley's supporter, Bedford, had now been replaced by Lord Holdernesse, however, and neither Newcastle nor Holdernesse had any intention of allowing their ambitious ministerial colleague, Lord Halifax, to manipulate British foreign policy through Halifax's control over one of the British commissioners in Paris.[64] Shirley had allowed his own ambition and his genuine concern for what he saw as the best interests of the colonists of New England to subvert his duty to his political master, Lord Holdernesse, and he had also seriously underestimated Mildmay's ability to influence the outcome of their dispute through his personal relationships with Fitzwalter and Holdernesse.

Shirley's removal as a commissioner in April 1752 is a subject on which historians have differed in their reports on this commission. The authors of the biographies of William Shirley in the *Dictionary of American Biography* and in the *Dictionary of National Biography* did not mention why he left Paris; both of these authors merely stated that Shirley was a member of the commission and that he returned to Boston in 1753.[65] Max Savelle's detailed history of the five-year commission virtually ended in 1752 and he did not, in fact, mention that Shirley had left the commission in April of that year. John Schutz's biography of William Shirley is the only account that describes Shirley's departure from Paris in detail, but with a great deal of speculation that is unsupported by any cited documentation.[66] In this section of his book Schutz appears to consider it self-evident that Shirley's behavior was completely praiseworthy and above reproach, and that Mildmay's motivation and activities were entirely deceitful and self-serving.

Without a careful study of the two volumes of commission documents, and of Mildmay's letters to Lord Fitzwalter—all of which are in the Mildmay Papers in the William L. Clements Library—it is possible to misinterpret the reason why William Shirley left the joint commission halfway through its life. If, however, one examines the language used in the commissioners reports from 1750 to April 1752, all of which were written by William Shirley,[67] and looks at some of the opinions and phrases in Mildmay's letters and his journal, it seems that although neither of these men were conniving or dishonest, both were strongly motivated by a contradictory and, increasingly antagonistic, self-interest. Shirley intended to return to Massachusetts as its governor, and by early 1752 he had such a deep distrust of French government motives that if the eventual outcome of these negotiations would allow his opponents to gain the slightest military advantage, he would rather that they fail. Mildmay, on the other hand, had no such inherent dislike of the French and he had a strong incentive to achieve a breakthrough; he saw a successful negotiation as an significant advancement to his diplomatic carrier or, possibly, to a parliamentary one. With these divergent aims and opinions, a confrontation between these two men was inevitable. Shirley's overconfident enthusiasm, coupled with a complete lack of diplomatic experience, caused him to assume, quite mistakenly, that with the support of Lord Halifax he could ignore any instructions from the southern secretary with which he disagreed.

Apart from the antagonism shown by Mildmay and Shirley in their commission work, however, John Schutz also sees yet another, and more sinister activity behind Shirley's dismissal. The authors of the material on Shirley in the Biographical Dictionaries mention that in 1751 he married a lady called "Julie," who was the daughter of his landlord in Paris, but they do not imply that this marriage was in any way a contributing factor to Shirley's disgrace.[68] Schutz, however, makes a major point of his discussion on Shirley's recall that this marriage was seen as a great scandal in London, Paris, and Boston, and that the adverse reactions of Shirley's political and diplomatic enemies, among whom he certainly includes William Mildmay, contributed to Shirley's downfall.[69]

As the documentary evidence about Julie is extremely limited, and as there is no mention of Shirley's marriage either in the letters that Mildmay sent to Lord Fitzwalter between 1750 and 1752 or in any of the official and private correspondence that Lord Albemarle and Joseph Yorke exchanged with Lord Holdernesse during these years, it seems that if this alliance actually took place, Shirley's contemporaries in Paris and London did not see it as particularly important, let alone as a notorious scandal. If, in fact, there was such a marriage, his colleagues may, perhaps, have considered the legal ceremony to be somewhat eccentric and unnecessary and as there is no record that Mrs. Shirley accompanied her husband on his return to London, or that she later traveled to Boston. Shirley may also have come to see his marriage as a mistake. In all events Shirley seemed to have abandoned his French wife because there is no evidence that she reappeared in the remaining twenty-five years of his life.

Although Shirley was not notified until 18 April (NS), 7 April (OS), the duke of Newcastle had already decided to make changes in the personnel of the commission by the end of March. On 30 March 1752 (OS), 10 April (NS), two royal warrants were issued, both of them signed by Newcastle, and they were sent to the Chancellor, Lord Hardwicke. The first revoked the commissions of both Shirley and Mildmay, and the second appointed "William Mildmay and Ruvigny De Cosne Esqs." to be the British commissioners.[70] It was one thing to dismiss Shirley, but it was quite another to be able to defend this action not only to Shirley but also to his supporters in London and New England, and to the French Foreign Ministry. In a letter to Fitzwalter on 19 April 1752 Mildmay revealed the details of what, in present-day terms, would be called the beginning of "official deniability."

In his letter of 19 April 1752 (NS) Mildmay told Lord Fitzwalter of Shirley's reaction when he heard the news from Lord Albemarle on the previous day, saying: "my colleague . . . received his dismission (sic) without any remark further than that he was not conscious he had done anything that might give offence."[71] Mildmay had been careful to conceal his own activities, and told Fitzwalter his reply to Shirley's remark was that if this were the case, then the reason for Shirley's recall was probably that the British government wanted to save the expense of paying two commissioners: "for Mr. De Cosne is to have no salary [as he was already on the embassy staff as First Secretary]." Feeling that this might seem an inadequate explanation, Mildmay said he then ventured to Shirley that: "the reason for recalling him, in particular, probably was because he had another commission of being Governor of one of His Majesty's colonies, his presence might be more necessary in that part of the world than in Paris."

In the second of these explanations, and its attempt to put the best face possible on Shirley's dismissal, Mildmay confirmed to Lord Fitzwalter: "This, My Lord Holdernesse has also hinted as the most plausible account and the most proper reason to be given to the French Court." Nevertheless he warned Fitzwalter he had been told that when Shirley returned to England he was going to charge Mildmay with manipulating events through his correspondence with Lord Fitzwalter and, through Fitzwalter, to Lord Holdernesse: "he knowing, to make up of his own phrase, the connection between Your Lordship and Lord Holdernesse. But I shall leave it your Lordship and to Lord Holdernesse's judgement what answer to return to those who shall presume to ask such questions."[72]

Lord Holdernesse made his own attempt to reassure Shirley that his dismissal did not indicate any disapproval of his behavior. In his reply, written on 23 April 1752 (OS), to Shirley's brief letter of 19 April (NS) Holdernesse told him: "I have the King's command to signify to you an entire approbation of your conduct during your residence at Paris."[73] John Shutz sees the tone of this letter as "friendly," and evidence that Shirley was not under an official cloud[74] and, but for Mildmay's remarks to Lord Fitzwalter about Lord Holdernesse's stated desire to have a "plausible account" to give to Shirley as reason for his removal, on the face of it this letter might well seem benign; it may also have served its required purpose at the French court.

Whether or not Shirley appeared to believe the official reason for his removal, Mildmay was still nervous and attentive to any signs that his own position might be threatened. On 3 May he reacted swiftly, and with some distress, when in a short letter to Lord Holdernesse he informed him that a completely inaccurate report on Shirley's removal had appeared in the Utrecht *Gazette* of 28 April 1752. In this letter Mildmay enclosed a copy of the Dutch article and on reading the report it is easy to understand Mildmay's unhappiness, for the correspondent of the *Gazette* had confused the names of the British commissioners. In the main, however, its substance was curiously accurate, and it gives added confirmation both of William Shirley's motives and behavior and on how these were seen at the foreign courts. The *Gazette* informant reported from London on 21 April:

> A courier who has arrived at the office of Lord Holdernesse, Secretary of State, has brought notice that the king disembarked at Hellevoetsluys [the Dutch port that served both the Hague and Hanover] on the 18th [of April]. The Lords of the Regency Council [acting in the king's absence] at once assembled and made arrangements for [a change of personnel] in the commission. Mr. Mildmay, one of the commissaries for Great Britain, who had been employed in Paris to make decisions on the limits in America, had given notice that he wished to be recalled from this commission. He left it without regret [and] the government had agreed that Mr. Shirley, his colleague, would continue to be employed there. It is believed that the place of Mr. Mildmay will be given to Mr. De Cosne, the Secretary of the British Embassy in France under Lord Albemarle. The current rumor has it that this commissary, despite his good intentions, has hindered the progress of this business, and one hopes that his recall will produce a good effect and speed up its success.[75]

If the name "Shirley" is substituted throughout for that of "Mildmay," the "current rumor" mentioned in the last paragraph would appear to be well founded, and, although the *Gazette* correspondent confused the names, in the statement that this commissioner had expressed a desire to be recalled to London, leaving Paris "without regret," one can perhaps see this particular piece of information being supplied by a helpful source in the Southern Department. Mildmay found the confusion of identities too much to endure in silence, however, and he told Lord Holdernesse that he had already written to Joseph Yorke, now British ambassador at The Hague, "in order to have a recantation of the falsity and the abuse." Nevertheless he added: "the reason of my addressing myself to Your Lordship is to assure you that this fact of the change which His Majesty has been pleased to make in the Commission with which I am honoured, has never transpired from any persons in this place."[76] Holdernesse knew, of course, precisely how Shirley's dismissal had been achieved, as he, Mildmay, and Lord Fitzwalter had been parties to it, but Mildmay obviously felt he must still make this official declaration of his innocence to the southern secretary.

The first part of April 1752 had been a worrying time in general for Mildmay. In the letter of 5 April (NS) that contained his complaints of Shirley's behavior, he had also asked Fitzwalter whether the government would agree to have him stand for Parliament in the forthcoming general election.[77] On 12 April (NS) he wrote again, saying that he hoped by the next courier to have some direction from: "the Secretary of State's Office [as] to my destination; of which I should be so far satisfied as it will relieve me from by present state of uncertitude."[78] A week after Shirley had been dismissed Mildmay, apparently, had still not been notified about his prospects because on 26 April (NS) he told Fitzwalter that since he had not yet received a letter from Lord Holderness confirming his appointment as senior commissioner, he must be cautious in his behavior.[79] His official position was about to change, however, and with it his power and ability to direct the work of the commission.

# 6.
# THE MISSED OPPORTUNITY: MAY 1752 TO DECEMBER 1753

ALTHOUGH AT THE BEGINNING OF MAY 1752 Mildmay had not yet received the official document that gave him his "full powers" as the senior commissioner, he decided that with Shirley's imminent departure he could now take charge of the negotiations. On 2 May he called a conference at his apartment on a matter that at the time, and given the earlier, mild reaction of the French commissioners, must have seemed somewhat minor: namely the French objections to twelve contentious words and phrases in the French translation of the British memorial on the ownership of St. Lucia that had been presented on 17 November 1751.

In his conference journal Mildmay said that the initial purpose of this conference was to allow Shirley to take his official leave of Galissonière and Silhouette, but after these diplomatic courtesies were concluded he then informed the French commissioners that his government had refused to change the words to which they had objected. He explained that this decision had been taken on the grounds that such changes could not be made without: "weakening the force of the Argument" and that as great care had been taken to draw up this document, any inaccuracies, or objectionable words that may have appeared in the French translation, should be blamed solely on the work of the translator. He said he had, in fact, offered to let them read the original English version so they could make sure that in this document there were no such offensive remarks, but that Galissonière and Silhouette replied: "we could do what we pleased, however if we did not alter the expressions objected to, they would take equal Liberty in the expressions of their reply."[1]

It is probable that in May 1752 both Mildmay and the British government saw this threat as merely an unhelpful irritant that could, if necessary, be lived with. Ten months later however, in March 1753, the French government was to use the British refusal to change these words and phrases as a reason to demand that the original and official version of all future British memorials must now be written in the French language: a requirement that would cause a critical, and ultimately fatal eighteen-month suspension of the territorial negotiations. Mildmay could not, of course, have anticipated these future consequences to the work of his commission and on 31 May 1752 he was able to give Lord Fitzwalter the encouraging news for which they had both been waiting. He noted: "the last messenger brought the new commission wherein Mr. De Cosne and I, or rather I and Mr. De Cosne, for I am named first, are jointly appointed to proceed with the commission in which I was before joined with Mr. Shirley."[2] By the same post he informed Lord Holdernesse that his royal warrant of appointment had now arrived, and thanked Holdernesse both for this honor and: "for your kind attention in joining such a one to me with whom I am entirely satisfied."[3]

Mildmay was now the leading British commissioner, unhampered by a suspicious and uncooperative colleague, and he thus felt able to negotiate in a manner that he believed might achieve a greater success. In his 31 May letter to Lord Fitzwalter he said he believed that without Shirley's presence the work would be both easier and more agreeable, but even before he had received his official warrant, Mildmay had already taken advantage of his new authority to discuss with Lord Holdernesse the changes he believed should be made in the conduct of future negotiations. On 3 May, a day after his first conference as leader, he wrote a private letter to Holdernesse with his proposal for an attempt to break the negotiation deadlock, observing that if the work of the commission was allowed to continue in the same manner as before, the four-year dispute over the contested issues would never be resolved. He therefore suggested to Holdernesse that as he felt a change in the negotiation method had a possibility of success he proposed a new strategy that he described as "a plan De Novo."[4]

In Mildmay's official commission correspondence is a second letter that he and De Cosne wrote to Lord Holdernesse, also on 3 May, and in which they gave a brief summary of this proposal. They reviewed the past two years of failure to resolve the territorial disputes and said that, as things now stood, there were only three possible choices: either the commission could be ended, it could continue to negotiate in the same manner, or the process could be changed. As both of them strongly favored the third option, they urged that instead of continuing the repetitive justifications of their respective territorial claims, both governments should now try to establish an agreement that neither side would attempt to invade: "the undisputed settlements already established."[5]

In his private and more detailed description of this "plan De Novo" Mildmay told Lord Holdernesse that, as he saw it, the present problem centered on the endless and unfruitful arguments about the territorial rights of each government and the equally detailed exchanges on the "ancient" historical justifications for these rights. He appreciated that such claims must ultimately be dealt with by this method of an historical determination, because this was the customary and traditional way by which all territorial ownership had to be decided under the rules of eighteenth-century diplomacy,[6] but Mildmay's immediate concern was to stop the dangerous escalation of local conflicts that were now taking place both in North America and in the West Indian islands. In order to achieve this he proposed to Holdernesse that there should be an immediate attempt to contain these conflicts by an agreement between the two countries not to interfere with the subjects of the other while the negotiations were in progress. He laid out the terms that this agreement should be covered in a series of "heads," or points. The first stipulated that the British would not attempt to prevent French subjects from settling: "on such coasts of Nova Scotia and Acadia as are towards the River of the Gulf of St. Laurence [the present coasts of eastern New Brunswick and the Gaspé peninsula]," in exchange for an agreement from the French government that all British subjects should be secure in their settlement of any other part of this coast "towards the Bay of Fundy and the Atlantic Ocean; the inland parts comprised within the above coasts to be settled by neither."

In his reference to the status of the "inland parts" of Nova Scotia and Acadia Mildmay was exploring an idea that eventually became known as the "*Liziere*," or neutral zone corridor, that the French government demanded as a necessity in order to secure a protected passage from Quebec to Cape Breton: passing across the isthmus of Nova Scotia and then along the eastern coast to the Strait of Canso. The British answer to this French demand is contained in a document headed "The Draft of an Agreement," which carries no date but is filed in a volume of the Leeds Papers containing documents from 1756. As it also makes reference to "His Majesty's entire confidence in the King of Prussia" it would thus appear to have been written soon after the signing of the Treaty of Westminster between Britain and Prussia in March 1756. This document states that: "[the status of] the peninsula and isthmus of Nova Scotia and the bay (*sic*) of Fundy, together with the *Liziere* adjoining thereunto, [is] to be adjusted between the two Courts," together with an assurance that: "France may have a passage from Quebec to a certain point on the continental part of Nova Scotia intended to be left neutral [the inland areas], and from thence to a certain point on the coast opposite the island of St. John [Prince Edward Island]."[7] By the time that this proposal was being advanced in 1756, however, the commission had long since been wound up and any possibility of an agreement between Britain and France had been overtaken by the serious incidents of warfare in North America. Nevertheless, in May of 1752 such an idea might have had the chance of success that Mildmay gave it in his proposal to Lord Holdernesse.

Mildmay's second proposal was that a similar agreement on "established settlements" should protect the existing French settlers on the island of St. Lucia in exchange for an equal guarantee by France to protect British settlers now on Tobago, and that the islands of St. Vincent and Dominica should be off limits to any colonists from both countries. The provisions in this clause were designed to resolve one of the disagreements that had preoccupied the negotiators in Paris for the last two years: namely that these islands must be entirely evacuated before any negotiations could take place on their ownership.

The Treaty of Aix-la-Chapelle had stipulated that certain of the Windward Islands whose ownership was still under dispute should be declared "neutral islands," or islands protected from any incursion by the subjects of either France or Britain while their status was negotiated. France had a considerable interest in adding Dominica and St. Lucia to the chain of French islands stretching from Guadeloupe to Martinique, and Britain wanted to acquire Grenada, St. Vincent, and Tobago—all of which could be governed from the British island of Barbados. Mildmay had already put forward the idea of an accommodation between Britain and France on these "neutral islands" in the earlier proposals he made to Lord Holdernesse and to the duke of Newcastle in August 1751.[8] At that time he said he had been informed the French government was afraid that if their military forces and settlers were forced to leave St. Lucia British settlers would promptly occupy it, and he therefore told Lord Holdernesse the French commissioners had indicated to him that in order to prevent this evacuation of St. Lucia, they might be prepared to make substantial territorial concessions in Acadia. The clause in Mildmay's May 1752 proposal that concerned the "neutral islands," and the "inland parts" in Nova Scotia and Acadia, was thus an attempt to provide some security to the present French and British inhabitants, and to prevent any further aggressive activities from either while a trade on the ownership of these territories was being explored in Paris.

Mildmay's third point covered the problem of the intrusion by the subjects of other countries and in this clause he stated that all settlers from other nations should be prevented from occupying any of these disputed territories in North America and the West Indies. This clause might seem superfluous in the context of the northeast coast of North America where, by 1752, no European country other than Britain and France had any colonial ambitions. It was still a very lively concern in the Caribbean, however, and Britain, France, Holland, and Spain watched each other's activities there with great suspicion. The Leeward Islands were largely divided between Britain and France, where Britain was in possession of Anquilla, Barbuda, St. Christophe, Nevis, Antigua, and Montserrat, and France occupied St. Bartholomew, Guadeloupe, La Desirade, Marie Galante, and Martinique. Lying midway between the Virgin Islands of St. Bartholomew and Barbuda was the Dutch island of St. Eustatius, and in the southern Caribbean Margarita and Trinidad belonged to Spain, Holland claimed Curacao and Bonaire, while Britain had possession of the central Windward island of Barbados. The ownership of the other islands in the Windward group was still under dispute when the Treaty of Aix-la-Chapelle was signed in April 1748 and, accordingly, Dominica, St. Lucia, St. Vincent, Grenada, and Tobago were declared to be "neutral islands," whose ownership was to be discussed at the negotiating table. The "off-limits" clause in Mildmay's proposal to Lord Holdernesse thus reflected the fact that while Britain and France reserved the right to dispute with each other the ultimate ownership of these neutral islands, neither nation had any intention of allowing Holland or Spain to acquire any more territory among these potential colonies in the West Indies.

Mildmay's fourth, and crucial point was that: "All the above agreements [are] to be entered into without prejudice to the rights set up by one Crown or the other," or, in other words, that these immediate agreements to limit further conflict would not preclude any future discussion of the rights of both sides. This document thus outlines the classic method for the negotiation of disputes, in which any additional aggravations are prevented by establishing an agreement to respect the existing status quo without prejudice to the eventual outcome, after which the real problems of the initial grievance can be addressed in a climate of some kind of reciprocal trust. Mildmay's proposal, made to Lord Holdernesse at the beginning of May 1752, is thus another crucial piece of direct evidence that he was engaged in a genuine attempt to negotiate an agreed settlement of the Treaty of Aix-la-Chapelle, and that he played a significant role in these negotiations.

It also directly contradicts the thesis that the true purpose of these British and French negotiators, and the governments that sent them, was nothing but a cynical exercise to buy time: that at no point was there any real expectation, by either side, that these negotiations would succeed, and, indeed, success in a peaceful settlement was never the actual objective of these governments, or of their commissioners.[9] Mildmay's letters to Lord Holdernesse in the Leeds Papers, and particularly this memoranda sent by Mildmay to Holdernesse, on 3 May 1752, seems to challenge the accepted view both of the insincerity of these negotiations and of Mildmay's lack of influence as a commissioner.

From the evidence of letters written by Lord Holdernesse to Lord Albemarle, and in further correspondence between Lord Hardwicke, the duke of Newcastle and Henry Pelham, it seems that in the late spring and early summer of 1752 members of the British Cabinet certainly did not believe that the negotiations were a futile, pointless exercise. On 17 May 1752 (NS), 6 May (OS), Albemarle sent a map to Holdernesse that showed the French government's proposal for the limits to the boundaries of Acadia,[10] and in his reply, written on 14 May (OS), Holdernesse told Albemarle that the map had been examined that day at a Cabinet meeting and: "I am to write to Hanover (to George II, in residence there for the summer) in consequence of it, so that you will have your future instructions from there."[11] On the strength of this map and of the Cabinet discussion that followed, Holdernesse seemed convinced that a breakthrough was possible. He summed up the sense of the meeting for Albemarle by saying: " . . . it is allowed as a first principle that concessions are mutually to be made. That is a nice step for *us* (*sic*) to take. If they are in earnest at Versailles it is not too difficult for them to come to a kind of *ultimatum* (*sic*) and if they would make a proposal tolerably occasionable, it might perhaps be adopted, but even an extravagant one would be ground for us to work upon."[12]

In a further letter to Albemarle, on 28 May (OS), Holdernesse expanded on this hope that the French government would make its own proposal but, bearing in mind the somewhat delicate political conditions under which the British ministers were forced to work, he said he was unable to understand: "what M. de Rouillé [minster of Marine] means by saying *He is determined to make none until you shall have received your Instructions (sic)*." Unlike the ministers in the absolutist government of France, the Cabinet of George II was compelled to respond to the political demands of an open parliament and public opinion. Holdernesse thus commented to Albemarle: "Mirepoix has always been sensible of the difficulties an English Administration must be under in these kinds of affairs. On their side they know what they would be at and can support it, while we are obliged to have a strict regard to other people's opinions and he [Rouillé] cannot but be sensible how much easier it is for us to adopt a scheme of theirs, than to lower our own proposals if we are forced to speak first."[13]

Despite Holdernesse's urging, it was impossible for Albemarle to have a serious discussion with Rouillé. In a letter he had written to the minister of Marine, on 23 March 1752, Albemarle had told Rouillé that he had made several attempts to meet him at Versailles in order to discover whether he had read Albemarle's note on the latest British government response, but had been unable to find him there.[14] Two months later, in a letter written on 17 May (NS), Albemarle confirmed to Holdernesse that Rouillé was, indeed, very difficult to pin down. He reported: "I have a man to treat with who is always on the Ramble with the King, his master, and when I thought to fix him at Compiègne for six weeks, he told me last week that he had to leave to make his father-in-law a visit in Lorraine, and I was not to see him till the 25th of next month."[15] Nevertheless, and despite what Lord Holdernesse described to Lord Albemarle in his 28 May letter as the "dance" of negotiation, it appeared that at last there was the beginning of some movement forward in the process.

The French map and its proposals on Acadia had definitely created some enthusiasm in Whitehall. On the day after the Cabinet meeting of 14 May (OS) Lord Hardwicke wrote to the duke of Newcastle, in Hanover, telling him that although he agreed with the proposals in general, he had certain differences with his ministerial colleagues on their timing: assuring Newcastle that: "there was no difference of opinion amongst the Lords that met, 'tho I think some seemed inclined to go rather faster than I was." Hardwicke said he estimated that in exchange for the demolition of their fort at Crown Point, the French would demand: "a Tract, or Lisere (*sic*) of Land, on the Southern

Bank of the River St. Lawrence, to be left to them," but he felt this would be difficult to accommodate, as: "it will be ceding to France, in possession, part of what is now understood here to be the Right of the Crown of Great Britain." He admitted that Lord Halifax and Lord Anson (First Sea Lord) thought a major success would have been achieved if the removal of Crown Point could be included as a part of this trade, however Hardwicke said he did not think such an arrangement would be agreed to by the French unless: "they can get the Possession of Ste. Lucia, of which you know my Lord Granville [president of the Privy Council] makes no account."[16]

However promising the situation might appear to some members of the Cabinet in London, and despite Lord Holdernesse's encouragement to Lord Albemarle to talk with M. Rouillé, the final decision must be made by George II, who had the sole constitutional right to determine British foreign policy. By the end of the month no such decision from Hanover had, as yet, arrived in Paris, and Albemarle was far too cautious to move on Holdernesse's instructions alone. On 31 May (NS) he told Holdernesse the negotiations on the issues central to British interests had not moved forward, but he said he hoped that as a consequence of the Cabinet advice sent to Hanover he would soon hear from the duke of Newcastle. Albemarle was dubious about proceeding any further without these royal instructions and told Holdernesse that as he did not know enough about what was being discussed, either in London or in Hanover, until he heard from Newcastle he did not feel he could approach Rouillé. He said he felt that to depend solely on a report of the minutes of the 14 May Cabinet meeting: "is no ground for me to tread on. Pray forgive my nicety, but in being cautious in this affair, I follow the example of my betters [members of the Cabinet]."[17]

On 4 June 1752 (NS) the duke of Newcastle finally sent the king's instructions to Lord Albemarle and in the accompanying letter he said he had read Lord Holdernesse's report of the Cabinet meeting of 14 May, with its proposal for British concessions on the boundaries of Acadia in exchange for the removal of Crown Point. Newcastle told Albemarle he agreed with his Cabinet colleagues that such an exchange seemed reasonable to ask under the circumstances, and repeated the same opinions as those of Lord Holdernesse: "that the rights on either side should not be too strictly adhered to, but that means should be found for a mutual security of the undisputed possession of each Crown."[18] By the end of June Henry Pelham seemed to be even more optimistic. In a letter to Newcastle on 19 June (OS),

30 June (NS), Pelham said that when he, Lord Holdernesse, Lord Granville, Lord Anson, Lord Hardwicke, and Lord Halifax had studied the proposed boundary lines: "We all agreed that if he [Albemarle] can procure such an agreement as that map points out, it is the greatest work for this country which has been done for many years. And the credit of His Majesty's government, as well as the abilities of those employed in this negotiation, will be transmitted to posterity with the greatest honour. We fear it is too good. However it is to be tryed (*sic*) and considering the present disposition of France with regard to peace, I am satisfied more is to be got now than we can reasonably expect another time."[19]

It was in this climate of hope for the success of the negotiations that Mildmay began his new responsibilities in Paris, in concert with his new colleague Ruvigny De Cosne. He was confident that with this collaboration the negotiation prospects were now much brighter because he had worked with De Cosne since arriving in Paris in 1750, and knew him to be a very competent diplomat. Ruvigny De Cosne was, in fact, an interesting man, whose contribution to the commission has also been seriously overlooked. His surname was French because he was descended from Huguenot refugees, who had fled to England after the revocation of the Edict of Nantes in 1685, but De Cosne was English and in May 1752 he was First Secretary at the British embassy in Paris. The position of First Secretary in Paris was an important diplomatic post; it carried with it the designation of minister plenipotentiary and "second minister," or acting *chef de mission* in the absence of the ambassador. De Cosne first came to Paris in September 1749 as Lord Albemarle's private secretary and on 16 October 1751 he was appointed First Secretary following Joseph Yorke's promotion as British ambassador to the Dutch United Provinces. On the sudden death of Lord Albemarle, in late December 1754, De Cosne took over the Paris embassy as its acting ambassador and he remained in that position until, with the complete breakdown in diplomatic relations, the embassy was closed on 27 July 1755 and he was withdrawn to London.[20]

De Cosne was not one of the golden young men from good families who looked on the diplomatic work at British embassies as a place to acquire a cosmopolitan polish and as a brief stepping-stone to political office. He was an intelligent career diplomat and was thought of highly by Sir Benjamin Keene, British ambassador to Spain. Immediately after Lord Albemarle's death, and while De Cosne was acting as *chef de mission* at the Paris embassy, in January 1755 Keene wrote to his friend Abraham Castres, British consul at Lisbon: "De Cosne is a very able and agreeable man and will be of infinite service to a new Minister [ambassador]." In May 1755 Sir Benjamin told Castres that, in his opinion, De Cosne: "is an excellent creature." No new ambassador was, in fact, appointed to Paris and when De Cosne returned to London in July 1755 Sir Benjamin requested that he be sent to Madrid to become First Secretary. De Cosne remained there as First Secretary until Sir Benjamin's death in Madrid in 1760, when, once again, he became the *chef de mission* and acting ambassador to the Spanish Court. He continued in this post for the next two years until he was replaced by the new British ambassador, Lord Bristol, in 1762.[21] Although his work as negotiator has not been mentioned in any analysis of the history of the commission, Ruvigny De Cosne was no more a light weight and nonentity than was William Mildmay.

From the optimistic reports that Mildmay was getting from Lord Albemarle on the boundary negotiations, he felt that by the end of June he could congratulate himself for their apparent success. On 21 June 1752 (NS) he wrote to Lord Fitzwalter: "it is some satisfaction to me and indeed does me no little honour to find the very scheme I proposed for an amicable determination of this entangled affair [in his report to Lord Holdernesse of 3 May (NS)] is equally approved by both Courts."[22] In his journal report on the next conference that he and De Cosne held with the French commissioners, on 26 June (NS), he said he had informed Galissonière and Silhouette that there was some hope that discussions between Lord Albemarle and the duke of Mirepoix, French ambassador to Britain, might resolve at least some of the territorial disputes in Nova Scotia and Acadia: ". . . M. de Mirepoix being now in Paris on leave of absence for some time."[23] The French commissioners told him they agreed with his hopes in this respect, however serious difficulties still appeared to remain with the problem of the prize ships. Mildmay said that on being asked whether they had prepared their list of those ships they wished to claim as "unlawful seizures," once again Galissonière and Silhouette replied that their list would include ships that were captured before, as well as after the late war.

At this point De Cosne had his first exposure to one of the fundamental disagreements that had persisted throughout the negotiations. In his journal report Mildmay stated that: "in order that Mr. De Cosne might be appraised, as they said, of what had passed at the former conferences," a great deal of time was taken by the French commissioners in a restatement of the general principles on which the French position on the prize ships was based, while Mildmay said he: "expressed surprise that they would renew a Demand [to include pre-war prizes] which had been before, so often and so peremptorily refused." This lengthy conference, in fact, resolved neither the overall sum of the indemnities to be settled by each Court, nor the time during which such prizes would be accepted as a legitimate claim, and the end result was only an agreement to disagree on these two basic points.

Three days after this conference, and realizing its pointlessness, Mildmay made two determined and creative efforts to solve the contentious issues of the ransoms and the prize ships: one in a letter to Lord Holdernesse and the other in a letter to the duke of Newcastle. On 29 June (NS) he informed Holdernesse that he had just written to Newcastle about the problems he was having in his negotiations on the French prisoners: specifically his attempt to obtain the compensation requested by Britain for the maintenance of the French marine soldiers who had been captured on the prize ships. Mildmay told Holdernesse that throughout their meetings M. Seigneur, the French commissioner appointed to deal with this particular subject, had always insisted that these negotiations should be bound by the terms of the Cartel of Frankfurt (an agreement made in Frankfurt in 1743 for the exchange of prisoners), and that these terms could be neither extended nor changed. Since this cartel had only mentioned "soldier prisoners," and the French maintained that in their navy such marines were regarded not as soldiers, but as sailors, he said Seigneur thus refused to discuss any such maintenance costs. Mildmay pointed out to Holdernesse, however, that in the negotiations on the damages due for the prize ships, the French government was refusing to accept the time limits for such prizes laid down in the document that governed the majority of the negotiations: namely the Treaty of Aix-la-Chapelle. This being the case Mildmay proposed that he should draw this contradiction to the attention of Galissonière and Silhouette, and suggest that if they insisted that the British abide by the strict terms of the first agreement (the Frankfurt Cartel), the French should then do likewise with respect to the second (the Aix treaty).[24]

Although Mildmay said it would give him some satisfaction to insist on this point of logic, he was more interested in getting these two problems solved. He told Holdernesse he had made a careful study of the total sums due to Britain for the French soldiers and the French marines, and said he had discovered that the final balance between all these prisoner ransoms and the cost of the indemnity to France for her prizes—both pre-war and post-war—was virtually the same. He therefore suggested that Lord Albemarle be instructed to ask the French Ministry if they would agree that rather than continuing the endless reiteration of the present dispute, they would contemplate some kind of mutual financial accommodation that would offset both the full cost of all the prisoners claimed by Britain, and of all the prizes claimed by France. With the elimination of these contentious monetary questions, he felt that nothing would then remain to negotiate, since even the issue of the sea limits would, at this point, become moot and at least two of the three mandates of the commission—the prisoners and the prizes—would thus be ratified successfully.

Mildmay also told Lord Holdernesse that in order to be able manage the smooth passage of these negotiations he felt it was imperative to get a new French commissioner in place, as Seigneur had proved quite useless in this respect. Indeed, Mildmay said that Seigneur was not even properly accredited: "for as yet I have been only referred to one who was, as he tells me, a former French commissioner of War during the last campaign in Flanders [in 1747], and who has no particular commission to treat with me, upon equal terms, and who indeed seems to have no other Authority, nor Qualification, than only to Chicane and Bluster in order to put off the just demands of His Majesty [George II]."

In the letter that Mildmay and De Cosne sent to the duke of Newcastle on the same day, 29 June (NS), they gave him a summary of the latest conference, and proposed two alternative suggestions. In the first they asked whether, in response to a similar document they had been told was being prepared by the French commissioners, Newcastle now wished them to prepare: "a formal declaration in writing" on the prize issue, and they advised that this declaration should clearly state the reasons why the British government refused to allow any damage claims for pre-war prizes. They said that as the 1748 Treaty of Aix-la-Chapelle was a mutually agreed settlement of the war that Louis XV had declared on Britain in 1744, and as the clear and unambiguous terms of this treaty precluded the present French demands, they urged that this British declaration should include a strong protest that such demands were still being made by the French government. In their second suggestion they repeated the proposal that Mildmay had sent to Lord Holdernesse; that a linkage should be established between the costs of the ransoms and the prizes, and asked that Newcastle instruct Lord Albemarle to consult with the French ministry to obtain their view of such a possible joint solution to these two disputes.[25]

The summer had now arrived, however, and in the middle of July Mildmay and De Cosne left with Lord Albemarle to visit the French Court in its summer residence at Compiègne where, in a letter sent to Fitzwalter on 17 July (NS), Mildmay described his participation in a royal hunting party.[26] From Compiègne Mildmay then traveled to the Champagne district and enjoyed his favorite occupation: studying the social and economic conditions of the French countryside.[27] On 17 June (OS), 28 June (NS), or the day before Mildmay had made his innovative proposal to Lord Holdernesse and the duke of Newcastle, Holdernesse had already given Albemarle his opinion about the unsatisfactory state of negotiations on the prize ships.

Lord Holdernesse appreciated that the British government's insistence that its commissioners were entirely bound by the terms of the Treaty of Aix-la-Chapelle was causing a compete stalemate in these negotiations. He told Lord Albemarle that although he had just sent a letter to Mildmay and De Cosne which informed them that they were not to consider the merit of any prizes that had been taken before this treaty was signed, he also said that as many of the disputes on prizes that France claimed had been taken unlawfully during the war had already been decided in favor of their French owners by the British Board of Admiralty court: "they [the British commissioners] are permitted to throw out an insinuation that tho they cannot exceed the bounds of their Commission, the Court of France may, if they please, apply to your Excellency, or to His Majesty's Ministers at London, upon this point."

This suggestion seems to indicate that the Cabinet had decided that the negotiations between Lord Albemarle and the duke of Mirepoix on the territorial disputes that Mildmay had mentioned to the French commissioners might now be extended to cover the prize ships, but only to any prizes taken *during* the late war. It is perhaps unfortunate that when he wrote this letter to Albemarle Holdernesse had not, as yet, received Mildmay's information that the overall costs for the prizes and the prisoners' maintenance might well cancel each other out, since he might thus have been able to include this important fact in his instructions to the ambassador. In the absence of this information, the instructions that Albemarle received were, at the least, provocative and unlikely to help Mildmay's negotiations with M. Seigneur. Albemarle was told to inform the French government ministers that if, contrary to the terms of the Treaty of Aix-la-Chapelle, they persisted in presenting a list of prizes taken before 1748, the British government expected to be reimbursed for the subsistence and transport of the French marines taken prisoner in the course of the war, regardless of any argument that these marine prisoners were not covered under the terms of the Cartel of Frankfurt.[28]

Holdernesse's letter to Mildmay and De Cosne had also been written on 17 June (OS), 28 June (NS), and in it he told them that the Lords Justices (the members of the Regency Council, acting in the king's absence in Hanover) had been consulted on this matter and had ruled that the legitimacy of all ships taken in the six months following the signing of the peace treaty had already been declared as those covered under the fourth Article of the Treaty of Aix-la-Chapelle: "Upon which, and only upon which, your commission, so far as it relates to unlawful captures at sea, is founded."[29] He then discussed the issue of the ships taken during the war and told them to point out there was no reason to change the established legal practice: "as I send you a list of a number of causes of this nature which have been heard and determined by the ordinary course of law [in the British Admiralty courts], many of which, you will observe, have been equitably and impartially determined in favour of France."

However, he repeated the suggestion he had written to Lord Albemarle, stating that although this: "exceeds the bounds of your Commission," they should find out whether the French government could be persuaded, given their previous success under British law, at least to agree that discussions on compensation for these ships, together with the questions of any damages other than for the ship and its cargo, could be removed from the commission negotiations and given to Albemarle and the duke of Mirepoix. As the senior diplomatic representatives of their two kings, they could then make a joint application to the British Court of Admiralty for a final determination on the legitimacy of each case.

Holdernesse said that although he thought this approach might be worth trying, he was very concerned about a formal, written protest that the French commissioners had announced that they proposed to issue. He stressed the importance of trying to prevent them from going to these lengths and instructed Mildmay and De Cosne "to shew (*sic*) them how little ground there is for such an offensive proceeding, and represent, in moderate terms, to them the consequences of it." Holdernesse further ordered that if their moderate attempts at persuasion failed, Mildmay and De Cosne should draw up a: "Counter Protest, setting forth your reasons for adhering strictly to the Letter of the Treaties between the Two Crowns," and instructing them that they were also to make sure that Lord Albemarle approved the wording of this document before it was submitted to the French side.

Lord Holdernesse sent a further letter on 26 June (OS), 6 July (OS), but addressed only to Mildmay, informing him that notice had been taken of his complaints about Seigneur's lack of status. He was told that Lord Albemarle had now received instructions to ask the French Court to appoint a properly accredited commissioner to negotiate the ransom of prisoners, and Holdernesse also told him that all letters on his progress over the ransoms should be sent both: "to the Duke of Newcastle at Hanover, and to me [in Whitehall]."[30] This order from Lord Holdernesse illustrates a serious problem for the successful momentum of the negotiations in 1752; one that had already become evident in the unfortunate delay caused by Lord Albemarle's need to wait for directions from Hanover in May, and the equal difficulty that Mildmay and De Cosne experienced in obtaining instructions from both Holdernesse and the duke of Newcastle in late June.

Each year of his reign George II insisted on visiting his electorate from late April, early May, until the end of October and during this interval all crucial decisions on British foreign policy were made from Hanover by the king and the northern secretary of state, whom he took with him.[31] The transmission of letters between Hanover and London, via the embassy at The Hague, inevitably took at least a week in each direction, and since their delivery was also dependent on the weather in the Channel, the elapsed time between asking for directions and receiving them might be considerably longer than the requisite two weeks. This lengthy, triangular process for the exchange of information and decisions between the southern secretary in London, the northern secretary in Hanover and the British ambassador in Paris, delayed the necessary instructions to Lord Albemarle and the British commissioners considerably: a problem that did not exist for the French commissioners. The difficulty that the king's absence from London caused to the timely arrival of diplomatic information is revealed in two letters from Lord Holdernesse to Lord Albemarle. On 14 May 1752 (OS), and at a time when Albemarle said he urgently needed information on what to say to St. Contest, Holdernesse told him: "as everything material will for the future will come from Hanover to you . . . I think it will be needless to continue your weekly messenger [to and from London]."[32] On 11 June (OS) Holdernesse wrote a brief letter, of two short paragraphs, in which he remarked: "My Dear Lord, . . . you must be sensible I have nothing material to say to you during the King's absence . . . I write at present more to keep up the correspondence than for anything else."[33]

In his letter of 14 May to Lord Albemarle, Lord Holdernesse had touched on yet another aspect of the information problem: namely the six-month interruption of regular visits by the kings messengers to the embassy in Paris. The British diplomatic service in the eighteenth century was not funded by parliament, but was paid by the king as a royal expense that stemmed from the prerogative right of the monarch to determine foreign policy. All British diplomats were, quite literally, the king's servants and while he received the advice of his ministers on the choice of a specific diplomat, the final decision on the appointment was made by the king, who also paid their salaries and all the expenses of maintaining his diplomatic posts abroad.[34] One of these expenses was the cost of the king's messengers, who traveled between each post and London, and whose diplomatic bags were reasonably secure from examination by the host government. Between April and October the route of the royal messengers was changed from the direct Dover to Calais crossing to one from Harwich to Helvoetsluys, which serviced The Hague and Hanover, and the diplomats in Paris had to depend on a returning British visitor to carry a particularly urgent letter to Whitehall, as its security could not be trusted to the French postal service.

The uncertainties and insecurities this caused are shown in a letter Mildmay sent to Fitzwalter on 27 May 1752. Here Fitzwalter was told: "Since by the new disposition that has been made, no more messengers are to go directly from hence to England during His Majesty's stay in Hanover, I must restrain my pen from writing subjects of a public [or sensitive] nature, or at least I must only write upon such topics as every one may be permitted to talk of, without making any additional remarks."[35] On 8 November 1752 Mildmay was able to assure Fitzwalter that "His Majesty setting out, as we are informed, this day from Hanover, our messengers will be dispatched directly to Calais, which will again reinstate my correspondence with your Lordship in the usual regular course."[36] During the preceding summer Mildmay had been forced to wait for infrequent royal messenger service that went via The Hague for all his official dispatches, as in a letter on 29 August 1752 he advised Fitzwalter: "I shall write to the Earl of Holdernesse by the next courier concerning diverse affairs which I dare not trust to the [direct] Post."[37]

Mildmay was right to be cautious, for the problem of preventing letters from being opened by the French authorities was always a constant concern. Within two months of his arrival in Paris Mildmay wrote to Lord Fitzwalter, on 2 July 1750, that he needed a: "safe conveyance," because: "I am thought a person of such consequence that all letters suspected to come from me, or directed to me, if trusted to the Post here are certain to be opened."[38] Without the security of the diplomatic bag Mildmay's private correspondence with Fitzwalter during the summer of 1752 was therefore guarded on the details of his negotiations, but in his letter of 29 August 1752 he informed Fitzwalter that he would be able to have a copy of the various pieces of information Mildmay was sending to Lord Holdernesse, via the royal messenger service, for: "I am engaged in drawing up the same, as well as in other matters relative to my own commission."[39]

Despite these communication difficulties, Mildmay and De Cosne persevered with their attempts to solve at least one issue in the dispute over the prize ships. On 2 August (NS) they wrote from the royal palace of Compiègne to thank Holdernesse for the information contained in his 28 June (NS) letter concerning the Regency Council's ruling, and the success of French cases before the Admiralty courts. They told him they had been able to take the opportunity of their visit to Compiègne to explore with the foreign minister, M. St. Contest, Holdernesse's suggestion that cases of indemnity for the prize ships captured during the war could be determined by these Admiralty courts alone.[40] They reported that they had given St. Contest specific details of a case that had been heard in 1741, and which had been decided in favor of France: "to the amount of £1000 ordered to be restored to the French proprietors." They said that St. Contest had then stated that since the case had been first mentioned to him by Lord Albemarle he had been unable to obtain any details of it from the Admiralty court records, and Mildmay and De Cosne therefore asked that such information be sent to them at once, especially as M. Rouillé had also expressed his disbelief on this point.

By the middle of August it also appeared that Mildmay's suggestion of a possible financial linkage on the issues of the prisoners and the prize ships might finally be bearing some fruit. Mildmay had now returned to Paris and on 17 August (NS) he wrote a private letter to Lord Holdernesse, thanking him for instructing Lord Albemarle to ask for a new French commissioner to negotiate the prisoner ransoms and saying that during the previous week he and Lord Albemarle had visited M. St. Contest at Versailles for this purpose.[41] Mildmay was pleased to be able to report that at this meeting: "M. St. Contest had promised to engage the same French Commissaries who are appointed to adjust the Demands on Captures at Sea [Galissonière and Silhouette] to settle likewise Demands on account of the Ransoms and Subsistence of Soldier Prisoners." Although the disputed question of the marine prisoners did not yet seem to have been addressed, he still saw this amalgamation of the two claims, to be negotiated by the same commissioners, as a positive step toward his stated goal. He told Holdernesse: "If these two accounts can be adjusted by setting the Balance of both Demands against each other, I believe it will be the most proper and speedy Method of putting an End to all further Disputes upon these subjects."

In their official letter to Lord Holdernesse, also written on 17 August, Mildmay and De Cosne reported that the French commissioners had recently requested a clarification of some of the proof documents that had been submitted with the British memorial on St. Lucia of 17 November 1751, and that they also seemed to be preparing a reply to this British document. With the prospect of this reply they once again asked Lord Holdernesse whether: "we ought not to be, on our part, prepared also with a Reply to their Answer to our memorial concerning the Limits of Acadie," and assured Holdernesse that if the commissioners of the Board of Trade had any points that they wished to be made, he and De Cosne would be careful to incorporate them in the document.[42]

The urgent need for such preparation was amply demonstrated by an event at the end of August which Mildmay and De Cosne regarded as so serious that, in addition to the official letter that they sent to Lord Holdernesse, they also sent a précis of the contents of their letter to the duke of Newcastle in Hanover, and to the Board of Trade in Whitehall. On 30 August they informed Holdernesse that Lord Albemarle had received a private and confidential message from the duke of Mirepoix: "*comme d'Ami, à Ami,* (*sic*) [which was the only way His Lordship would accept it]," that the French government intended to print and distribute their reply to the British memorial on Acadia and Nova Scotia, concurrently with the delivery by Galissonière and Silhouette of the long-awaited reply on the British claim to St. Lucia. Even beyond this extraordinary breach of diplomatic protocol,

Mildmay and de Cosne informed Holdernesse that in the margin of this printed version would be: "a number of Annotations which have never been communicated to us" and which, in their opinion, were there specifically: "to make an Appeal to the Publick in such a manner without giving any Opportunity of [our] making an Answer."[43]

Thankfully, in this letter they were able to report that: "by Lord Albemarle's Interposition a Stop was put to their Publication soon after they [the copies] were Printed, and as at present we come to the knowledge of them only through private Confidence, we cannot presume to make formal use of them." Nevertheless, they told Holdernesse that they had used the limited time in which Lord Albemarle had possession of a copy to transcribe this document: that they now enclosed with their letter. They said that in the margin of their copy they had been careful to note those "annotations" that had been inserted in the proposed manuscript, so that a response could be prepared to these French objections that: "were thus Clandestinely intended to be Insinuated."

Mildmay and De Cosne also told Holdernesse that, along with the text of this document, the French government had inserted a map: "and as this map is often referred to in their notes, we have thought it proper to send Your Lordship a copy of it on which are marked . . . the Lines that describe the Limits by several Governments." In order that Holdernesse and the Board could make a geographical comparison with the British claim, they said that they had also included their own map, prepared in the same fashion as that drawn by the French cartographer. They pointed out, however, that their map might contain some inaccuracies, as the French map had been carefully researched and prepared specifically for this occasion, while they had been forced to produce a somewhat hasty response from the only information they could obtain.[44]

With this apparent French diplomatic duplicity, by the middle of October Mildmay appeared to be resigning himself to the fact that despite all his earlier hopes for a speedy and successful end to at least a part of his commission work, this event was unlikely to take place in 1752. On 15 October he wrote to Fitzwalter from the palace of Fontainebleau, where he was again enjoying a royal hunting party, and after he had described the lack of interest of Louis XV and his Court in discussing any subject other than hunting, he continued: "it may be of some consolation to me to have done no harm, since I can do no good. This is all the merit I can hope for from this Court, which so far from being eager to finish the affair I am charged with, don't seem inclined to talk about them. This makes me desirous of entering into the scenes of private life."[45] Mildmay then expanded on the nature of this "private life" by stating his wish to be able to spend his entire time "enjoying the happiness . . . of your Lordship's company" at Moulsham Hall in Essex. Two days later, on 18 October, he reported to Lord Holdernesse from Fontainebleau that despite St. Contest's stated intent in August, during the last two months neither the French government nor the French commissioners had made any serious attempt to negotiate a compromise, either on the ransoms or the prizes.[46]

Despite what seemed a setback to their hopes, on 23 November 1752 Mildmay and De Cosne made yet another determined effort to convince the French commissioners that although the British government did not intend to move from its stated position on the pre-war prize issue, there was still room for some flexibility on the question of indemnities. Mildmay's journal report for 23 November noted that on that day they attended a conference at Galissonière's apartment at which they were finally given the list of prizes that the French government had prepared for settlement.[47] Far from producing a solution to the problem, however, Mildmay said that once again they discovered that this list was in fact a: "*Book, or volume of Papers, tacked together, entitled Etat des Prizes sur Mer (sic)*." This book contained a list of all the French ships captured since 1738 and was divided into three different headings: the first being ships seized from 1738 up to the first six months of the war, the second containing those taken during the rest of the war, and the third a list of prizes taken since the war had ended. He noted that the preface to this book was a statement, backed with a long, supporting argument, which said that notwithstanding the decision of the British commissioners not to discuss any prizes taken before the Treaty of Aix-la-Chapelle, the French commissioners had been instructed by their Court to demand indemnity for all the ships on this list: "from which claim, the King their Master could never desist, nor think it ought to be postponed to any further term."

This list was filed in the correspondence of the French Foreign Ministry and from the date given on its title page it had, in fact, been prepared a month earlier, on 24 October. Its three sections gave the names and descriptions of some 70 French ships, over a half of which (37 ships) were claimed to have been taken before the war had been declared, while 7 were declared to have been captured in the first six months of the war, and a further 26 seized within six months of the signing of the preliminary peace treaty in the spring of 1748. From their descriptions, most seem to have been either merchantmen or fishing vessels and they came from ports around the southern, eastern, and northern French coasts: Frejus, Arles, Marseille, Bayonne, Bordeaux, La Rochelle, Cherbourg, and Dunkirk.[48]

Mildmay reported that once they had seen the list, he and De Cosne fell back on a restatement of their steady argument that the commission mandate was bound solely by the terms of the Treaty of Aix-la-Chapelle, but he suggested that if the French commissioners would agree to detach the first two parts of their list (the pre-war and wartime ships), he and De Cosne would now accept the third part in exchange for a similar list of British claims that they had already prepared. Without such a division, Mildmay told them he was unable to accept this document as it now stood, however in accordance with his instructions from Lord Holdernesse in June, he said he pointed out that this refusal would not deny justice to French claimants, since the French commissioners could still give the list of those prizes taken during the war to Lord Albemarle, or to the duke of Mirepoix, for their judgment. He stated he had repeated the information given him by Lord Holdernesse: that the British Admiralty court was available for a decision on these wartime claims and these court records showed that many had already been decided in favor of French subjects. He reported that Galissonière and Silhouette: "pretended to express great surprise" at this refusal to accept their list and its attachments, stating that that they did not think it was within the power of the British side to reject any documents presented by the French, but: "so that the proceedings might not seem too violent on either side," he said that both sets of commissioners agreed to postpone further discussion of this issue until after they had consulted with their governments.

The conference concluded with some discussion on the limits of the Channel and the North Sea previously claimed by Britain, and Mildmay reported that on this issue the French commissioners said they did not agree that the Irish Sea and the seas around the Orkneys and the west coast of Scotland should be claimed as "British Seas." From their response it appears that even after fifteen months of negotiations by the joint commission, the French position on the Channel limits had not changed from those laid down in 1749 at the meetings at St. Malo. In their counter-proposal Galissonière and Silhouette stated, yet again, that the limits of the western end of the Channel should be established on a line drawn between Cape Ushant and the

Scilly Islands (not the British boundary of Cape Finistère to the south coast of Ireland), and that the outer limits of the North Sea should be at a line drawn between "the Naise Point [at the mouth of the Narvik fjord, in northern Norway] to the opposite shores of Scotland [the west coast of the Shetlands]"; these, they said, being the limits laid down in previous treaties of peace. Not surprisingly, Mildmay and De Cosne disagreed on the grounds that Britain must have a secure protection for all of her coastline (including the whole of southwestern England, Wales, eastern Scotland, and the east coast of Ireland) and not just from the tip of Cornwall to the western Shetlands. Mildmay said he also indicated to Galissonière and Silhouette, whom, he said, agreed this minor point with him, that as only one of the French prizes seemed to have been taken outside of the middle of the Channel, and the one exception on the British list was only worth £150, the indemnity claims for the post-war prizes could thus be settled without having to make any final decision on the boundaries of the Channel and the North Sea.

In the official letter that Mildmay and De Cosne sent to Lord Holdernesse on 6 December 1752, they described this long and fruitless discussion on the sea limits, and on the unsatisfactory list of prizes that had been produced by the French commissioners, and for the first time they summed up their feelings on this whole phase of the negotiation. They told Holdernesse that, in their opinion, the French commissioners did not intend to deviate from their position on the validity of pre-war prizes for, regardless of any optimism he and De Cosne may have had for an immediate settlement in early August: "it is now more than two years since we demanded their list of prizes . . . they have never thought fit to offer us their list till now and, at the same time, by casting our eyes cursorily over it, [discovered] that they had not set down the amount of the value of the damages." They said that having asked Galissonière and Silhouette the reason for this fundamental omission, and on receiving the reply that it was up to the "individual sufferer" to determine his exact loss, they had concluded: "This, we humbly submit, is a mark of their not having a disposition to come to an amicable Accommodation."[49]

The negotiations on the prize ships and the sea limits now appeared to be at a complete standstill and during the autumn and winter of 1752 two things seemed to occupy Mildmay's mind. The first was how to orchestrate the proceedings in his commission work so that he could receive permission to visit Lord Fitzwalter, and the second was to find out, yet again, whether Fitzwalter thought that he would be acceptable to the Pelham ministry as a parliamentary candidate in a possible general election. His urgency to visit England may have been increased by a letter that he had received during the summer from Edward Johnson, who had been a valued, senior servant of Lord Fitzwalter for the past thirty years.[50]

After Johnson had talked about the state of the corn harvest in Essex and his opinion of Mildmay's suggestion to Fitzwalter that with the current French prices, English grain could be exported to France at a profit, he admitted: "But my Lordship does not know of my writing now. I was in hopes that you would have been over to England by this time for my Lord is very much alone now."[51] Johnson explained that this summer Lord Fitzwalter was living at Moulsham Hall without the accustomed company of his stepdaughter and stepson because Lady Caroline Ancram and her husband, Lord Ancram, were visiting their estates in Yorkshire, and Lord and Lady Holdernesse were spending their time between London and the spa at Tunbridge Wells. Johnson did not need to remind Mildmay that his lonely friend and patron, of whom Mildmay was the heir presumptive, was now in his early eighties and a frail widower.

Mildmay continued to keep up a correspondence with Edward Johnson and in early November 1752 Lord Fitzwalter was also encouraging Mildmay to return to London, but the difficulty lay in trying to find a time when Mildmay could leave the commission safely and could also find a reasonable excuse to have to return to Whitehall for consultations. On 22 November Mildmay was forced to tell Fitzwalter he had heard from William Shirley, who was now in London working with the Board of Trade, that the Board would shortly be sending him a long memorial on the Acadian boundary limits. This, Mildmay knew from experience: "would perhaps occasion me some further disputes with the French commissaries upon those points," and he said Lord Holdernesse had also written, privately, that he would be sending an: "*official* (*sic*) letter of business."[52]

Regretfully Mildmay advised Fitzwalter that, under these circumstances, it would appear to be extremely difficult for him to leave Paris. In an effort to explore the possibility, however, he said he intended to make use of John Pownall, the friend at the Board of Trade who had served him well in his problem with Shirley in 1751 and who was now the chief clerk (or undersecretary),[53] telling Fitzwalter that he would ask Pownall to let him know the precise date on which he could actually expect the memorial from the Board to arrive. The presentation of this British memorial on the limits of Acadia had already been postponed several times and, at this point, Mildmay was still counting on the fact that the French commissioners had told him they wanted a meeting to deliver their revised list of the prizes they claimed had been unlawfully seized. He thus informed Fitzwalter that, having received this French list, he anticipated he would need to make an official investigation in order to allow the Admiralty Court to examine each case on its merits, and for this inquiry to proceed speedily it would obviously be much easier if he was in London, where he could question in person the: "several merchants and owners of privateers in the City" about whom the French were complaining.

This may have seemed an excellent, indeed, a very rational reason for his need to return to England, however at the conference that was held on the next day he discovered that, unfortunately, the French commissioners' list remained completely unacceptable and so, with no cases to be judged, there could be no prior inquiry in London. In his report to Lord Fitzwalter on this unsatisfactory conference Mildmay told him: "The French commissioners, with their usual chicanery, have proposed such unreasonable terms of proceeding as to oblige us to write to our Masters for further instructions." He therefore concluded, regretfully, that this: "will oblige me to stay here for the due execution of them."[54]

On 2 December 1752 John Pownall replied to Mildmay's inquiries about the memorial from the Board of Trade on the boundaries of Acadia. In his letter Pownall revealed the lack of any effective coordination between the Board and the Department of State when he informed Mildmay that the memorial he had sent to Lord Holdernesse at the beginning of May, with its considered and creative suggestions for solving these disputes: "in support of His Majesty's Right to of Acadia, has not been communicated to the Board of Trade and is therefore not taken notice of in the course of their Memorial, which I doubt not you will have received ere this."[55] With some thinly disguised sarcasm on the political aspirations of the young Charles Townshend, Pownall also told Mildmay that this new memorial on Acadia from the Board of Trade was the work of: "Mr. Charles Townshend of their Board . . . except in some immaterial parts, and is such a one as I hope will be as much utility to the Cause as it is to him." Although the text of Pownall's letter does not confirm this, from Mildmay's remarks to Lord

Fitzwalter in his letter of 22 November on Shirley's present employment with the Board of Trade, it is probable that Shirley had also contributed to this memorial in concert with the ambitious Charles Townshend, later to be the ministerial author of the notorious duty on tea that so enraged the inhabitants of Boston. If, in fact, Shirley was involved with the preparation of this memorial, Mildmay's earlier proposal would have stood very little chance of being well received in any case, since it proposed important territorial concessions to be made by the British in Nova Scotia and Acadia that Shirley would have found completely unacceptable.

Unfortunately for Mildmay's careful plans to orchestrate his return to Essex, he was forced to remain in Paris over the Christmas holidays and into the New Year. On 6 December 1752 he told Lord Fitzwalter the French commissioners were raising difficulties about his proposed absence and Lord Holdernesse had also asked him for a full report on the commission meeting of 23 November, of which report Mildmay said: "my colleague and I, acting together in perfect harmony, have sent [to London] by this opportunity and My Lord Holdernesse's answer will probably fix me here for some time longer, or give me an opening to ask leave to come home for a time." Nevertheless Mildmay took this occasion to ask Fitzwalter, yet again, whether: "it would be proper for me to solicit me being a member [of parliament] . . ." in a possible general election the next year.[56]

There is no evidence in any of his letters to Fitzwalter that Mildmay was ever encouraged to become a member of parliament and, in fact, this is the last time that he asked Fitzwalter the question. In any case, his duties as a commissioner occupied him fully in the last three weeks of 1752. In a private letter he sent to Lord Holdernesse on 13 December, assuring Holdernesse that it was completely confidential, Mildmay gave his detailed overview of the exchange of memorials that had taken place in the last eighteen months. He advised Holdernesse that despite the information he had received that the Board of Trade had already prepared the British memorial on Acadia, this document still had not arrived, and he said he was concerned that this memorial should be given to the French commissioners before parliament was due to meet on 11 January 1753. He gave as his reason that he had heard: "some captious Members of the House of Commons intend to move soon after their meeting [the opening of Parliament] for an examination of our Proceedings in the execution of the commission." Under these circumstances, he said he thus believed it should be shown that: "every step has been taken [by the British commissioners] to vindicate His Majesty's right" to this territory in Nova Scotia, though he also admitted: "I apprehend, from the disposition of this [French] Court, that [the right] will never be established but by argument of another kind."[57]

It appears that Mildmay's opinion on the present conduct of the French government was also shared by Lord Holdernesse. In a letter to Lord Albemarle on 20 December 1752 Holdernesse told him that the French government's continued insistence on the pre-war prize issue had made George II very angry. He said: "I hope you will talk roundly to St. Contest on the subject of *prizes (sic)*. He must not expect we will push our complaisance so far as to give up everything. I can tell you in confidence that the King was so provoked that I had no small difficulty to prevent our Commission being recalled in a hurry and it will certainly come to that if things go on as they have hitherto." Holdernesse reassured Albemarle that the next messenger would be bringing: "a strong memorial relating to North America . . . I believe you will agree with me that it is very ably drawn up and lays all the French arguments upon the ground, and particularly breaks the last memorial of theirs as it deserves." On 27 December Albemarle replied that he was eagerly awaiting the arrival of the memorial on Acadia, but it was not until 28 December that Holdernesse was able to announce that this long-awaited document had, at last, been sent, and he confirmed John Pownall's information to Mildmay in stating that it had been: "drawn up by young Townshend of the Board of Trade."[58]

Even though Mildmay was now leading the British negotiations on territorial disputes and the prize ships, he still continued with his sole responsibility for the prisoner ransoms and on 30 December 1752 he wrote a letter to Lord Albemarle that outlined the present, unsatisfactory state of these ransom meetings. The only surviving copy of this letter that is now in the Newcastle Papers is in French and is a translation of the document Mildmay sent to Lord Albemarle. A later inscription that is written on the copy states that Albemarle subsequently translated this letter from Mildmay and sent the translation to M. St. Contest, who filed it in the correspondence of the Ministry of Foreign Affairs. Since this translated letter is also contained in the correspondence of the duke of Newcastle, Albemarle must also have sent another copy to Whitehall.[59]

In his letter Mildmay repeated to Albemarle his earlier request that St. Contest be asked to appoint a suitable person to receive and reply to the claims of the British government, as this had now become a matter of urgency. He complained that nothing had been done since the summer to implement St. Contest's proposal to combine the two disputes (the ransoms and sea limits) in his negotiations with Galissonière and Silhouette. He also said he had made many fruitless attempts to get a reply to his memorials from Mr. Seigneur, at the Ministry of Foreign Affairs, only to discover that Seigneur had recently been instructed to transfer the responsibility to reply to the bureau of the comte d'Argenson, minister for war. This Ministry was now raising a new point of dispute on whether the French king ought to be asked to pay the prisoners' maintenance costs in advance of being able to recover them from the prisoners themselves, which only added a further and, in his opinion, unnecessary delay to an already protracted process. He therefore asked that Albemarle pass on a copy of his letter to St. Contest, if it was found to be satisfactory.

The substitution of the Ministry of War in the ransom negotiation had immediate consequences. A letter written by the comte d'Argenson to M. St. Contest, on 19 December 1752, shows that Mildmay's appeal to Albemarle was only a culmination of a series of acerbic exchanges that had taken place over several weeks, involving Seigneur, Mildmay, Albemarle, d'Argenson, and St. Contest. In this rather curt letter d'Argenson began by referring St. Contest to his previous letter of 9 December in which he had commented on the statement of record that Albemarle (or rather Mildmay) had produced on the total maintenance costs demanded by the British government for their French prisoners. This, he said, came to some £20,860 incurred since 1745 and the battle of Culloden, but he noted that £300 of this sum was charged to the maintenance of: "marines, and thus, consequently, to M. Rouillé [or the responsibility of the Ministry of the Marine and not that of the Ministry of War]." D'Argenson pointed out that since the king had now ordered his Ministry to take responsibility for the major part of these prisoners, any attempt by George II, through Lord Albemarle, to have Seigneur replaced now needed his concurrence. Seigneur, he said, was an experienced: "commissioner of war and our choice for conducting this matter" and he did not intend to give such an agreement for a new negotiator simply because Albemarle, in his preamble to the British statement, had indicated that such a change would be: "indispensable to his comfort."

D'Argenson concluded by pointing out to St. Contest that although Mildmay had been given two commissions—the first to negotiate the prisoner ransoms and the second to settle the territorial problems in America—he said:

> He has not, in fact, consistently attended to his first responsibility because he has not yet produced any justification documents, but only certificates by the English commissaries [for the hospitals and prisons], in which the land troops [soldiers] and the marines [sailors] are combined, and which, in consequence, M. Seigneur is not able to accept, as you can see from a copy of the attached memoir on this subject.[60]

The contents of d'Argenson's letter reveal three things: that the two-year disagreement over the status of the sailor prisoners was far from being resolved; that the war minister was in a "turf battle" with the minister for foreign affaires in which any attempt by St. Contest to intervene in what could be classed as strictly military matters would be strongly opposed; and, lastly, that any momentum to settle the question of the ransoms was rapidly eroding. Unfortunately for his hopes, Mildmay was now faced with an example of the bitter, factional politics that existed inside the Council of State, where St. Contest and M. de Machault, the controller general, were protégés of Madame de Pompadour, who had secured their appointment, and the comte d'Argenson and the chancellor, Lamoignon, were implacable enemies of the marquise. As Louis XV was incapable of decisive leadership over his warring ministers, any sensible attempt to negotiate that entangled itself in this constant rivalry was unlikely to succeed.

Nevertheless, Mildmay was anxious to extricate himself from Paris and on 3 January 1753 he told Lord Fitzwalter that he still hoped to bring all of his commissions (the negotiations on territory, on prizes, and on the ransom of prisoners): "to be finished together, or at least put into such a train of being finished as my asking leave to come home without any imputation of neglect of duty."[61] Unfortunately this was not to be achieved easily, as Mildmay found out, for although he may have thought that his problems with the ransom and the prizes were difficult enough, these ongoing irritants were about to be eclipsed by another and, potentially, far more threatening challenge to his commission.

On the same day on which he wrote in optimistic terms to Lord Fitzwalter (3 January), Mildmay and De Cosne acknowledged to Lord Holdernesse the arrival of the long memorial from the Board of Trade on the limits of Acadia, and said that they were busy having a copy of it transcribed.[62] The copy of the Acadia memorial was completed within three weeks but when Mildmay called a conference at De Cosne's apartment on 23 January to hand over the document he discovered that the territorial negotiations, for which he had high hopes in the previous year, were about to become the subject of a series of deliberate political maneuvers that would close them down completely for the next eighteen months.

Following the instructions that Lord Holdernesse had given him in March 1752, in his conference journal Mildmay said that he submitted this memorial on Acadia to the French commissioners not in its customary French translation, but in English, and it was at this point that a price was exacted for the British government's May 1752 refusal to alter the twelve contested words in the French translation of the St. Lucia memorial that was presented in November 1751. In his entry for 23 January 1753 Mildmay reported that when he and De Cosne handed over the memorial they explained that it was in English "lest any mistakes might happen in the translation of it into French."[63] The initial reaction from Galissonière and Silhouette was surprise: apparently they had not expected a document in English, and Mildmay said they declared that as they were worried about the accuracy of the French translation they were now being asked to make, they felt that he and De Cosne should inspect their efforts "from time to time."

At first sight this request would seem to be eminently reasonable, but Mildmay, who, doubtless, remembered the earlier threat by the French commissioners to respond with equal harshness to the offensive words they had found in the November 1751 St. Lucia memorial, told Holdernesse that he and De Cosne refused to give any definite answer: "not thinking it incumbent upon Us to give a Sanction to their expressions in their language any farther than to guard against their altering the sense of ours." He reported that the only reaction of Galissonière and Silhouette to this refusal was to state that if the British side was now going to deliver its memorials in English, then, in fairness, Mildmay and De Cosne should supply the original English version of the St. Lucia memorial (an offer which had, in fact, been made by Mildmay when the French commissioners protested the French wording in March of 1752, but which Galissonière and Silhouette had declined to accept at that time).

Mildmay said he and De Cosne promised to write to Whitehall for the original, as they no longer had a copy of the English version, and this phase of the conference had ended with his insistence to Galissonière and Silhouette that with the many "incontestable proofs" supplied with this present Acadia memorial: "there was no room for further conferences upon these [boundary] Limits in Question." The French commissioners answered that until they had translated this British document they would not be making any further response and, given its obvious length, they did not feel that this could be accomplished in less than six months. Such a cautious timetable would seem to be reasonable, since the report on this British memorial on Acadia that Galissonière and Silhouette sent to St. Contest, on 4 February 1753, stated that the British memorial consisted of 219 pages, and thus would obviously take some considerable time to translate: "with precise accuracy and fidelity" to the English original.[64] The only other issue raised at this meeting of 23 January was an inquiry from Galissonière and Silhouette on whether the British would now accept their list of prizes and, to this, Mildmay said he restated the position that his government completely refused to accept any prizes other than those taken after the peace treaty had been signed. He said the conference closed with Galissonière's observation that the six months that it would take to translate the British memorial on Acadia would give the French government ample time to prepare their reply to the British claim to St. Lucia.

The outcome of this conference was to be so far-reaching and crucial to the commission's work that Mildmay's journal report of this meeting of 23 January 1753 is worth studying in some detail, for on this evidence it seems as though both sides had suddenly reversed the previous behavior and positions that they had steadily maintained over two and a half years. On Mildmay's part, his manner seemed deliberately confrontational and a complete departure from the temperate, conciliatory style of negotiation that he had previously advocated on the Acadia boundary limits, and which he was still proposing for the resolution of the prize issues. The initial reaction of the French commissioners also appeared to be a sudden change of position; their response suggested that, tacitly, they accepted the British right to supply their documents in English and their only concern was the accuracy of their own French translation. Unlike the caustic retort that they had made in March of 1752, here they only observed that in order to establish some consistency Mildmay should now give them the English version of the British St. Lucia memorial. They also said they anticipated being able to present the French answer to both British memorials: albeit in six months time.

This statement from Galissonière that it would now take a further six months to produce the expected French statement of their claim to St. Lucia may, perhaps, explain Mildmay's uncharacteristic behavior; however, as from the evidence of a letter that he wrote to Lord Fitzwalter on the following day (24 January) it seems he felt a genuine disappointment and frustration at these endless delays. In this letter Mildmay told him that although he was: "in full business with the French commissioners," yet he was: "heartily sick of their chicanery, but it is to be hoped that His Majesty will put an end to all wrangling and disputes by a happier method of accommodation, or more persuasive arguments than what are delivered in written memorials."[65]

Although Mildmay's reaction to Fitzwalter may be understandable, the curious aspects of these events appeared to continue. Also on 24 January Mildmay carried out his promise to the French commissioners by writing to Lord Holdernesse with a request that the English original of the 1751 memorial on St. Lucia be sent to Paris. In his letter he gave Holdernesse a short summary of the conference and, in a footnote, Mildmay told him that he had also sent a letter to the members of the Board of Trade that informed them he had delivered their latest memorial, but: "pursuant to Your Lordships' instruction, in English, without accompanying it with any French translation."[66] Three weeks later, on 14 February, Mildmay and De Cosne thanked Lord Holdernesse for the arrival of the original version of the St. Lucia document, which they assured him they would copy and transmit to the French commissioners as soon as possible; however, they went on to say that they were "extremely unhappy" to have received a rebuke from Holdernesse that they had sent a letter to the Board of Trade. As they pointed out to him: "We beg leave to observe, in justification of the Irregularity imputed to us of having corresponded with the Lords of Trade, that we are directed so to do by the last article but one of His Majesty's instructions to us, dated at Herrenhausen (the king's palace at Hanover) 3rd July/10th August 1750."[67]

It is inconceivable that Holdernesse was not aware of these instructions, as they were the standard directions given to all British commissions abroad. Not only had Mildmay and Shirley been instructed to keep both Lord Albemarle and the Board informed of anything in the negotiations that was of their direct concern, the British commissioners had been doing so assiduously over the past two years. There are three different constructions that can, therefore, be put on Holdernesse's apparent discomfort that the Board had been informed: either Holdernesse so distrusted the president of the

Board, Lord Halifax, that he intended to keep him ignorant of events in Paris; Holdernesse had forgotten the details of the language instructions that he had given to Mildmay ten months earlier; or before this document had been sent to Paris Holdernesse had not taken the precaution of asking both the duke of Newcastle and the king whether Mildmay and De Cosne were to give the French commissioners the customary French translation of this memorial.

Any one of these three reasons is possible. There was, indeed, bad blood between Lord Holdernesse and Lord Halifax; for some time Halifax had been attempting to get the administration of the North American colonies away from the legislative authority of the Southern Department and under the control and patronage of the Board, and Shirley's dismissal from the commission in April 1752 had been one of the consequences of Halifax's political intrigue. It is also possible that the mistake could have been caused by some confusion, or lack of communication, between Lord Holdernesse and the commissioners. Confusion on such a major issue is difficult to understand, however. Although these language instructions had been given to Mildmay ten months earlier, they had been very specific and Mildmay was a precise man who kept careful records. By contrast, Holdernesse was certainly known as a somewhat relaxed Cabinet minister, who had an active social life, but in Claudius Amyand he had an experienced chief clerk who usually kept him out of trouble in his ministerial responsibilities. The most likely explanation is the third: a lack of prior approval, and if one remembers the caution with which Lord Albemarle sought the duke of Newcastle's confirmation of Holdernesse's instructions in the summer of 1752, there is some evidence that Holdernesse occasionally took too much on himself and did not consult with his superiors before he acted.

Whether the language used in this memorial, and its lack of any accompanying translation, was a genuine oversight or a deliberate act, the result on the negotiations was calamitous. A month after the French commissioners had received the British memorial on Acadia, the language problem took on a life of its own: one in which each government took up fixed positions that could not be altered without a complete loss of face on both sides. The first move came from the British government. In the hope that this would solve the problem, the British Cabinet attempted to withdraw the contested French translation of the 1751 St. Lucia memorial as an official commission document, since this solution would still allow it to preserve its position on the language to be used in future British memorials. Accordingly, Lord Holdernesse instructed Mildmay to ask that the French translation be returned to them, and that the original English version be substituted in its place as the only official British government memorial. In his journal Mildmay reported that he held a conference at Galissonière's apartment on 26 February to deliver the English original of the memorial on St. Lucia, as the French commissioners had requested, but said he: "offered it only upon the condition that they would accept it as the Original, and consent to return the French translation of it which we had some time before given them, of which they found fault with several expressions." He continued: "we hoped there would be no such exception when they examined the meaning in the English Tongue, which as it was our natural Language, We must naturally be supposed best to understand, and consequently it was the only one we could abide by."[68]

Four weeks had now passed since the English memorial on Acadia had first been presented, however, and it seems that the French Court had now decided that it did not intend to let the British government off the diplomatic hook this easily. In his 28 February report on this conference to Lord Holdernesse, Mildmay told him that although the French commissioners had asked for this English version of the Acadia memorial, he was astonished when Galissonière refused to accept it, saying, at the same time, that he and Silhouette would soon be returning the British memorial on Acadia, which they had been criticized by their minister for receiving in English. Mildmay told Holdernesse his response was to remind Galissonière that he and Silhouette had been in possession of this memorial on Acadia for over month and as it was on the specific instructions of his government that it was written in English, he and De Cosne could not take it back again without further government orders to do so.[69]

The French government had spent the intervening time in preparing the ammunition for its argument. The French commissioners now presented a statement of precedents that had been put together two weeks earlier, on 10 February, and as evidence of the long standing custom of using French as the language of diplomacy it cited documents written in French by Charles II to Louis XIV in 1660 and 1664, together with a more recent example of a letter reportedly written in French from Whitehall to the Prussian minister.[70] In his report on this 28 February conference Mildmay told Holdernesse that Galissonière had now asked them to write to Whitehall as quickly as possible, and to point out: "it was unprecedented that in a negotiation with this [French] Court, Papers be offered in English whilst we [the British] acted differently with other Courts." Galissonière also said he felt it was unfortunate that the British Court had, apparently, decided to abandon what, till then, had been "constant Usage," referring Mildmay and De Cosne to the paper given to the Prussian minister that, he was assured, had been written in French.

In an effort to defuse what had suddenly become a serious problem, in a footnote to this letter Mildmay told Holdernesse he had asked that if a French translation was delivered at the same time as this latest English memorial on Acadia, could Galissonière and Silhouette accept that: "we had not then the Right to abide by the Original in our own tongue?" He reported their only response was: "We might abide by what we liked, but they should only regard what was delivered in their Language." This unsatisfactory conference ended with Galissonière's statement that although they now had their list of prizes ready to deliver, they had been informed that the duke of Mirepoix had been instructed to renew with the British government the French demands that pre-war prizes should be included, and they therefore would not put the list forward until they had received Mirepoix's answer on this issue.[71]

By the middle of March 1753 both sides had hardened their official positions completely. In his journal Mildmay reported that on 17 March Galissonière requested a conference at which he told them that the French government had decided to return the British memorial on Acadia. Mildmay said he replied that he and de Cosne considered the interval of two months, during which this document had been held by the French government, had been ample time in which to have it translated. He also said he told Galissonière that they could not accept his government's position that it had had the right to receive memorials only in French, and pointed out that although it had previously been the custom for the British government to present their documents in a French translation, this step had been taken "for the sake of mutual convenience," not as any acknowledgment of a right. Mildmay said he then remarked that the British government, having considered the matter, had now concluded that it had an equal claim to such "convenience." He emphasized that this equality was claimed on the grounds that the British commissioners had been sent "to treat with them [the French government] in their own capital," and had also agreed to conduct the meetings in French, even though M. Silhouette spoke perfect English and had translated several English books. He asked what was the function of the many expert translators employed by the French Court, if all diplomatic documents were required to be presented in French, and ended by declaring that it was the manner in which their French translation had been treated in 1751 that had caused the British government to decide to use English from now on.[72]

The other side of the negotiating team was feeling equally badly used. In his report to St. Contest, written in the absence of Silhouette on other government business, Galissonière was scathing on his suspicions about this language debate. He told St. Contest that, in his view there had been attempts, for some time, to break off the conferences, since the British commissioners had interrupted the work with all kinds of difficulties, and he felt that this presentation of their memorial in English, knowing that it could not be acceptable to France, was nothing but the latest excuse.[73]

It appears that in person he was less hostile, or perhaps more diplomatic. In Mildmay's 28 March report to Lord Holdernesse he added the information that when the official conference business had concluded Galissonière had mentioned to him that in order to examine the argument that had been used by his government about the use of French in diplomacy, he had read the cited Prussian document. Having examined this answer given by the British government to the Prussian Court on the ransom of Prussian prisoners after the recent war, Mildmay said Galissonière: "acknowledged it to be a very solid and complete answer . . . but pretended [claimed] that the complaints of his Court on the subject of Prizes were in some measure different." Nevertheless, and despite this more positive response, Mildmay said Galissonière had still repeated that he would receive no orders from his Ministry about their list of pre-war prizes until the negotiations now taking place between Lord Holdernesse and the Marquis of Mirepoix had ended.[74]

In these discussion on the prize ships there was, however, no agreement on the chief issues, even though Mirepoix was acting with full authority from St. Contest. On 15 February 1753 Holdernesse confirmed to Lord Albemarle that the French ministers were still instructing Mirepoix to insist that any claims that involved compensation would be decided by the commissioners, rather than by the British Admiralty courts: even including those cases whose verdict had already been decided. On this proposal Holdernesse commented: "This would never be submitted to. It is indeed absurd to think of it . . . [as] it would be establishing a new Court of appeal which His Majesty cannot legally grant."[75]

The hopeful diplomatic climate in the early summer of 1752 had now deteriorated to the point where if it were to be restored, it was imperative that both Lord Albemarle and Lord Holdernesse should have a French government negotiator whom they believed had the full support of his Court. Neither of them trusted the intentions of St. Contest and Rouillé, and, in retrospect, it appears that a major cause of the eventual failure of the commission negotiations was the lack of confidence shown by the French Court in the duke of Mirepoix: a man whom Holdernesse felt had a genuine desire to achieve a peaceful settlement of the various national disputes.

On 4 January 1753 Holdernesse sent two letters to Lord Albemarle: one of them private and the other official. In his official letter Holdernesse informed Albemarle that George II was becoming more than a little impatient to see Mirepoix's words translated into some effective action by his Court, as the ambassador's assurance of the stated desire of Louis XV to adjust: "in an amicable manner the several points in dispute between the two Crowns" did not seem to indicate any immediate urgency in Paris. Holdernesse pointed out that fifteen months had passed since France had first asked to allow the disputes on the prize ships to be determined by himself and Mirepoix "de Cour en Cour," and very little had, in fact, happened. He observed that the same conduct had taken place over the neutral islands in the West Indies; promises had been made about evacuating these islands, but had not been kept and, indeed: "it might not, perhaps, be unnatural to conclude that the French Ministry aim at gaining time, concluding nothing, and in the mean while going on in their own way, without much regard for their engagements [promises]." In this light Holdernesse said that St. Contest seemed very anxious that the joint commission should remain in session in Paris while he and Mirepoix negotiated in London, but said he could not see what useful purpose this would serve: "[for] if every point is to be referred to commissaries . . . things will remain for ever in the present litigated situation . . . and I suspect this as the reason of their desire of keeping the commissaries assembled. . . ."[76]

His private letter told Albemarle he was saddened by his inability to work effectively with Mirepoix, whom he respected, but under these circumstances Holdernesse now advised Albemarle to stand firm with St. Contest and: "Shew (sic) him that . . . tho' we mean to be civil . . . don't let him think to cajole us, or that we will let things remain much longer as they are." He noted that on the instructions of George II he had held a discussion with

Mirepoix to complain about French intransigence over the prize ships, but although he said he felt his words made an impression on the ambassador: "it will signify little, for I believe he is not even trusted [by St. Contest] much less consulted." Quite apart from the difficulties this caused, Holdernesse admitted: "I am sorry for it, for he is really a man of honour, and above the *chicanery* (*sic*) with which a friend of yours [St. Contest], whom you now have to deal with, entertains you."[77]

In early April Mirepoix received instructions from Louis XV to return to Paris, where he was to remain for the following six months, and on 9 April 1752 Holdernesse wrote to Albemarle that at a time when the commercial and territorial disputes with France were in such a delicate state he very much regretted the ambassador's absence. Holdernesse encouraged Albemarle to do what he could to restore the confidence of the French Court in Mirepoix, for: "we are parted prodigious good friends, and I beg your Excellency would omit no opportunity of testifying of the King's regard for him. You'll find him in excellent principles for adjusting our national quarrels, for the settling of which there must be some mutual concessions."[78]

Although Lord Holdernesse appeared to believe that such compromises were still possible, the directions that Mildmay and De Cosne received from the king at the beginning of April did not allow them much flexibility in their negotiations. On 5 April Lord Holdernesse told them that by order of George II they were instructed to refuse the demand to provide documents in French, indeed if the French continued to insist on this point the king had said that, as under accepted diplomatic protocol: "all nations whatever have the right to treat with each other in a neutral language," perhaps both sides should now present their memorials in the "neutral" language of Latin. Although Latin had been the official language in which all previous treaties prior to that of Aix-la-Chapelle were issued, considerable problems would be caused by the need to translate all the preliminary negotiation documents into Latin and Holdernesse did not seriously advance this as a solution. He pointed out, however, that the custom adopted by the English side of supplying a French translation with all British memorials was given as an act of: "complaisance to the French Court." As this practice seemed to have been poorly received by the French government and they had: "found fault with many expressions in the translation" of the British memorial on St. Lucia, he said the British government had now decided that: "all written papers [by the British side] be [only] in the English language, the force of which being better understood by yourselves, you might not be liable to make use of terms and expressions that might carry a [translated] meaning you do not intend to convey."[79]

Lord Holdernesse concluded his remarks by saying that George II felt this gesture of supplying a French translation, taken: "out of delicacy to the Court of France," had now been abused by turning the language used in memorials into a matter in which: "the French Commissaries, having demanded this as a point of right, were the King to comply with this demand it would be establishing a precedent which the King cannot and will not consent to." Holdernesse told Mildmay and De Cosne to demand a conference with their French counterparts and inform them of the contents of his letter while, at the same time, asking whether the French commissioners were now ready to deliver their list of prizes on the basis of Article IV of the Treaty of Aix-la-Chapelle (or the limitation of all prizes to those taken after the war had ended).

Although diplomatic protocol entitled George II, or rather his ministers, to ask that Latin be adopted as the language for all future memorials, there was a certain malicious satisfaction to be found in this demand, or that is how Lord Albemarle saw it. In a letter to Lord Holdernesse, written on 8 April, Albemarle told him: "I am delighted with the orders you have sent to the commissioners here. If the French do not wish to use the Latin language, into which position they have boxed themselves under the pretext that the language must be *universal* [neutral], they must now be forced [either] to express themselves in good English or else be in great error [make serious mistakes].[80] However amusing this self-inflicted dilemma may have seemed to the British diplomats at the time, however, with a hindsight knowledge of the eventual consequences of this language dispute, it is possible that in April 1753 the ultimate "great error" might have been made by both governments.

If Lord Holdernesse still had any hopes that "mutual concessions" might solve the present disputes over language, these ended at the conference held in Mildmay's apartment on 15 April 1753. In accordance with the firm instructions that Mildmay had received, in his journal report he said that at this meeting he told the French commissioners he had been told by the king to refuse to accept the return of the British memorial on Acadia, since the king believed: "every Nation has a Right to present their Memorials either in their own, or in a neutral Language."[81] Mildmay repeated the reason why the British government had decided to revert to submitting their memorials in English, and stated that the king felt that to agree with the French demand would be establishing a precedent that he could not, and would not consent to. On the French objection that as the British government used French in their diplomacy with other nations they (the French government) felt they had a right to be addressed in their own language, Mildmay said he replied: "with regard to other Nations, French was a neutral tongue, which all Nations might treat in . . . and in that Light it must be understood we treated with the [German] princes of the Empire [in French]." So far as negotiations between France and Britain were concerned, however, the only neutral language was Latin, and in conclusion he said he told Galissonière and Silhouette that, on the orders of George II, unless the French government was prepared to accept any further memorials in English, he was instructed: "to consent to accommodate this dispute by both sides treating in Latin."

From the evidence in Mildmay's journal it appears that even at this late stage, and despite the intransigence of the two governments, the joint commissioners might have been able to be achieve an amicable arrangement if they had been allowed to do so. After some discussion on who had, in fact, been responsible for the present impasse, at this 15 April conference Galissonière proposed that: "we might enter into a kind of Preliminary Agreement that the giving and accepting of any written Papers in the French Language should not be drawn into a Precedent for the future." Further evidence that there was still a genuine desire on the part of the French commissioners to prevent a diplomatic rupture appears to come in Mildmay's concluding remarks on this issue. Having noted that Galissonière and Silhouette had brought the Acadia memorial with them, he said: "they only asked us, in gentle tone, whether we would accept it, without insisting on returning it, nor did they seem to contest the Solidity of the principle that all Nations had the right to treat with each other in a Neutral Tongue. So the British Memorial remained in their hands."

The territorial issues may have reached a stalemate but the matter of the prizes was still under active discussion in London, and in his concluding paragraph Mildmay stated that when he again asked the French commissioners if they had now adjusted their list of prizes, he reported they replied that they still waited for further instructions from their government. When the conference had ended, however, Galissonière told Mildmay that in the answer that the British government had given to the king of Prussia there were: "some Principles laid down in that Answer which they believed their Court would not admit to," but he said that, in this, he was only expressing a personal opinion. Mildmay also stated that Galissonière did not mention any observation that his government intended to make on this point, and nor did he discuss any memorial that might be in preparation at the moment. In a note that Mildmay wrote at the bottom of the report, and which he added later, he said that a few days after this conference was held, St. Contest had delivered a memorial to Lord Albemarle that listed all the French claims to be compensated for prizes: "taken from Them by Us at Sea *before the War* (*sic*)." By the time that he wrote this Mildmay obviously saw Galissonière's silence on the subject of this memorial as yet another piece of French "chi-canery," as from the evidence of a letter written by Lord Albemarle to Lord Holdernesse on 9 May, in which he refers to: "M. Silhouette's Last Memorial," it appears that its actual author was, in fact, Galissonière's fellow commis-sioner, Silhouette.[82]

Whatever Mildmay may have thought of the merits of a "preliminary agreement" when Galissonière had suggested it in mid-April, two weeks later he had received his instructions to reject this proposal as well. In a let-ter to Lord Holdernesse on 2 May, Mildmay assured him: "we shall adhere to our former Instructions and refuse entering into any kind of Preliminary Agreement concerning the giving, or accepting any Papers in the French language, nor that we take any further steps on the Article of Prizes." He also told Holdernesse that as Lord Albemarle had shown them the memori-al he had received from St. Contest on the French pre-war prize claim, the enclosed document contained observations on this claim that he and De Cosne considered were pertinent to their commission."[83]

Even if both the territorial and prize negotiations now appeared at an impasse, Mildmay still seemed hopeful for a successful conclusion to the question of the ransoms. On 24 February 1753 he had reported to Fitzwalter that on this subject he was trying: "to disentangle myself [from Paris] as fast as possible. I have a long account to lay before my Masters relating to the ransom of prisoners, but I hope that they will think it right in not doing it till the whole is finished, that there may be but one trouble in giving me their orders therein."[84] Apparently Lord Fitzwalter was unaware of Mildmay's current negotiation problems, however, as throughout the spring he contin-ued to press Mildmay to ask for permission to return to England.

Even if he was allowed to return for consultations with Lord Holdernesse, the negotiations were at a very critical stage and as a careful lawyer Mildmay always made sure that he was as prepared as possible. In their last conversation Galissonière had referred to a British statement on prizes that was given in letters to the Prussian minister, and since he was unaware of the details, on 24 February he told Lord Fitzwalter he had been informed by Lord Albemarle that these letters had now been published, and said: "I should be much obliged to your Lordship if you would be pleased to order your Porter to buy half a dozen for me and send them by the first favourable opportunity."[85] On 5 March 1753 Fitzwalter's private secretary, John Liddell, wrote to Mildmay with a message from Fitzwalter that a packet containing the second installment of the duke of Newcastle's letters to the king of Prussia were now on their way to him, via Lord Albemarle's address in Paris. It also appears that Fitzwalter's need to see Mildmay had, by now become acute, as Liddell closed his letter by reporting that even though Fitzwalter's health had not deteriorated: "My Lord bids me tell you that . . . [he] would be extremely glad to see you in England again,"[86] and at the bottom of this letter Fitzwalter emphasized this hope with a note in his own hand that said: "I wish I could have a prospect when that would happen."

Such a prospect did not seem bright, however, for complications in the dispute over the prisoner ransoms were now growing. On 14 March 1753 Mildmay repeated to Lord Holdernesse his previous information on the ransoms and the prize ships, and added that in their claims for subsequent damages on these two issues the French commissioners were still maintaining two quite contradictory positions; they cited the strict terms of Cartel of Frankfort for the first, but were refusing to accept the same terms under the Treaty of Aix-la-Chapelle for the second.[87] In marked contrast to his earlier behavior over the Acadia memorial, Mildmay seemed eager to obtain a mutually agreeable settlement of the ransoms and prizes, and in the same spirit as his previous attempt to solve the vexed problem of the marine prisoners by equating their costs against the time and boundary limitations placed on the prizes, he explored with Holdernesse the possibility of striking a balance between these two damage claims.

He asked whether, in return for an agreement by the British government to conform to the terms of the Cartel of Frankfurt, and to give up its right to a further subsistence amount for each prisoner, he could then insist that France must observe the same principles established in the Treaty of Aix-la-Chapelle, and give up its right to any: "subsequent damages [claimed] for these Prizes at Sea." He told Holdernesse that as in his calculations, he had already determined that the sum of these two claims for subsequent damages (the prize ships and the prisoners) came to almost equal amounts, the settle-ment could easily be adjusted. He said he hoped that if this joint concession could be negotiated successfully: "my proceedings in the one commission [the ransoms] might facilitate the conclusion of the other [the prizes]."[88]

Despite his best attempts nearly two months passed without any such agreement, but Mildmay persevered. On 2 May he assured Fitzwalter that he was working to speed up negotiations on the ransoms and the prize ships so that he could come to England, and he noted the care with which he had doc-umented all of the conferences when he told Fitzwalter that he had: "kept a careful journal of all proceedings under my commission in order to lay it before his Lordship [Lord Holdernesse] upon my return."[89] Mildmay con-tinued working on his mandate and on 20 June 1753 he sent Lord Holdernesse his itemized list of all the ransoms, hospital expenses, subsis-tence allowances, and transportation costs he calculated that the British gov-ernment had incurred in the care of French prisoners taken since 1744. This expense total came to £55,097–0s-11d, for which Mildmay stated that Lord Albemarle had informed him the French were delaying payment on the grounds that after all the accounts were tallied there might still be a balance due to the French Court. He said that such a balance would, in fact, be in the British favor and, unless he heard from Holdernesse to the contrary, he would now give this expense account to the French commissioners.[90]

In June the campaign to have Mildmay return to Essex became even more intense. On 11 June 1753 Lord Ancram wrote a letter to Mildmay, on behalf of his father-in-law, Fitzwalter, in which Ancram said he agreed with Mildmay's tactical: "schemes and veins" to receive permission to return for the summer: "and [I] heartily wish you was (*sic*) here." However, he remind-ed Mildmay: "the season is more far advanced and your Principal [Lord Holdernesse] going away into the Country [for the summer], as all the rest of the world is." Under these circumstances Ancram said he was "amazed" that Mildmay had not already sent such a request to Holdernesse: "alleging much specious and plausible reasons as your own judgement will furnish you with." Ancram was aware that Mildmay expected to inherit Lord Fitzwalter's estates, and in a plain and frank observation on Mildmay's seem-ing inattention to Fitzwalter's needs, he asked: "How could you neglect your own interests so much?"[91]

Within two weeks of receiving Ancram's letter Mildmay noted in his journal that he had now found his successful excuse to return to England in

THE MISSED OPPORTUNITY 171

the departure of both French commissioners to their family estates "for this Vacation."[92] He wrote a private letter of request to Lord Holdernesse on 20 June and on 28 June he finally received his Lordship's official permission to leave.[93] In a letter to Lord Fitzwalter, written on 4 July, he said that he presumed that his absence from Paris would only be for the summer vacation, but that he intended to use this opportunity to discuss with Fitzwalter: "several observations . . . towards accommodations of affairs relative to my Commission in a manner more suitable to His Majesty's Service." In some triumph he announced that he had visited Versailles yesterday to make his official farewells to the French ministers and would be on the road to Calais tomorrow, and in London a week later. Once there, he promised that having made his official visits of ceremony to the various ministries, he would then travel to Moulsham Hall to spend the summer with Fitzwalter.[94]

Although Mildmay might still have some confidence that when he returned to Paris he could succeed in his limited objectives, Lord Holdernesse's bright hopes in the summer of 1752 that the treaty of Aix-la-Chapelle could be successfully ratified had turned, one year later, into an irritable distrust of French government intentions and behavior. On 3 May 1753 he had written a private letter to Lord Albemarle in which he deplored St. Contest's latest memorial on pre-war prizes (written by Silhouette and given to Albemarle in April, and told him: "we are not for a paper war, but a short, firm answer will be necessary to that curious piece and I hope H.M. [His Majesty] will consent that such a one will be prepared."[95] Albemarle was as incensed as Mildmay over the deception that had been practiced in this memorial, both by the French commissioner and by the French foreign minister, and in his reply, on 9 May, he referred to St. Contest as: "a shuffler, and no truth can be expected from him." In Albemarle's opinion, the only honest Frenchman was the duke of Mirepoix, with whom: "we should soon settle our differences, despite the emotions, systems and arguments of M. Silhouette's last Memorial."[96]

By September Holdernesse was further angered by what he saw as the dissembling of both St. Contest and Rouillé in their reports that the French settlers had now evacuated the island of St. Dominique. Armed with some contrary intelligence that had been supplied to the Admiralty by two British sea captains, in his 19 September private letter to Albemarle Holdernesse told him: "St. Contest and Rouillé are the most notorious deceivers I have ever met with . . . if it is proved they have amused themselves with false affirmations, I'll publicly expose them for the greatest Lyers (*sic*) this day existing in the Univers (*sic*)."[97] On 26 September Albemarle's reply to this emotional outburst was to give Holdernesse his frank and unflattering opinion of those members of the royal family who ought to be providing the leadership in France, but were only: "poor servile courtiers and without any spirit"; interested in nothing but hunting, overeating, womanizing, or religious bigotry. He described what he saw as the inferior behavior and characters of the king's brothers and nephews: the Dukes of Orléans and Penthièvre, the Princes of Condé and Conti, and the Counts of Charolais, Clairmont, and Manli, and concluded: "There is no successor to the Grand Condé to be found amongst Princes of the Blood. . . . The above characters are the safety of the French State!"[98]

Although Mildmay was in England for the summer, he and Ruvigny De Cosne kept in touch with each other when an issue relating to their commission arose: indeed they seemed to have taken their responsibilities far more seriously than did their political masters. On 29 August De Cosne had sent Mildmay a map of Acadia, drawn by a Robert de Vaugondy, which claimed to have been produced by the royal printing house and with the permission of the comte d'Argenson.[99] De Cosne pointed out that this map contained all of the boundaries that had been claimed by France in the memorial on Acadia they had presented on 16 November 1750, and told Mildmay that, in his opinion: "this is a strange proceeding, to offer to determine by an apparent authority, before the question is decided, the Limits of a Country that are actually in dispute." He said that he considered this printed map to be: "an imposition on the Public Faith, in a great irregularity to say no more of it, with respect to the Commission now subsisting between the two Courts, [one] that can tend to no good purpose," and asked Mildmay to bring it to the attention of Lord Holdernesse.

Mildmay wrote his reply from Fitzwalter's London residence of Schomberg House, in Pall Mall, and in this letter, written on 6 September, he said that he considered the matter of the printed map to be so scandalous that he had returned from Essex especially to meet with Lord Holdernesse.[100] He reported to his colleague that Holdernesse had: "been pleased to observe that since the French Court thought fit to treat the negotiations in so slight a manner . . . It was high time for us to insist that the Affair between us should be brought to an Accommodation at once . . . or else to attend to [result in] some more serious consequences." As the other Cabinet members were still at their country estates, however, Lord Holdernesse said that any official response would have to wait, but Mildmay reported he was expecting instructions from the duke of Newcastle, now in Hanover, on the continuing negotiations over the prizes and ransoms and, as these instructions would not arrive for at least two weeks, he therefore told De Cosne to expect him in Paris in about three weeks' time.

When Mildmay returned to Paris at the beginning of November he found that far from receiving the urgent attention that Lord Holdernesse had demanded of the Ministry in September, the French commissioners had not even arrived back in the city to begin negotiations.[101] Frustrated in his ability to continue any official work, he spent the balance of 1753 writing weekly letters to Fitzwalter that gave detailed accounts of the politics at the French Court, and the ongoing battle that the king was having with his rebellious *Parlement* of Paris.[102] Such apparent disinterest in the negotiations was in sharp contrast to the sense of urgency so evident a year earlier, but in this Mildmay was only reflecting the curious indifference now being shown by both governments. After three and a half years of unproductive work on these intractable problems, a universal, weary inertia seemed to have replaced any real hope for a solution.

# 7.

# THE LAST CHANCE LOST, AND WINDING DOWN: 1754–1755

BOTH THE BRITISH AND THE FRENCH governments were later to regret the time they had wasted on the negotiation process in 1753, for in 1754 the colonists in British North America, the French administrators in Canada, and the directors of the British and French East India companies all took the initiative in attempting to solve the territorial disputes in their own way. By the end of 1754 any theoretical control that the governments of Britain and France held over the military strategy in their colonies had, in reality, become limited to decisions on how many troops and warships to send to each place and when and how to send them. The people on the ground were now driving the foreign policies of their remote colonial masters toward what they conceived to be their own best strategic and commercial interests. It took some time for this reality to become appreciated in Whitehall and Versailles, and it was not until the autumn of 1754 that both sides began a new round of negotiations with a fair degree of panic. Belatedly, at the beginning of September the British and French government ministers realized that they were at the point of being driven into a war in North America for which neither country had any real enthusiasm, and that neither would be properly equipped to fight.

During the first eight months, however, the British government did not seem to regard the worsening military situation in North America as an urgent priority. This apparent lack of concern is reflected in the subject matter of the correspondence that Lord Holdernesse (now promoted to be the northern secretary) and the new southern secretary, Sir Thomas Robinson, exchanged with the various British ambassadors in continental Europe.

Throughout the spring and early summer of 1754 the topics in this body of diplomatic documents are focused on defending British interests at the courts of Spain, the Hapsburg Empire, Russia, and Saxony; on alarms about the skirmishes that were now taking place on the coast of India between the French and British East India companies; and, most particularly, on apprehensions about the aggressive activities of the king of Prussia. There are many letters to and from the British ambassadors in Madrid, Vienna, St. Petersburg, and Berlin that contain worried discussions about the true political and military intentions of Maria Theresa of Austria and Frederick of Prussia, together with letters on the growing disquiet of the British government about the belligerent encroachments of the French East India Company.[1]

In the opinion of Lord Holdernesse, the chance of an accidental war with France might well come from agitation in Whitehall at the news that a fleet of armed ships had been sent to the east coast of India by the French East India Company to counter a similar fleet the British government had recently dispatched to defend the trading factories of their East India Company. On 2 February 1754 Holdernesse told Lord Albemarle that even so: "I cannot persuade myself that they [the French government] wish a war at present and yet the measures they pursue in different parts of the world will force *us* and *themselves* (*sic*) into one before either of us think of it."[2]

The content of Mildmay's letters to Lord Fitzwalter echoes Lord Holdernesse's view of the danger of the crisis now growing in India, and from his letters it seems that during the first half of 1754 British diplomats in Paris also did not see any great importance in the continual territorial clashes taking place in North America. In the twelve letters that Mildmay wrote to Lord Fitzwalter from January to August 1754, seven of them were solely concerned with his views on the considerable commercial benefit of obtaining a settlement of the disputes between the two British and French trading companies in India, while four were detailed descriptions of the French king's constitutional disputes with the *Parlement* of Paris. In only one letter, written on 16 January 1754, did he mention the potentially dangerous results of the boundary disputes in North America and, even then, simply as a part of a remark about the chances of a war in general. He told Fitzwalter that if such a war came it would be caused by the urgent need of the French government to divert the attention of its population from the serious political defiance now being asserted by the magistrates of the Paris *Parlement*, for:

"It is common knowledge here that France must rather have a War abroad, or at home, so restless a disposition are the people of this country."[3]

In his preoccupation with a possible threat to British trade in India, Mildmay was reflecting British merchant opinion on the relative geographical importance of the areas of British colonial trade in the early 1750s. If there was any feeling in London in the spring of 1754 that vital British commercial interests were at stake, these concerns centered primarily on the continuing British ability to be able to expand the lucrative trade with India and the Far East, and on the considerable financial importance of retaining ownership of certain West Indian sugar islands. In comparison to New England the population of Nova Scotia and Acadia was very small, gathered around a few harbors, and, except for the settlers in the new military town of Halifax, the main occupations were fishing and subsistence farming. Other than as a source of excellent timber for shipbuilding, British traders had very little interest in the export potential of these territories in the mid-1750s.

As the British West Indian merchants saw it, the strategic problem posed by the French ownership of Acadia, and particularly of Cape Breton, lay in the threat that the fortress of Louisbourg represented to their ships coming up from the West Indies. The direction of the wind and sea current in the Caribbean and the North Atlantic had always dictated that the best route from the West Indies was to sail with the prevailing westerlies to the Grand Banks and then turn east for the run across the Atlantic to Europe. For the French government, the importance of Louisbourg was to be able act as a defense against any British blockade of the Gulf of St. Lawrence for vessels bound for Quebec, to give protection to their West Indian convoys and the French fishing fleets on the Grand Banks, to harass both the British fleets coming from the West Indies and the fishing boats from the ports of Massachusetts, and to maintain a secure harbor for a large and very profitable trade in salt cod to Europe and the French West Indies.[4]

To the colonists of New England, and particularly to the fishermen and merchants of Boston, the question of who commanded access to the coastline and hinterland of Acadia and Nova Scotia was of supreme commercial and strategic importance and very much worth fighting for. The West Indian trading interests in the City of London had a great influence on government policy in the early 1750s. If the British government had to make a hard economic choice between a secure settlement of the disputed islands of St. Vincent and Tobago and a agreement to cede to France the coastline from

178 THE FORGOTTEN COMMISSIONER

the Isthmus of Nova Scotia to the entrance to the Gulf of the St. Lawrence, and to guarantee a land access to Cape Breton for the French settlers in Acadia, both government and merchant opinion would have favored the former option.

The evidence in a letter from the duke of Newcastle to Lord Hardwicke, written in 1751, demonstrates that such an exchange of territory was, in fact, the basis of the mutual concessions that were discussed by the British Cabinet in September of that year. In his letter of 6 September 1751 Newcastle had told Hardwicke of Mildmay's information that France might agree to give up her claim to Tobago, St. Vincent, and land around the Bay of Fundy and the Northumberland Strait in exchange for St. Lucia and the northern coast of Nova Scotia toward the St. Laurence. He then observed: "this would be sufficient for us . . . I beg you to turn your thoughts how far this expedient may be practical and advisable. I think we should go to any reasonable lengths . . . to get rid of these constant pretences for quarrel."[5]

In the colonies of New England, however, such a land accommodation would never have been thought "sufficient" or "practical," let alone "advisable." Possession of the hinterland around the Bay of Fundy and the coastline of the Northumberland Strait would do nothing to solve the problems caused by the Atlantic fortress of Louisbourg. Moreover, by agreeing that France would retain possession of the southern half of Nova Scotia the French fleet would also have effective control of the seas around the entire south and west coast, from Cape St. Mary to the tip of Cape Breton. The fishermen of Boston had no financial interest in the ownership of the islands of Tobago and St. Vincent, or in any other part of the lucrative West Indies sugar trade, and it was the fear of such an agreement between Versailles and Whitehall that was the driving force behind the determination of the New England colonists to disrupt these negotiations and, if necessary, to find their own solution.

At the beginning of 1754, Mildmay had no prophetic insight into the future and although the language dispute had stalled territorial negotiations for the past twelve months, he continued his work in the belief that a resolution of all these disagreements was still possible. The effects of four years of frustration were now evident in his letters, however, and he began what was to be his last full year as a commissioner in Paris with some reflections to Lord Fitzwalter on the advantages and disadvantages of what we would now call a preemptive first strike. In his letter of 16 January he speculated that if

an external war would allow the French government to distract the population from their present social, political, and economic problems, then
Britain's best interest might best be served by denying the French government the first opportunity to declare one. He noted that given the bitter
antagonism between Louis XV and his *Parlement* of Paris, there were those
in Britain who thought: "we, if such be their situation, ought to declare war
against them, from an imagination of gaining an advantage by attacking
them amidst the time of their own disputes and diversions." Against this
Machiavellian argument in one direction, Mildmay offered another. "Why
should we think of knocking them on the head whilst they are so very ready
to cut their own throats? Let them alone and they will do themselves much
more mischief than we can do. But if we draw our swords we shall only cut
the knot of their disputes and they will come at once with a united force
against us."[6]

In this letter Mildmay also outlined another argument against the
prospect of an immediate war, and one that he was to repeat to Fitzwalter
throughout the year. From his own careful observations and from the paid,
private intelligence reports he had collected from French informants,
Mildmay was convinced that the military capacity of France, and most particularly that of the French navy, was in no way large enough to fight a successful war. Furthermore, he was certain that the French government was
well aware of this fact, despite all their bellicose threats to the contrary. He
told Fitzwalter that in its present financial dilemma the French Court had
only two choices. The first was to raise its necessary revenue by an attempt
to collect a new tax; however, he said that in the present circumstances this
option was virtually impossible. Under French law the *Parlement* of Paris
must register any tax edict presented to it by the king before such tax collection could be enforced, and at the moment this defiant legal authority was
consistently refusing to do so. The second course was to: "reduce the public
expense and consequently lay aside all projects for aggrandising (*sic*) their
Marine and Commerce." Mildmay was convinced that given the present
social unrest in France, this alternative action was already being taken. He
reported: "for this purpose I have been well informed that the yearly fund of
20 million [*livres*] destined for their Marine is, for the year ensuing, reduced
to 14 million . . . that no more works are carried on in that Quarter . . . that
out of some 2000 workmen employed in their Dockyards [at Rochefort] last
year only 600 are remained for the year ensuing—that these are paid only

for the days in which they work . . . and, for a further saving, the Dockyards are to be shut up one day in each week, besides the Sundays and HolyDays (*sic*). There is only one Frigate now building in that Port . . . ."[7]

Mildmay's remarks on the precarious state of French government finances, and on the perceived need by the French government to reduce its military expenditures, are confirmed in a letter that M. de Rouillé sent from Paris on 1 June 1754 to *Intendant* François Bigot in Quebec. He told Bigot that the defense of Canada had become such an insupportable drain on the French treasury that either the colonists must pay the costs of their own protection, or this growing expense would lead to the dismissal of the present military governor, M. Duquesne.[8]

With his belief that the obvious benefits of colonial trade might still persuade both nations to avoid a war, at the end of January Mildmay asked Lord Fitzwalter how the negotiations were progressing on a convention of neutrality that was being explored in London by directors of the British and French East India companies, and by representatives of their respective governments. He reported that in Paris there was considerable enthusiasm among the French merchants for an agreement that would state that even if a war should break out in Europe between Britain and France, the inhabitants of the trading settlements of both countries in India should remain neutral. As the only beneficiaries in the present disputes between these two trading companies seemed to be the various Indian rulers, Mildmay said he was thus disturbed that despite the best efforts of the president of the French Company, M. Duvalear, who was in London to negotiate, no agreement appeared to have been signed between the British ministers and the duke of Mirepoix.[9]

Mildmay had been a long-term advocate of the expansion of British overseas commerce, and in this letter he emphasized to Lord Fitzwalter that the first concern for Britain ought to be to look after her trade, being careful not to be drawn into a war for other and "remote interests," a conviction he was to repeat in his letters to Fitzwalter as the political situation worsened during the year. Unfortunately for his hopes in the sanity of a neutrality agreement in India, on 11 February Mildmay reported to Fitzwalter the information that Lord Holdernesse had given Lord Albemarle on 2 February: namely that armed ships had now been sent by the French government to the east coast of India, and this despite the verbal assurances of the duke of Mirepoix that no such move would be made by France while negotiations were in progress in London. Mildmay told Fitzwalter that when he had asked about this contradiction he was told: "he [Mirepoix] had no orders from hence to make any such promises." After describing this as typical French Court "chicanery," he continued: "all sensible people in this Country, as well as in ours, are convinced that a flourishing Commerce cannot be carried on by either Side without a mutual agreement to keep Peace with one another."[10]

Nevertheless, however reasonable peace might be for commercial interests, the British government response to the French action was to send their own, armed contingent to India for defense purposes. On 6 March Mildmay noted to Fitzwalter that French merchants in Paris were becoming alarmed, and he with them, for: "forces having been sent by one in pretence of recruits [under the claim of reinforcing their troops] and the other in pretence of defence [against this reinforcement], whilst these troops of two rivals of Commerce come near to each other, with considerable Booty between them, it may be apprehended that the prospect of Lucre will tempt them to break though all orders of restraint, and a war begun in these parts from motives of private interest may occasion a national War in Europe."[11]

With a hindsight knowledge of the open warfare that was to break out in North America four months later, it might seem ironic that Mildmay did not appear to appreciate that exactly the same acute danger also existed in the Ohio Valley, and for very much the same reasons. The early spring, however, was a time in which he again hoped to arrange his work in Paris to allow him a long summer in England at Fitzwalter's estate of Moulsham Hall, but in March the first of three events took place that over the course of the year were to change both the workings of the commission and Mildmay's own position on it.

On 6 March 1754 Henry Pelham died suddenly, at the age of fifty-nine, and an immediate shift of political power took place in London. George II asked the duke of Newcastle to form a ministry as the First Lord of the Treasury and Newcastle recommended to the king that Lord Holdernesse be appointed as Newcastle's replacement in the senior post of secretary of state for the Northern Department. On 3 April Mildmay wrote two letters to Lord Holdernesse from Paris. The first was a formal, joint letter from himself and Ruvigny De Cosne, in which they acknowledged that in Lord Holdernesse's letter of 25 March he had informed them of his new position, and that Sir Thomas Robinson, as the new secretary for the Southern Department, was now in charge of their commission.[12] Mildmay's second letter was a private communication to Holdernesse in which he thanked him for his patronage and assured him: "although I am no more to receive your Lordship's orders in my publick capacity, yet I shall esteem it the greatest happiness to be employed in the execution of any other commands you may be pleased to honour me with during my residence in these parts."[13] Mildmay's position of influence with his minister had ended with Lord Holdernesse's move to the Northern Department, however, for Sir Thomas Robinson was a very different political master from Holdernesse.

Sir Thomas was a career diplomat of fifty-nine, who had been in the foreign service since he had first been sent to the British embassy in Paris in 1722 as secretary to the ambassador, Horatio Walpole. In 1730 he was appointed British ambassador to the Court of Vienna where he stayed until 1748, acting with considerable skill through eighteen years of stressful diplomacy and the political crises of the War of the Austrian Succession. On his return to London, in the early spring of 1748, Henry Pelham sent him to join the peace negotiations at Aix-la-Chapelle because Lord Sandwich and the duke of Bedford were having great difficulty in bringing all of the combatants to an agreement. The Treaty of Aix-la-Chapelle was substantially the work of Sir Thomas Robinson and he certainly knew as much about the nuances in its clauses as anyone in the present government. In December 1748—eight months after the preliminary treaty had been signed—he was appointed to the Board of Trade as one of the Lords Commissioners and remained there until his appointment to the Southern Department in March 1754.[14]

On the Board of Trade Sir Thomas worked closely with its new president, Lord Halifax, and he assisted in drawing up those memorials that were sent from the Board to the commission in Paris. In April 1754 he was thus in a position to take charge of the commission work in a way that had eluded Lord Holdernesse, who had never been more than a competent amateur, working under the direction of the duke of Newcastle and on the advice of Lord Albemarle, William Shirley, and William Mildmay. As a consequence of the length of time he had spent in Vienna Sir Thomas also spoke fluent German and was thought of highly by George II, who had insisted on choosing him for this post of southern secretary.[15] According to Horace Walpole, Sir Thomas Robinson: "had German honour, loved German politics . . . [and] if the Duke had intended to please his Master, he could not have succeeded more happily than by presenting him with so congenial a servant.

The King, with such a Secretary in his closet, felt himself in the very elysium of Herrenhaussen [the palace of the Elector in Hanover]."[16] George II, like his father, distrusted amateurs and Sir Thomas represented a professionalism that the king respected and preferred, for in the opinion of James, second earl of Waldegrave: "Sir Thomas was diligent in his office, did as he was directed, understood foreign affairs and pretended nothing further."[17]

Although on his appointment as the northern secretary Lord Holdernesse had told Lord Albemarle that under Sir Thomas Robinson's direction there would be no substantial change of policy, since: "the Foreign System will be supported upon the right principle, with consistency and dignity,"[18] with Sir Thomas' arrival there was an immediate change in how this policy was administered. His sense of formality and his need for such dignity can be seen in the tone of his letters to Lord Albemarle; in this correspondence there was none of the easy exchange of opinions and cheery gossip that had marked the letters between Albemarle and Lord Holdernesse. He frequently began his letters to Albemarle with the ministerial convention: "My Lord, I have been honoured with your Excellency's letter of the [date] instant and have laid it before the King . . ." and they always contained detailed and specific instructions for Albemarle's immediate attention. Albemarle's replies were equally formal and to the point, and included none of the customary banter and snippets of current French satire with which he had entertained Lord Holdernesse.[19]

Sir Thomas's appointment may have seemed an immediate improvement to George II, but in March 1754 it did not produce any sense of urgency to negotiate so far as the French government was concerned and Mildmay returned to England for the summer of 1754 largely as a consequence of this lack of interest shown by the French Court. By the end of April the senior French commissioner was no longer in Paris, for on the 17th of April Mildmay told Lord Fitzwalter that Galissonière, who was also a distinguished admiral of the fleet, had now reported that he was on the point of being sent to the naval port of Toulon, from where he had been ordered to sail with a squadron of ships and proceed to Algiers, to "bombard" that port and clear the surrounding area of Barbary Corsairs.

Mildmay said that when he had asked Galissonière how long he expected to be away he had replied "five to six months," but despite being assured that Silhouette would remain in Paris to continue the negotiations, Mildmay did not believe the reason that Galissonnière had given for his naval expedition was the truth. He told Lord Fitzwalter he was convinced that the French government had not detached such a valuable and experienced naval officer from the commission simply to chase pirates around the southwestern Mediterranean, and he argued a case to Fitzwalter that the real objective of this fleet was a summer campaign against the British forts on the coast of Guinea in order to disrupt the British trade in African slaves.[20] Mildmay's reasoning was sound and well thought out but in this case he was giving the French government too much credit for ingenuity and intelligent strategy. Galissonière did, in fact, go with his squadron to Algiers, where he spent from May to mid-November scouring the Barbary coasts of Morocco, Tunisia, Tripoli, and Algeria, and Mildmay acknowledged this when, on 27 November, he announced in a letter to Fitzwalter that Galissonière had just returned to Toulon.[21]

Mildmay may have been mistaken in this instance but he was not being overly suspicious about Galissonière's movements during the summer of 1754, for there were others who also did not believe the story about the Corsairs. William Shirley had now returned to Massachusetts as its governor and in a letter he wrote to Lord Halifax from Falmouth, Massachusetts, on 20 August he speculated: "I confess the appointment of Mons. de la Galissonière to command the Toulon Squadron makes me think it possible that the destination of some part of their armament may be for an attempt on Nova Scotia; he being the most proper Officer which France could employ on such an enterprise."[22] The British government was, it appears, equally skeptical. On 25 July 1754 Sir Thomas Robinson informed Lord Albemarle he had received reports from captains in the British Navy that Galissonière's squadron was now anchored in the harbor of Cadiz, and had been reinforced by several ships sent out from Brest. Sir Thomas told Albemarle that even George II had said he found it somewhat strange that: "the French Court such be at such an expense for an expedition [to the Barbary coast] that will appear to have no great utility to it."[23] On 24 May, in the last letter Mildmay wrote to Lord Fitzwalter before he received permission to visit England for the summer, he reported that before Galissonière had left for Toulon: "he [Galissonière] and M. de Silhouette were for several days together busy settling a long memorial, which I suppose in a short time will be offered to us."[24] Even here Mildmay was to be disappointed; this second French memorial on the claim to St. Lucia was not presented to him until 4 October, a month after his return to Paris.[25] In this May letter to Fitzwalter Mildmay also admitted he would be: "heartily glad to finish all affairs abroad," but news of the dangerous hostilities that had resumed in North America in late June made it clear to the governments in Whitehall and Versailles that if they wished to avoid a full-scale war, they must make one last, serious effort to negotiate these boundary disputes.

It was this sudden understanding that caused the enthusiasm at Versailles to reactivate the joint commission, and this change of strategy began in early August while Mildmay was still in England. In his commission journal Mildmay noted that on 3 August his colleague, De Cosne, received a visit from Silhouette, who informed him that the French governments had now prepared its reply to the British claim to St. Lucia and asked whether De Cosne had received any further instructions: "on the difficulty we had made of using the French tongue only, in our negotiations?"[26] On 4 August De Cosne reported the content of this meeting to Lord Holdernesse, saying that his response to Silhouette's question was that the fault for any delay lay entirely with the French Court, who had raised the language question in the first place. He stated he had informed Silhouette that the British government maintained the same position on the use of English that they had held when their memorial on Nova Scotia had first been turned back at the beginning of 1753: namely that they had the right to present their memorials in English, with a French translation. However, he told Holdernesse that he had also said that if the French government were now prepared to accept the original of the British memorial on Nova Scotia and Acadia in English, he would then be able to accept their reply to the British claim to St. Lucia in French."[27] To this, Silhouette replied that he had no official authority to make such an agreement and must seek further instructions from M. Rouillé, now the new foreign minister, but De Cosne informed Holdernesse that Silhouette had privately admitted: "he wished this point was settled, that our Conferences might resume their activity."[28]

In his journal Mildmay stated that ten days later, on 14 August, Rouillé met Lord Albemarle at Versailles and told him the French Court had agreed that in order "to prevent further delay in this Punctilio about Language," it would accept the British memorial on Nova Scotia and Acadia in English: "only desiring that as a Translation was to be made of it in French, His Majesty's Commissaries might revise and certyfy (*sic*) it to be just and conformable to our original." In his report on this meeting Mildmay noted that Albemarle had informed Sir Thomas Robinson of this development on the same day (14 August), but before Sir Thomas could act he must first contact Hannover in order to get the king's permission. Mildmay stated that it took until 30 August to receive the agreement of George II to Rouillé's proposal. Mildmay's instructions from Sir Thomas arrived somewhat more swiftly it seems, as in his journal he reported: "I had orders to depart forthwith to Paris for that purpose, and setting out from London on Tuesday September 3$^{rd}$, arrived in Paris on the Saturday following, September 7$^{th}$ 1754."[29]

It certainly appears that Rouillé's indication of a softening of the French government position on its language demands was taken seriously in Whitehall. Three days after Sir Thomas had received the king's consent to reopen the territorial negotiations, on 2 September he wrote to Lord Albemarle and informed him: "I am to acquaint your Excellency that Mr. Mildmay sets out for Paris this day, charged with his Majesty's instructions"[30] Within three days of Mildmay's arrival, he recorded in his journal that on 10 September he, Albemarle, and De Cosne met with Rouillé at the latter's Paris town house.[31] At this meeting Mildmay said Rouillé expressed his hope that now this language dispute had been settled, these two memorials (the present French reply to the British claim to St. Lucia and the British memorial of 15 November 1753 on the extent of Nova Scotia) could be exchanged and the conferences: "be carried on in such a manner as would lead to reconcile the Disputes between the two Crowns in America by an amicable negotiation. . . ." Although Mildmay still intended actively to pursue such a settlement, by this point in the negotiations he privately admitted he was worried that the chance of success was diminishing rapidly. In a letter to Lord Fitzwalter on 11 September Mildmay told him: "I fear my Lord that we shall begin too late, for from the last news from that Quarter [North America] we are told both sides are endeavouring to decide the differences in a more hostile manner."[32]

Mildmay was here referring to some disturbing news that had reached London at the beginning of September, and had caused the sudden Cabinet concern about the situation in Nova Scotia. On 3–4 July 1754 a battle had taken place at Fort Necessity—a British fort established at the forks of the Ohio and Monongahela Rivers—in which a French force that had been sent out by Governor Duquesne of Canada had totally defeated and annihilated a company of 200 of the Virginia militia under the command of Colonel George Washington. Washington had been attempting to retake Fort Necessity after its capture the previous April by the French, who had then considerably strengthened its defenses and renamed it Fort Duquesne. Washington's troops had been sent into the Ohio Valley by Governor Dinwiddie of Virginia, acting not so much on behalf of the whole colony of Virginia but for the interests of the Ohio Company of Virginia, of which he and Washington were both stockholders. The burgesses of Virginia were, in fact strongly opposed to Dinwiddie's attempt to involve their colony in what they saw as an unnecessary and dangerous activity, carried out solely for the financial benefit of the Ohio stockholders.[33]

The full details of the military disaster at Fort Necessity first appeared in the copy of the *Virginia Gazette* of Williamsburg on 19 July 1754 and were taken from the report on the battle submitted to Governor Dinwiddie by Colonel Washington and Captain James Mackay.[34] From the tardiness of Governor Dinwiddie, who had received this report in the second week of July but did not send it to Whitehall until 29 July, and given the usual four-week sea passage, the news of the loss of Fort Necessity did not arrive in London until 1 September. Once informed, however, the Cabinet reaction was immediate. According to a letter that the duke of Newcastle wrote to Lord Albemarle on 5 September 1754, three days after Mildmay had been sent to Paris to renew negotiations, he told Albemarle: "the results of encroachments by the French have alarmed the inhabitants of our colonies to such a degree that many of them have left their habitations, with troops on their lands. All North America will be lost if these poachers are tolerated and no war can be worse to this country than the suffering of such insults as these."[35]

In this letter Newcastle also reported that although Rouillé's response to the protest by the British government had been to ask for the renewal of the commission negotiations, he said he felt that "they [the French] get into possession by force and afterwards, or at the same time, to show their pacific disposition, they offer to refer the disposition of those rights to Commissaries." With some exasperation Newcastle admitted: "I own I am quite sick of Commissaries, tho' I don't well know how to get rid of them. I am sure they will do no good, and therefore hope we shall not be so far amused [distracted] by their conferences as to suspend or delay taking the proper measures to defend Ourselves, or recover our lost Possessions." Albemarle was in total agreement with Newcastle on this. In his reply of 12 September he told his Grace that although he felt that "Commissaries will never do" as a solution, nevertheless, in accordance with his instructions from Sir Thomas Robinson: "I carryed (*sic*) ours yesterday to M. de Rouillé. . . ."[36]

Even without the news from Fort Necessity, in August the duke of Newcastle already believed he had good reason to be concerned about the direction that French foreign policy seemed to be taking. The death of the French foreign minister, M. St. Contest, at the beginning of August 1754, had resulted in a general exchange of personnel on the king's council. On 11 August Newcastle wrote a anxious letter to Lord Albemarle in which he discussed the implications of the appointment of Rouillé to be the new foreign minister, the replacement of M. de Machault as *Garde des Sceaux* (Keeper of the Seals) by M. de Sechelles, and the appointment of Machault to be the successor to Rouillé as minister of Marine. Newcastle's concern was that Machault's new position appeared to be a demotion and he asked Albemarle that if this was so, did it then mean that the hitherto pacific influence of the marquise de Pompadour, Machault's patron, was also on the wane and thus that the fortune of M. d'Argenson, minister for war and the enemy of both the Marquise and Machault, was now on the rise.[37] With the growing belligerence of France in both India and North America, Newcastle said he believed that this kind of shift of influence, if that was what was taking place, could be very disquieting news to the British government.

In his reply of 21 August Lord Albemarle was at pains to reassure Newcastle that he had learned: "Machault had relinquished the Seals, and had been removed from the Head of Finances to the *Bureau de la Marine* by his own choice and no ways by compulsion." Albemarle explained that for some time Machault had been under great pressure from the senior French clergy, who deeply resented his unprecedented imposition of the *vingtiéme* tax (a twentieth part of total income) on the Galican Church, and from the unhappiness of Louis XV, who, as a devout Catholic, was disturbed by the outrage of his archbishops and bishops.[38] Although Albemarle's information proved to be correct, and Machault remained in a position of power in the royal Council, Newcastle was correct to be concerned that the negotiations could be adversely affected by this alteration in the Foreign Ministry; such a change of masters would inevitably cause some revisions and delicate readjustments to Silhouette's own position at a critical time in the negotiation.

By early September it was evident that the military situation was, indeed, critical both for Britain and for its North American colonists. On 4 September Lord Albemarle, who had just been informed by Sir Thomas Robinson about Washington's defeat on the Ohio, sent a concerned letter to the duke of Newcastle. In it he stated that since it appeared the colonial militia was not up to the task of defending British territory in North America: "Officers, and good ones, must be sent to Discipline the militia, and to lead them. . . ."[39] While the advice of Albemarle, as an experienced soldier, might have merit, the Cabinet had realized that time was not on their side. As a result of the battle of Fort Necessity, a renewed attempt to defuse the military situation in North America had now become imperative to George II and his ministers, and Rouillé's proposal to restart the negotiations on these territorial disputes was therefore studied with great interest in Whitehall.

In any such solution, however, the problem for both governments lay in the economic aims of their colonial subjects, since the commercial motives that were behind these military forays were not confined simply to the Ohio Company of Virginia. Governor Duquesne of Canada was, himself, indirectly involved in the trading interests of a company called the "Great Society" run by a large group of Quebec merchants and profiteers supplying military material, and operated under the direction of the *Intendant*, François Bigot. General Montcalm was later to state: "War came and it was this Great Society, whose criminal acts were perpetrated in its own self interests, that provided the English with the pretext their ambitious schemes required to light the blaze."[40] Patrick Higonnet, in his article "The Origins of the Seven Years' War," blames both sides equally, stating that between the beginning of 1752 and the end of 1755 the commercial interests of the colonists of Virginia, New England, and Canada had caused an escalation of their small-scale skirmishes to gain territory into a situation that was now: "involving their governments in a shooting war."[41]

Curiously enough, despite the desire expressed by the French government to begin immediate conferences, this urgency did not seem to have been communicated to the two French commissioners. Mildmay had been sent to Paris on only three days notice, but when he met with Rouillé on 10 September he reported he found that: "M. Galissonière was yet out to Sea with his Squadron [in the Mediterranean]" and Silhouette was still at his country estate near Orlèans. Even though Mildmay said Rouillé had told them he would send an immediate message to Silhouette: "to come up and settle with Us all matters in question," it took until 4 October 1754, or a further three weeks, before Mildmay and De Cosne could hold a conference with Silhouette at Mildmay's apartment.

From a letter that Mildmay sent to Fitzwalter on the day before this conference was held it appears he felt that he and Silhouette could now negotiate the boundary problems with some success. In his letter of 3 October he told Fitzwalter they had already met and jointly agreed they should: "proceed with all diligence to finish the work on hand. It would really add great honour to us both, could we by any accommodation prevent differences between the subjects of both Crowns in America."[42] On the face of it, and given the mutual mistrust shown by both governments over the previous four years, such a sudden "accommodation" would seem highly unlikely. It is therefore difficult to say whether, on 3 October 1754, Mildmay actually believed that the commissioners on either side had the ability to make such a breakthrough independently, or whether his confidence was based on his understanding that the two kings and their ministers seriously intended to bring the territorial disputes to an end.

Both in his journal and in a letter to Sir Thomas Robinson Mildmay described the events of the 4 October conference that he and De Cosne held with M. Silhouette, and from his comments it is obvious that his initial expectation of some immediate and substantial progress was not realized. Far from beginning any talks on specific proposals for a resolution of the disputed North American boundaries—an essential component in reducing the present armed conflicts—Silhouette merely apologized that he could not hand over the promised French translation of the English memorial on Nova Scotia and Acadia as it was not yet complete. Mildmay said Silhouette stated that the translation that had so far been made was of such poor quality that he had sent it back for revision, but promised that it would soon be presented: "in a fair copy, for our certifying the Justness of it."[43] This translated document was one of the ostensible reasons stated by the French government for the renewal of talks but, although Silhouette had not produced it, he now offered his government's reply to the British memorial on the right to St. Lucia. Even at this point there was still a problem, however, for despite M. Rouillé's indication to Lord Albemarle that he wished the commission to resume serious negotiations, Mildmay said "he [Silhouette] hinted that perhaps we might think some of the [French] expressions in this Memorial a little too harsh."

The unfortunate and foolish pettiness that had now become endemic in these negotiations is revealed when Mildmay reported to Sir Thomas that Silhouette had admitted that this "harsh" language was a deliberate retaliation for the British government's refusal to modify similar expressions in its French translation of the original memorial on Nova Scotia—first presented nearly two years earlier, in November 1752—and to which the French government had objected in February 1753. Mildmay said he replied that he and De Cosne were still prepared to withdraw this French version of their Nova Scotia memorial and to substitute the English original as the official conference document, but Silhouette refused, on the grounds that he had been given no such authority. He reported that, nevertheless, Silhouette had emphasized that his government's present agreement to make its own translation of this British memorial on Nova Scotia should be taken as proof of its sincere intention to resolve these boundary disputes. On the next day Mildmay and De Cosne informed Sir Thomas Robinson that on the understanding that the French translation of the Nova Scotia memorial would soon be produced, they had accepted this French memorial on St. Lucia, and in a note at the end of his 4 October conference report Mildmay said they duly sent a translated copy of it to Sir Thomas. On 20 November, however, they were forced to write and say that the translation of the memorial on Nova Scotia had still not yet arrived, but as: "M. de Silhouette, we hear, has just arrived back from his country house . . . we expect in a few days he will give us the French translation of our last English memorial. . . ."[44]

At this point Mildmay and De Cosne did not yet know that the 4 October 1754 conference with Silhouette was, in fact, the last that they would hold as commissioners,[45] and from the evidence of the enthusiasm Mildmay expressed in his letters to Lord Fitzwalter during September and October, it appears he was also unaware that during the summer certain ministers in the British government, and in particular the duke of Newcastle, had already expressed a complete lack of confidence both in the commission and in the outcome of its work. Despite the new appetite to negotiate that appeared to be coming from the French court, this skepticism remained. On 12 September Sir Thomas Robinson told Lord Albemarle: "His Majesty will not suffer himself to be amused by negotiation, or by referring pretensions which have no foundation to commissaries, while the French are in possession of countries belonging to Great Britain and are acting hostilely (*sic*) in the manner which they are now doing in North America." Sir Thomas also reported that although George II was pleased that Albemarle had cultivated a sincere friendship with Rouillé, the king also said he believed that Rouillé's stated desires for a settlement of the territorial disputes "arise more from his own private inclinations than from any general desire of the whole French Court."[46]

Mildmay's letters to Fitzwalter in early October on the territorial negotiations are in direct contrast to this government pessimism but although he expressed some hope of success in this sector, it appears he had little expectation of any settlement of his ransom accounts. In the 3 October letter in which he had commented to Fitzwalter on his new rapport with Silhouette, he explained that his aim was to set up a secure and undisputed claim for a non-recoverable debt on the ransom demands, "because Payment I *do not* expect (*sic*) . . . which [claim] I may then leave against any other demand they may have against us." The North American boundary disputes, he felt, were a different matter and it was with an evident sense of optimism that on 9 October Mildmay reported to Lord Fitzwalter the results of the conference that had been held five days earlier. Silhouette, he said, had agreed to accept the British memorial on Nova Scotia without demanding that it first be written in French, and he remarked "This point of form and punctilio being settled, I could wish we might bring the more substantial matters into as easy a method of accommodation. We have discovered to one another which are our favourite points [on the ownership of St. Lucia and the boundaries of Nova Scotia] and by mutually yielding these, the differences might be reconciled."[47]

This remark to Fitzwalter clearly demonstrates the apparent unreality of the diplomacy taking place in Paris in the autumn of 1754, proceedings that had now become totally disconnected from decisions being made in the colonies of New England, Virginia, and Canada. So far as the colonial leadership on both sides was concerned, any discussion of the differences in these "favourite points" concerning an island in the West Indies was irrelevant, and by October 1754 the French and British colonists had reached the stage where they were long past any interest in a mutual accommodation, let alone a reconciliation. During the spring of 1754 constant small-scale skirmishes had been taking place between the British and the French colonial militia, and long before the July defeat at Fort Necessity the British colonists had decided they were no longer prepared to rely on regiments of the British army for their entire defense. In response to the renewed fighting that had broken out in Nova Scotia, on 19 April 1754 Governor William Shirley sent a report to Lord Holdernesse from Boston, telling him that on the direction of the Board of Trade he had successfully proposed to the "General Assembly of the Colony of Massachusetts Bay" that they should: "joyn (*sic*) with the Commissaries of New York, and the Commissaries which should come from Virginia, Maryland, the New Jerseys and New Hampshire" to

meet with their Indian allies at a conference to be held in Albany. At this
meeting, he said, it had been agreed that these colonies should unite in what
it was hoped would become a: "General Union which it is His Majesty's
pleasure that all his Colonies enter into."[48]

When Shirley wrote this letter from Boston on 19 April he was not yet
aware that on 25 March 1754 Lord Holdernesse had been replaced as the
southern secretary, because with the delay of a four-week sea crossing this
news had not yet reached North America. His letter was delivered to the new
secretary, Sir Thomas Robinson, and on 8 May Shirley wrote to Sir Thomas,
giving him lengthy advice on the military method by which to dislodge the
French from their forts on the Kennebeck and St. John Rivers, and on the
Isthmus of Canso, and proposing that a contingent of troops should be sent
to reinforce the garrison at Halifax.[49] By 24 June 1754, the British Cabinet
had decided to send such a force—of at least 1,000 regular soldiers—who
would join the men to be raised and paid for by the colonies themselves,
since, as the duke of Newcastle wrote in a letter to Horatio Walpole three
days after this Cabinet meeting: "The first point we have laid down is that
the Colonies must not be abandoned, that our rights and possessions in
North America must be maintained and the French obliged to desist from
their hostile attempts to dispossess us."[50]

When, on 9 October, Mildmay wrote his optimistic letter to Lord
Fitzwalter about the progress he felt had been made at the 4 October conference, he had not yet heard the news that the duke of Newcastle sent to Lord
Albemarle. On 10 October Newcastle informed Albemarle that in the first
week of October (while this conference was, in fact, taking place) a British
force, under the command of General Braddock, had finally sailed for North
America; but what was supposed to have been a secret expedition had now
been made public by the War Office in a detailed announcement in the official government publication, the *Gazette*. As Newcastle's agitated letter
informed Albemarle, this foolhardy and premature release of information
had: "set all the Foreign Ministers on fire and made them believe we are
going to war, which is, I hope, the farthest from our thought." Unlike the
majority of his more belligerent Cabinet colleagues, Newcastle had a realis-
tic misgiving about the danger of yet another war with France, and he thus
continued to Albemarle: "But whoever begins it [the war], it will be the
greatest misfortune to this Country . . . and therefore everything should be
done to preserve it [the peace]."[51] Sir Thomas Robinson had a similar concern

both for French government opinion and for possible military retaliation, though his tone was more restrained. In a letter to Lord Albemarle in which he announced that Braddock's fleet had sailed from Cork with two regiments, bound for Virginia, Sir Thomas asked Albemarle to be: "very attentive in observing what effect this measure . . . may have on the minds of Mor. de Rouillé and the other Ministers."[52]

Lord Albemarle replied to the duke's letter on 23 October 1754 and in his reply he reassured Newcastle that there had been no general public reaction to the announcement: "by these abominable writers of [British] Daily Newspapers," since the Royal control of information in France was total, and the ministers: " . . . prefer silence to flamour [from 'flambée,' or 'outburst'] and they have so far succeeded that nothing is mentioned in Publick." However Albemarle admitted that, for himself: "I must own that it requires a better head than mine to distinguish with proper nicety what we are doing now, from hostile preparations."[53] With such contradictory messages coming from Newcastle and from other Cabinet members, perhaps it is not surprising that both Lord Albemarle and Mildmay should have some confusion about their diplomatic responses in the autumn of 1754.

Lord Albemarle's letter of 23 October had been sent to the duke of Newcastle from Fontainebleau, where he had been joined by Mildmay and De Cosne. The French Court went to Fontainebleau each year in late October to hunt during the fine weather of "St. Martin's Summer" [54] and Mildmay and De Cosne had been instructed that they were to continue their negotiations with Silhouette at Fontainebleau between royal hunts, while Lord Albemarle carried out the same activity at the Ministerial level with Rouillé. Mildmay did not actually arrive in Fontainebleau until 24 October because, as he told Lord Fitzwalter, he had been busy finishing his translation and transcription of the French memorial on St. Lucia (received on 4 October), so that he and De Cosne might be able to review the document while they were away.[55] By 13 November Mildmay had returned to Paris, and he reported to Fitzwalter that the Feast of St. Martin having: "concluded the vacation here, the Ministries are returned from Fontainebleau, the Courts of Justice reassembled and my conferences with the French Commissary [M. Seigneur] renewed, which in a short time I hope to put upon such an issue as to admit my being absent from hence."[56]

Underlying this desire for a permanent return to London was a problem that Mildmay had faced since he came back to Paris in September, for by the autumn of 1754 he found that his private responsibilities were now in conflict with his loyalties as a diplomat. When he was ordered back to Paris at the beginning of September Mildmay expressed a concern about the state of Lord Fitzwalter's health, and said he hoped that Fitzwalter's present recovery would continue. In every letter thereafter Mildmay continued to make some reference to this subject and in each of these letters he also reassured Fitzwalter that he was making every effort to try and conclude his commission on the accounts of the prisoner ransoms as quickly as possible. From Mildmay's correspondence during the early winter of 1754 it is obvious that Fitzwalter's health had now deteriorated to the point where Mildmay felt a considerable conflict between his duty to the government and his equal duty to his long-time friend and benefactor, of whom he was the heir presumptive.

Such a duty to the elderly head of the family from his heir was taken very seriously in eighteenth-century society and under normal circumstances the heir would be allowed to leave a government post abroad and return to take up the private responsibilities of his future inheritance. The diplomatic situation in late 1754 was not a normal one however; although Mildmay was only a commissioner, the continued presence in Paris of the British commission had become a sensitive issue for the British government and, by this point, neither side wished to be seen by other European powers as contributing to a breakdown in negotiations by the withdrawal of its commissioners. At the beginning of September the duke of Newcastle had already admitted to Lord Albemarle that he was: "sick of the commissaries" and their deliberations, but neither he nor his ministers could think of a way to recall them. Mildmay's only chance to return was based on the hope that with Albemarle conducting skillful negotiations of the boundary disputes at the senior level, and with his colleague, De Cosne, in place on the commission as a permanent employee of the Embassy, Mildmay might be allowed to leave Paris for good if he could settle his single commission on the ransom of prisoners successfully.

When Lord Fitzwalter received Mildmay's 13 November letter it appears that he had asked for an explanation of Mildmay's cryptic statement about his hope to be able to return to England, and on 20 November Mildmay wrote a somewhat despondent reply to Fitzwalter's query in which he summed up his present feelings about his four-year mission in Paris. Since he had now begun to doubt his earlier belief in the promises that Silhouette had made in October, he told Fitzwalter: "and to you only I mention it in confidence, that with regard to our American disputes, I find neither side inclined towards an accommodation by yielding up part of their Pretensions, and that the Right which each Crown endeavors to support by reason and argument must remain to be decided by the force of those reasons and arguments contained in their respective written Memorials, mutually delivered. Since We have, on both sides, delivered the State of all our Demands, with all our Answers and Replys (*sic*), I don't find any further advances can be made if we stay here even 10 years longer."[57]

This was also the position he now held with respect to the ransom question. He told Lord Fitzwalter he had answered every objection put forward on the sums of money due from France, and therefore felt he was wasting his time waiting for a payment from the French government that he was sure would never arrive. He concluded: "I have gone, in one Commission [the territorial disputes] as far as either side cares for going, and in the other I can go no further." Given this situation, Mildmay said that as he was most anxious to be able to return to Essex to care for Fitzwalter he wondered whether: "after waiting a little while longer to see if any new offers are made, I may not take the liberty of asking leave to come home, for since I can be of no more Service to the Publick, why should I be deprived of paying my private Duty to you, to whom I owe such infinite obligations?"

The note of quiet despair in this letter is in such contrast to the high hopes expressed by Mildmay to Lord Fitzwalter from 1750 until the end of 1752, and even in his qualified optimism of three months ago in his talks with Silhouette, that it provides strong evidence he went to Paris in April 1750 with the aim of succeeding in his commission and that he continued to believe this to be possible for nearly four years. If, in 1750, Mildmay had understood he was engaged in what was simply a cynical diplomatic exercise, designed for failure, he would not have been so distressed at what appeared to be the final collapse of these negotiations. He would also not have written about his four wasted years of failed hopes in a private letter to an old friend with whom he had no reason to keep up pretenses.

In an effort to extricate himself from Paris, on 27 November 1754 Mildmay reported to Lord Fitzwalter that, in order to expedite matters, he had held three separate meetings with commissioner Seigneur during the previous week. He also said that, after a six-month absence, Galissonière had finally returned with his fleet to Toulon, but he told Fitzwalter it remained to be seen whether his arrival would cause the French government to show any renewed interest in the territorial negotiations.[58] On 4 December he wrote a long letter to Fitzwalter in which his frustration was apparent. Far from Galissonière's presence in Paris being any sort of a catalyst to negotiations, he said Galissonière had now informed him that since he had not yet been able to report to Rouillé, he had nothing new to propose. This being the case, Mildmay said he approved of the: "glorious resolution by us lately to defend our colonies [the intent to unite the militia forces of the various colonies, as reported by William Shirley at the Albany conference]." He stated that in his opinion, the French government only understood such a display of force, for: "as soon as that appears to be more formidable than theirs, they will skulk back into their old habitations" and with such a "single United Power . . . this new Project will alter the system in that part of the World and will be the surest means of aweing (sic) our Limitropes (sic), or [French] Borderers, into a more peaceable conduct for the future."[59]

On 18 December he was pleased to be able to tell Lord Fitzwalter that within a week he would have finished his accounts, ready to hand over to Seigneur, and, after sending a detailed report to Whitehall, he would: "with impatience, await my final orders."[60] Unfortunately for all these plans, however, just before Christmas an event took place that was to end all Mildmay's hopes of an immediate return. On 21 December Lord Albemarle was coming home alone from a supper party when he collapsed in his coach from a stroke, and died at six o'clock on the following evening without regaining consciousness. Later that same night Mildmay sent two shocked letters— one to Lord Fitzwalter and the other to Lord Holdernesse—in which he told them what had happened and that De Cosne, as first secretary, had now taken charge of the post as its acting ambassador and was in the process of informing Sir Thomas Robinson of Lord Albemarle's death.[61]

In one day Mildmay's responsibility in Paris had changed. There was now no experienced British ambassador to negotiate with the French ministers, and at the same time he had also lost the full-time services of his other colleague on the commission. As if these events were not disruptive enough, at the end of a year of changes that had begun in March, with the death of Henry Pelham, on Christmas Day Mildmay received the news that Lord Fitzwalter had resigned from his post as treasurer of the king's household. He told Fitzwalter that his: "distraction had been augmented by this new information" and, in an uncharacteristically emotional response, he also said that unless this had been a "free and voluntary resignation," Fitzwalter could count on Mildmay's own resignation of his commission post in protest, for "as you are my protector and leader, and as I fight under your banner, so by you, my Lord, I am always ready to rise and fall."[62]

Mildmay was not called on to make this loyal sacrifice as he subsequently found out that Lord Fitzwalter had asked to be relieved of his post from ill health, but for the first time since he had arrived in Paris in 1750 he realized that he had now no protector with influence at the English Court. As he was very anxious to have the king's permission to leave the diplomatic service, this lack of help was only going to make his problem more difficult. Without a patron who had direct access to the Court or to a member of the Cabinet, any minor diplomat in a foreign post could become a forgotten man within days.

## WINDING DOWN

At the beginning of 1755, and despite this growing concern about his diplomatic position in Paris, events now began working in Mildmay's favor. With the death of Lord Albemarle his work became considerably reduced, as direct responsibility for determining the boundaries of Nova Scotia and Acadia, the ownership of St. Lucia, and the sea limits was transferred from the British commission in Paris to Sir Thomas Robinson in London. On 16 January 1755 the duke of Newcastle, Lord Holdernesse, Lord Hardwicke, Sir Thomas Robinson, and Lord Anson, the First Sea Lord, held a Cabinet meeting at Newcastle House, at which they discussed whether Sir Thomas should now negotiate these disputes directly with the duke of Mirepoix.[63] At a further Cabinet meeting, on 7 February, Sir Thomas was instructed to tell Mirepoix that the British government expected him to be given "Full Powers," or comprehensive authority from Louis XV to negotiate for this purpose.[64] Although the British Cabinet seemed unaware of it on 7 February, such powers had already been granted to Mirepoix by the French king on 3 February in a document that was a seven-page restatement of all the areas of disagreement that existed in the territorial disputes in North America.[65]

Mirepoix and Sir Thomas conducted their negotiation throughout the spring and into the summer of 1755, but the series of dispatches that Mirepoix sent to Rouillé and the French Court—both his own presentations and those of Sir Thomas to him—indicate that these efforts were more in the nature of a justification by which each nation would subsequently be able to claim it had done all it could to negotiate in good faith. Nevertheless, formal presentations of the present state of the negotiations were exchanged by both sides and some three months (February to May) were spent discussing a British suggestion for a "counter project," a part of which proposed an agreement to divide the territory bounded by the headwater of the St. Lawrence River and Lakes Ontario and Erie into two uncontested areas, one owned by France and the other by Britain. In this "project" it was intended that these areas would be divided on a line drawn at the entrance to Lake Ontario. The land along the south bank of the St. Lawrence River to the east of this line would become part of Canada, owned by France, while to the west all the hinterland around the southern shores of Lakes Ontario and Erie would become attached to the British colonies of New York and Pennsylvania.[66] This was a last minute, completely unrealistic proposition that had never before been discussed, either in any previous memorial or at any commission meeting. As it would effectively have cut off all French forts along the Ohio River from their base in Canada, it was vehemently rejected by the French government, who used it as part of the justification of their charge of false dealing against the British. The clerks in the French Ministry of Foreign Affairs, who had transcribed this document, noted at the end of each copy the names of the various French ambassadors to the Courts of Europe who had received one.[67]

By the beginning of May Mirepoix, at least, was under no illusions about his role as a negotiator. At the end of yet another dispatch to Rouillé that discussed the impossibility of any acceptance of the terms offered by the British government, he admitted: "Yesterday I saw the Minister [Sir Thomas Robinson] but, as I have had the honour to mention to you, I have no hope for any conciliation. I am, however, comforted that I will [soon] be allowed to make my departure. This will be the most expedient way to stir things up (*pour hâter la revolution*)."[68] The withdrawal of the ambassador would certainly bring the negotiation to an end but neither side was yet ready for a public rupture, and it was, in fact, 24 July 1755 before the First Secretary at the French Embassy, M. Boutet, was able to inform his Court that M. Mirepoix had, that day, left for Paris.[69]

Although Mildmay had not yet received the official notification, by the middle of January 1755 he was aware that that everything except the ransom question would probably be removed from his commission responsibilities, and he therefore felt more positive that he would finally be allowed to return to England. On 15 January he was able to report to Lord Fitzwalter that, having sent his account of the state of prisoner ransoms to Sir Thomas Robinson, Sir Thomas had informed him of the king's: "approbation of my diligence in executing this commission." Mildmay said he had been instructed to deliver to the French minister a formal document that stated the king's financial demands, and to insist that this balance would be accepted as: "a Debt from the Court of France towards His Majesty."[70] This instruction corresponded with Mildmay's own suggestion that the British government should not pursue an actual repayment any further, but should try to balance this debt against any future financial demands from the French government. He thus told Fitzwalter he felt satisfied that not only had his advice been followed, but that he would soon be: "free for ever from any further engagement in this affair" and his work in Paris would, at last, be over. Later in this letter of 15 January he sounded a warning note to Fitzwalter when he pointed out that there seemed no government enthusiasm to appoint another British ambassador to Paris. To add to Mildmay's difficulties, he also reported that most of the other embassy staff had returned to England with the body of Lord Albemarle and he and De Cosne were now the only senior British officials left in Paris to carry out all public business at the embassy: not the least of which were their desperate attempts to stave off the late Lord Albemarle's numerous French creditors.

Mildmay doggedly continued his attempt to bring his single, remaining commission to a conclusion but at the end of January he had to admit to Fitzwalter that it was not an easy process. On being informed by commissioner Seigneur that his government still had some comments to make on the British ransom demands, Mildmay told Fitzwalter, on 29 January: "I keep my temper, as well as my resolution, which is not to mind his observations but to deliver my accounts not to him, but to his Ministers."[71] By the beginning of February Mildmay was speculating to Fitzwalter that perhaps an outbreak of war might solve his problem for him, since the warlike preparations in both countries made further peace unlikely, and: "if these American disputes which brought me over hither are to drive me back again, the publick (sic) peace and my commission are to expire together."[72]

Once again Mildmay was to be disappointed. Two weeks later he was forced to tell Lord Fitzwalter the Treasury Board was concerned that in his debit list he had omitted the cost of transporting the French prisoners from

England to France. Accordingly, the Board was afraid that this would establish a precedent and in his letter of 19 February Mildmay said Sir Thomas Robinson had now instructed him to include this sum in the official claim. To add to his frustration with this late delay, the letter from Sir Thomas had given him no idea of the exact transportation amount per prisoner that the Treasury officials expected him to include, so once again he was forced to wait until he had been sent this information from Whitehall. He told Fitzwalter he was also concerned that in the present delicate state of diplomacy and rumors of imminent war: "it is suggested to me going from hence would greatly encrease (*sic*) the alarm, and since appearances of peace are to be preserved, it is hinted to me from Mr. De Cosne . . . that should I apply to my Superiors for leave just at this instant, it would not be attended with success."[73]

Indeed Ruvigny De Cosne was quite correct in his opinion. When Mildmay wrote to Lord Fitzwalter on 5 March he also enclosed the original of a letter he had just received in which Sir Thomas Robinson refused his request for leave, despite the solicitations of some of Mildmay's friends on his behalf, and told Fitzwalter it thus it appeared that he was: "confined, if not imprisoned here, by constraint and order."[74] By 12 March, however, he was more hopeful, as he wrote to Fitzwalter that, although the present situation had not changed: "it cannot be long before the negotiation [between Sir Thomas Robinson and the duke of Mirepoix] now on the *tapis* will be decided, either amicably or otherways (*sic*), and let it be one way or the other, as I have before told your Lordship, it will be the means of bringing me over . . ."[75]

It was, in fact, to be two more months before Mildmay was "brought over" to England permanently, but during these eight weeks between late March and the middle of May 1755 he was able to perform one last important diplomatic service for the British government. After a period in which his weekly letters to Lord Fitzwalter were brief and did not discuss the possibility of warfare between England and France, on 26 March Mildmay said he felt he should continue with his political observations and sent Fitzwalter a long analysis of the reason why he considered that France could not mount a successful naval challenge to Britain in the North Atlantic.[76] He pointed out that the French fleet: "had neither sufficient canon (*sic*), nor provision to put on board" and the French Ministry of the Marine, well aware of this lack of essential materiel, "talk only of their forces at land, surmising that if we send out our ships, they will march their army, but where, and against whom?" He also speculated that the French government might take out its frustration at not being able to revenge itself in North America by turning Europe into a battleground.

North America, however, was to become the first of the battlegrounds, for in March 1755 with reports of dangerous French incursions along the whole of the colonial frontiers the British Cabinet decided to send General Edward Braddock, together with two regiments of Irish infantry, to Virginia to take command of the militias of Virginia, Massachusetts, and New York. The aim of this combined force was to remove the increasing French presence in the Ohio Valley, Upper New York, Crown Point (*Fort Frédéric*), and along the headwaters of Lake Champlain. As it was imperative that the French must not receive any military reinforcement that would allow them to resist this British land campaign, the Cabinet also decided to try intercept any French warships sailing to Canada, and Admiral Edward Boscowan was appointed to take a British fleet to intercept a reported French fleet due to sail for Louisbourg almost immediately.

By mid-April Mildmay was trying to keep abreast of reports that this French fleet was ready to sail from Brest to supply the French garrisons in Acadia, the Ohio Valley, and the city of Quebec with fresh troops and materiel. On 16 April 1755 he told Lord Fitzwalter he had been given information that orders had been sent on that day (16 April) to John Macnamara, the French Vice-Admiral in charge of this fleet, to sail from Brest and: "If the wind prove favourable he will go out with sixteen ships of the line and four fregates (*sic*) and 3000 land forces, all destined for Louisbourg to forti-fye (*sic*) their possessions in America."[77] It was obviously extremely important that the British government have accurate information on the sailing of this French fleet, but in his letter of 26 March Mildmay had already told Fitzwalter that such information was now very hard to come by, as he was: "in an awkward situation in this country, treated as a friend and yet suspected to be an enemy."[78]

Mildmay decided that with the help of the several intelligence contacts he had made in France over the years, he must now do his best to overcome this problem and his information certainly seems to have proved more useful to the British government than a report it received from another intelligence source in France. In a letter that Horace Walpole wrote to Sir Horace Mann, Walpole admitted that even by 22 April 1755 his government friends in

Whitehall were still very much in the dark on the exact location and destination of the French fleet; their only information was contained in a letter
that had been sent from France on 27 March and received in London on 8
April, or two weeks earlier. Walpole said that the intelligence in this letter
told them that: "in the night between the 18th and 19th past [of March] a
squadron of 5 or 6 men of war, with troops on board, sailed silently out of
Brest for America."[79] This information was not only out of date, but was
also inaccurate.

From his own sources Mildmay was able to discover that on 30 April 1755
this French fleet was still in the harbor at Brest, as it was being kept in that
port by a combination of high winds and inadequate victualing supplies. He
told Fitzwalter that since he had been informed the British fleet, commanded by Admiral Boscowan, was reported at that moment to be waiting in
Portsmouth, he considered it would equally be prevented from sailing by the
same bad weather. He therefore speculated: "if these [two fleets] do not
meet, there is no likelihood of any hostilities being yet awhile committed,"
and if this were the case, then Mildmay said he again hoped that he would be
permitted to return to England when George II made his annual visit to
Hanover.[80]

The king's departure for Hanover in the early summer of 1755 caused a
great deal of uneasiness, even alarm, in Whitehall. George II refused to give
up the pleasure of his regular visit to his electorate, despite the obvious danger of an immediate war in Europe and the constitutional difficulties his
absence from England would cause his ministers. On 6 August 1755 Sir
Thomas Robinson wrote a worried letter to Lord Holdernesse, who was
with the king in Hanover as his northern secretary. Sir Thomas informed
Holdernesse that a delegation of government ministers who were on the
Regency Council—led by the duke of Newcastle and including Lord
Hardwicke, Lord Anson, and himself—had met with the council president,
the duke of Cumberland, to discuss how the Council was to direct the active
warfare that was now taking place in North America.[81]

Sir Thomas pointed out to Holdernesse that: "a delay of twelve or fourteen days for receiving His Majesty's pleasure" might very well have a disastrous effect on the ability of the king's ministers to give proper instructions
to Admiral Hawke, who was about to sail with a British military force to
reinforce the colonial militia in New England. Sir Thomas said the duke of
Cumberland and the other Council members therefore asked Holdernesse to

press the king to return as soon as possible, as apart from the danger of such delayed royal instructions, if the French king decided to issue a declaration of war only George II had the constitutional ability to be able to respond to such a declaration.

The date and place of Lord Holdernesse's answer to this 6 August letter from Sir Thomas is symptomatic of the sense of unreality and drift that now determined crucial diplomatic decisions; when Holdernesse finally replied his letter was dated 5 September, and it came from Amsterdam. Far from being with the king in Hanover, able to advise and to discuss with George II the details of the present crisis faced by his country, Holdernesse told Sir Thomas that he was now in Holland meeting with the Dowager Princess of Orange, eldest daughter of George II and regent for her seven-year-old son. Holdernesse apologized for his delay in replying to Sir Thomas' two previous letters: "but I was obliged to postpone answering them until today [because] the Princess Royal commanded me to attend her at Soesdyck on Tuesday."[82] Despite the threat of war, and the appeals of his ministers, the king did not, in fact, return to London until the end of October, his usual time of arrival.

In contrast to the inertia at the Court in Hanover, in May of 1755 Mildmay felt a great sense of urgency in his obligation to provide timely, strategic information to his government. As the bad weather was holding both the British and the French fleets in port, Mildmay decided to see if he could find out the exact composition of the French fleet that was still in Brest. On 9 May 1755 he wrote his discoveries in a letter to his relative and friend, Carew Hervey Mildmay of Marks, who had been keeping him informed of Lord Fitzwalter's health throughout the previous winter.[83] Carew Mildmay had good political connections and as William Mildmay's letter contained important information for the British government on the size, condition, and destination of this French fleet, he asked Carew to pass this letter on to Sir Thomas Robinson.[84] As there is no letter from Carew Hervey Mildmay in the collection of Sir Thomas's official correspondence it is impossible to know whether Carew did what he had been asked,[85] but on 28 May, a week after William Mildmay had returned to London, he sent Sir Thomas Robinson a complete report of this information he had given to Carew on 9 May, including the ultimate destination of the troops being transported in these ships.[86] Three days later, on 31 May, Mildmay was also able to respond to a request from Viscount Royston, the eldest son of Lord Hardwicke, that

Mildmay should send him the list of the ships in the French fleet at Brest, together with the: "General List of Ships belonging to the Crown of France" that he had been carefully collecting from his various French sources over the previous four years.[87]

In Mildmay's 9 May letter to Carew he said he had obtained this report on the French fleet by the simple, if somewhat unorthodox, method of taking advantage of a dinner party with a *"conseilleur d'Etat"* to steal a list of the French ships and make an instant copy. He reported that the list: "being negligently thrown upon a table, I honestly stole it from thence, whilst the rest of the company were at cards and in another room, marking down the following particulars, [and] conveyed this paper [back] to the same place without being observed."[88] With the information gained from his secret coup, Mildmay observed that from this list the British government could see that the French fleet was not nearly as powerful or as well equipped as its apparent size would indicate. He pointed out that although there were twenty-seven ships in this fleet and seventeen of them, on paper, were described as "ships of the line," among these seventeen capital ships there were eight with very limited armaments that were being used as troop transports, one that was now a hospital ship, and two others that were filled with stores and ammunition.

From this information Mildmay estimated to Carew that the purpose of the remaining six fully armed ships of the line was not to engage the British fleet, but to act as a convoy for the eight troop carriers until the fleet was just off Louisbourg and the coast of the Île Royale (Cape Breton). He predicted that at this point these troop transports would then unload their soldiers to smaller craft sent out from Louisbourg, which would then transport them to other parts of the Île Royale while the main French fleet turned back for France. He said he had confirmed his conviction that Quebec was the ultimate destination of many of these soldiers from an independent report he had received that the newly appointed governor of Canada, M. de Vaudreuil, and his family would be on the Admiral's flagship, the *Parmier*. The most important message Mildmay wished to convey, however, was that the eight ships of the line used as troop carriers would be coming back lightly armed: "like empty hulks, to be made a prey of with ease. Supposing such hostilities then to have been begun in the country they are destined to as may justify us in attacking them on their return, how inexcusable it will be to let them escape!"

Among the collection of Mildmay's papers now in the Essex Record Office is a document, in his handwriting, entitled "List of Ships set sail from Brest May 3rd 1755," and as the writing seems to be hurried and not as careful and controlled as his normal script, it is possible that this may be secret copy that he made at the dinner party.[89] The list is laid out under the headings of "*Noms des Vassaux*, Times [dates] de Construction and *Nombre d'Equippage*," and it describes the tonnage, the number of cannon and the age of each ship. Mildmay had divided the list into the six fully armed, 80- to 69-gun "*Vaissaux Ligne*" (Ships of the Line), the seven 39- to 22-gun "*Fregates*" and "*Ceux n'ont que 24 Cannons*," or the eight capital ships that were being used as troop transports and had only this reduced number of guns.[90] Such advance information on the composition and the armament of the French fleet was to prove invaluable to Admiral Boscowan when the British ships *Dunkirk* and *Defiance* were able to sink the 230-ton French frigate, *le Lis*, and the 580-ton ship of the line, *l'Alcide*, on 8 June 1755 off Louisbourg. Boscowan would thus have had prior knowledge of which French ships were formidable threats and which were the "empty hulks" identified by Mildmay; however, when these two fleets actually met there was a heavy fog coming off the Grand Banks and the great majority of the French ships were, therefore, able to unload most of their soldiers and supplies before escaping back to Brest.[91]

Mildmay had now been able to justify his long-standing and passionate interest in the collection of useful information about France and with this last effort his work in Paris was indeed over. On 10 May 1755 Sir Thomas Robinson sent him an official letter of permission to leave Paris, but the permission was still granted on a provisional basis only. As the British Cabinet was concerned that France should not be given an excuse to declare that Britain was abandoning the negotiations, Sir Thomas told Mildmay that his permit to return was granted for one month: the Lords Justices (the Regency Council) were told that Lord Fitzwalter was dangerously ill, was not expected to live, and Mildmay thus had "to attend to the affairs of the family." Sir Thomas also instructed Mildmay to visit M. Rouillé and inform him of this reason: "in order that your coming away at this conjuncture may not be misunderstood as in any way affecting the Commission with which you are charged, or arising from the present situation of affairs between the two Courts."[92]

There is nothing from Mildmay's correspondence to confirm that Lord Fitzwalter was in any sudden and immediate danger in early May of 1755. If

Horace Walpole's gossip is to be believed, Fitzwalter may very well have been feeling somewhat unwell from an unwise diet, as in a letter to Sir Horace Mann on 21 December 1755 Walpole told Sir Horace: "I must mention the case of Lord Fitzwalter, which the [medical] faculty say exceeds anything known to their practice. He is past eighty-four . . . He has lived many months upon fourteen barrels of oysters and twenty bottles of port and, some think, seven bottles of brandy per week."[93] Walpole was mistaken in Lord Fitzwalter's age but, if his report has any accuracy, perhaps by the age of eighty-five Fitzwalter had decided that in a generally hard-drinking society he could consume whatever he liked. Whether or not Fitzwalter's health had been used as an excuse, after his departure on 17 May 1755 Mildmay did not return again to Paris, and he was able to look after Lord Fitzwalter at Moulsham Hall until Fitzwalter died on 29 February 1756.[94]

He did not spend these nine months rusticating in Essex, however, as from June to December 1755 he was commissioned by the British government to write a detailed history of the past five years of diplomatic negotiation. One last event in the commission's history took place after Mildmay had left Paris. On 18 May Galissonière sent De Cosne a large package that contained the manuscript of the long-awaited French memorial in reply to the British claim to Nova Scotia and St. Lucia, together with a collection of justification documents. In the letter that De Cosne wrote to Sir Thomas Robinson on the same day (18 May), he said Galissonière had also included a second copy of this memorial for Mildmay, but as the three-volume package was "too bulky for the common carrier and I have no direct means of sending it to the Earl of Holdernesse" (who was with the king in Hanover), he asked that Sir Thomas would arrange to have a messenger sent from Whitehall to collect the copies for Lord Holdernesse and William Mildmay, together with his own accompanying letter.[95]

De Cosne also told Sir Thomas that as he had discovered that the French government intended to publish this latest memorial, he found it: "out of Rule, to say no more of it," that the two French commissioners had added their own notes at the bottom of several of its pages: none of which had been shown either to him, or to Mildmay, in advance. He enclosed a copy of a letter that Galissonière had sent with this package, in which he requested that De Cosne would review the memorial and send back his observations before it was printed, but as De Cosne said he felt that to take any notice of this request would appear to be giving his consent to the contents, he asked for

Sir Thomas' instructions on this point. The wording of the letter from Galissonière that accompanied Mildmay's copy of the memorials was more revealing in its intent. His letter to Mildmay contained the same request for a critique; but with what was, doubtless, a reference to yet another series of "harsh" expressions in this French document, Galissonière specifically drew Mildmay's attention to: "the observations that we have made at the bottom of the pages of yours [your copy], in case, contrary to our intentions, we have covered those things [in such a way] that would wound [offend] your Court."[96]

The final letter in the collection of official commission correspondence is a letter from De Cosne to Sir Thomas Robinson, written on 23 May 1755. The French government obviously wished to be able to print its memorial as quickly as possible, for on 21 May Galissonière had called on De Cosne to find out whether he had yet read the manuscript, and in his letter De Cosne told Sir Thomas that he had taken this opportunity to ask Galissonière the reason why the French government wished to publish it in the first place. He said Galissonière had replied that his government was concerned about the reports that were appearing in: "the papers and writings that are, every day, published in England . . . which, he said, would gain Credit in the World and become unavoidable Prejudices against the Right of this [French] Crown, if some measures are not taken to oppose them."[97] Implicit in Galissonière's statement on this need to publish, however, is the admission that by May 1755 the French government was providing this belated memorial not as an act of diplomacy, but of politics.

During the summer and fall of 1755 the governments of both France and Britain were actively engaged in justifying their reasons why they should resort to war against each other. This kind of justification of legal rights and national honor in the waging of war was as much a vital part of international diplomacy as was an attempt to avoid a war; a successful justification could have a considerable effect on the future state alliances in that war. In this context the British naval offensive that took place off Louisbourg in July 1755 was a delicate, indeed embarrassing point for the British government, since this belligerent action had been taken without a prior declaration of war. Sir Benjamin Keene, the British ambassador in Madrid, was acutely aware that in order to guarantee Spanish neutrality it was important that he was able to counter French charges of the bad faith of British behavior. In a letter Sir Benjamin sent in July to Abraham Castres, in Lisbon, he described the diplomatic outrage of the French ambassador in Madrid, M. Duras, as a: "raree show . . . [that] got no great credit in Court or City," but he said he felt that if these accusations of British false dealings remained unchallenged, they could be dangerous.[98]

In Florence, Sir Horace Mann agreed with this assessment. He spent a large part of his letters to Horace Walpole during the summer of 1755 complaining that, as the British resident to the Court of Tuscany, he was being kept in the dark about diplomatic events elsewhere, and was thus unable to mount a proper defense to the French charges. On 16 August 1755 Sir Horace told Walpole: "it is incredible how they [the French] abuse us, which looks as if they would vent all their anger that way, unless they are waiting for answers from Spain to know what they may depend on, in hopes that upon their assertion that we are the offenders, because we have fired the first cannon at sea [in the battle off Louisbourg], that all the Bourbons will fall on us at once."[99]

The international alignment of potential allies had begun and it was vital for both governments to get their version of the history of the negotiations published as quickly as possible. Mildmay had kept very careful records during the last five years and he was now employed in London as the author of the official British statement on all these conferences and memorials. Among Mildmay's papers in the Essex Record Office is a government memorandum that was sent to him outlining how the documents were to appear in published form. It stated that all the memorials from the British side were to be presented in English, with an accompanying French translation on each page, and the edition was also to include, in a separate volume, all of the historical justifications produced by the British government in the course of preparing these memorials. In the same document bundle as this memorandum are Mildmay's copies of twenty-four of these justifications, going back to 1669, and a land grant in North America by Charles II. Mildmay's instructions further ordered that all French observations on these British justifications were to be omitted, and only the relevant clauses in the various treaties that dated from the 1713 Treaty of Utrecht were to be printed.[100]

The French commissioners were equally busy putting all their records together. Silhouette had been given the prime responsibility of preparing the work and Galissonière was put in charge of supervising the printing and distribution of the official volumes. On 2 June instructions were sent to M Auisson de Perron, director of the royal printing house at the galleries of the

Louvre, to prepare an edition of the French memoirs on Acadia and St. Lucia. He was told he had the authority to ask for copies of any documents that were held by the Ministry of the Marine and to include a copy of the Treaty of Aix-la-Chapelle.[101] M. Perron had progressed to the point that on 6 July he wrote to ask how many copies he should reserve for the treasury officials, saying he had been in touch with M. de la Galissonière for the distribution of what were now seven volumes, and he now needed an immediate decision on the number of sets he would be required to print. He was given this authority on 8 July and in the same month he issued *Mémoires des Commisaires du Roi et de ceux de sa Majesté Britanuque, sur les possessions et les droits respectifs des deux Couronnes en Amérique: avec les Actes publics et Pièces justicatives.* On 23 August he submitted his bill, which stated that the main work contained 290 pages, in three separate volumes, and as he had printed 200 of these, the cost came to 3,600 *livres.* Accompanying these three volumes were a further 336 pages, in four volumes, that contained all of the justification documents concerning the ownership of Acadia and St. Lucia, and for these he billed 4,800 *livres:* a total of 8,400 *livres* all together.[102]

When he arrived in England Mildmay had one last problem that had been caused by the political need to disguise his departure. In order to keep up the impression that he would return, he had been forced to leave most of his possessions in Paris and in early July he was still trying to be reunited with his two trunks. In a letter De Cosne wrote from Paris on 9 July, he told Mildmay that he regretted he could not do as he had been asked: "for I do not see which way I can send you your two trunks as you desire without giving suspicion of what you apprehend. . . ." What was more: "these trunks, being with me, the world would swear that it is I, as Minister [acting ambassador], am sending my goods, and to steal away afterwards, as well as knowing [they will say] that War is at hand." De Cosne promised Mildmay that he would look after these trunks with the same care he gave his own belongings, and with the immediate prospect of a war being declared, De Cosne said that he also expected to be summoned home within a short time.[103]

The present existence of the large amount of documents written both by and to Mildmay in Paris is evidence that his two trunks must have come back safely to England with De Cosne when he returned at the end of July 1755.[104] The main reason for De Cosne's letter to Mildmay was not only to reassure him about his luggage, however, but also to send him some information about a copy of the official, printed version of the latest French memorial on

St. Lucia and Acadia, first presented by Galissonière to De Cosne in draft form on 18 May. According to the information in De Cosne's letter, this copy of the official document had afterward been lent to Silhouette (presumably for his work on the writing of the French version of the commission history), but Mildmay had already told De Cosne that it was important to recover this document from Silhouette, together with the numerous "proofs" that had accompanied it, since he needed all of this material to complete his own work on the British justification.

De Cosne now informed Mildmay that he had acquired this copy of the French memorial, with its proofs, and in his letter he also demonstrated one of the technical problems experienced by eighteenth-century diplomats and their staff when he said, with some triumph, that the four, separate packets of material he was sending contained not only the printed copy of the lengthy French text, but an English translation of it. De Cosne informed Mildmay that Galissonière had only given him this official version of the memorial a few days earlier but, despite the short time available to do so, the four people who still remained at the British Embassy had been able to make this translation because: "all hands have been so diligent that it is copied . . . though it contains 270 pages—there for you!"[105] De Cosne included in these four packets an itemized list, written in French, that recorded the three memorials on the boundaries of Acadia and Nova Scotia and the four on the ownership of St. Lucia that had been produced by both sides, beginning with the first British memorial of 21 September 1750 and ending with the memorial issued by France on 24 October 1754, together with all of the supplementary maps and justifications.[106] Mildmay's official commission report was based on these memorials, on the official commission correspondence, and on his own records; this account, which included copies of the memorials themselves, was published by the British government in the winter of 1755 as *Memorials of the English and French Commissioners concerning the limits of Nova Scotia, or Acadia, and St. Lucia* (volume 1: Acadia, and volume 2: St. Lucia).[107]

In early December 1755 the French government also printed an additional summary of their justification material on Acadia in *Discussion sommaire sur les Ancienne Limittes de l'Acadie*, again published by the royal printing house in Paris,[108] and both governments circulated all of their justification reports during the spring of 1756. On 21 December 1755 M. Rouillé sent a letter to Henry Fox, minister for war, that contained a memorial addressed to George II, and he asked that Fox give it to the king.[109] It contained a summation of examples of the perceived bad faith demonstrated by the actions of the George II and his ministers toward Louis XV and the French Court, culminating in the attack by the fleet of Admiral Boscowan in April 1755, carried out in the absence of any declaration of war. The document demanded that George II make immediate reparations for these unprovoked acts of aggression by taking steps to restore all French warships and merchant ships seized by the British navy, together with their armaments and cargoes, or the French king would be forced to declare war on Britain. Rouillé also sent a copy of this memorial to the French Court with his observations, a part of which stated: "the essence of the state of the negotiation is *The authentic proofs, by which The Most Christian King is ready to prove [his claims] to the whole world (sic),*" and that the *Discussion sommaire* was the written evidence of such proofs.[110]

At the same time that Mildmay was making his contribution to the official British government publication he also wrote his own book, designed to counter the French version of events. At the beginning of January 1756 he published *A Fair Representation of His Majesty's Right to Nova Scotia and Acadia briefly stated, with an answer to the objections contained in the French Treatise entitled Discussion sommaire sur les Ancienne Limittes de l'Acadie,* and on 27 January Mildmay sent several printed copies of this book to Joseph Yorke at The Hague for Yorke's information and possible distribution. Mildmay told him: "I thought it my duty to offer a vindication of His Majesty's Right by recapitulating the proofs of it in as short a compass as is, in moderate terms, possible; observing herein the invitations of my Superiors, when they permitted me to attempt what I have the honour of submitting to your perusal." He said his book had been written to counter the adverse reports being put out by the French government (both in the *Discussion sommaire,* and in copies of the memoir by Rouillé) to: "numerous foreign courts in a very unfair manner," and if Yorke approved its contents, Mildmay asked whether: "it would be of any service to His Majesty's interests in this dispute to have this Treatise translated into any other language. They who are willing to enrich their skills and talent to the hazard of gaining by the sale of it are welcome to the Copy."[111]

Joseph Yorke replied on 3 February 1756, thanking Mildmay for his work and telling him that he found it: "very solidly and politely wrote and in a stile (*sic*) which I ever did and will approve of in public affairs . . . what you have given us is in a masterly way." Yorke said he was especially pleased with Mildmay's evidence of: "the new proofs, which I own I was surprised to find had never been produced before. . . . I shall make good use of your work and in some shape or otherwise give it to the foreign worlds [courts]."[112] There is now no evidence that Mildmay's treatise was translated for foreign distribution and the only existing copy is in English in the British Library.

A final example of the underestimation of the work of William Mildmay on the Anglo-French commission is shown both in a British Library catalogue entry, and in the extensive bibliography of contemporary imprints that Max Savelle provides in his book *The Origins of American Diplomacy*. In Savelle's comprehensive five-page list of these imprints, *A Fair Representation of His Majesty's Right to Nova Scotia* is the only one that has no named author.[113] The British Library catalogue does not identify William Mildmay as the author of this work; however, the information that Mildmay gave in the letter to Joseph Yorke on 27 January 1756 clearly indicates that this sixty-four page book—containing both the detailed progress of the British negotiating position over a period of five years and a point-by-point rejection of the claims of the French commissioners on their boundary rights in North America—was the work that Mildmay wrote in 1755, and sent a printed copy of to Joseph Yorke.

Further evidence of Mildmay's authorship of this work was confirmed by Henry Kent Causton, the editor of a nineteenth-century edition of Mildmay's book *The Method and Rules of Proceeding upon all Elections, Polls and Scrutinies at the Common Halls and Wardmotes of the City of London,* first published in 1743. Causton stated that *The Method and Rules* was reprinted three times during Mildmay's lifetime, and in his bibliographical note on Mildmay in the introduction to this fourth edition, published in 1861, he also said that that on the publication of the diplomatic justification by the French commissioners in late 1755, and called *A Summary Discussion of the Limits of Ancient Acadia:* "Mr. Mildmay immediately answered it with a concise pamphlet, of which a very large impression was speedily sold, so well was it approved by the public. This was entitled *A Fair Representation of his Majesty's Right to Nova Scotia and Acadia.*"[114]

Three months later, on 17 May 1756, Britain declared war on France. After his letter to Yorke there is nothing further in the collections of Mildmay's papers on any details of the diplomacy on which he had been engaged so completely for five years. Other than in his book *A Fair Representation*, he left no printed record of the scope and value of his negotiation activities, but the details in his unpublished letters and conference journal remain a unique account of this crucial five years of British and French diplomacy. They tell the story of a group of men—diplomats and politicians—who slowly and almost inexorably allowed themselves to be driven into a war that few of them wanted, and that could, possibly, have been avoided.

Mildmay was a bureaucrat who was charged with carrying out the orders of his government masters, but, like many talented civil servants, he had his own views on the best way to implement his instructions. With his first-hand experience of the ongoing events at each conference, his growing appreciation of the personalities of his opponents, and above all, with his sense of the timing needed to keep up the momentum, he gradually built up a clear view of what was required from the British side. He sincerely believed that an honorable compromise by both governments could achieve success. Unfortunately, a legacy of unresolved wars fought between Britain and France over the past century, the deep suspicions of the colonists—both French and British—about the true intentions of their respective governments, and the ambition, antagonism, and personal agenda of certain politicians within the British Cabinet and the French Court all combined to frustrate Mildmay's determined attempts and were ultimately to decide that the only outcome was yet another war. The failure of this commission was neither inevitable nor designed in advance, and it is arguable that once William Shirley had been removed in May 1752, the negotiations to ratify the Peace Treaty of Aix-la-Chapelle might have stood a chance of success if the process had been left solely to the ingenuity of the four remaining commissioners.

When Lord Fitzwalter died in February 1756, Mildmay inherited Fitzwalter's considerable Essex estates, and in 1765 he was knighted and became Sir William Mildmay, Bart.[115] There is one last piece of evidence, however, that in his new life as an Essex landowner he had not lost all interest in his previous work. On 27 August 1763 Mildmay wrote a letter to Lord Egremont, secretary of state for the Southern Department in the new government of George III. Four years earlier, in 1759, the British had acquired the territorial right to most of North America, and on 10 February 1763 a peace treaty had been signed in Paris that laid out the boundaries of a new political world; yet six months after this treaty had been signed, Mildmay still appeared to be concerned about claims that the French government continued to make on the limits of the Channel and the North Sea.

He pointed out to Lord Egremont that having been one of the British commissioners in Paris from 1750 to 1755, and responsible for:

> among other points, the mutual demands between the two Crowns on account of the prizes taken at Sea after the time taken for the cessation of hostilities in the British and Northern Channels, according to the terms of the treaty of Aix-la-Chapelle, I think it is my duty to inform your Lordship that in the course of that negotiation the French Commissaries offered several proposals injurious to His Majesty's undoubted right to the Sovereignty of those Seas.[116]

In his letter Mildmay told Lord Egremont he that had already spoken to Lord Bute on this subject and as Bute had referred him to the southern secretary, he now asked Egremont whether his informed historical contribution might be useful, both to his Lordship and to the British government. If Egremont should feel that Mildmay's detailed knowledge could, in fact, be helpful, he said: "I shall be proud to await on your Lordship any time you shall be pleased to appoint for that purpose." A week before Mildmay's letter was written, however, Lord Egremont died unexpectedly of a heart attack on Sunday, 21 April 1763, and after his death there was a hiatus of over a week while George III decided whom to appoint as the new secretary of state for the Southern Department.[117] The king finally, somewhat reluctantly, decided on George Greville, but in the confusion caused by this change of minister, it is not surprising that neither in Mildmay's papers, nor in the documents from the Foreign Office correspondence, is there any existing record of a reply to Mildmay's offer of assistance.

# Epilogue

LORD FITZWALTER DIED ON 29 February 1756. His will instructed that after the payment of his debts, funeral expenses, and bequests to his servants, to Lord and Lady Holdernesse, to Lord and Lady Ancram, and to his grand-daughters—Lady Amelia Darcy and Lady Louisa Kerr—the residue of his estate was to go to William Mildmay, who thus became the Lord of the manors of Chelmsford and Moulsham and the owner of Fitzwalter's London property, Schomberg House.[1] The Seven Years' War began three months after Mildmay had moved into Moulsham Hall and he spent several of these years as a captain in the militia and as the commanding officer of the regiment that guarded French prisoners of war in Winchester Castle. In recognition of his military service, in February 1765 he was created a baronet and served as sheriff of Essex in the same year.[2] He was also given important recognition by his legal peers; in 1758 he was elected a bencher of the Middle Temple and in 1768 he was nominated to be that year's "reader," or a senior member of the Bench who is given the distinguished responsibility of describing and clarifying a legal statute before the assembled Middle Temple Parliament.[3]

When Mildmay returned from France in 1755 he brought back the considerable quantity of collected papers and notes he had accumulated over a period of nearly seven years, and from 1756 to 1765 he used this material to write and then to publish four books. The first, *A Fair Representation of His Majesty's Right to Nova Scotia and Acadia* (1756), was his report of the diplomatic negotiations on which he had been engaged for five years. In his second, *The Police of France* (1763), he gave a detailed description of the centralized legal and regulatory authority used by the French Crown in the mid-eighteenth century to control the conduct of society. The third, *An Account of the Southern Maritime Provinces of France* (1764), was the economic survey of the provinces of Languedoc and Provence that he had made during his travels there in 1748–49, and written with particular attention to the vulnerability of these two provinces to attack in any future war. The last, *The Laws of England in Relation to Trade Examined by the Maxims and Principles of*

*Trade in General* (1765), contained his views on the advantage that could be gained by British merchants in examining the methods used by their European trading rivals. Copies of the first editions of all of these books are now in the British Library, and two of them—*The Police of France* and *An Account of the Southern Maritime Provinces*—were reprinted in 1811.[4]

Now that he had become a major landowner Mildmay had the financial ability to organize and to direct important projects, unhampered by any superior authority, and Chelmsford and Moulsham benefited considerably from the benevolent activities of their new Lord of the manor. He rebuilt the Moulsham almshouses that had originally been established by Sir Thomas Mildmay in 1620, extended the Chelmsford Grammar School that had been founded by Sir Walter Mildmay in 1552, and fought for the interests of Chelmsford in his successful opposition to the attempt by the town of Colchester to acquire the prestigious and highly lucrative County Assizes. In an effort to reduce the cost of hauling grain and coal between Chelmsford and Maldon, in 1762 he also recommended that the Chelmer River should be dredged and embanked to allow barge, rather than road, transport. He collected a group of interested landowners and after four years of planning the work, surveying the proposed embankments, collecting the necessary financial backing, and petitioning parliament, on 6 June 1766 Sir William Mildmay and his backers were able to have their application passed in "An Act for the Navigation of the River Chelmer." Mildmay and his friends, as large-scale grain growers, would benefit from cheaper transport, but there had been some considerable opposition, especially from local carters, from the owners of fish weirs, and from Maldon merchants with a financial interest in the status quo. When the bill was finally approved the combined efforts of Bamber Gascoyne (member of parliament for Midhurst, Sussex), John Strutt (Gascoyne's friend and the owner of a large grain mill on the river), and the Mayor and Council of Maldon were strong enough to have a clause inserted that was so restrictive it ultimately killed Sir William's navigation scheme.[5]

For the last four years of his life Sir William was involved in a fierce dispute over the location of the new county jail. In 1767 the Essex justices of the peace complained to parliament about the poor condition of the jail at Chelmsford and in 1768 a Commons Committee tabled a proposal to have this prison rebuilt. Rather than erecting the new building on the present, riverbank site, however, the Committee initially recommended a location in the marketplace opposite Shire Hall: the place where criminal trials were held. This might seem a practical solution to the serious problem of transporting the Assize prisoners through Chelmsford, but it was pointed out by a delegation of townspeople, led by Sir William, that for several reasons the chosen site was unsuitable. They told the Committee that the prison and its prisoners would spread disease, that its demands for water would disrupt the already overtaxed town water supply, and finally, that the marketplace at Chelmsford was not only the hub of activity for the town and surrounding countryside, but was the location of most of the inns where the gentry and the respectable inhabitants gathered during the Assizes. The fact that Sir William and several members of his group also owned the land by the river, while some of the market site proponents had a financial interest in that location, was not entirely coincidental in this dispute.

After three years of fierce debate, counterproposals, competing surveys and building designs, parliamentary hearings, and substantial legal expense incurred by both sides, Sir William and his supporters succeeded in having the riverbank site approved in "An Act for Rebuilding the Common Gaol (*sic*) of the County of Essex," passed by the Commons on 28 March 1770 and enacted by the Lords on 11 April. The promoters of the marketplace, however, did not give up. The Journals of the House of Commons record that a year later, in the beginning of May 1771, Sir William Mildmay was an active member of a delegation that petitioned the Crown to have this act enforced and requested that a beginning be made to the construction of the jail.[6]

In 1772 a large and imposing prison was finally erected on the banks of the Chelmer, next to Moulsham Bridge, but Sir William did not live to see the work begun. In the early summer of 1771 he went to Bath for his health, and died there on 8 August 1771 at the age of sixty-six. His body was brought back to Chelmsford and buried in the Fitzwalter family tomb by his widow Anne, Lady Mildmay, but even at his death Sir William was still initiating improvements to his town. Part of the water supply of Chelmsford ran in underground pipes from Burgess Well to a conduit near the market, but these pipes were in such bad condition that the system lost water through leaks into nearby cellars. In his will Sir William left a donation for the installation of new water pipes in the center of the town.[7]

William Mildmay's life spanned four reigns. Born in Surat, India, in the beginning of the reign of Queen Anne, he was educated during the reign of George I, spent his working life under George II, and died a knight and wealthy Essex landowner in the eleventh year of the reign of George III, five years before the outbreak of the American Revolution. None of the wealth and social position he eventually achieved was apparent at the beginning of his life. In 1705 Charles Mildmay (Baron Fitzwalter), Benjamin Mildmay (Charles' bachelor brother), and William's father (William Mildmay senior) all stood between William and any inheritance of the Chelmsford and Moulsham estates.

William Mildmay senior died when his son was five, and in 1726 Charles Mildmay died childless, but two years earlier his brother Benjamin had married Frederica, dowager countess of Holdernesse, and in 1725 Benjamin and Frederica had a son. For William, now twenty-one, this would appear to have ended the matter, but in April 1727 this child also died, and although Frederica had several more pregnancies during the following eight years, they all ended in miscarriages. As the last surviving male heir in the direct line, William could now expect to inherit the Mildmay estates but it took until February 1756, and the death of the eighty-six-year-old Lord Fitzwalter, before William Mildmay, at the age of fifty-one, was finally able to enjoy his inheritance.

The letters, journals, and reports that he wrote in the early 1750s reveal the characteristics of a patient man who had already waited for a long time, and with some trepidation, to achieve his goal. Until Mildmay became the owner of the manors of Moulsham and Chelmsford he was outwardly circumspect, deferential, and careful not to appear to be anticipating his change of status. His letters to Fitzwalter show that he genuinely liked the old man, but whether he appreciated the lectures on his behavior from Lord Ancram, Fitzwalter's son-in-law, or indeed from any of the other members of Fitzwalter's household, is another matter that his guarded words do not reveal.

At very rare intervals there is a hint in the tone of Mildmay's letters that there was a price to be paid for this patient concealment, and in an unusually personal letter to Lord Fitzwalter, sent on 12 July 1752, he demonstrated both his anxiety, and how completely his behavior was ruled by his patron's requirements. With uncharacteristic emotion, he assured Fitzwalter there was absolutely no foundation to the gossip that his sister Mary had warned him was circulating in London concerning his courtship of a young English visitor to Paris. He noted that he had visited a Mr. and Mrs. Colebrooke and Miss Shadwell, "a companion to the latter," simply as a courtesy: a part of his diplomatic responsibility to entertain English visitors to Paris. He continued: "This lady [Miss Shadwell] was, long before I knew her, engaged if not married to another. Add to this that her departure from Paris has broke off all acquaintance, nor do I believe it is probable that I shall ever see her again as long as I live."[8]

In case Fitzwalter suspected that Miss Shadwell had, in fact, been something more than just a diplomatic chore, and anxious to repair any possible damage, in this letter Mildmay gave Fitzwalter his promise that he would never think of marrying without first obtaining Fitzwalter's consent to his choice. Indeed, he went further; this prospective wife, he wrote, must be able join with him to care for Fitzwalter with equal gratitude and respect, and "if such a one I can find, or rather if your Lordship would recommend such a one to me, I am ready to take her to wife with my best endeavours to propagate our name."

Mildmay was unable to return on a visit to England until May 1754, however in February of that year he was still assuring Lord Fitzwalter: "I have neither wife, nor mistress, though it is the fashion here to have both." Until this correspondence from Paris ends, in May 1755, there is no further mention of a possible wife, but when William did marry it was not for love. He married his cousin Anne, sole heiress to the Mildmay estate of Shawford, in Hampshire, in a strategic alliance within the family that was in the best Mildmay tradition. Unfortunately, this custom of the intermarriage of cousins in order to assemble larger family estates had been practiced too often; over the last century there had been a progressive failure of heirs, and particularly of sons.[9]

Sir William and Lady Mildmay had no children, and although the Chelmsford and Moulsham estates were inherited by Anne's niece, Jane St. John Mildmay, she chose to live at her husband's estate in Hampshire. The death of Sir William in 1771, and that of his wife in 1796, ended a family history that had continued, unbroken, in Chelmsford for nearly three hundred years but as the last of the Mildmays of Essex, Sir William had proved himself an admirable representative of his family. Beyond his benefit to the citizens of Chelmsford, however, in his diplomatic work he served his country well and, through his writings, he is a major contributor to future historical scholarship. It is hoped that with this book, and its detailed examination of his working papers, William Mildmay will now be seen both as a important source for the study of European and North American eighteenth-century history and as the author of an invaluable but, until now, completely over-looked record of the crucial diplomatic attempt that was made to prevent the outbreak of the Seven Years' War.

ENGLISH AND FRENCH MAPS ON FOLLOWING PAGES—*Remarks on the French memorials concerning the Limits of Acadia, printed at the Royal printing House at Paris* (Printed for Thomas Jeffries, Geographer to his Royal highness the Prince of Wales. London: (1754) B.L.


THE FRENCH MAP:

Limits proposed by the English Commissaries, the 21st of September 1750 and the 11th of January, 1751, exclusive of cape Breton, with short strokes - - - - -

Limits of Acadia and its Banks, by the treaty of Utrecht, marked thus + + + + +

District of Port Royal, by the same treaty, enclosed with a strong line ══════

Limits of Nova Scotia, as granted to Sir William Alexander, the 10th of September, 1621, with dots • • • • •

Cromwell's grant to La Tour, Crown and Temple, on the 7th of August, 1656. ━━━━━━

La Tour's government in 1638, shaded perpendicularly. |||||||

Charnesay's government in 1678, shaded obliquely. \\\\\\\\

The government of Denys in 1654, shaded horizontally. ≡≡≡

The Country restored (to France) (*sic*) by the treaty of Breda, includes all granted by Cromwell, with the country of Mirlega to Canseau.


THE ENGLISH MAP

Nova Scotia. or Arcadia, as claimed by the English Commissioners, under the Treaty of Utrecht in 1713—short strokes  - - - - -

Nova Scotia as granted to William Alexander, 1612, and divided by him into two provinces—Alexander and Caledonia—all to the east of this line • • • • •

Acadia according to Champlain, from 1603 to 1629, the same as Nova Scotia (excepting) (*sic*) Cape Breton, with the country west of the Penobscot (Pentagoet) river, the small pricked line • • • • •

La Tour's government in 1683 marked thus + + + + +

The Etchemin coast, according to Champlain and Denys, shaded obliquely \\\\\\\\

Acadia proper, according to the triparte division, mentioned by Charlevoix, upright strokes |||||||


Note: The French Map is an exact copy from the French, and both are drawn to the same scale with it.

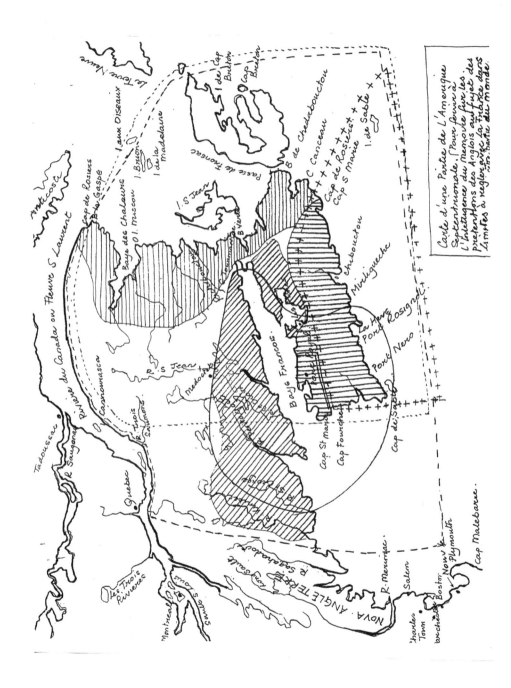

Carte d'une Partie de l'Amérique
Septentrionale. (Pour servir à
l'intelligence du mémoire sur les
prétentions des Anglois au sujet des
Limites à réglergxec. la France dans
cette partie du monde.

Le Terre Neuve

I aux Oiseaux

I. de Cap Breton

O Cap Breton

Passe de Fronsac

I. Bruon

I du la madelaine

B. de Chedabouctou

C Canceau

Cap de Rosiers

Cap S. Marie

I. de Sable

Anticosti

Cap de Rosiers

Baye de Gaspé

O I. Miscou

Baye des Chaleurs

I. S. Jean

Pivière du Canada ou Fleuve S. Laurent

Chibouctou

Mirliqueche

La Herve

Port Rosignol

Port Nero

R. S. Jean

Medoctek

Baye Francois

Cap St marie

Cap Fourchu

Cap de Sable

Tadoussac

R. Saugenay

R. Trois
Saumons

Caconnasca

Quebec

Cap Malebarre

Cap Plymouth

R. Merrimac

Salem

Nous York

fond Sud

R. Seacokabou

NOVA ANGLETERRE

Montreal

Sault S. Louis

Les Trois Rivieres

Charles
Town

burcheston Boston

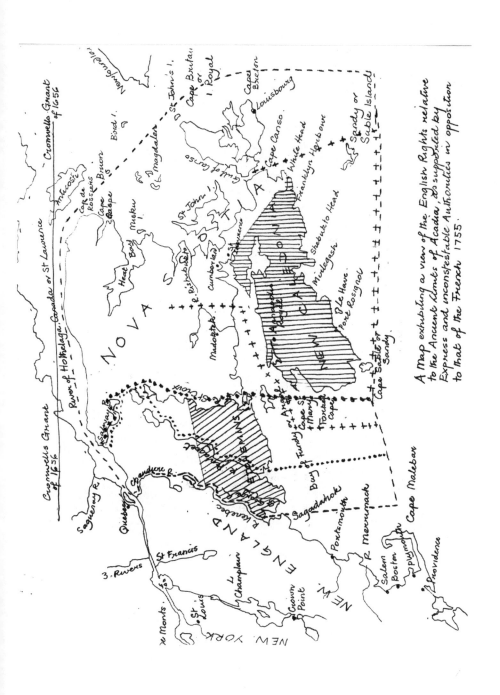

A Map exhibiting a view of the English Rights relative to the Ancient Limits of Acadia, as supported by Express and incontestable Authorities in opposition to that of the French 1755.

A room in the house on the rue St. André des-Arts, Paris, where Mildmay lived from 1750-1755 (presently a part of the Lyceé Fenelon)

Enid Robbie.
February 2000.

Enid Robbie. 1942.

THE ALMSHOUSES BUILT BY SIR WILLIAM MILDMAY AT MOULSHAM, IN 1758.

Enid Robbie
1993.

MOULSHAM HALL, ESSEX IN THE 18TH CENTURY (SINCE DEMOLISHED)
DRAWN FROM A CONTEMPORARY ENGRAVING IN: *The Account Books of Benjamin Mildmay, Earl Fitzwalter*, BY A.C. EDWARDS. (1977) PAGE 33.

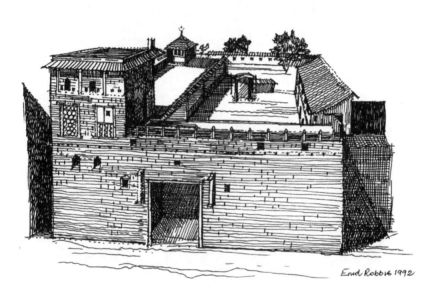

The English Factory at Surat in 1638, from the engraving facing page 226 in *A Voyage to Surat in The Year 1689*, edited by H.G. Rawlingson (1929)

THE MEMORIAL TO LORD FITZWALTER, THE COUNTESS FITZWATER, SIR WILLIAM
MILDMAY AND ANN, LADY MILDMAY, IN CHELMSFORD CATHEDRAL.

# Appendix 1. The Inscription on the Fitzwalter Tomb in Chelmsford Cathedral

HERE LYETH BENJAMIN MILDMAY: EARL FITZWALTER, WHO HAVING MANY YEARS SERVED HIS COUNTRY IN SEVERAL GREAT OFFICES OF STATE WITH DIGNITY AND INTEGRITY, DIED FEBRUARY 29$^{TH}$ 1756, AGED 86. HE INHERITED THE BARONIES OF FITZWALTER, EGREMONT, BOTETOFT AND BURNELS FROM SIR HENRY MILDMAY, HIS GREAT GRANDFATHER, SON OF SIR THOMAS MILDMAY, WHO MARRIED IN 1580 LADY FRANCIS, ONLY DAUGHTER AND HEIR OF HENRY EARL OF SUSSEX, IN WHOM THESE BARONIES IN FEE WERE VESTED. HE MARRIED IN 1724 FREDERICA, COUNTESS DOWAGER OF HOLDERNESS, BY WHOM HE HAS ONE SON WHO DIED AN INFANT. HE WAS CREATED EARL FITZWALTER AND VISCOUNT HARWICH IN 1730, BUT DYING WITHOUT ISSUE, DEVISED HIS ESTATE TO WM. MILDMAY ESQR., HIS NEAREST RELATIVE IN THE MALE LINE, BY WHOM IN GRATITUDE THIS MONUMENT IS ERECTED.

HERE ALSO LYETH FREDERICA COUNTESS FITZWALTER, WIFE OF THE SAID EARL, A LADY OF EXCELLENT ACCOMPLISHMENTS, EMINENT VIRTUES AND MOST NOBLE BIRTH, WHO DIED AUGUST 7$^{TH}$ 1751, AGED 63. SHE WAS THE DAUGHTER OF MINEHARDT DUKE OF SCHOMBERG, COUNT OF THE ROMAN EMPIRE, BY THE LADY CHARLOTTE, DAUGHTER OF CHARLES LEWIS, ELECTOR PALATINE. BY HER FIRST HUSBAND SHE HAD ISSUE ROBERT EARL OF HOLDERNESS, WHO SUCCEEDED TO HIS FATHER'S HONOURS IN 1721, AND LADY CAROLINE, WHO MARRIED WM. EARL OF ANCRAM.

HERE ALSO LIE THE ABOVE MENTIONED SIR WM. MILDMAY, BART., OF MOULSHAM HALL AND ANNE, HIS WIDOW, DAUGHTER OF HUMPHREY MILDMAY ESQR, OF SHAWFORD, HANTS.

# Appendix 2.

Extract from a letter by Lord Albemarle (British ambassador to France) to Lord Holdernesse (secretary of state for the Southern Department), dated 4 April 1753, giving Albemarle's opinion of the members of the French king's Court and Council. B.L. Leeds Papers, vol. 134, Egerton 3457, f. 68.

"Your Lordship desires to know the <u>Composition of this Court, with whom power and influence is really lodged</u> (*sic* underline). This, in the second particular, is a very difficult task to answer. The first is easy. What appears to us is a Mistress in high credit, almost absolute, but with many enemies, jealous of her influence. At the head of them the Royal Family, without any exception. A Council composed of nine persons, six in places, three with pensions and a few favourite companions of the King's amusement, all (except the Prince de Conti and the Duke de Richelieu) (sic brackets), attached to Madame de Pompadour, to whom the members of the Council pay their respects with assiduity, and who are ill or well with her according to their readyness, or rather exactness, to execute her commands. But the *Garde des Sceaux* (Machault) is looked upon to be of the first rank, as he has the disposition of the money, which he never refuses her.

"The Ministers differ frequently among themselves. D'Argenson (*comte* d'Argenson, Minster for War) and Machault are at the Head of the two principal Cabals and daily trye to turn each other out. Some changes have been talked of amongst the others, but these rumours have soon vanished. It has been said that Maurepas was to displace Rouillé (Minister of Marine), that St. Contest (the Foreign Minister) was to make way for Courteil, one of the *Intendants* of Finance. I wish to God this report was true, but I never gave credit to either, or else I would have informed your Lordship of it.

"The Chancellor (Lamoignon) is a heavy, sleepy idiot. The Marechal de Noailles's quality, rank and age gives him more freedom of speech and liberty than any of the others presume to take. This is all I can say relating to the powers and influence of the individuals comprising the Government of this country, which, I own, is no satisfactory answer to your question, but it is, I assure you, the best that can be given by anybody . . ."

# Appendix 3. The Family Tree of the Waterson/Bonnell Family

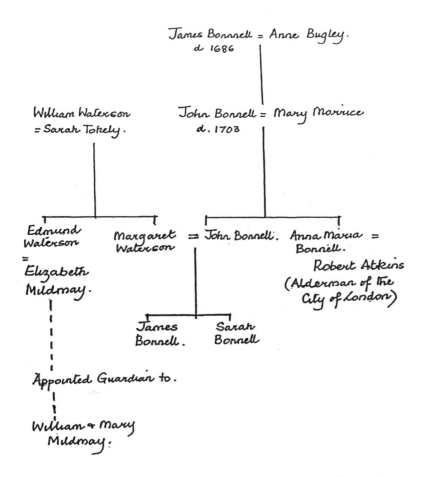

James Bonnell = Anne Bugley.
d 1686

William Waterson = Sarah Tokely.

John Bonnell = Mary Morrice
d. 1703

Edmund Waterson = Elizabeth Mildmay.

Margaret Waterson = John Bonnell.

Anna Maria Bonnell. = Robert Atkins (Alderman of the City of London)

James Bonnell.    Sarah Bonnell

Appointed Guardian to.

William & Mary Mildmay.

* : From information supplied to the Essex Record Office by Mr Herbert Hudson, June 1947 in E.R.O. Mildmay Papers D/DM. L2/2.

= Margery Everard.

y = Agnes Read of High Easter

lliam of = Elizabeth
ungfield | Paschell
1570

John = Francis
of Terling Raynbow.
d 1580

Sir Walter = Mary
(Chancellor to    Walsingham
Queen Elizabeth    d 1577
d 1589.

3 other
daughters

Sir Thomas. = Agnes Winthrop
d 1612      daughter of Adam
             Winthrop of Groten

Sir Thomas = Margaret
d.w.i.      Whitall.

Sir Anthony
= Grace
Sharington.

Humphrey = Mary Capel
of Danbury
Place

Mary = Francis Fane
1st Earl of Westmorland.

William = Margaret Hervey
a  d before     of Marks.
   1612

Anthony    Sir Henry    = Alice
           of Shawford  Halliday
           d 1664

Sir Humphrey = Jane   John   2 others
d 1692     Crofes.        is.1d

Sir Thomas = Mary
d 1657      Enniey

Carew Mildmay = Dorothy
of Marks      Gerrard
d 1676

William.   Henry of = Alice
           Shawford  Brimstone
           d 1704

John
= Mary
Bancroft
d.w.i.

Mary = Thomas
      Duckett.

William of = Sibilla
Springfield   Palmer

Francis = Mathew
Hervey    Honeywell.
d 1703    d 1717

Halliday of = Alice Bawden
Shawford
d 1734

William = Sarah
ent of the   Wilcox
ust India Co.)
d 1715.

Carew Hervey = Anne Barret -
of Marks      Leonard
d 1758

Carew Hervey of
Marks  d 1784
d.w.i.

1726
Humphrey = Letitia Mildmay of Shawford
d 1761      d 1749

1756
Sir William = Ann Mildmay
Mildmay of    d 1796
Moulsham
d 1771 w.i.

Carew Hervey of Shawford = Jane Pescod
d 1768                      d 1799

1786
Sir Henry Paulet St. = Jane
John of Dogmersfield | Mildmay
Park, Hampshire      d 1857
d 1808
(took the name of St John
Mildmay in 1786)

Ann.    Letitia.

Sir Henry Carew St. John
Mildmay
d 1848

The Rev. Anthony St.
John Mildmay
(Rector of Chelmsford)
d 1878

14 other children

Sir Henry Bouverie Paulet
St. John Mildmay
d 1902

Sir Henry Paulet
St. John Mildmay
d 1916

Sir Gerald Shaw - Lefevre St. John Mildmay
d 1928

# Appendix 4. The Mildmay Family Tree

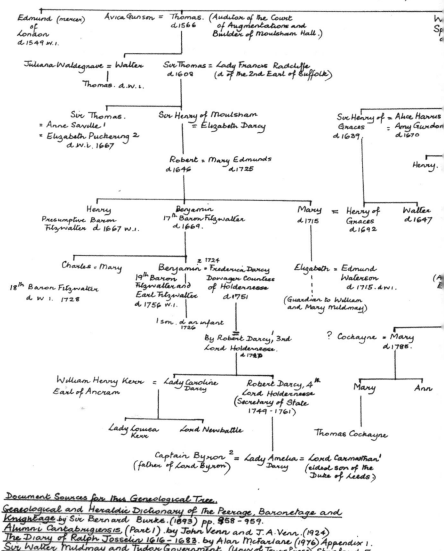

Walter Mildma
(Bailiff)

Thomas. Mildm
(mercer) d 1551.

Edmund (mercer) of London d 1549 w.i. — Avica Gunson = Thomas. d 1566 (Auditor of the Court of Augmentations and Builder of Moulsham Hall.)

Juliana Waldegrave = Walter — Thomas. d.w.i.

Sir Thomas = Lady Frances Radcliffe d 1608 (d of the 2nd Earl of Suffolk)

Sir Thomas. = Anne Saville 1 = Elizabeth Puckering 2 d.w.i. 1667

Sir Henry of Moulsham = Elizabeth Darcy

Sir Henry of Graces d 1639 = Alice Harris = Amy Gurdon d 1670

Henry.

Robert = Mary Edmunds d 1646 d 1725

Henry Presumptive Baron Fitzwalter d 1667 w.i.

Benjamin 17th Baron Fitzwalter d 1669.

Mary d 1715 = Henry of Graces d 1692

Walter d 1647

Charles = Mary

18th Baron Fitzwalter d w i. 1728

z 1724
Benjamin = Frederica Darcy 19th Baron Fitzwalter and Earl Fitzwalter d 1756 w.i. Dowager Countess of Holdernesse d 1751

Elizabeth = Edmund Waterson d 1715. d w i. (Guardian to William and Mary Mildmay)

1 son. d an infant 1726

By Robert Darcy, 3rd Lord Holdernesse. d 1721

? Cockayne = Mary d 1786.

William Henry Kerr Earl of Ancram = Lady Caroline Darcy

Robert Darcy, 4th Lord Holdernesse (Secretary of State 1749-1761)

Mary       Ann

Lady Louisa Kerr       Lord Newbattle

Thomas Cockayne

Captain Byron 2 (father of Lord Byron) = Lady Amelia Darcy = Lord Carmarthen 1 (eldest son of the Duke of Leeds)

Document Sources for this Geneological Tree.
Geneological and Heraldic Dictionary of the Peerage, Baronetage and Knightage by Sir Bernard Burke. (1893) pp. 958-959.
Alumni Cantabrigiensis, (Part 1) by John Venn and J.A.Venn. (1924)
The Diary of Ralph Josselin 1616-1683. by Alan McFarlane (1976) Appendix 1.
Sir Walter Mildmay and Tudor Government, (Univ of Texas Press) Stanford E Lemburg (1984) p. 311.
Sir Humphrey Mildmay: Royalist Gentleman. Ralph Phillip Lee. (1947)
The Accounts Book of Benjamin Mildmay: Earl Fitzwalter. A.C.Edwards (1977)
The Sleepers and the Shadows. Part 1. Hilda Grieve. (1988)
The Mildmay Papers: The Essex Record office. Chelmsford.
Feet of Fines for Essex. Vol. 4. edited by Mark Fitch and H. Reaney (1963)

# Appendix 5.

MEMORANDUM BY WILLIAM MILDMAY ON THE COMMODITY PRICES HE
RECORDED IN MONTPELLIER AND IN LANGUEDOC IN 1748–49.

E.R.O. Mildmay Papers, D/DM, 01/28.

*Prices of provisions in Montpellier.*

|  | *Livres* | *sous* | *deniers.* |
|---|---|---|---|
| Beef, per pound | 0 | 4 | 6 |
| Mutton, per pound | 0 | 5 | 6 |
| Pork, per pound | 0 | 8 | 0 |
| Lamb, per pound | 0 | 6 | 0 |
| Veal, per pound | 0 | 8 | 0 |
| Bread. . . . | 0 | 2 | 0 |
| Refined Sugar . . | 1 | 4 | 6 |
| Common Sugar . . | 0 | 15 | 0 |
| Butter. . . . |  | 12 | 0 |
| A Hare . . . | 2 | 10 | 0 |
| A Rabbit. . |  | 18 | 0 |
| A Partridge. . | 1 | 5 | 0 |
| A Fowl. . | 1 | 0 | 0 |
| A Chicken. . | 0 | 15 | 0 |
| A Pigeon. . | 0 | 15 | 0 |
| A Turkey. . | 2 | 0 | 0 |

Price of ploughing land with an oxen     3 *livres* a day
A Day labourer in Winter, without victuals,     22 *livres* a day
In Harvest or Vintage time     25 *livres* a day

Price of Land in Languedoc
An acre, or *Quartiere* or *Septiere*, which will demand 90 *(sic)* pd. [pound] in
seed, costs 100 *livres*.

An acre planted in vineyard costs 130 *livres* p. [per acre].
Mulberry trees, if large, will yield one with another, 40 *livres* per annum.
Land of 1000 *livres* per annum, if noble and exempt from the *taille*, will cost 3000, but if subject to the *taille*, without privileges, will cost 2400 *livres*.

The *taille* is imposed on the value, be it more or less, of the land, divided into *dioceses*, each *diocese* into communities.
General impositions about 4 to 5 *livres* in 20
A Gentleman, if he has no land, yet pays *capitation*.
If he has 20,000 *livres* rent he pays 400–500 [*livres*] *capitation*.
A merchant worth 100,000 *livres* pays about 60 livres *capitation*
Men pay 20 *sols* a year *capitation*.

The Province (Languedoc) pays for the :

| | |
|---|---|
| *Taille* to the King, yearly. | 3 million [*livres*] |
| *Capitation*. | 1 mill. 600,000 |
| For the *Dixième*, compounded. | 2 mill. |
| | 6 mill. 600,000 |

The Province is at present 80 millions [of *livres*] in debt, for the most of which they pay interest at 5 per cent, but for the other moiety from 3 to 2 and a half per cent.
The Province has a revenue every year of 800,000 *livres* by tax on meat and for the sale of wine in public houses.
Its riches consist of the manufacture of cloths which are made for the Levant and Turkey, and comes to 20 million [*livres*] per year.
The silk produced by the mulberry trees comes to 5 millions [of *livres*].

The City of Montpellier
There is a manufacture of Verdegrease in which they annually make about 600,000 pounds of Verdegrease and employ there about 1800 *quintals* of copper.[1]
There is likewise a manufacture of woolen quilts for beds, which brings in near 2 millions [of *livres*]. Also a manufacture of diminties, (*sic*) made with cotton, which brings in about 100,000 *livres* per year.

The King takes from the port of Sette (*sic*, Sète) by duties, about 12 million [*livres*].

Montpellier pays its proportion of *capitation, Dixieme,* 80,000 [*livres*] per year. It owes 300,000 [*livres*]. It gets, by its revenues on weight and measures and upon the entry of grain and wine, 25,000 *livres*.

# Appendix 6.

Mildmay's Lists of Information on the French Economy

E.R.O. Mildmay Papers, D\DM, 01\28.

*An Account of the Revenue of France. Consisting of the Domaines, Aydes, Gabelles, as they are termed, Extracted from the Accounts of Monsieur Fonceville, one of the Forty General Farmers.*

This general farm is let for the term of this year, which expired in 1748, at the general rent of 91,083 *livres*, besides 300,000 *livres* payable at different times during the term. On these conditions the Farmers General are entitled to the sale of all the salt and tobacco vended and distributed throughout the Kingdom, paying the proprietor for the salt at the several *Salines*, or Salt Pits: 4 *livres* for each *minot* of salt, and selling the same at the price hereafter mentioned in the following districts.

|  | *Livres* |
|---|---|
| Provence, Marseilles and Arles. Per. *minot* | 15- |
| Avignon and Dauphiny, from 20 to | 21- |
| Lyons and thereabouts | 27- |
| Vivarez | 20- |
| Forez, from 27 to | 28- |
| Ville Franche, from 27 to | 28- |
| Maconois | 29- |
| Brest | 28- |
| Languedoc | 20- |
| Generality of Paris | 40- |

The Revenues from Tobacco arises by the Licences granted for the sale and distribution thereof throughout the Kingdom, the Licence duty being proportioned to the quality each one sells in a year, raised and diminished according to the increase or decrease of the sale by each particular trader. These two Revenues from the salt and tobacco tax are distinguished under the denomination of the *Gabelle* and annually yield 70,900,000 *livres*.

The other Revenue arising from the *Domaines*, being the rents due to the Crown, and the *Aydes*, being the Inland duties upon the sale of Wines and several other commodities. These are fermed (*sic*) as above, at the annual payment of 20,183,000 *livres*, clear money, payed to the King, after which the General Farmers, by letting the same to under Farmers, make a clear gain to themselves of 27,471,000 *livres* during the term, as appears in the following recapitulation.

*An Account of what is raised by the under Farmers upon the Domaines.*

| | |
|---|---:|
| Cities and Generalities of Paris, Bordeaux and Pau. | 2,867,000 |
| Flanders, Hainault and Artois | 100,000 |
| Tours, Bourges and Moulins | 957,000 |
| Bretagne | 1,150.000 |
| Toulouse, Montpellier, Montauban and Roussillon | 1,333,000 |
| Franche Comte, Dijon and Riom | 1,164.000 |
| Poitiers, Limoges and La Rochelle | 815,000 |
| Amiens, Soissons, Chalons, Metz and Sedan | 1,216,000 |
| Provence, Dauphiny and Lyons | 1,290,000 |
| Rouen and Alençon | 1,184,000 |
| Orleans | 343,000 |
| Total of the Amount of the *Domaines* (*livres*) | 12,416,000 |

*An Account of what the Farmers General raise by the Aydes.*

| | |
|---|---:|
| Amiens and Soissons | 2,060,000 |
| Paris | 1,350,000 |
| Chalons and District | 1,550,000 |
| Caen | 1,112,000 |
| Orleans and Montargis | 750,000 |
| Tours | 1,620,000 |

| | |
|---|---:|
| Poitiers and La Rochelle | 1,420,000 |
| Lyons, Bourges and Moulins | 1,060,000 |
| Alençon and District | 690,000 |
| Rouen | 1,630,000 |
| Inspectors of the *Boucheries* | 750,000 |
| Imposts and Billets, Bretagne | 820,000 |
| Tallow, Fermed | 190,000 |
| Stamp and Mark from Iron | 320,000 |
| Stamp and Mark from Gold and Silver | 400,000 |
| Total of the *Aydes (livres)* | 15,055,000 |

| | |
|---|---:|
| *Gabelles* | 70,900,000 |
| *Domaines* | 12,416,000 |
| *Aydes* | 15,055,000 |
| Raised *(livres)* | 98,371,000 |
| Payed to the King | 91,083,000 |
| Annual to the Farmers | 7,288,000 |

*A General Account of all the Revenue of France.*

|  | Livres |
|---|---:|
| The Farms of the *Gabelle, Aydes* and *Domaines* | 91,083,000 |

Capitation, *Dixième, Don Gratuit* of the Several
Provinces, *Don Gratuit* of the Clergy, Sale of
Offices, Duties of the Exports and Imports.
In Total amount to about         1,400,000 pounds sterling.
The National Debt, in Total,
amounts to about        110 million pounds sterling

*Provincial Debts since 1740 for Corn.*

| | |
|---|---:|
| In 1740, by Ditto, with exemptions | 860.000 |
| In 1747, by Ditto | 1,200,000 |
| In 1748, by Ditto | 700,000 |
| In 1748, by Ditto 150,000 | |

By expenses in 1747 and 1748, exceeding in
Income, as by the Treasury Documents                 1,500,000
Total of the Debts of the Provinces                  7,910,000
Total of the Debts of the Community                 18,586,000
Expenses of the War                                 26,990,000


[The above, beginning "Provincial Debts for Corn," is a scribbled note, with some crossing out, in William Mildmay's handwriting.]


*An Account of the French Fisheries and Colonies.*

English Colonies

| | Hogs of Sugar at hundred per hogshead] | Value of the[40 sh. Per 100 | Tons | Ships of 200 tons | Men, at 25 men to a ship of 200 tons |
|---|---|---|---|---|---|
| Jamaica | 600,000 | £1,440,000 | 36,000 | 180 | 4,500 |
| Barbados, | 150,000 | £360,000 | 9,000 | 45 | 1,125 |
| Antigua, | 18,000 | £432,000 | 10,800 | 54 | 1,350 |
| Nevis, | 8,000 | £192,000 | 4,800 | 24 | 600 |
| Montserrat, | 4,000 | £96,000 | 2,400 | 12 | 300 |
| | 120,000 | £ 2,880,000 | 72,000 | 360 | 9,000 |


*French Colonies*

| | Hogs of Sugar at 10 hundred[per hogshead | 100 weight of coffee | Value of the Sugar at 40 sh The coffee at 3 pounds per 100 weight | Tons | Ships | Men |
|---|---|---|---|---|---|---|
| Guadeloupe | 20,000 | 20,000 | £460,000 | 13,500 | 70 | 1,750 |
| St. Domingo | 80,000 | ——— | £160,000 | 40,000 | 207 | 5,175 |
| Grenada | 6,000 | ——— | £120,000 | 3,000 | 15 | 375 |
| Grenadines | ——— | ——— | ——— | — | — | — |
| | 126,000 | 40,000 | £2,640,000 | 73,000 | 362 | 9,050 |

Miscellaneous Products
Guadeloupe        Sasparilla, Ginger, 5000 bags of cotton
Grenadines        Coffee, Ginger, 5000 bags of cotton.


*French Fishery*

Mud Fishery (coastal fishery).
The ships employed are from 50 to 100 tons and carry from 12 to 25 men. Of
21 persons employed, 18 matelots, 2 novices and 1 mousse
The costs of fitting out a ship for the Mud Fishery, from 50 to 100 tons, is
from 12,000 to 36,000 *livres.*

Cod Fishery.
The ships employed are from 120 tons to 350 tons and carry from 45 to 140
men and cost from 34,000 to 130,000 *livres.* Fitting out they employ from 8
to 26 boats, with 3 men in each boat, except the *Bateaux caplanier* (sic underline), which should have about 4 to 5 men in each.

| Mud Fishery. | Ships |
|---|---|
| From the port of Granville | 55 to 60 |
| From Cherbourg, Dieppe, Barfleur | 75 to 80 |
| Nantes, Koune, Rochelle | 55 to 60 |

| Cape Breton Fishery. | Ships |
|---|---|
| From St. Malo, Rochelle, Bayonne | 70 to 80 |

| Gaspe Fishery for Dry Cod. | |
|---|---|
| From St. Malo, Granville, Bayonne | 40 to 50 |

| Petit Nord Dry Cod Fishery. | |
|---|---|
| From St. Malo, Granville, Benie | 80 to 90 |
| Some likewise from Brest and Morlaix | |

The navigation of the Mud Fishery and
Cod Fishery employ 15,000 to 16,000 men
including 1,800 or 2,000 *novices* (*sic* underline)

Mud Fishery.

| | |
|---|---|
| 190 vessels, 100 tons each | 19,000 tons |
| 190 vessels, at 18 men each | 3,425 men |

Cape Breton Fishery.

| | |
|---|---|
| 75 vessels at 75 tons each | 6,625 tons |
| 75 vessels at 18 men each | 1,350 men |

Gaspe, Labrador, Petit Nord and Cod Fishery.

| | |
|---|---|
| 140 vessels at 250 tons each | 35,000 tons |
| 140 vessels at 80 men each | 11,200 men |

Vessels . . . . . . . . . . . . . . . . . . . . .450
Tons . . . . . . . . . . . . . . . . . . . . .9,625
Men . . . . . . . . . . . . . . . . . . . . .15,970


*Different Jurisdictions in France.*

1  Justices Seignorials, *Basse, Moyen, Haut*
2  Justices Royalty, *Ordinaires*
3  *Prévôt des Maréchaux,* Vice Bailiffs, Vice *Senéchaux*
4  *Conservateurs des* Privileges
5  *Prévôts des Marchands, Maires et Échevins*
6  Judges and Consuls
7  *Tresoriers de France* and *Bureau de finance, 7 chambres de domaines*
8  *La jurisdiction des Eaux et Forêts*
9  *L'Amiraute*
10  *La Jurisdiction de la Grand Pannetier*
11  *La Jurisdiction des Massons*
12  *Les Arbitres*
13  *La Requête de l'Hotel*
14  *Les Parlements*
15  *Les Élus Grontiers [Grenetiers]et autre juges qui connaissent des droits, Ferme de Roi et dont les Appellants ressortissent aux Cour des Aydes.*
16  *Les Cours des Aydes*
17  *Le Prévôt de l'Hotel, grand Broote [Bureau] de Finance*
18  *Le Grand Conseil*

19  *La Cour des Monnayes*
20  *Les Conseils du Roi*
21  *Le Chancellery*
22  *La Jurisdiction particulatique [particulière]*


*Revenue of France 1760* [from taxation].
E.R.O. Mildmay Papers, D/DM, 01/28
        *Livres*

| | | |
|---|---|---|
| Ordinary Revenue of France 1751 | | 233,880,000. |
| Extraordinary, a *vingtième*, including the tax on industry. | 23,944,500. | |
| The 2 s*ols en suite* on 2 *vingtièmes* | 4,492,500. | |
| | 28,447,000. | |
| Taxes of ordinary and extraordinary, 1751 | | 252,317,000. |

Additional taxes in 1760

| | | |
|---|---|---|
| Additional extraordinary since, viz one time *vingtième* and the tax on industry laid on 1760, say | 23,944,500. | |
| A Third *vingtième*, without the 2 *sols en suite* and the tax on industry laid on 1760, say | 20,000,000. | |

| | | |
|---|---|---|
| A Double *capitation* which adds, viz | | |
| *Pais d'Élection* | 12,600,000. | |
| *Pais d'États* | 2,200,000. | |
| *Reunies et conquis* | 4,300,000. | |
| All of which are included in the *recettes générales*. | | |
| Taxes of ordinary and extraordinary, 1760 | | 315,361,500. |

# Appendix 7.

WILLIAM MILDMAY'S LIST OF SHIPS.

E.R.O. Mildmay Papers, D/DM, 01/41.
This list appears to be the one that he refers to as the "enclosure" he sent in his letter to Carew Hervey Mildmay on 9 May 1755. E.R.O. Mildmay Papers, D/DM, 01/30

List of Ships set sail from Brest, May 3rd 1755 (The fleet sent to Louisbourg).

| Noms des Vaissaux | Time de Construction | Nombre d'Equippage (tons) | (guns) | |
|---|---|---|---|---|
| Le Formidable | 1746 | 1100 ------------80 | | |
| La Parmier | 1752 | 750 -------------4 | | |
| Le Heros | 1754 | 750 ------------99 | | |
| Le Bisarre | 1750 | 580 ------------69 | | Vaissaux |
| L'Entrepenart | 1751 | 750 ------------79 | | Ligne |
| L'Alcide | 1740 | 580 ------------69 | | |
| L'Oiselle | 1751 | 580 ------------69 | | |
| L'Inflexible | 1751 | 580 ------------69 | | |
| La Fleur de Lys | 1753 | 230 ------------30 | | |
| L'Amethest | 1753 | 220 ------------26 | | |
| L'Herrine | 1752 | 220 ------------26 | | Fregates |
| La Sirene | 1745 | 230 ------------30 | | |
| La Comete | 1752 | 220 ------------22 | | |
| L'Aigle | 1751 | 350 ------------50 | | |
| La Diane | 1751 | 230 ------------39 | | |

Noms des Vaisseau, *Armes en Flute*. [See the following page for the note on this type of ship, and Mildmay's description in his letter].

| Le Difference | 1723 | 750------------79 |
| L'Esperence | 1724 | 750------------79 |
| L'Algonquin | 1752 | 750------------79 |
| Le Dauphin | 1735 | 750------------79 |
| L'Huitre | 1750 | 580------------69 |
| Le Leopard | 1747 | 580------------69 |
| Le Lis | 1747 | 580------------69 |
| L'Aihis | 1752 | 500------------69 |
| L'Opiniatre | 1750 | 500------------69 |
| L'Apolion | 1741 | 350------------69 |
| L'Aquilion | 1730 | 350------------50 |
| La Fidelle | 1748 | 220------------22 |

*Ceux ci n'ont que 24 Cannons.* [All the ships in this group had been reduced to 24 guns from the normal armament stated in the list.]

*Note on the Flûte Ships.*

A *Flûte* was a type of sailing ship that was first invented by the Dutch, and was used to transport cargo.[2] The *Flûtes* in this list, however, were large ships of the line that had been stripped of most of their guns because they were being used as troop transports for the army being sent to defend Quebec.

In a letter that William Mildmay wrote from London on 28 May 1755 to Sir Thomas Robinson, secretary of state for the Southern Department, he informed Sir Thomas that in the list of ships of the French fleet leaving Brest on 3 May, and enclosed with his letter, those marked as "*Armes en flûte*" were "ships of the line" that had been converted into troop transports and, therefore, were only carrying: "24 guns of 12 pounders each" (12-pound shot). He reported that one of the frigates had also been converted into a victualling ship for the rest of the fleet. Mildmay also told Sir Thomas that six battalions of troops, or 3150 men, had been embarked for this voyage to Louisbourg, but 400 of them had become ill and had been put ashore in Brest before the fleet sailed and, of these, "12 had died the same day." He confirmed that their destination was ultimately the city of Quebec, as he had discovered that "Mons. de Vaudreuil, the newly appointed Governor of Quebec, is embarqued with his wife and family on the Parmier."[3]

This list of ships is the composition of the fleet that was intercepted by Admiral Boscowen off Louisbourg in June 1755, and in this encounter the ships *L'Alcide* and *Le Lis* were sunk. The sea battle took place after the troops had been landed at Louisbourg, however, and these soldiers went on to join the army that Montcalm commanded on the Plains of Abraham.

1. Mildmay was using the anglicized spelling for a *Verdigris* industry whose production was centered in southern France, and particularly in Languedoc. Reed Benhamou, in her study of this manufacture, states that this product was copper acetate (made by the action of acetic acid on copper) and it produced a spongy blue-green mold that was used in dyes, paints, and drugs. The industry was largely controlled by women, both as workers and brokers, and the *verdigris* was made by packing thin copper strips in earthenware jars filled with grape juice. The resulting mold was scraped from the copper and pressed into blocks, and over 80 percent of it was exported to Holland. The Dutch made it into a dark green weatherproof paint, used to protect their houses from the sea air. War interfered with these exports and the export figures from 1744 to 1748 showed that the normal value of the trade, estimated at 1,011,145 *livres* per year, dropped by over two thirds during the War of the Austrian Succession. Reed Benhamou, "The Verdigris Industry in Eighteenth Century Languedoc: Women's work, Women's Art." *French Historical Studies* 16 (spring 1990): 560–76, 562, 563, 564, 566, 569, 571.

2. Paul Bamford, *Fighting Ships and Prisons: The Mediterranean Galleys of France in the Age of Louis XIV* (Minneapolis: University of Minnesota Press, 1973), 323.

3. E.R.O. Mildmay Papers, D/DM, 01/41.

# Notes

## List of Abbreviations

BL: The British Library, London.

ERO: The Essex Record office, Chelmsford, England.

WCL: The William L. Clements Library, University of Michigan, Ann Arbor.

C.A.M. Canadian Archives Manuscripts Division: Public Archives, Canada. Ottawa.

France: *Archives du Ministere des Affaires Etrangères, Correspondance Politique: Angleterre.*

## INTRODUCTION

1. Fred Anderson, *Crucible of War: The Seven Years' War and the Fate of Empire in British North America, 1754–1756* (New York: First Vintage Books Edition, Random House, 2000), vii.
2. Ibid.; Fred Anderson, *A People's Army: Massachusetts Soldiers and Society in the Seven Years' War* (Chapel Hill: University of North Carolina Press, 1984).
3. Anderson, *Crucible of War*, xvii.
4. William L. Clements Library, Ann Arbor, The Mildmay Papers, 7 vols.; British Library, The Leeds Papers, Egerton Additional Manuscripts, vols. 3432, 3456, 3457, 3458; Essex Record Office, Department of Manuscripts, The Mildmay Papers, D/DM Series.
5. W.C.L. Mildmay Papers, vol. 3 (This volume has been given the title "Private Letters from Paris" by the William L. Clements Library); A. C. Edwards, *The Account Books of Benjamin Mildmay, Earl Fitzwalter* (London: Regency Press, 1977), vii; F. G. Emmison, *Guide to the Essex Record Office* (Chelmsford: Essex Record Office Publication 52, 1969), part 2, 10; Essex Record Office, Mildmay Papers, D/DM, 01/24.
6. See the details of these relationships in chapter 1.
7. William Mildmay, *The Police of France* (London: Edward Owen and Thomas Harrison, 1763); *An Account of the Southern Maritime Provinces of France* (London: Thomas Harrison, 1764).
8. Max Savelle, *The Diplomatic History of the Canadian Boundary 1749–1763* (New York: Russell and Russell, 1940). This journal is in volume 2 of the Mildmay

Papers in the William L. Clements Library; Alan Williams, *The Police of Paris 1718–1789* (Baton Rouge: Louisiana State University Press, 1979).

9. Hilda Grieve, *The Sleepers and the Shadows, Chelmsford: A Town, Its People and Its Past*, 2 vols. (Chelmsford: Essex Record Office Publications, 1988 and 1944), 2:142.

10. Sir Richard mentioned that when he was elected sheriff, he asked William Mildmay to write a report that would outline the scope of the work and duties of London sheriffs and the regulations for the administration of the city. The publisher of Sir Richard's book, Richard Crutwell, stated that this manuscript, "dedicated to Richard Hoare, Esq.," was now in his possession and that he intended to publish it. Sir Richard Hoare, *A Journal of the Schrievalty of Sir Richard Hoare Esq. in the Years 1740 to 1741, printed from a manuscript in his own handwriting*, 1743 (Bath: Richard Crutwell, 1815), 4. Sir William Mildmay had first published this manuscript in 1768 (see the following note).

11. William Mildmay, *The Method and Rule of Proceeding on all Elections, Polls, Scrutinies at Common Hall and Wardmotes within the City of London* (London: William Johnson and Thomas Harrison, 1768).

12. E.R.O. Mildmay Papers, D/DM, 01/29 (A letter from Sir Thomas Robinson, secretary of state for the Southern Department, dated 10 May 1755, giving Mildmay official permission to return to England).

13. Sir Bernard Burke, *A Genealogical and Heraldic Dictionary of the Peerage, Baronage and Knightage of Great Britain* (London: H. Colburn, 1893), 959.

14. E.R.O. Mildmay Papers, D/DM, T/33/29, D/DM, T/52/20.

15. Burke, *Genealogical Dictionary*, 959.

16. H. A. St. John Mildmay, *A Brief Memoir of the Mildmay Family* (privately printed, 1913), 197–98; Grieve, *The Sleepers and the Shadows*, 2: 240, 241.

17. F. G. Emmison, *A Guide to the Essex Record Office*, part 2, 111.

18. *Seventh Report of the Historical Manuscripts Commission*, part 1 (London: Public Record Office, 1879), 593, 594. Hazelgrove House, in Somerset, had been owned by a branch of the Mildmay family since the early seventeenth century. This estate was inherited by Jane Mildmay, the wife of Sir Henry Paulet St. John Mildmay, on the death of her cousin Anne Hervey Mildmay, who was the sole heir of her father, Carew Hervey Mildmay of Marks and Hazelgrove. H. A. St. John Mildmay, *A Brief Memoir of the Mildmay Family*, 196.

19. H. A. St. John Mildmay, *A Brief Memoir of the Mildmay Family*.

20. Howard H. Peckham, *Guide to the Manuscript Collection in the William L. Clements Library* (Chicago: University of Chicago Press, 1942), 190. This sale of William Mildmay's papers probably took place either in late 1933 or in early 1934, when the last member of the family to own Dogmersfield Park, Sir

Anthony St. John Mildmay, sold the house and moved to London. *Who's Who* (London: A. and C. Black Ltd., 1933, 1935). Sir Anthony's address is given as "Dogmersfield Park" in the 1933 edition (2250) and "The Cottage, Aesop Place, Baker Street" in the edition of 1935 (2008).

21. Emmison, *A Guide to the Essex Record Office*, part 11, 111.

22. *Dictionary of National Biography*, vol. 5, ed. Leslie Stephen and Sidney Lee (London: Smith Elder and Company, 1908), 48 (Biography of Robert Darcy, 4th Lord Holdernesse).

23. B.L. Leeds Papers, vol. 133, Egerton Add. Mss. 3456, vol. 134, Egerton Add. Mss. 3457.

24. E.R.O. Mildmay Papers, D/DM, A17 (accounts and receipts for fees paid on the creation of Sir William Mildmay as a baronet ).

25. W.C.L. Mildmay Papers, 3:19 September 1752.

## CHAPTER 1

1. "A Pedigree of the Mildmay Family compiled from the Visitation of Northampton in 1618 and from the Harl. MSS, 1553, f. 77," *Genealogical Memorabilia Relating to the Family of Mildmay*, 12; Hilda Grieve, *The Sleepers and the Shadows: Chelmsford, a Town, Its People and Its Past*, 2 vols. (Chelmsford: Essex Record Office Publications, 1988, 1994), 1:90.

2. Details of the land and buildings purchased by Thomas Mildmay are in the *Feet of Fines for the County of Essex 1423–1547*, ed. H. Reaney and Marc Fitch (Colchester: The Society, 1934), 4:30, 83, 161, 195, 196, 276. The youngest son, now Sir Walter Mildmay, did not inherit any of his father's property in 1550. Before 1540, only those monasteries whose annual income was less than £200 were closed down. A. C. Edwards, *A History of Essex* (Chichester: Phillimore, 1958), 57.

3. Grieve, *The Sleepers and the Shadows*, 1:102; H. A. St. John Mildmay, *A Brief Memoir of the Mildmay Family* (London: Privately Printed by John Lane, 1913), 13.

4. See the Mildmay Family Tree, appendix 2; Grieve, *The Sleepers and the Shadows*, 1:102.

5. Walter Cecil Richardson, *History of the Court of Augmentations, 1536–1554* (Baton Rouge: Louisiana University Press, 1961), 9.

6. Ibid., 8, 118.

7. Ibid., 118.

8. Stanford E. Lehnberg, *Sir Walter Mildmay and Tudor Government* (Austin: University of Texas Press, 1957), 48, 49.

9. Grieve, *The Sleepers and the Shadows*, 1:93, 94.

10. *Fifth Report of the Historical Manuscript Commission*, part 1 (London: Historical Manuscripts Commission, 1876), 307; Philip Morant, *The History and Antiquities of the County of Essex*, 2 vols. (London: T. Osborne, 1763–1768; reprint, London: E. P. Publishing Ltd., 1978), 2:3n. 1; Grieve, *The Sleepers and the Shadows*, 1:96.

11. "Queen Elizabeth granted the manor of Chelmsford, with its appurtenances, also called Bishops Hall, in Chelmsford, and the capital mansion of the said manor unto Thomas Mildmay Esq. and his heirs for ever." Morant, *The History and Antiquities of the County of Essex*, 2:2; Grieve, *The Sleepers and the Shadows*, 1:108.

12. Sir Bernard Burke, *Genealogical and Heraldic Dictionary of the Peerage, Baronage and Knightage of Great Britain*, 55th ed. (London: H. Colburn, 1893), 958.

13. Ibid.; Grieve, *The Sleepers and the Shadows*, 1:109; See also the Mildmay Family Tree, appendix 2.

14. See the Mildmay Family Tree, appendix 2.

15. Mildmay, *A Brief Memoir of the Mildmay Family*, 167. Sir Henry Mildmay had inherited the manors of Moulsham and Chelmsford on the death of his brother, Sir Thomas Mildmay, who died in 1625 without a male heir. Grieve, *The Sleepers and the Shadows*, 2:33.

16. Burke, *Genealogical History*, 958. In his autobiography, written in 1683, Sir John Bramstone (1611–99) stated that Sir Benjamin Mildmay obtained the right to assume the title of baron Fitzwalter from Charles II by paying 1,000 guineas to the duke of Buckingham and the king's mistress, the duchess of Cleveland. Given the mercenary appetites of both Buckingham and the duchess, this may well be true, but Sir John Bramstone was also a bitter political enemy of the Mildmay family. At the time of the Titus Oates plot, in 1672, Sir John had been accused of being a Papist by Sir Henry Mildmay of Graces, the cousin of Sir Benjamin Mildmay. *The Autobiography of Sir John Bramstone of Skreens K.B., in the Hundred of Chelmsford*, ed. P. Braybrooke, vol. 32 (London: Camden Society, 1844), iv, 120, 121.

17. Mildmay, *A Brief Memoir*, 169; Burke, *Genealogical Dictionary*, 958.

18. A. C. Edwards, *The Account Books of Benjamin Mildmay, Earl Fitzwalter* (London: Regency Press, 1977), vii, viii

19. See the Mildmay Family Tree, appendix 2.

20. Morant, *The History and Antiquities*, 2:9 (record of the sale), 2:vi (list of subscribers).

20. Morant, *The History and Antiquities*, 2:9 (record of the sale), 2:vi (list of subscribers).

21. Burke, *Genealogical and Heraldic Dictionary*, 959.

22. Ibid.; *Alumni Cantabrigienses: A Biographical List of All Known Students, Graduates and Known Office Holders at the University of Cambridge*, ed. J. Venn and J. A. Venn (Cambridge: University of Cambridge, 1922–54), part 1, 3:183 (references to the company status of Mildmay's father); Morant, *The History and Antiquities*, 2:9 (a reference both to the father of Sarah Mildmay [Wilcox] and to her husband's position in the company ).

23. The will of William Mildmay senior is dated 1707. E.R.O. Mildmay Papers, D/DM T 96/97. The family documents are in E.R.O. Mildmay Papers, D/DM L2/1, L2/2.

24. Lucy Sutherland, *The East India Company in Eighteenth Century Politics* (Oxford: Clarendon Press, 1977), 2, 45.

25. John Ovington, *A Voyage to Surat in the Year 1689*, ed. R. G. Rawlinson (London: Oxford University Press, 1929), 227, 228, 233.

26. Ibid., 301, 302.

27. The date of Mildmay's entry into the Middle Temple is given as January 1723, in bond number 6017. The original bond is now in the archives of the Middle Temple Library. A record of this bond is printed by Herbert A. C. Sturgess in *A Register of the Honourable Society of the Middle Temple from the Fifteenth Century to the Year 1944* (London: Butterworth and Co., 1949), 1:295.

28. Mildmay, *A Brief Memoir of the Mildmay Family*, 34 (a history of Graces), appendix E (a record of the marriage of Elizabeth Mildmay and Edmund Waterson on 7 September 1696). Henry and his wife Mary, who was Benjamin Mildmay's aunt, owned the estate of Graces, near Little Baddow. They were the neighbors of the Reverend Ralph Josselin, and Mary and her family are mentioned in Josselin's diary. Alan MacFarlane, *The Dairy of Ralph Josselin, 1616–1683* (London: Oxford University Press, 1976), 669.

29. E.R.O. Mildmay Papers, D/DM, L2/1.

30. Ibid. When this bill was sent in 1717, Benjamin Mildmay was still the younger brother of the eighteenth baron Fitzwalter, Charles Mildmay. See the Mildmay Family Tree, appendix 2.

31. Ibid. (This information is in a letter from R. Poole, dated 26 February 1717.)

32. Robert Atkins was married to the sister of Margaret's late husband, John Bonnell, and these heirs were thus his nephew and niece. The family tree of the Waterson/Bonnell families is in E.R.O. D/DM, L2/1, and was supplied to the Essex Record Office by Herbert Hudson in June 1949. See appendix 3.

33. E.R.O. Mildmay Papers, D/DM, L2/1.

34. Ibid.

35. Ibid.

36. Ibid. (A document stating: "Particulars of Mrs. Waterson's estate . . . A copy given by me to Mrs. Waterson July 24th 1722" and signed B.M.).

37. E.R.O. Mildmay Papers, D/DM, L2/2.

38. Fitzwalter's journal for 18 May 1751 noted that Lord Holdernesse had just been appointed Southern secretary. Edwards, *The Account Books of Benjamin Mildmay*, 212. The two secretaries of state—Northern and Southern—were amalgamated into the single office of foreign secretary in the nineteenth century.

39. Venn and Venn, *Alumni Cantabrigienses*, part 1, 3:188 (a record of Mildmay's entrance date, matriculation date, and dates of the degrees awarded, together with the names of all the other members of the Mildmay family who attended the University of Cambridge). Mildmay went up to Emmanuel College as a pensioner because this Cambridge college had been founded by his ancestor, Sir Walter Mildmay, in 1584 and since its foundation it had been the preferred college for many members of the Mildmay family. Sir Walter Mildmay, *The Statutes of Sir Walter Mildmay Kt., Chancellor of the Exchequer and One of Her Majesty's Privy Councillors, Authorised by Him for the Government of Emmanuel College, Founded by Him*, trans. with an intro. Frank Stubbings (Cambridge: Cambridge University Press, 1983).

40. Sturgess, *Register of Admissions*, 1:292. Membership in the Middle Temple required that two senior members of the Inn sign a legal undertaking, in the form of a bond, that the prospective entrant would pay all of his dues, and had also agreed to the rules of the society. During the early eighteenth century, the fee for this bond was £4. *Middle Temple Records, Minutes of the Parliament*, vol. 5 (1703–47), ed. with a preface Cyril L. King (London: Society of the Middle Temple, 1970), xvi.

41. The record of the legal career of William Mildmay is in the list of the Middle Temple Benchers who were elected in 1758. *The Middle Temple Bench Book, Being a Register of the Benchers of the Middle Temple from the Earliest Records to the Present Time*, 2d ed., ed. J. Bruce Williamson (London: Chancery Land Press, 1937), 175; Sturgess, *Register of Admission*, 1:292.

42. "Admissions to the House and Chambers 1695–1737" MS., vol. G (London: Middle Temple Society Archives), 376, 387.

43. E.R.O. Mildmay Papers, D/DM, 01/19 (Fitzwalter); E.R.O. Mildmay Papers, D/DM, F24 (Pelham).

44. E.R.O. Mildmay Papers, D/DM, F10.

45. *Middle Temple Records, Minutes of the Parliament, 1703–1747*, vol. 5, ed. King, 326.

46. "The Case of Hartopp. Bart. Against Hoare and others before Sir William Loo, Knight, Chief Justice, and a Jury." The appeal was heard in the Court of the King's Bench on 2 June 1741. E.R.O. Mildmay Papers, D/DM, L5. Defendants were given the right to be represented by legal council in the Westminster

Courts after the 1730s. J. M. Beattie, *Crime and the Courts in England 1600–1800* (Princeton: Princeton University Press, 1986), 356.

47. "The Declaration of the Barristers and Students Assembled in the Vacation Parliament concerning the Rights of Continuing their Parliament . . . presented by me . . . [William Mildmay] to the Masters and Benchers of the Middle Temple, as the man appointed spokesman of the said Parliament," (1745). E.R.O. Mildmay Papers, D/DM, F23.

48. The word "parliament" was used at the Middle Temple to describe the meetings of Benchers. At Lincoln's Inn these meetings were called "councils" and Gray's Inn described them as "pensions." *The Middle Temple Bench Book*, 108n. 1.

49. The "vacations" at the Middle Temple were set periods of time between the four legal "terms," during which the Westminster Courts were in session. There were two such vacations and one of them was the "learning vacation," or a period when students received instruction in the law at a "moot," or teaching process that imitated the procedures at the Court of Common Pleas. One of the required nine "exercises," or dissertations made by a student on a point of law, took place during this vacation. The Parliament Chamber was in the lower end of the Middle Temple Hall and such parliaments were supposed to be held on the first and last Friday of every month. *Middle Temple Records: Minutes of the Parliament*, 1:106.

50. The Chambers at the Middle Temple were supposed to be reserved entirely for members of the bar of this Inn. This criticism by Mildmay was, apparently, not the first time such a complaint had been made. In 1708 the Bench itself complained that there were "a great number of persons, not members, residing in the Inn." The Benchers in that year decided that members who allowed "any strangers, or families of women and children " to live there should have their privileges removed, but the Parliament Minutes state: " This order has been preceded and followed by many others of the same sort." *Middle Temple Records: Minutes of the Parliament*, 5:xvi.

51. Mildmay, *A Brief Memoir of the Mildmay Family*, 173.

52. There are 129 letters from William Mildmay to Lord Fitzwalter, written between 1750 and 1755, in W.C.L. Mildmay Papers, vol. 3. Further correspondence between William Mildmay and Lord Fitzwalter is in E.R.O. Mildmay Papers, D/DM series.

53. E.R.O. Mildmay Papers, D/DM, T 33/29, T/ 52/20. See also the Mildmay Family Tree, appendix 2.

54. Frederick Chancellor, *The Ancient Sepulchral Monuments of Essex* (Chelmsford: Edmund Durrant and Co. 1890), 59; Grieve, *The Sleepers and the Shadows*, 2:240, 241.

55. By 1987, Dogmersfield Park had become the property and the head office of an insurance and development company, called Amdhal. This information, together with the date of the fire that destroyed its interior, was supplied to me by Miss C. J. Humphreys, senior archivist, Hampshire Record Office, Winchester. Amdhal is in the process of developing Dogmersfield Park into a series of private apartments.

## Chapter 2

1. W.C.L. Mildmay Papers, vol. 2 (Mildmay's journal on the commission meetings); W.C.L. Mildmay Papers, vol. 3 (Mildmay's letters to Lord Fitzwalter); W.C.L. Mildmay Papers, vol. 4 (Mildmay's reports on the conferences he held on the ransom of prisoners); W.C.L. Mildmay Papers, vol. 5 (The official reports of the St. Malo meetings and of the commission conferences in Paris); B.L. Leeds Papers, vol. 133, Edgerton 3456 (Mildmay's official letters to Lord Holdernesse); E.R.O. Mildmay Papers, D/DM series (further letters, both private and official, from Mildmay to Lord Fitzwalter, Lord Holdernesse, and Sir Thomas Robinson).

2. William Coxe, *Memoirs of Horatio, Lord Walpole, Selected from his Correspondence and Papers . . . from 1678 [to?] 1757*, 2 vols. (London: Longman, Hurst, Rees and Orme, 1808), 2:251; William Mildmay, *An Account of the Southern Maritime Provinces of France* (London: Thomas Harrison, 1764), 25. The signatories to the treaty were Lord Sandwich, secretary of state for the Southern Department, and Lord Montague for Britain, the Comte de Saint-Sévérin, minister of state, for France, and Counts Bentinck and Hasselear for Holland. W.C.L. Mildmay Papers, 1:2–7 (a copy of the preliminary treaty, signed on 30 April 1748).

3. W.C.L. Mildmay Papers, 5:1–5; W.C.L. Mildmay Papers, 1:20–23 (reports from Messrs. Allix and Hind to the duke of Bedford); *British Diplomatic Instructions 1689–1789*, ed. L.G. Wickham Legg (London: The Royal Historical Society, 1934), 2–4 (instructions from the duke of Bedford, secretary of state for the Southern Department, to Joseph Yorke, first secretary to the British embassy from 16 January 1749, and to the duke of Albemarle, British ambassador to France from 8 May 1749).

4. Instructions to M. Guillot from Louis XV, dated 19 May 1749, W.C.L. Mildmay Papers, 1:18–19.

5. Reports on the negotiations at St. Malo during 1748 and 1749, sent by Messrs. Allix and Hinde to the duke of Bedford, are in W.C.L. Mildmay Papers, 1:20–23 and 5:1–5. These fundamental disagreements—both on the limits of the Channel and the North Sea and on whether payment for ships taken before

the war began should also be covered in the negotiations—were to continue throughout the entire series of negotiations from 1749 to June 1755.

6. In a "Sketch of a Plan of Instructions for the Commissioners who are to meet in Paris (in 1750)," the lack of an agreed definition of these sea limits is the reason given for the breakdown of negotiations at St. Malo in 1749, W.C.L. Mildmay Papers, 1:28, 29. The "Memorial in Reply to the Answer and Objections of the French Court to the British Instructions for the Commissaries on the Limits and Prizes" states: "the want of a proper Harmony in the Principles the Commissaries were to proceed upon rendered this meeting at St. Malo fruitless," W.C.L. Mildmay Papers, 5:22–26. The instructions given to Lord Albemarle in April 1749 on the British government's position regarding the sea limits are in W.C.L. Mildmay Papers, 1:40–44.

7. In a letter Mildmay wrote to Lord Fitzwalter on 22 August 1750, he stated that it was proposed to hold a meeting of the full commission on this date, W.C.L. Mildmay Papers, vol. 3. Mildmay's journal entry, made after this first meeting, gave the date as 31 August 1750. W.C.L. Mildmay Papers, 2:1.

8. B. L. Hardwicke Papers, vol. 774, Add. Mss. 36,122, f. 24, "Warrants for Affixing the Great Seal to Messers Shirley and Mildmay, Full Powers." This document of April 1750 contains the instructions of George II to Lord Hardwicke; it was signed on the king's behalf by the duke of Bedford, and describes the scope of the responsibilities of both British commissioners. The establishment of this commission was insisted on by the French government and the British agreed to participate; however, some members of the cabinet were not entirely convinced that it would be beneficial to British interests. *British Diplomatic Instructions*, xv. In the spring of 1752, William Shirley was replaced as a British commissioner by Ruvigny de Cosne, first secretary to the British embassy in Paris. (See chapter 5, The Year of Possibilities 1751–1752.)

9. *British Diplomatic Instructions*, 7, 9, 10. In a memorandum that he wrote at the beginning of his commission journal, Mildmay described his French colleagues as "Monsr. de la Galissonière, *Chef d'Escadre* (fleet admiral) and late Govr. of Canada, and Monsr. de Silhouette, *Maître des Requêtes* and Chancellor to the Duke of Orleans." W.C.L. Mildmay Papers, vol. 2. The spelling of the Marquis de la Galissonière's name as "Galissonnière" by Max Savelle throughout his book *The Diplomatic History of the Canadian Boundary 1749–1763* (New York: Russell and Russell, 1940) is an error. (Ibid., 28 and passim). I have used the same spelling of Galissonière's name as that given by William Mildmay, both in his letters and in all of his journal reports of the commission conferences. (W.C.L. Mildmay Papers, vol. 2, passim.) It is also the spelling that was used in all the official documents and in the marquis's own letters, all of which were filed between 1750 and 1755 by the French Foreign Ministry. *Ministére des*

*Affaires Etrangeres, Correspondance Politique: Angleterre,* 1720–1755, vols. 429–39. Canada, Public Archives, Manuscript Division, MG5 A1, Microfilm reels C 12544–C 12546. Under a French law of 1663, the territory originally known as "New France" was renamed "Canada," except for Acadia and Louisiana. As Mildmay also referred to the land along the St. Laurence River as "Canada," I have used this name, rather than "New France," to describe this French territory.

10. "His Majesty's Declaration of War against the French King." Robert Beatson, *Naval and Military Memoirs of Great Britain from 1727–1788,* 3 vols. (London: Longman, Hurst, Rees and Orme, 1804), 3:102–4.

11. Guy Fregault, *Canada: The War of the Conquest* (1955; reprint, Toronto: Oxford University Press, 1969), 8–10; Samuel S. Drake, *A Particular History of the Five Years French and Indian War in New England and Parts adjacent, from its declaration by the King of France, March 15th 1744, to the Treaty with the Eastern Indians, October 16th 1749, sometimes called Governor Shirley's War* (Albany, N.Y.: 1870); Hayes Baker-Crothers, *Virginia and the French and Indian Wars* (Chicago: University of Chicago Press, 1928); Edward P. Hamilton, *The French and Indian Wars: The Story of Battles and Forts in the Wilderness* (Garden City, N.J.: Doubleday, 1962).

12. Jeremy Black, *Natural and Necessary Enemies: Anglo French Relations in the Eighteenth Century* (London: Duckworth, 1986), 58, 59; Olwen Hufton, *Europe: Privilege and Protest 1730–1789* (Ithaca, N.Y.: Cornell University Press), 113, 114, 115.

13. Max Savelle, *The Diplomatic History of the Canadian Boundary,* chap. 2, "Diplomatic Futility" (New York: Russell and Russell, 1940), 37.

14. Drake, *A Particular History of the Five Years French and Indian War,* 172.

15. Coxe, *Memoirs of Horatio, Lord Walpole,* 2:271. Horatio Walpole was not created a peer until 1756; ibid., 2:429.

16. In the eighteenth century the word "commissary" was used to describe a modern-day commissioner. Leo Francis Stock, *Debates and Proceedings of the British Parliaments Respecting North America,* vol. 5, 1739–54 (Washington, D.C.: Carnegie Institution, 1941), 5:368

17. Joseph Yorke was the third son of Lord Hardwicke, the lord chancellor. In 1745, he became lieutenant colonel of a regiment of foot soldiers and *aide-de-camp* to the duke of Cumberland. He was sent to the Paris embassy as first secretary in 1749. *Dictionary of National Biography,* ed. Sidney Lee and Leslie Stephen (London: Smith Elder, 1909), 21:1259.

18. B.L. Add. Mss. 32822, f. 89, cited by L.G. Wickham Legg, *British Diplomatic Instructions,* xi. The insertion in parenthesis is mine.

19. Savelle, *The Diplomatic History of the Canadian Boundary*; John A. Schutz, *William Shirley: King's Governor of Massachusetts* (Chapel Hill: University of North Carolina Press, 1961).

20. Max Savelle and Margaret Anne Fisher, *The Origins of American Diplomacy: The International History of Angloamerica 1492–1763* (New York: Macmillan, 1967).

21. Ibid., 392n.12.

22. Fregault, *Canada: The War of the Conquest*, 21n. 67, 24n. 81, 26n. 89; Schutz, *William Shirley*, 159n. 30, 162n. 38; George Stanley, *New France: The Last Phase 1744–1760* (Toronto: McClelland and Stewart, 1968), chap. 9 passim; James A. Henretta, *Salutary Neglect: Colonial Administration under the Duke of Newcastle* (Princeton: Princeton University Press, 1972), 163n. 120, 215n.102, 291n. 44; Black, *Natural and Necessary Enemies*, 53n. 32.

23. Theodore C. Pease, *Anglo-French Boundary Disputes in the West 1749–1763* (Springfield, Ill.: U.S. Historical Library, 1936).

24. Howard H. Peckham, *Sources of American Independence: Selected Manuscripts from the Collection of the William L. Clements Library* (Chicago: University of Chicago Press, 1978), 190; F. G. Emmison, *A Guide to the Essex Record Office* (Chelmsford: Essex Record Office, 1969), part II, 111.

25. Schutz, *William Shirley*, 153–67.

26. Ibid., 159, 159nn. 30, 31.

27. Savelle, *The Diplomatic History*, 40–42.

28. E.R.O. Mildmay Papers D/DM, 01/26.

29. Ibid.

## CHAPTER 3

1. John Schutz, *William Shirley, King's Governor of Massachusetts.* (Chapel Hill: University of North Carolina Press, 1961), 1–5; (William Shirley), *Dictionary of National Biography*, ed Sidney Lee and Leslie Stephen (London: Smith Elder and Co., 1897–1908), 52: 152. William Mildmay's letters to Lord Fitzwalter, W.C.L., Mildmay Papers, vol. 3.

2. William Mildmay, *A Fair Representation of His Majesty's Right to Nova Scotia and Acadia briefly stated, with an Answer to the objections contained in the French Treatise entitled Discussion sommaâtre sur les Ancienne Limites de l'Acadie* (London: T. Harrison, 1756); William Mildmay, *The Police of France* (London: Edward Owen and Thomas Harrison, 1763); William Mildmay, *An Account of the Southern Maritime Provinces of France* (London: Thomas Harrison, 1764); William Mildmay, *The Laws and Policy of England Relating to Trade Examined*

*by the Maxims and Principles of Trade in General and by the Laws and Policy of Other Trading Nations* (London: Thomas Harrison, 1765).

3. Mildmay, *An Account of the Southern Provinces*, 1, 43.

4. For specific details of these various sources of information, see Mildmay's comments both in this chapter and in his reports on the work of the Anglo-French commission.

5. D. B. Horn, *The British Diplomatic Service 1689–1789* (Oxford: Clarendon Press, 1961), 37, 190, 253, 254, 275.

6. W.C.L. Mildmay Papers, 3:22 March 1752, 3 May 1752.

7. Ibid., 3:14 February 1753.

8. E.R.O. Mildmay Papers, D/DM, 01/19 (Mildmay's letter to Lord Fitzwalter). The record of Lord Fitzwalter as chief commissioner of the Board of Trade is in E.R.O. Mildmay Papers, D/DM, 01/24. A letter from William Mildmay in 1754 confirms Lord Fitzwalter's position as the treasurer of the royal household. W.C.L. Mildmay Papers, 3:25 December 1754.

9. E.R.O. Mildmay Papers, D/DM, F24.

10. E.R.O. Mildmay Papers, D/DM, 01/28. Mildmay is here referring to the losses suffered by the French navy during the War of the Austrian Succession.

11. E.R.O. Mildmay Papers, D/DM, 01/19 (Headed "Middle Temple, 16th August 1748").

12. E. R.O. Mildmay Papers, D/DM, 01/19. Information on the activities of the *intendants* and French merchants in these "Chambers of Commerce," first established by Louis XIV during the War of the Spanish Succession, is given by J. S. Bromley, "The Decline of Absolute Monarchy," *France: Government and Society*, ed. J. M. Wallace-Hadrill and J. McManners (London: Methuen, 1957), 153.

13. E.R.O. Mildmay Papers, D/DM, 01/19.

14. E.R.O. Mildmay Papers, D/DM, 01/28. See appendix 6 for the full transcription of this document. The information that Mildmay gives here is not accurate, as Jacques Forceville was not one of the Farmers General, but was only the "straw man," or agent, who was nominated by the Company of the General Farmers in 1738 to sign a six-year lease with the Crown for the rent of the Royal General Farm on their behalf. The lease was signed for the period from 1738 to 1744, for a sum of 91,830,000 *livres*, and George Matthews states that the Forceville lease was "the last lease printed and published in full during the eighteenth century, and was regarded as a standard lease." George T. Matthews, *The Royal General Farms in Eighteenth Century France* (New York: Columbia University Press, 1958), 78n. 1, 82n. 13, 285. The Forceville lease was published under the title *Bail des Fermes-Royales-Unies fait à M. Jacques Forceville le 16 Septembre 1738. Registre en la Chambre des comptes le 31 Decembre*

*1738, et en la Cour des Aydes le 22 des mesmes mois et an* (Paris: *De l'Imprimerie Royale*, 1739).

15. This farm was let in 1738, but as its term ran to 1744 it would have been in effect during the first half of the War of the Austrian Succession. See the previous note on the Forceville lease.

16. E.R.O. Mildmay Papers, D/DM, 01/28. (Contains both the information and the letter to Holdernesse.)

17. W.C.L. Mildmay Papers, 3:23 February 1752. Information on Lord Holdernesse' interest in foreign newspapers, and on these *gazettes à la main*, are given by Horn, *The British Diplomatic Service*, 280, and Leon Bernard *The Emerging City: Paris in the Age of Louis XIV* (Durham, N.C.: Duke University Press, 1970), 79.

18. W.C.L. Mildmay Papers, 3:31 May 1752 (Montgon); B.L. Leeds Papers, vol. 133, Egerton 3456, f. 283, 13 December 1752 (Maintenant).

19. B.L. Leeds Papers, vol. 133, Egerton 3456, f. 320, 2 January 1753. M. d'Anville was a famous French cartographer who, in 1746, was used by the French government to support its claim to the territory of Nova Scotia, *The Conduct of the French with Regard to Nova Scotia, from its first settlement to the present time*, signed "A Letter to a Member of Parliament." (London: Printed for T. Jeffreys, 1754), 47, 48. Lord Holdernesse and the British government would be interested in the map sent by Mildmay, as it had a direct bearing on the claims of the French East India company to an exclusive trade in the territories governed by the princes of the Carnatic, together with the present rivalry between the interests of the French trading post at Pondicherry and the British East India Company post at Madras.

20. Norman Hampson, *The Enlightenment: An Evaluation of its Assumptions, Attitudes and Values* (1968; reprint, London: Penguin Books, 1984), 133.

21. W.C.L. Mildmay Papers, vol. 3, 12 December 1753.

22. Henry A. St. John Mildmay, *A Brief Memoir of the Mildmay Family* (London: Privately Printed, 1913), 173, 174, 175; E.R.O. Mildmay Papers, D/DM, 01/41 (a letter from Mildmay confirming their arrival on 6 October, dated 10 November 1748). In Paris, the party stayed for several weeks at a *hôtel de séjour* called the *Hôtel d'Orléans*; this hotel had existed as a lodging house since at least the thirteenth century. The first building on the site at the corner of the rue *Saint-Andre-des-Arts* and the rue *Éperon* was called the *Hôtel de Navarre*, and later the *Séjour d'Orléans*. The *Hôtel d'Orléans* was rebuilt in 1728 and lasted as a hotel until 1883, when it was pulled down to construct a girls' *lycée*. Jacques Hillairet, *Dictionnaire Historique des Rues de Paris*, 7th ed. (Paris: *Éditions de Minuit*, 1961), 375, 477. In the present *Lycée Fénelon* there is one room, now used as the principal's sitting room, which, together with the original staircase, has been preserved from the building in which Mildmay stayed in 1748.

23. E.R.O. Mildmay Papers, D/DM, 01/41. Britain and Spain were at war with each other by 1740, but France did not declare war on Britain until 1744.

24. Ibid.

25. Ibid.

26. Britain declared war on Spain at the beginning of 1740. Voltaire stated: "The war was at first carried on by sea, and the privateers of both nations (Britain and Spain), authorized by letters of marque, attacked the merchant-men in Europe and America. Thus they were destroying the trade (in slaves and supplies to the Spanish West Indies) which had occasioned the rupture between the two nations." Voltaire, *The Age of Louis XV, being the Sequel to the Age of Louis XIV, Translated from the French of M. de Voltaire* . . . , 2 vols. (London: G. Kearsly, 1774), 1:78.

27. E.R.O. Mildmay Papers, D/DM, 01/41.

28. Garden, *Lyon et Les Lyonnais au XVIIIe Siecle*, 16, 179, 180.

29. Mildmay, *An Account of the Southern Maritime Provinces*, 21 (on the wheat dependency). See the details that Mildmay gave on the comparative prices in appendix 5. The main transport of grain in the eighteenth century was usually by sea or by river, as the land transport cost of such a bulky and heavy item would make this basic commodity far too expensive. The importance to the south of France of the sea traffic in grain into Marseille from North Africa, England, and the Baltic lay not only in its plentiful supply, but also in its much lower transportation costs. Charles Tilly, "Food Supply and Public Order in Modern Europe." *The Formation of National States in Western Europe*, ed. Charles Tilly (Princeton: Princeton University Press, 1975), 416.

30. Mildmay, *An Account of the Southern Maritime Provinces*, 25, 26.

31. E.R.O. Mildmay Papers, D/DM, 01/41.

32. Mildmay, *An Account of the Southern Maritime Provinces*, 18, 19, 26n. 26, 27.

33. Again with no indication of whom this person might be, whether Henry Pelham or another.

34. Among his papers Mildmay kept his original manuscript draft of a part of his book on the southern provinces. Here he explained the reason why the English ship owners were selling these ships, stating: "Several corn vessels were destined to this harbour (Marseille), and as the French are most fond of ships of their own build, some of which have been taken from them during the war were now loaden and sent there for sale." These sales, apparently, were thus a trade in some of the prize ships captured by the English during the War of the Austrian Succession. E.R.O. Mildmay Papers, D/DM y, 15/ M 50 / 1324.

35. E.R.O. Mildmay Papers, D/DM, 01/19, 1 January 1749.

36. Mildmay, *An Account of the Southern Maritime Provinces*, 42.

37. Ibid., 92–95.

38. St. John Mildmay, *A Brief Memoir of the Mildmay Family*, 181 (the date of Mildmay's return to England); B.L. Hardwick Papers, vol. 774, Add. Mss. 36, 122, f.24 (warrants for the appointment of William Shirley and William Mildmay as commissioners); W.C.L. Mildmay Papers, 3:8 May 1750 (letter confirming the date of Mildmay's arrival in Paris).

39. David Garrick visited Paris with his wife in the summer of 1751. In his travel diary he mentioned a dinner he enjoyed at the house of Sir John Lambert (a banker friend of William Mildmay), at which Mildmay was present, followed by a visit to the theater to see "ye Comedie Italienne with Mr. Mildmay, belonging to the Embassy." *The Diary of David Garrick: Being a Record of His Memorable Trip to Paris in 1751*, ed. Ryllis Clair Alexander (New York: Oxford University Press, 1928), 20.

40. W.C.L. Mildmay Papers, 3:19 December 1750.

41. Ibid., 3:7 June 1752. The "Visits of Ceremony" that were an essential part of the upper-class social life in Paris were described in William Cole's journal in 1765. Cole described a visit made by the duke of Bedford to Horace Walpole and another made to the salon of Madame Geoffrin. These visits were conducted with strict observance of the social protocol and attendance was regarded as a mark of status and acceptance in society. William Cole, *A Journal of my Journey to Paris in the year 1765*, ed. Francis Griffen Stokes, (London: Printed for J Hawman by T Gillet, 1805), 80–83.

42. Horn, *The British Diplomatic Service*, 17, 182.

43. The Marquis d'Argenson, *The Journal and Memoirs of the Marquis d'Argenson*, ed. E. J. B. Rathery, trans. Katherine Prescott Wormeley (Boston: Hardy, Pratt and Co., 1902), 2:159, 194; Jean Egret, *Louis XV et l' Opposition Parlementaire 1715–1774* (Paris: Librarie Armond Colin, 1970), 246; Marcel Marion, *Dictionnaire des institutions de la France aux XVIIe et XVIIIe siècles* (Paris: Auguste Picard, 1923), 299.

44. W.C.L. Mildmay Papers, 3:15 December 1751. The book M. Trudaine probably wanted was *Mr. Ogilby's and William Morgan's Pocket Book of the Roads, with their computed and measured distances* (London: Christopher Wilkinson, 1689), and reprinted in 1721, 1732, 1741, and 1745. The 1745 printing was the 10th edition of this popular book of maps, first published in 1675 by John Ogilby as *Britannia . . . or an Illustration of the Kingdom of England and the Dominion of Wales, by a geographical and historical description of the principal roads thereof.* Copies of both books are now held by the British Library. Daniel Charles Trudaine was an intelligent and far-sighted administrator. As an *intendant des finance* he controlled the finances of the department of the *Ponts et Chaussées*, and in 1754 he founded the *École des Ponts-et-Chaussées* to train engineers in the design of bridges, roads, and harbors in France. Shelby T.

McCloy, *Government Assistance in Eighteenth-Century France* (Durham, N.C.: Duke University Press, 1946), 82.

45. B.L. Leeds Papers, vol. 133, Egerton 3456, f. 228.

46. Président de Brosses, first president of the *Parlement* of Dijon, mentions Daniel Charles Trudaine as a member of the Council of State. *Lettres du Président de Brosses a Ch.-C.Loppin de Gemeaux*, Introduction by Yvonne Bezard (Paris: Firmin-Didot, 1929), 290n. 1.

47. W.C.L. Mildmay Papers, 3:6 March 1754.

48. Ibid., 3:17 January 1753.

49. Ibid., 3:17 January and 11 April 1753. M. Duvalear, a director of the French East India Company, is recorded by the politician George Bubb Doddington as having been one of his dinner guests at Bubb Dodington's house in Hammersmith, near London, on 15 July 1753. George Bubb Doddington, *The Political Journal of George Bubb Doddington*, ed. John Carswell and Lewis Arnold Dralle (Oxford: Clarendon Press, 1965), 226.

50. W.C.L. Mildmay Papers, 3:17 May 1752. Mildmay also told Fitzwalter in January 1753 that "as my chief acquaintance lys (*sic*) among these gentlemen of the robe, so I not only hear their complaints of what is passed, but otherwise the intentions and designs of their future conduct." Ibid., 3:10 January 1753.

51. B.L. Leeds Papers, vol. 133, Egerton Add. Mss. 3456, f. 271. This correspondent may have been someone he had known from his visit in 1749, and from whom he had obtained the map of Toulon harbor.

52. W.C.L. Mildmay Papers, 3:24 February 1753.

53. Ibid., 3:16 January 1754 (Toulon and Rochefort), 3:22 January 1755 (Rochefort and Brest). St. John Mildmay, *A Brief Memoir of the Mildmay Family*, 179 (quoting from Mildmay's travel journal on the numbers of ships in the royal fleet at Marseille and on the conditions in Toulon in 1749). In his book on the economy of the provinces of Provence and Languedoc, Mildmay gave further information on the French navy. In the section called "The Marine of France" he gave an extensive description of the state of the royal dockyards of Marseille and Toulon, of the French marine as he observed it 1749, and further information he obtained about the French navy at Toulon, Rochefort, and Brest in 1753, 1754, and 1755. Mildmay, *An Account of the Southern Provinces*, 103–11.

54. W.C.L. Mildmay Papers, 3:16 January 1754. Mildmay's written extract from this Rochefort letter is in his papers in the Essex Record Office. It gives the names and details of the warships now in harbor at Rochefort, those that have already sailed, the numbers of troops on the ships commanded by the French admiral of the Fleet, M. Macnamara, and the information that M. Bigot, the intendant of Quebec, has been ordered home to make his financial report and

is to be replaced by M. Robert, commissioner general of the Department of Brest. E.R.O. Mildmay Papers, D/DM, 01/28.

55. W.C.L. Mildmay Papers, 3:22 January 1755. The weight of a quintal has been estimated at approximately 110 lbs. Robert Forster, *The Nobility of Eighteenth Century France* (Baltimore: Johns Hopkins University Press, 1960), 67, 68. Based on 110 lbs. per quintal, Mildmay was talking about 660,000 lbs. of biscuit to feed 400 men for six months. At 165 lbs. per head, this comes to 27 lbs. of biscuit per month for each sailor.

56. W.C.L. Mildmay Papers, 3:5 February 1755. This information is an enclosed list of the names of ships in the French fleets that had just sailed from Brest, with a description of the tonnage of each ship, the date on which it was built, and its armament. In his letter of 5 February, Mildmay told Fitzwalter that he had given this list to Ruvigny de Cosne, first secretary of the British embassy. He also sent another copy of it to Carew Hervey Mildmay on 9 May 1755 and to Sir Thomas Robinson, secretary of state for the Southern Department, on 28 May 1755. E.R.O. Mildmay Papers, D/DM, 01/30 (Carew Mildmay); E.R.O. Mildmay Papers, D/DM, 01/41 (Robinson). The full transcription of this list is in appendix 7. On 31 August 1752, Mildmay reminded Lord Holdernesse of some earlier information on the composition of the French fleet in Toulon that he had collected during his visit to the port in 1749 and which, on his return to England, he had subsequently delivered to the duke of Bedford. B.L. Leeds Papers, vol. 133, Egerton 3456, f. 271, 31 August 1752.

57. E.R.O. Mildmay Papers, D/DM, 01/29. See appendix 6 for the full list of these export figures. Arthur Young, in noting the details of the exports from the French West Indies, stated that by 1770 the total value of export trade in sugar from these islands had increased to "three million sterling." He also stated that in 1770 "the . . . [sugar] produce of the French island . . . [of] Hispaniola (Haïti) amounts to as much as all the British islands together." Arthur Young, *Letters Concerning the Present State of the French Nation* (London: W. Nicoll, 1770), 56, 58n.

58. In a manuscript draft for his book on the political economy of Languedoc and Provence, Mildmay stated that this particular manuscript was "written in the year 1756, soon after the War was declared against France." E.R.O. Mildmay Papers, D/DMy, 15 M 50/1324.

59. Mildmay, *An Account of the Southern Maritime Provinces*, 119. In 1760, Mildmay was stating an opinion on these French islands that would cause William Pitt to resign in protest from the Cabinet in 1761. During that year George III and Lord Bute were negotiating the return of the captured West Indian islands in order to achieve a treaty with France in the Peace of Paris (1763): a decision with which Pitt profoundly disagreed.

60. W.C.L. Mildmay Papers, 3:9 February 1752. The word "fustian" described both a course cotton twill and a cheap form of cotton velveteen. It was a part of the "New Draperies" that competed for a textile market with traditional English woolen cloth. Charles Wilson, *England's Apprenticeship 1603–1763*, 193.

61. John Holker (1719–86), who was a Catholic, owned a cotton mill in Manchester. He joined the army of Prince Charles Edward Stuart in 1745 and after he was captured at Carlisle with the other Jacobites from Manchester, he was sentenced to prison in Newgate. In June 1748 he escaped to France by bribing a Newgate turnkey, and in 1751 he asked the British government for a pardon. This appeal was rejected. In 1752 he got the permission of Controller General Machault to open a fabric factory in Rouen. *Dictionary of National Biography*, ed. Lee and Stephens, 9:1026.

62. Holker was appointed the inspector general of manufacture by Controller General Machault in 1754 and introduced improvements to the manufacture of velvet and corduroy in his Rouen factory. There he also established a spinning school for the training of French artisans. He was granted *lettres de noblesse* by the French government in 1775 and was buried in Rouen in 1786. Andre Remond, *John Holker, manufacturier et grand fonctionnaire en France au 18e siècle, 1719–1786* (Paris: M. Riviere, 1946).

63. John Bosher reports that François-Pierre Billard, *caissier-général des Postes* and a businessman, formed an agricultural company in the early 1750s to develop new farming methods in Berry. It may have been this company that Mildmay reported was attempting to acquire British sheep for breeding purposes in Berry. John Bosher, *French Finances 1770–1795: From Business to Bureaucracy* (Cambridge: Cambridge University Press, 1970), 107.

64. W.C.L. Mildmay Papers, 3:9 February 1752.

65. Ibid., 3:30 March 1753. It seems likely that Kay's invention was used in Holker's spinning school, where French artisans were trained for his factory in Rouen.

66. Ibid., 3:20 February 1754. Among the documents that Mildmay kept in his papers is a proposal from an inventor of several machines, one of which was entitled "*Description d'un movement ou machine, et de l'usage à quoi elle doit etre appliquée.*" This appears to be a machine for cutting boards of wood, up to eight feet long, which could be operated by one man. Its inventor stated that it would replace the normal work carried out by 12 men and he was asking 800 *livres* for the full details of his invention. Another machine, for which he wanted 2,400 *livres*, could grind grain also by using the labor of one man, and was capable of operating at a 50 percent profit over the conventional method. The third machine was a new kind of fulling mill, able to raise water and turn water pumps, and its inventor considered it to be worth 1,600 *livres* to a prospective buyer. E.R.O. Mildmay Papers, D/DM, 01/28.

67. B. L. Leeds Papers, vol. 133, Egerton 3456. f. 271.

68. W.C.L. Mildmay Papers, 3:6 December 1752.

69. E.R.O. Mildmay Papers, D/DM, 01/26. As this document is in Mildmay's papers, entitled *"Projet de Loterie de Banque ou de Commerce de la part de M. Mildmay,"* Pelham must have done so. E.R.O. Mildmay Papers D/DM, 01/27.

70. W.C.L. Mildmay Papers, 3:20 February 1754. In Mildmay's papers this invention appears as *"Projet d'un Moulin à Sucre"* and it was submitted to Mildmay by a M. Robert. E.R.O. Mildmay Papers, D/DM, 01/27.

71. This information is in a letter from Mildmay to Lord Fitzwalter, written on 2 December 1750, that mentions Pownall's help. W.C.L. Mildmay Papers, vol. 3. In his letter of 2 December 1752, which reveals further private information from the Board of Trade, John Pownall passes on to Mildmay the best wishes of "all our friends and relations." E.R.O. Mildmay Papers, D/DM, 01/26.

72. The chief clerk was the administrative head of a department, or board, and had the same position as a later permanent secretary. Thompson, *The Secretaries of State,* 96.

73. W.C.L. Mildmay Papers, 3:20 February 1754.

74. E.R.O. Mildmay Papers D/DM, 01/27.

75. William Beckford was elected to Parliament in 1749 and in 1752 he was elected an alderman for Billingsgate Ward, in the city of London. He was a strong promoter of the West Indian sugar trade and in Tobias Smollett's estimation, "The cause of the sugar planters was defended vigorously and managed in the House by Alderman Beckford." Tobias Smollett, *The History of England from the Revolution in 1688 to the Death of George II,* 4 vols. (London: R. Scholey, 1805), 4:165.

76. E.R.O. Mildmay Papers, D/DM, 01/28. This report by Mildmay's French friend is in W.C.L. Mildmay Papers, vol. 7, and its title is *"Lettre á Monsr. Mildmay sur la commerce de St. Dominique et sur l'etât present de cette colonié, par Monsr. V—l—s."*

77. Jansenism was a religious movement that began in the seventeenth century, inspired by the book *Augustinius,* written by the bishop of Ypres, Cornelius Jansen, in 1640. Their belief in predestination as a prerequisite for Christian salvation came very close to the teachings of Calvinism and, as a result, the Jesuits and the papacy thus accused them of being subversive schismatics and potential heretics.

78. W.C.L. Mildmay Papers, 3:17 January 1752.

79. Ibid., 3:17 May 1752. This council consisted of two cardinals, two bishops, and three councilors of state, one of whom was Trudaine. With his 17 May letter, Mildmay sent the official announcement of 10 May 1752, printed by the French government, that gave the names and titles of the commissioners.

80. B.L. Leeds Papers, vol. 133, Egerton 3456, ff. 59–62 (Albemarle's report to Holdernesse, dated 11 December 1751). W.C.L. Mildmay Papers, 3:1 December 1751 (Mildmay's letter to Fitzwalter in which he stated that he had obtained his enclosed information from one of the magistrates of the *Parlement*).

81. Edmond Barbier, *Journal Historique et annecdotique du régne de Louis XV par Edmond Barbier*, ed. A.de Villegille (Paris: Renourd, 1847–56); d'Argenson, *Journal and Memoirs of the Marquis d'Argenson*, ed. Rathery, trans. Prescott-Wormeley; *Memoires and Letters of Francois-Joachim de Pierre, Cardinal de Bernis*, intro. C. A. Stainte-Beuve, trans. Katherine Prescott-Wormeley (Boston: Hardy Pratt and Co., 1902); J. H. Shennan, *The Parlement of Paris* (London: Eyre and Spottiswoode, 1968); Jean Egret, *Louis XV et l'Opposition Parlementaire 1715–1774* (Paris: Libraire Armand Colin, 1970); Francois Bluche, *Les Magistrats du Parlement au XVIIIe Siècle* (Paris: Economica, 1986); John Rogister, *Louis XV and the Parlement of Paris 1737–1755* (New York: Cambridge University Press, 1995); Franklin L. Ford, *The Regrouping of the French Aristocracy after Louis XVI* (Pittsburgh: University of Pittsburgh Press, 1976); James Hardy, *Judicial Politics in the Old Regime* (Baton Rouge: Louisiana State University Press, 1967); Norman Ravitch, *Sword and Mitre, Government and the Episcopate in France and England in the Age of Aristocracy* (The Hague: Mouton Press, 1966); Bailey Stone, *The Parlement of Paris, 1774–1789* (Chapel Hill: University of North Carolina Press, 1981); Bailey Stone, *French Parlements and the Crisis of the Old Regime* (Chapel Hill: University of North Carolina Press, 1986); Dale Van Kley, *The Jansenists and the Expulsion of the Jesuits* (New Haven: Yale University Press, 1985); Dale Van Kley, *The Damiens Affair and the Unraveling of the Ancien Régime* (Princeton: Princeton University Press, 1984).

82. The problems caused by the lack of a supreme court of appeal had spread throughout France. The difficulties that this was causing to the court of the *Parlement* of Burgundy were commented on by Charles de Brosse, one of the senior presidents of this court in the 1750s. Charles de Brosse, *Lettres du President de Brosse à Ch-C.Loppin de Gemeaux*, intro. Yvonne Bezard (Paris: Firmin-Didot, 1929), 6, 252.

83. W.C.L. Mildmay Papers, 3:30 May 1753.

84. Ibid., 3:26 April 1752. Mildmay was referring to the religious riots in London caused by the Whig impeachment of the High Church clergyman, Dr. Henry Sacheverell, in 1710.

85. Mildmay was discussing the constant military skirmishes taking place between the British colonial militia and the French forces on the borders of New England and in the Ohio Valley.

86. W.C.L. Mildmay Papers, 3:12 December 1753.

87. Ibid., 3:19 December 1753.

88. E.R.O. Mildmay Papers, D/DM, 01/27.

89. W.C.L. Mildmay Papers, 3:23 April 1755.

90. E.R.O. Mildmay Papers, D/DM, 01/28.

91. Ibid. Mildmay was referring to Ferdinand VI of Spain (1713–59), third son of Philip V, duke of Anjou, who had inherited the Spanish throne in 1746. Although Ferdinand VI did not die until 1759, the Bourbon Charles III (1734–59), ruler of the Kingdom of the Two Sicilies from 1734, had only been restored to his throne at Naples, in 1746, as a part of the agreement with Austria in the Peace Treaty of Aix-la-Chapelle. No British consulate was established at Naples until 1786 and the signing of the commercial treaty between Britain and the Kingdom of the Two Sicilies.

## CHAPTER 4

1. B.L. Hardwicke Papers, vol. 774, Add. Mss. 36, 122, f. 24. A royal warrant of appointment, dated April 1750, and signed by the duke of Bedford, as secretary of state for the Southern Department.

2. W.C.L. Mildmay Papers, 2:1, "Memorandum."

3. E.R.O. Mildmay Papers D/DM, 01/42.

4. B. L. Newcastle Papers, Add. Ms. 32,737, f. 550. "A list of Foreign Ministers with their Several Ordinaries and Extra-Ordinaries." This list covers the year 1752, and in the second part, among the residents and commissioners, is "William Mildmay (Commissary re Prizes and America) 3. l. (£3) per day. Do. (ditto) 20s (£1) a day for a Secretary."

5. Benjamin Keene, *The Private Correspondence of Sir Benjamin Keene, K.B.*, ed. Sir Richard Lodge (London: University Press, 1933), 58, 59, 60, 85, 86.

6. D. B. Horn, *The British Diplomatic Service, 1689–1789* (Oxford: Clarendon Press, 1961), 16.

7. B.L. Newcastle Papers, vol. 125, Add. Mss. 32,820, f.202.

8. Ibid., f. 395. Bedford's instructions to William Shirley and William Mildmay, dated 29 March 1750, together with the king's instructions that were sent from Hanover, are printed in full in D. B. Horn, *British Diplomatic Instructions, 1689–1789*, ed. L. G. Wickham-Legg (London: Royal Historical Society, 1934), 307–13.

9. B.L. Newcastle Papers, vol. 125, Add. Mss. 32,820, f. 429.

10. W.C.L. Mildmay Papers, 3:22 April 1752.

11. W.C.L. Mildmay Papers, 4:5.

12. B.L. Newcastle Papers, vol. 125, Add. Mss. 32,820, f. 436.

13. B.L. Leeds Papers, vol. 93, Egerton 3416, f. 214.

14. Mildmay's official instructions stated that the States General of Holland, as parties to the treaty of Aix-la-Chapelle, had also appointed commissioners to look after their interests, and he was to give "friendly advice and assistance" to the Dutch commissioners in order to show "Our sincere regard for Our good allies," Horn, *British Diplomatic Instructions*, 308.

15. B.L. Leeds Papers, vol. 93, Egerton 3416, f. 228.

16. A. C. Edwards, *The Account Books of Benjamin Mildmay, Earl Fitzwalter* (London: Regency Press, 1977), 212. Lord Fitzwalter notes Holdernesse's appointment as British ambassador to Holland on 24 May 1749, ibid., 212, 213. Holdernesse was made southern secretary on 18 June 1751. Horace Walpole gives an inaccurate date of 1750 as Holdernesse's appointment as the British ambassador to Holland. Horace Walpole, *Memoirs of the Reign of King George II*, ed. Lord Holland, 2 vols. (London: Henry Colburn, 1846), 206.

17. Edwards, *The Account Books of Benjamin Mildmay*, vii, viii (the date of the marriage of the Honorable Benjamin Mildmay to Frederica, countess dowager of Holdernesse). After Fitzwalter became Mildmay's financial guardian in 1716, Mildmay was a frequent visitor to Lord Fitzwalter's estate of Moulsham Hall, near Chelmsford, Essex. E.R.O. Mildmay Papers, D/DM L2/1, L2/2. Also see chapter 1.

18. E.R.O. Mildmay Papers, D/DM L2/1 (Fitzwalter's guardianship records, from 1716 to 1722).

19. W.C.L. Mildmay Papers, 3:28 November 1750 (seven letters, dating from 22 July to 19 December 1750).

20. Ibid., 3:2 July 1750 (Paris).

21. F. G. Emmison, *A Guide to the Essex Record Office* (Chelmsford: Essex Record Office Publication no. 52, 1969), part 2, p. 110 (on Lady Frederica Fitzwalter's family); W.C.L. Mildmay Papers, 3:25 December 1754 (confirming Lord Fitzwalter's position on the Board of Trade).

22. Horace Walpole, *Memoirs of King George II*, ed. John Brooke, vol. 2, March 1754–59 (New Haven: Yale University Press, 1985), 133n. 1 (Schomberg); Edwards, *The Account Books of Benjamin Mildmay*, vii; append. 1, the Fitzwalter Tomb inscription (Lady Frederica Fitzwalter as daughter of the duke of Schomberg, and granddaughter of Charles-Lewis, the Elector of the Rhine Palatine). Also see chapter 1.

23. W.C.L. Mildmay Papers, 3:30 December 1750.

24. Savelle, *The Diplomatic History of the Canadian Boundary*, 32, 33.

25. Horn, *British Diplomatic Instructions*, 308.

26. W.C.L. Mildmay Papers, 4:5–7.

27. Ibid., 4:7, 8, 10, 11, 12, 13.

28. Ibid., 4:5, 6. In a letter to Lord Fitzwalter, written on 4 August 1752, Mildmay gave the value of the *livre* as just under one English shilling. W.C.L. Mildmay Papers, vol. 3. The total sum of the ransom demanded by France for the Hanovarian and Hessian troops was, therefore, approximately just under £4,000.

29. W.C.L. Mildmay Papers, 4:11, 12. Based on the exchange value given by Mildmay in 1752 (see note 27 above), these sums would have been approximately £33,000 and £29,000 respectively.

30. Ibid., 4:12.

31. Ibid., 3:22 August 1750.

32. Ibid., 3:2 July 1750.

33. Horn, *British Diplomatic Instructions*, 307–13.

34. W.C.L. Mildmay Papers, 5:6–8.

35. Ibid., 3:171, 31 January 1753.

36. B.L. Newcastle Papers, vol. 125, Add. Mss. 32,820, f. 431–35. This document is headed: "Memorial in reply to the Answers and Objections of the French Court to the plan of Instructions relating to Prizes taken at Sea during the War." A note on the title page also states: "The Memorial from whence this copy is taken was in the Duke of Bedford's letter of 16th April 1750 [to the Duke of Newcastle] and the answer set back for alteration on 25th April." A copy of the French memorial, presented to Lord Albemarle by M. Puysieulx, and to which this document is an answer, is in W.C.L. Mildmay Papers, 5:29–34.

37. W.C.L. Mildmay Papers, 5:20–26. A boundary based on Cape St. Vincent would thus take in all of the northwest and west coast of France, and include the Bay of Biscay.

38. Ibid., 5:26.

39. B.L. Newcastle Papers, vol. 125, Add. Mss. 32,820, f. 429.

40. Ibid.

41. W.C.L. Mildmay Papers, 3:22 August 1750. The official notice of the appointment of William Shirley and William Mildmay by George II was written in Latin, signed by Shirley and Mildmay, dated August 1750, and presented to the French Court. It was filed by the French Ministry of Foreign Affairs in their document collection for 1750. C.A.M., *Correspondence Politique*, vol. 430, reel C 12544, pp. 7–9.

42. E.R.O. Mildmay Papers D/DM, 01/41.

43. Ibid.

44. W.C.L. Mildmay Papers, 5:18, 19.

45. Ibid., 2:5–8.

46. Ibid., 2:5–8.

47. Ibid., 5:35–37 (dated 2 September 1750).

48. Ibid., 2:5–8.

49. Ibid., 2:8–10. In the official report that Mildmay and Shirley sent to the duke of Bedford the name of the new governor of Martinique is given as M. Bompar, who had just left Brest with: "strict orders given him for the immediate evacuation of these islands [St. Lucia, St. Vincent, and Dominique], in conjunction with M. Granville (the British governor of Barbados)." W.C.L. Mildmay Papers, 5:38–41.

50. Mildmay and Shirley sent copies of their official report on this meeting to the duke of Newcastle, in Hanover, and to the commissioners of the Board of Trade, in London, W.C.L. Mildmay Papers, 5:38–41. They also tried to get a speedy response to their request by writing to the duke of Bedford's secretary, Richard Neville Aldworth, asking that if Bedford were not in town, would Aldworth please forward their recent, urgent dispatches. W.C.L. Mildmay Papers, 5:42.

51. Keene, *Private Correspondence*, 25.

52. A French translation of this British memorial, signed by Shirley and Mildmay, is in W.C.L. Mildmay Papers, 5:43–45, and the French memorial, signed by Galissonière and Silhouette, is in the same volume on pages 45, 46.

53. W.C.L. Mildmay Papers, 2:12–14. These two memorials of September 1750 are noted in the final list of all the memorials exchanged during the course of the commission's work. E.R.O. Mildmay Papers, D/DM, 01/41. The maps of both the French and the British claims to Acadia and Nova Scotia were printed in *Remarks on the French Memorials concerning the Limits of Acadia, printed at the Royal printing house at Paris and distributed by the French Ministers to all the Foreign Courts of Europe* (London, 1756), B.L. 8176 a.a. 39; B.M. 10470 c. 10. In present-day terms the geographical boundary given in this British map appears to cover the western part of Maine, the southwest shore of the St. Lawrence, the Gaspe Peninsula, New Brunswick, and Nova Scotia, but excluding Cape Breton. (Ile Royale) and Prince Edward Island (Ile St Jean), which had always been regarded as a French possession.

54. The 1713 Treaty of Utrecht had divided the Nova Scotia peninsula between Britain and France on a line from Cape St. Mary to the Strait of Canso. In the map supplied by the French in 1756, the territory of Acadia claimed by France was all of the land to the south of this line from Cape St. Mary to Canso, enclosing the entire Atlantic coastline, including the Island of Cape Breton, and leaving to the British the northern half of the peninsular, including Port Royal and the south shoreline of the Bay of Fundy, but not that of the Minas Basin.

55. W.C.L. Mildmay Papers, 5:47, 48.

56. Savelle, *The Diplomatic History*, 37.

57. These are the two complaints against the British in a printed copy of *"Ordonnance du Roy portant déclartion de guerre contre le Roy d'Angleterre, Du 15 Mai 1744,"* now in the W. C. L. Mildmay Papers, 3:53–56.

58. W.C.L. Mildmay Papers, 2:15, 16.

59. Ibid., 5:49–50.

60. C.A.M. vol. 430. C 12546, pp. 38–45.

61. W.C.L. Mildmay Papers, 2:17–19; ibid., 5:50–52 (the commission report).

62. Mildmay was using the French government's decision in 1663 to rename its territory in North America "Canada," rather than its previous name of "New France," as an example to demonstrate that the existence and ownership of a piece of land was not affected by any subsequent change to its name.

63. W.C.L. Mildmay Papers, 5:51, 52.

64. C.A.M. vol. 430, C 12546, pp. 81–85.

65. W.C.L. Mildmay Papers, 3:28 October 1750. In the thirty-seven following the Treaty of Utrecht, successive British governors complained that the French had allowed colonists to build settlements and small forts on land that the Treaty had given to Britain. To insist on the strict observance of the Treaty would mean that these must now be demolished, and the French encroachment ended.

66. Savelle, *The Diplomatic History*, 35, 37n. 89.

67. W.C.L. Mildmay Papers, 2:14. The letter to Bedford is the official report, sent by Mildmay and Shirley, and dated 23 September 1750, ibid., 5:47, 48.

68. Ibid., 3:28 October 1750.

69. Savelle, *The Diplomatic History*, 37, 38.

70. W.C.L. Mildmay Papers, 2:20–23.

71. Ibid., 5:53–54.

72. Ibid., 5:53.

73. Ibid., 2:23–27; ibid., 5:55 (letters to the duke of Bedford and the Board of Trade).

74. Ibid., 2:29–32.

75. C.A.M. vol. 429, C12546, p. 126.

76. W.C.L. Mildmay Papers, 3:28 October 1750.

77. Savelle, *The Diplomatic History*, 38n. 92.

78. Schutz, *William Shirley*, 1–5.; *Dictionary of National Biography*, ed. Lee and Stephen, 52: 152.

79. *Dictionary of National Biography*, 52:143.

80. Henry St. John Mildmay, *A Brief Memoir of the Mildmay Family* (London: privately printed, 1913), 186.

81. *Dictionary of National Biography*, 52:143; Schutz, *William Shirley*, 96–100.

82. Olwen Hufton, *Europe: Privilege and Protest 1730–1787* (London: Harvester Press, 1980), 112.

83. Schutz, *William Shirley*, 147, 152, 153.

84. Letter from William Shirley to the duke of Newcastle, March 28th 1750. *The Correspondence of William Shirley, Governor of Massachusetts and Military Commander in America 1731–1760*, ed. C. H. Lincoln, 2 vols. (New York, 1912), 1:499–504; Schutz, *William Shirley*, 154.

85. *The Correspondence of William Shirley*, vol. 1: letter from William Shirley to the duke of Bedford, 10 May 1749 (485, 486); letter from, the governor of New York, George Clinton, to William Shirley, 19 May 1749 (487); letter from William Shirley to the duke of Newcastle, 28 March 1750 (499-504); letter from William Shirley to the duke of Newcastle, 10 April 1750 (505-7).

86. Letter from William Shirley to Lord Holdernesse, 19 April 1754, B.L. Newcastle Papers, Add. Mss. 32,735 f. 110–18.

87. Letter from Lord Holdernesse to Lord Albemarle, B.L. Leeds Papers, vol. 133, Egerton 3456, f. 71–73. Letter from Lord Albemarle to Lord Holdernesse, ibid., f. 91–94.

88. W.C.L. Mildmay Papers, 3:28 October 1750.

89. This statement is in Mildmay's journal entry for 17 March 1753, ibid., 2:70.

90. Horn, *The British Diplomatic Service*, 182, 183.

91. W.C.L. Mildmay Papers, 2:30, 31.

92. Ibid., 4:20–22 (Mildmay's letter to the duke of Bedford; ibid., 4:98–121 (the printed text of the Cartel of Frankfurt).

93. Ibid., 3:22 September 1750.

94. In the eighteenth century the word "pretend" could also mean "claim."

95. W.C.L. Mildmay Papers, 4:23, 24.

96. Ibid., 5:60–61; ibid., 2:32–33.

97. Ibid., 5:61.

98. C.A.M. vol. 429, C 12546, p. 136.

99. W.C.L. Mildmay Papers, 3:22 November 1750.

100. Ibid., 3:22 November 1750. In the instructions given to the commissioners in May 1750 they had been told to send copies of their commission reports both to the secretary of state and to the Board of Trade, but only so long as these reports were on subjects in which the Board had a legitimate interest. This instruction did not indicate that they were also permitted to send to the Board, or to the president, any copies of Bedford's correspondence to the commission.

101. The actual identity of this clerk is revealed in a letter written by John Pownall to Mildmay on 2 December 1752, in which Pownall stated that he was now the chief clerk (undersecretary) at the Board of Trade. In this letter Pownall referred to his previous assistance, and gave Mildmay further confidential information on certain deliberations taken by the Board regarding Mildmay's

commission. E.R.O. Mildmay Papers D/DM, 01/26. The help that Pownall was giving Mildmay may not have been entirely disinterested, however. In his biography of John Pownall's elder brother, Thomas Pownall, governor of Massachusetts, John Schutz describes both John Pownall's considerable influence as a professional bureaucrat at the Board of Trade, and the animosity that both brothers had for William Shirley. John Schutz, *Thomas Pownall, British Defender of American Liberty* (Glendale, Calif.: Arthur H. Clarke and Co., 1951), 20, 21, 60, 61.

102. W.C.L. Mildmay Papers, 3:19 December 1750. These orders from the Board become apparent in the commission report sent to the duke of Bedford early in 1751. It is very unfortunate that Mildmay did not keep any of Fitzwalter's letters to him, as this is one case where it would have been useful to know the exact nature of the "advice" that he received.

103. Ibid., 5:62.

104. *The Memorials of the English and French Commissaries concerning the Limits of Nova Scotia and Acadia and St. Lucia*, 2 vols. (London, 1756), British Library.

105. W.C.L. Mildmay Papers, 5:63.

## Notes to Chapter 5

1. W.C.L. Mildmay Papers, 2:33, 34.

2. Ibid., 2:33.

3. Ibid., 5:64.

4. E.R.O. Mildmay Papers, D/DM, 01/20.

5. W.C.L. Mildmay Papers, 5:65; 2:34.

6. Ibid., 3:34 (8 April); 5:67–69 (13 April).

7. Ibid., 2:35; 5:67, 68, 69.

8. E.R.O. Mildmay Papers D/DM 01/20.

9. W.C.L. Mildmay Papers, 2:35–37.

10. Ibid., 2:37, 38. A copy of this French memorial, dated 29 April, is in the correspondence of the French Foreign Ministry. C.A.M. vol. 433, C 12545, pp. 212–14.

11. Horn, *The British Diplomatic Service*, 37.

12. W.C.L. Mildmay Papers, 3:7 June 1752.

13. Letter from Horace Walpole to Sir Horace Mann, 9 January 1755. *Memoirs of the Reign of King George the Second*, ed. Lord Holland (London: Henry Colburn, 1846), 458; Horace Walpole, *Horace Walpole's Correspondence with Sir Horace Mann*, vol. 4, 15th November 1748–18th September 1756, *The Yale Edition of Horace Walpole's Correspondence*, vol. 22, ed. W. S. Lewis and A. Doyle Wallace (New Haven: Yale University Press, 1954), 155, 156, 169, 170.

14. *British Diplomatic Instructions 1689–1789, Vol. VII: France, Part IV, 1745–1789*, ed. L. G. Wickham-Legg (London: The Royal Historical Society, 1934), Camden Third Series, 49:1, 2. Sir Benjamin Keene stated in a letter to Abraham Castres on 23 December 1754 that Albemarle had been a very popular ambassador at the French Court, Sir Richard Lodge, ed., *The Private Correspondence of Sir Benjamin Keene K.B.* (London: University Press, 1933), 394.

15. The following letter is the only one from Mildmay to Lord Albemarle that is to be found, either in Mildmay's own papers at the William L. Clements Library and the Essex Record Office or in the diplomatic material in the Leeds and Newcastle Papers.

16. B.L. Newcastle Papers, vol. 221, Add. Mss. 32,827, f. 251/2.

17. W.C.L. Mildmay Papers, 8:69.

18. C.A.M. vol. 432, C 12544, pp. 81–82.

19. W.C.L. Mildmay Papers, 5:71–73.

20. Ibid., 2:40–44.

21. Ibid., 2:44; *Correspondence of Horace Walpole with Sir Horace Mann*, 249n. 38.

22. B.L. Leeds Papers, vol. 133, Egerton 3456, f. 5. The Princess Mary, daughter of George II, had just become regent for her young son on the sudden death of her husband.

23. In volume 7 of the Mildmay Papers in the William L. Clements Library is a lengthy document headed "*Lettre à Monsr. Mildmay sur le commerce de St. Dominique, et sur d'état de cette colonié*." Using the body of information he had collected while in France, after he returned to England Mildmay wrote a book on the comparisons between British, French, and Dutch trade practices, entitled *The Laws and Policy of England Relating to Trade Examined by the Maxims and Principles of the Laws of Trade in General, and by the Policy of Other Trading Nations* (London: T. Harrison, 1765).

24. E.R.O. Mildmay Papers, D/DM, 01/28.

25. W.C.L. Mildmay Papers, 5:73–76.

26. Ibid., 5:76–78.

27. Ibid., 5:78.

28. B.L. Leeds Papers, vol. 133, Egerton 3456 f. 13. Cardinal Bernis stated that the influence behind the king's decision to appoint M. St. Contest was M. de Machault, *Garde du Sceaux*, (Keeper of the Seals) who, in turn, owed his own appointment to the patronage of Madame de Pompadour. C. A. Sainte-Beuve, ed., *The Memoirs and Letters of Cardinal Bernis*, trans. Katherine Prescott Wormeley (Boston: Hardy, Pratt and Co., 1902), 167.

29. B.L. Leeds Papers, vol. 133, Egerton 3456, f. 28.

30. W.C.L. Mildmay Papers, 2:46.

31. A. C. Edwards, *The Account Books of Benjamin Mildmay Earl Fitzwalter* (London: Regency Press, 1977), viii.

32. *Correspondence of Horace Walpole with Horace Mann*, 169, 170. Lord Albemarle (1702–54) was married to Anne, youngest daughter of Charles Lennox, first duke of Richmond and natural son of Charles II. J. C. D. Clarke, ed., *The Memoirs and Speeches of James, 2nd Earl Waldegrave 1742–1763* (Cambridge: Cambridge University Press, 1988), 137n. 429.

33. B.L. Leeds Papers, vol. 133, Egerton 3456, f. 87–90, 91–94, and passim.

34. William Coxe, ed., *Memoirs of the Administration of the Right Honourable Henry Pelham*, 2 vols. (London: Longman, Rees, Orme, Brown and Green, 1829), letter from Newcastle to Hardwicke, 2:407.

35. B.L. Leeds Papers, vol. 135, Egerton 3458, f. 9.

36. The wishes of inhabitants of this coast, and of the Ile St. Jean were, of course, immaterial. Given the deportation of the Acadians from Nova Scotia in 1754, and from the Ile Royale and Ile St. Jean after the fall of Louisbourg in 1758, this remark has a certain terrible irony to it.

37. B.L. Leeds Papers, vol. 135, Egerton 3458, f. 21.

38. E.R.O. Mildmay Papers, D/DM, 01/26.

39. W.C.L. Mildmay Papers, 3:12 November 1751; ibid., 2:46.

40. Ibid., 3:25 December 1754.

41. Ibid., 2:41.

42. Ibid., 2:47.

43. Ibid., 5:80.

44. Ibid., 2:47–49; C.A.M., vol. 433, C12545, pp. 168–69.

45. The War of the Austrian Succession broke out between England and Spain in 1741, and the activities of licensed privateers had been taking place since 1739, but although France opposed the claim of Maria Theresa to the Austrian throne, while Britain supported it, it was not until 15 March 1744 that France officially declared war on Britain. The British position that only French ships captured by British captains within the six-month period from 15 March to mid-August 1744 were covered under the Treaty, removed from the list of prize claims any ship captured before March 1744. The French position maintained by Galissonière, acting on the instructions of Louis XV, was that many of the French prizes had, in fact, been taken by privateers during the period from 1738 to 15 March 1744, when France was still, technically, neutral. The French assertions were that under the accepted conventions of sea warfare the capture of ships from a neutral nation, as well as those in foreign ports when war was declared, were acts of piracy. This is the background to the legal argument that was being used by Britain to insist on recognizing only those prizes taken from

270 THE FORGOTTEN COMMISSIONER

15 March to 15 August 1744, and in the six months following the peace treaty, signed in April 1748. By refusing to discuss any compensation both for French ships taken in British ports before mid-March 1744, and for the acts of privateers going back to 1738, Britain was able to deny any government responsibility for these captures. Regardless of anything they had signed in the Treaty of Aix-la-Chapelle, the French were determined to compel Britain to accept this legal responsibility, both now and in the future.

46. W.C.L. Mildmay Papers, 3:4 December 1751.

47. Ibid.; ibid., 5:79, 80, 24 November 1751.

48. B.L. Leeds Papers, vol. 133, Egerton 3456, f. 57.

49. W.C.L. Mildmay Papers, 3:22 December 1751(NS).

50. Ibid., 5:81.

51. "Mr Appy's Declaration concerning the French Memorial," E.R.O. Mildmay Papers. D/DM, 01/41. John Appy subsequently became the private secretary to Lord Loudoun, who replaced William Shirley as military governor of Massachusetts in 1756. John Schutz, *Thomas Pownall, British Defender of American Liberty* (Glendale, Calif.: Arthur A. Clark Co., 1951), 73.

52. E.R.O. Mildmay Papers, D/DM, 01/41. The reference to "a half margin" indicates that these pages were laid out in the usual method for writing a draft document; the pages were divided in half, lengthways, with one side of each page left for accompanying notes, comments, and suggestions. This reply was, apparently, a response to Shirley's draft on Acadia.

53. W.C.L. Mildmay Papers, 2:47–49; ibid., 5:78–80.

54. B.L. Leeds Papers, vol. 133, Egerton 3456, f. 71–73.

55. Ibid., f. 91–94. In the membership of the king's council, Machault was seen as a more powerful minister than St. Contest.

56. Horn, *The British Diplomatic Service*, 20.

57. W.C.L. Mildmay Papers, 3:8 March 1752.

58. Ibid., 2:50–53. There were twelve of these words and phrases, used in only thirteen separate instances, and Mildmay listed them as "*Gliseé* (slippery), *Prefourré* (prearranged), *Furtive* (furtive), *Tronqué.e et agencée* (casually laid out), *furtivement* (furtively), *plus interefie, qu' honourable* (more selfish than honourable), *invasion injuste* (an unjust invasion), *frivole* (frivolous), *chimerique* (illusory), *suggestions imaginaire* (fanciful suggestions), *furtivement, maniere tronquée* (a cursory manner), *compromise leur politesse et leur judgement,* and (compromise their courtesy and their judgement).

59. C.A.M., vol. 433, C 12545, p. 199.

60. W.C.L. Mildmay Papers, 3:8 March 1752 (NS).

61. Ibid., 3:15 April 1752 (NS).

62. Ibid., 2:52.

63. B.L. Leeds Papers, vol. 133, Egerton 3456, f. 192.

64. Mark Thompson, *The Secretaries of State 1681-1782* (Oxford: Clarendon Press, 1932), 50-53.

65. *Dictionary of American Biography*, 121; *Dictionary of National Biography*, 52:142.

66. Schutz, *William Shirley*, 164, 165.

67. Until mid-April 1752 all these reports are in Shirley's handwriting; thereafter they are written by Mildmay. W.C.L. Mildmay Papers, 5:passim.

68. *Dictionary of American Biography*, 121; *Dictionary of National Biography*, 52:142.

69. Schutz, *William Shirley*, 163, 164.

70. B.L. Hardwicke Papers, vol. 774, Add Ms 36, 122, f. 142 and f. 146, 30 March 1752. A second copy of these two warrants, both written in Latin, was presented by Mildmay and Shirley to the joint commission. They were then sent by the French commissioners to the French Foreign Ministry. C.A.M., vol. 433, C 12545, pp. 202, 203.

71. W.C.L. Mildmay Papers, 3:19 April 1952 (NS).

72. Ibid., 3:19 April 1752 (NS). William Shirley did not, in fact, return immediately to Boston as governor. Until the autumn of 1753 he was employed in London by the Board of Trade.

73. Public Record Office, State Papers, vol. 78, 239 f. 171/172.

74. Schutz, *William Shirley*, 165.

75. *Gazette d'Utrecht, XXXIV, Vendredi, 28 Avril 1752*. B.L. Leeds Papers, vol. 133, Egerton 3456, f.207/208. This article is in French, and the translation is mine.

76. B.L. Leeds Papers, vol. 133, Egerton 3456, f. 205.

77. W.C.L. Mildmay Papers, 3:5 April 1752 (N S).

78. Ibid., 3:12 April 1752 (NS).

79. Ibid., 3:26 April 1752 (NS).

## CHAPTER 6

1. W.C.L. Mildmay Papers, 2:53, 54.

2. Ibid., 3:31 May 1752. The commissioner named first on a warrant of appointment was regarded as the senior member. William Shirley was the first name in the 1750 warrant.

3. B.L. Leeds Papers, vol. 133, Egerton Add. Mss. 3456, f. 241. The warrant is in British Library Hardwicke Papers, vol. 774, Add. Mss. 36,122, f. 146.

4. B.L. Leeds Papers, vol. 133, Egerton 3456, f.203.

5. W.C.L. Mildmay Papers, 5:86, 87.

6. Horn, *The British Diplomatic Service*, 205.

7. B.L. Leeds Papers, vol. 135, Egerton 3458, f. 43. This proposed passage from Quebec would appear to pass through an inland area of Nova Scotia and would

exclude the whole eastern shore, except for this unnamed "certain point" facing the Northumberland Strait.

8. B.L. Leeds Papers, vol. 133, Egerton 3456, f. 9.

9. Savelle, *The Diplomatic History*, 41, 45.

10. B.L. Leeds Papers, vol. 133, Egerton 3456, f. 222–24, 252.

11. Ibid., f. 252.

12. Ibid., f. 253.

13. Ibid., f. 243–44.

14. C.A.M.., vol. 433, C12545, p. 201.

15. B.L. Leeds Papers, vol. 133, Egerton 3456, f. 252.

16. This letter from Hardwicke is printed in Theodore C. Pease, *Anglo-French Boundary Disputes in the West* (Springfield, Ill.: Illinois State Historical Society, 1936), 37. In a letter that Mildmay wrote to Sir Thomas Robinson on 28 May 1755, he stated that Crown Point was the name the British had given to given to Fort Frederic. E.R.O. Mildmay Papers, D/DM, 01/41. This fort had been built by the French at the headwaters of Lake Champlain, and it had been captured by the British in 1751. Fort Frederic, or Crown Point, had subsequently been retaken by a force sent from Quebec and as it commanded Lake Champlain, its removal as a military base was therefore of great importance to the British government.

17. B.L. Leeds Papers, vol. 133, Egerton 3456, f. 239–40.

18. Wickham-Legg, ed., *British Diplomatic Instruction*, 28.

19. Coxe, *Memoirs of the Administration of Henry Pelham*, 435.

20. Wickham-Legg, ed., *British Diplomatic Instruction*, 52; Horn, *British Diplomatic Service*, 18, 52, 112; D. B. Horn, ed., *British Diplomatic Representatives*, 3d series, vol. 46 (London: Camden Society, 1932), 21. (A letter from Sir Thomas Robinson, dated 22 July 1755, giving De Cosne instructions to leave Paris and return to London).

21. Benjamin Keene, *The Private Correspondence of Sir Benjamin Keene K.B.*, ed. Sir Richard Lodge (London: University Press, 1933), 395, 396, 406, 408, 395n.2.

22. His proposal to Lord Holdernesse made in May 1752. W.C.L., Mildmay Papers, 3:21 June 1752 (NS).

23. Ibid., 2:54–56.

24. Ibid., 4:27, 28.

25. Ibid., 5:83–84.

26. Ibid., 3:27 July 1752 (N.S.).

27. Ibid., 3:17 July 1752 (N.S.).

28. B.L. Newcastle Papers, Add. Mss. 32,838, f. 311.

29. Ibid., f. 317.

30. Ibid., f. 315.

31. Mark Thompson, *The Secretaries of State 1681–1782* (Oxford: Clarendon Press, 1956), 21.

32. B.L. Leeds Papers, vol. 133, Egerton 3456, f. 233.

33. Ibid., f. 250.

34. In 1750 the Civil List (the king's prerogative fund) covered the cost of British diplomacy, the civil service, the judiciary, and the salaries of government ministers. The Civil List amount voted each year for George II was £800,000, John Carswell and Lewis Arnold Dralle, eds, *The Political Journal of George Bubb Doddington* (Oxford: Clarendon Press, 1965), xvii.

35. W.C.L. Mildmay Papers, 3:7 June 1752.

36. Ibid., 3:8 November 1752.

37. Ibid., 3:29 August 1752.

38. Ibid., 3:2 July 1750.

39. Ibid., 3:29 August 1752.

40. Ibid., 5:85.

41. Ibid., 4:29.

42. Ibid., 5:87.

43. Ibid., 5:88; Companion letter to Newcastle and the Board of Trade, 5: 89.

44. Both of these maps were finally included in the printed justification of the negotiation issued by the British government in 1756. B.L. *Remarks on the French Memorials concerning the Limits of Acadia* (London, 1756), maps 1 and 2.

45. W.C.L., Mildmay Papers, 3:15 October 1752. This letter was written after the new dating convention was established in Britain. In order to conform to the dates used in the rest of Europe, the Act of 24 Geo. II, c. 23 decreed that 2 September 1752 should immediately be followed by 14 September 1752. From the beginning of September 1752 onward all of Mildmay's letters have, therefore, only one date.

46. Ibid., 4:30.

47. Ibid., 2:56–64.

48. C.A.M., vol. 433, C 12545, pp. 226–68.

49. W.C.L. Mildmay Papers, 5:93–95.

50. A. C. Edwards states that Edward Johnson had been Lord Fitzwalter's butler since before Fitzwalter married, in 1724, and he became Fitzwalter's steward in 1733. A. C. Edwards, *The Account Books of Benjamin Mildmay, Earl Fitzwalter* (London: Regency Press, 1977), 17.

51. E.R.O. Mildmay Papers, D/DM, 01/41, 2 August 1752 (letter from Johnson to Mildmay).

52. W.C.L. Mildmay Papers, 3:22 November 1752.

53. Schutz, *Thomas Pownall*, 20.

54. W.C.L. Mildmay Papers, 3:29 November 1752.

55. E.R.O. Mildmay Papers, D/DM, 01/26.

56. W.C.L. Mildmay Papers, 3:6 December 1752.

57. B.L. Leeds Papers, vol. 133, Egerton 3456, f.283.

58. Ibid., f. 309 (Holdernesse to Albemarle), f. 316, (Albemarle to Holdernesse), f. 317 (Holdernesse to Albemarle).

59. B.L. Newcastle Papers, vol. 154, Add. Mss. 32,841, f. 411; C.A.M., vol. 436, C 12545, pp. 104, 105.

60. C.A.M., vol. 435, C 12545, pp. 95, 96. In the margin a clerk has written the date of 27 October 1752.

61. W.C.L. Mildmay Papers, 3:3 January 1753.

62. Ibid., 5:96.

63. Ibid., 2:64.

64. C.A.M. vol. 433, C 12545, p. 278.

65. W.C.L. Mildmay Papers, 3:24 January 1753. In this remark Mildmay was probably alluding to the negotiations taking place between Lord Holdernesse and the duke of Mirepoix, discussed later in this chapter.

66. Ibid., 5:96, 97.

67. Ibid., 5:99. The text of this article stated: "You are also to correspond with Our Commissioners of Trade and Plantations, desiring their advice upon any difficulties that may arise," and further: "you are also to deliver to Our Commissioners for Trade and Plantations a duplicate of the said account [of your proceedings], so far as the same may relate to their cognizance." Wickham-Legg, ed., *British Diplomatic Instructions*, 49:313.

68. W.C.L. Mildmay Papers, 2:66–71.

69. Ibid., 5:99, 100.

70. C.A.M, vol. 433, C 12545, pp. 280–82. Although they are no longer in the official correspondence of Lord Holdernesse, copies of these documents were filed by the French Ministry of Foreign Affairs.

71. This information had been given to the French commissioners in a document sent from the office of M. Rouillé on 13 March. C.A.M, vol. 433, C 12545, pp. 286–88.

72. W.C.L. Mildmay Papers, 2:70, 71.

73. C.A.M., vol. 433, C 12545, p. 289.

74. W.C.L. Mildmay Papers, 2:101, 102.

75. Wickham-Legg, ed., *British Diplomatic Instructions*, 37, 38.

76. Ibid., 34, 35.

77. B.L. Leeds Papers, vol. 134, Egerton 3457, f. 3.

78. B.L. Leeds papers, vol. 133, Egerton 3456, f. 194.

79. B.L. Newcastle Papers, vol. 159, Add. Mss. 32,844, f. 34–35.

80. B.L. Leeds Papers vol. 134, Egerton 3457, f. 52.

81. W.C.L. Mildmay Papers, 2: 71–74.

82. B.L. Leeds Papers, vol. 134, Egerton 3457, f. 81. See p. 57.

83. W.C.L. Mildmay Papers, 5:105.

84. Ibid., 3:24 February 1753.

85. Ibid., 3:24 February 1752.

86. E.R.O. Mildmay Papers, D/DM, 01/26.

87. In the instructions Mildmay had been given when he took up his appointment on 29 March 1750 he had been told that "the Convention made in Frankfurt in the year 1743" was to be the basis of the negotiations on all subjects before the commission, Wickham-Legg, ed., *British Diplomatic Instructions*, 307. Under the cartel agreement signed in Frankfurt in 1743 the only sum due to the captor was for the actual ransom of each prisoner, while the sole compensation named in the 1748 treaty of Aix -la-Chapelle was restricted to the actual cost of the ship and its cargo. In each instance, however, both governments were trying to obtain additional damages, over and above the specific terms of these two agreements; in the case of the prisoners, for the cost of maintaining them, and on the subject of prizes, for the subsequent loss of revenue their capture had caused to the owner.

88. B.L. Newcastle Papers, vol. 164, Add. Mss. 32,851. f.118.

89. W.C.L. Mildmay Papers, 3:2 May 1753.

90. B.L. Newcastle Papers, vol. 160, Add. Mss. 32,845, f.121 (Mildmay's letter to Lord Holdernesse); ibid., f. 123 (Mildmay's expense list).

91. E.R.O. Mildmay Papers, D/DM, 01/26.

92. W.C.L. Mildmay Papers, 2:75.

93. Ibid., 5:106 [the request]: E.R.O. Mildmay Papers, D/DM, 01/41 [the permission].

94. Ibid., 3:4 July 1753.

95. B.L. Leeds Papers, vol. 134, Egerton 3457, f. 75.

96. Ibid., f. 81.

97. Ibid., f. 138.

98. Ibid., f.144.

99. W.C.L. Mildmay papers, 5:107.

100. Ibid., 5:108, 109.

101. Ibid., 3:3 November 1753.

102. Ibid., vol. 3. Letters written to Lord Fitzwalter on 6 November, 9 November, 14 November, 21 November, 2 November, 12 December, 19 December, and 26 December 1753.

## NOTES FOR CHAPTER 7

1. B.L. Leeds Papers, vol. 134, Egerton 3457. Diplomatic correspondence from January to December 1754.

2. Ibid., f. 273.

3. W.C.L. Mildmay Papers, 3: 16 January 1754. Mildmay was here referring to the potentially dangerous consequences for France in the ongoing constitutional and religious dispute that was taking place between the *Parlement* of Paris and the government of Louis XV.

4. Gilles Proulx, *Between France and New France* (Toronto: Dundurn Press, 1984), 51; J. S. McLennan, *Louisbourg From its Foundation to its Fall, 1713–1758* (1918; reprint, Halifax, N.S: The Book Room Limited, 1979), 3, 22, 23, passim.

5. Letter from Newcastle to Hardwicke, 6 September 1751, William Coxe, *Memoirs of the Administration of the Right Honourable Henry Pelham* (London: Longman, Rees, Orme, Brown, and Green, 1829), 2:407.

6. W.C.L. Mildmay Papers, 3: 16 January 1754.

7. Ibid.

8. Guy Fregault, *François Bigot: Administrateur Français* (Montreal: L'Institut, 1948), 2:78. Letter from Rouillé to Bigot, 1 June 1754.

9. W.C.L. Mildmay Papers, 3: 23 January 1754. In a letter from Lord Holdernesse to Lord Albemarle on 24 January 1754, in which he reviewed with Albemarle the history of the disputes between the French and British East India companies that had taken place in India over the previous year, he mentioned the arrival in London of "M. Duvalear and his brother" to negotiate a treaty of neutrality with a committee set up by the British company, *British Diplomatic Instructions*, 41–45.

10. W.C.L. Mildmay Papers, 3:11 February 1754.

11. Ibid., 3:6 March 1754.

12. B.L. Leeds Papers, vol. 134, Egerton 3457, f. 318.

13. Ibid., f. 322.

14. *Dictionary of National Biography*, ed. Sidney Lee and Leslie Stephen (London: Smith Elder and Co., 1897–1908), 49:47-49; Horn, ed., *British Diplomatic Representatives*, 46:46.

15. W. S. Taylor and J. H. Pringle, eds., *The Correspondence of William Pitt, Earl of Chatham*, vol. 1 (London, 1838-40), 96.

16. Horace Walpole, *Memoirs of the Reign of George the Second*, ed. John Brooke (New Haven: Yale University Press, 1985), 2:11.

17. James, Earl Waldegrave, *Memoirs from 1754 to 1758* (London: John Murray, 1821), 52.

18. B.L. Leeds Papers, vol. 134, Egerton 3457, f. 305.

19. B.L. Newcastle Papers, Add. Mss. 32,849, f. 232, 247, 256; Newcastle Papers, Add. Mss. 32,851, f. 129, 288, 305.

20. W.C.L. Mildmay Papers, 3:17 April 1754. Guinea was the name the British then gave to the entire territory along the Gulf of Guinea, consisting of what are now Guinea, the Cameroon, Nigeria, Ghana, and the Ivory Coast.

21. Ibid., 3:27 November 1754.

22. A letter from Governor William Shirley to Lord Halifax, 20 August 1754. *Military Affairs in North America 1748–1765, Selected Documents from the Cumberland Papers in Windsor Castle*, ed. Stanley Pargellis (Hamden, Conn.: Archon Books, 1969), 22.

23. B.L. Newcastle Papers, vol. 164, Add. Mss. 32,849, f. 376.

24. W.C.L. Mildmay Papers, 3:24 April 1754.

25. This date is given in "A List of Memorials sent to Mr. Mildmay." E.R.O. Mildmay Papers D/DM, 01/41. These memorials were sent to Mildmay from Paris on 9 July 1755 by Ruvigny De Cosne, as Mildmay was now in London preparing an official summary for the British government on the work of the commission over the past five years.

26. W.C.L. Mildmay Papers, 2:78.

27. Ibid., 5:113.

28. Sir Benjamin Keene told Abraham Castres on 8 August 1754 that a dispatch had just arrived from Paris reporting the sudden death of M. St. Contest, and of his replacement as foreign minister by M. de Rouillé. Benjamin Keene, *The Private Correspondence of Sir Benjamin Keene, K.B.*, ed. Sir Richard Lodge (London: University Press, 1933), 373.

29. W.C.L. Mildmay Papers, 2:79. In a commission letter to Sir Thomas Robinson Mildmay states that George II gave his consent to Rouillé's proposal on 30 August. Ibid., 2:116. This king's agreement, in August 1754, to have Mildmay and De Cosne review and certify the French translation of the Nova Scotia memorial was precisely what Mildmay had been instructed to refuse to do in the spring of 1753.

30. B.L. Newcastle Papers, vol. 164, Add. Mss. 32,850, f. 191.

31. W.C.L. Mildmay Papers, 2:79–81.

32. Ibid., 3:11 September 1754.

33. Hayes Baker-Crothers, *Virginia and the French and Indian Wars* (Chicago: University of Chicago Press, 1928), 28; Fred Anderson, *Crucible of War: The Seven Years' War and the Fate of Empire in British North America, 1754–1766* (New York: Knopf, 2000), 37, 40, 41, 50–59.

34. B.L. Newcastle Papers, 165, Add. Mss. 32,850, f. 231–34. Captain James Mackay was a British officer, commissioned by the king, who reluctantly, agreed to be seconded to the Virginian militia. Anderson, *Crucible of War*, 60.

35. B.L. Newcastle Papers, vol. 165, Add. Mss. 32,850, f. 218.

36. Ibid., f. 289.

37. Ibid., f. 6/7.

38. Ibid., f. 126.

39. Letter from Governor Dinwiddie to Sir Thomas Robinson, Louis Knott Koontz, *Robert Dinwiddie in His Career in American Colonial Government and Western Expansion* (Glendale, Calif.: Arthur H. Clarke Co., 1941), 391; Letter from Lord Albemarle to the duke of Newcastle, 4 September 1754, B.L. Newcastle Papers, vol. 165, Add. Mss. 32,850, f. 289.

40. The quotation is cited by Guy Fregault and is taken from Montcalm's memoirs. Guy Fregault, *Canada: The War of the Conquest*, trans. Margaret M. Cameron (Toronto: Oxford University Press, 1969), 68, 69, 70.

41. Patrice Higonnet, "The Origins of the Seven Years' War." *Journal of Modern History* 40 (1968): 57–90, 32, 33.

42. W.C.L., Mildmay Papers, 3:3 October 1754.

43. Ibid., 2:81–84 (conference minutes); W.C.L., Mildmay Papers, 5:117 (letter to Sir Thomas Robinson, 4 October 1754).

44. Ibid., 5:118.

45. Mildmay's report of the 4 October 1754 conference is the last item in his book of conference minutes and the letter that he and De Cosne sent to Sir Thomas Robinson on 20 November is their last official letter of 1754.

46. Wickham-Legg, ed., *British Diplomatic Instructions*, 46.

47. W.C.L. Mildmay Papers, 3:9 October 1754.

48. B.L. Newcastle Papers, Add. Mss. 32,735, f. 110–18. In 1754 the territory was called East Jersey and West Jersey.

49. B.L. Newcastle Papers, Add. Mss. 32,736, f. 259.

50. B.L. Newcastle Papers, Add. Mss. 32,735, f. 597.

51. B.L. Newcastle Papers, vol. 166 Add. Mss. 32,851, f. 56.

52. Wickham-Legg, ed., *British Diplomatic Instructions*, 49.

53. B.L. Leeds Papers, vol. 166 Add. Mss 32,851, f.82.

54. A period of warm weather in late October that frequently precedes the Feast of St. Martin of Tours, on November 11th.

55. W.C.L. Mildmay Papers, 3:23 October 1754.

56. Ibid., 3:13 November 1754.

57. Ibid., 3:20 November 1754.

58. Ibid., 3:27 November 1754.

59. Ibid., 3:4 December 1754.

60. Ibid., 3:18 December 1754.

61. Ibid., 3:22 December 1754; B.L. Leeds Papers, vol. 134, Egerton 3457, f. 347.

62. W.C.L., Mildmay Papers, 3:25 December 1754.

63. B.L. Newcastle Papers, Add. Mss. 32,996. f. 51.

64. B.L. Newcastle Papers, Add. Mss. 32,996, f. 25.

65. C.A.M., vol. 438, C 12546, pp. 62–68.

66. Ibid. At the conclusion of the Seven Years' War, in 1763, a portion of this proposal was, in fact, adopted when the hinterland of the entire south shore of the St. Lawrence River that begins across from the present city of Cornwall became the boundary of the new province of Lower Canada (later the province of Quebec), while the remaining territory along the St. Lawrence, beginning just east of Massena, was acquired by the colony of New York.

67. Ibid., 90–92, 106–10, 161–63, 266–67; C.A.M., vol. 439, C12546, pp. 19–20, 24–25, 31–32, 33–38.

68. C.A.M., vol. 439, C 12546, p. 25.

69. Ibid., 197–98.

70. W.C.L. Mildmay Papers, 3:15 January 1755.

71. Ibid., 3:29 January 1755.

72. Ibid., 3:5 February 1755.

73. Ibid., 3:19 February 1755.

74. Ibid., 3:5 March 1755.

75. Ibid., 3:12 March 1755.

76. Ibid., 3:26 March 1755.

77. Ibid., 3:16 April 1755.

78. Ibid., 3:26 March 1755.

79. Walpole, *Correspondence of Horace Walpole with Sir Horace Mann*, 474 and 474n. 5. John Brooke cites H. C. Richmond, *Papers Relating to the Loss of Minorca* (London, 1913), 60, for this information.

80. W.C.L. Mildmay Papers, 3:30 April 1755.

81. B.L. Leeds Papers, vol. 125, Egerton 3458, f. 289.

82. B.L. Leeds Papers, vol. 135, Egerton 3458, f. 300.

83. Carew Mildmay was William's third cousin, from a separate family branch, but he was also the only other surviving male in the family and the uncle of William's future wife, Anne. In a letter Mildmay sent to Lord Fitzwalter on 15 January he mentioned a letter he had received from Carew Mildmay about Fitzwalter's health, and in another letter, on 19 February, he stated that he had asked for Carew Mildmay's help in obtaining permission to return to England. W.C.L. Mildmay Papers, 3:15 January 1755, 19 February 1755.

84. Letter to Carew Hervey Mildmay, E.R.O. Mildmay Papers D/DM, 01/30. A list of ships in the French fleet at Brest in 1755, E.R.O. Mildmay Papers D/DM 01/40. The request from Philip Yorke, Viscount Royston, B.L. Leeds Papers, vol. 125, Egerton 3458, f. 289. As a young man Carew Hervey Mildmay (1690–1784) had been a member of parliament during the last years of the reign

of Queen Anne, and a secretary to Lord Bolingbroke. He was also well regarded by George II and still had regular contacts among the present members of the British government. Mrs. Paget Toynbee, *Letters of Horace Walpole* (London, 1903–5), 5:208; Philip Ralph Lee, *Sir Humphrey Mildmay: Royalist Gentleman, Glimpses of the English Scene 1633–1652* (New Brunswick: Rutgers University Press, 1947), 220, 221.

85. The correspondence of Sir Thomas Robinson during May 1755, B.L. Leeds Papers, vol. 135, Add. Mss. 3458.

86. E.R.O. Mildmay Papers, D/DM, 01/41.

87. B.L. Hardwicke Papers, Add. Mss. 35,606, f.140.

88. E.R.O. Mildmay Papers, D/DM, 01/30.

89. The date of 3 May, given in this French document, was the intended sailing date, but the bad weather forced a postponement before this fleet was able to leave the harbor at Brest.

90. E.R.O. Mildmay Papers, D/DM, 01/41.

91. A Letter from Horace Walpole to Horace Mann, 16 July 1755. Walpole, *Horace Walpole's Correspondence with Sir Horace Mann*, 4, 15th November 1748–18th September 1756, *The Yale Edition of Horace Walpole's Correspondence*, vol. 22, ed. W. S. Lewis, Warren Hunting Smith and George L. Lam (New Haven: Yale University Press, 1960), 484.

92. E.R.O. Mildmay Papers, D/DM, 01/29.

93. Walpole, *Horace Walpole's Correspondence with Sir Horace Mann*, 516. Walpole's information was inaccurate, as in December 1755 Fitzwalter was eighty-five. He died in February 1756 at the age of eighty-six. See appendix 1, The Fitzwalter Monument inscription.

94. A. C. Edwards, *The Account Books of Benjamin Mildmay, Earl Fitzwalter* (London: Regency Press, 1977), ix. The date of Mildmay's departure from Paris is given in a note inserted in the volume of official commission letters, W.C.L. Mildmay Papers, 5:118.

95. W.C.L. Mildmay Papers, 5:118, 119.

96. E.R.O. Mildmay Papers, D/DM, 01/30.

97. W.C.L. Mildmay Papers, 5:120.

98. Sir Benjamin Keene, *The Private Correspondence of Sir Benjamin Keene K.B.*, ed. Sir Richard Lodge (London: University Press, 1933), 412.

99. Walpole, *Horace Walpole's Correspondence with Sir Horace Mann*, 4:488, 489.

100. E.R.O. Mildmay Papers, D/DM, 01/41. This is the order and language of the justification documents as they are printed in *Memorials of the English and French Commissioners concerning the Limits of Nova Scotia, or Acadia and St. Lucia*, 2 vols. (British Government: London, 1755).

101. C.A.M. vol. 439, C12546, p. 123.

102. Ibid., 152, 153, 201.

103. E.R.O. Mildmay Papers, D/DM, 01/41.

104. *British Diplomatic Instructions,* 52. A letter to De Cosne from Sir Thomas Robinson, dated 22 July 1755, instructing him to close the British Embassy and to leave Paris.

105. E.R.O. Mildmay Papers, D/DM, 01/41.

106. Ibid.

107. The copy of this book in the British Library states that it was printed in 1755, and on the front cover is a note that this edition was presented to the library by Dr. Maty in November 1760. In this book the complete list of memorials differs somewhat, both in dates and content, from the list sent to Mildmay by De Cosne, and from those recorded by Mildmay in his journal. The book gives these memorials as three on St. Lucia—11 February 1751 (French), 15 November 1751 (British), 24 October 1754 (French)—and five on Nova Scotia and Acadia: 21 September 1750 (British), 16 November 1750 (French), 11 January 1751 (British), 4 October 1751 (British), 23 January 1753 (British). Missing from the book list is the memorial on Acadia that was described as "vague," and was presented by the French government on 21 September 1750. In his journal Mildmay did not record any British memorial as having been presented on 4 October 1751, and the memorial on St. Lucia and Acadia that was presented by Galissonière to De Cosne on 18 May 1755 does not appear on either list.

108. Thomas Jeffreys, *Remarks on the French Memorials concerning the Limits of Acadia, printed at the Royal Printing House at Paris and Distributed by the French Ministers to All the Foreign Courts of Europe* (London, 1756).

109. Rouillé's letter and memorial was sent to Fox via M. Bonac, French ambassador to Holland. It was then sent on to London by Joseph Yorke at The Hague, because Britain had no ambassador to France in Paris in 1755. Letter from Horace Walpole to Sir Horace Mann, 28 January 1756. *The Yale Edition of Horace Walpole's Correspondence,* 22:553, 554.

110. B.L. Leeds Papers, vol. 135, Egerton 3458, f. 154–65. This document is in French and the translation is mine.

111. E.R.O. Mildmay Papers, D/DM, 01/26.

112. Ibid.

113. Max Savelle and Margaret Anne Fisher, *The Origins of American Diplomacy: The International History of Angloamerica 1492–1765* (New York: Macmillan, 1967), 559.

114. *The Method and Rules of Proceeding upon all Elections, Scrutinies at Common Hall and Wardmotes within the City of London, by Sir William Mildmay, with additional notes . . . by Henry Kent Causton, Citizen and Skinner of London* (London: Henry Kent Causton, 1841), xiii.

115. Burke, *A Genealogical and Heraldic Dictionary*, 959.

116. E.R.O. Mildmay Papers, D/DM, 01/41.

117. Anderson, *Crucible of War*, 557, 558.


EPILOGUE

1. E.R.O. Mildmay Papers, D/DM T96/22 (Lord Fitzwalter's will). Schomberg House, 80–82 Pall Mall, was built in 1696 for Lady Frederica's father, the third duke of Schomberg, and it is now the offices of C. H. Elson and Partners. In 1769 it was sold by William Mildmay and was then divided into three, interconnected houses. From 1774 to 1788 Thomas Gainsborough had an apartment there. In the twentieth century the core of the building was converted into offices and only the shell of the original mansion remains.

2. This information is given in the introduction by Henry Causton to Mildmay's book, *The Method and Rule of Proceeding upon all Elections*, reprinted edition with additional notes by Henry Kent S. Causton (London: Henry Kent S. Causton, 1841), xiii.

3. J. Bruce Williamson, *The Middle Temple Bench Book, being a Register of the Benchers of the Middle Temple from the Earliest Records to the Present Time*, 2d ed. (London: Chancery Land Press, 1937), 175 (masters of the Bench), 557 (The office of reader).

4. William Mildmay, *A Fair Representation of His Majesty's Right to Nova Scotia and Acadia, briefly stated, from the Memorials of the English Commissioners* (London: Thomas Harrison, 1756); *The Police of France* (London: Edward Owen and Thomas Harrison, 1763); *An Account of the Southern Maritime Provinces of France* (London: Thomas Harrison, 1764); *The Laws and Policy of England Relating to Trade Examined by the Maxims and Principles of Trade in General and by the Laws and Policies of Other Trading Nations*, (London: Thomas Harrison, 1765).

5. In the center of the facade of the almshouses is a plaque stating that they were "Rebuilt by William Mildmay Esq." in 1758; E.R.O. Mildmay Papers, D/DM F 15/7 (papers on the grammar school addition); Philip Morant, *The History and Antiquities of the County of Essex, 1763–1768*, 2:5, 6 (information on the foundation of the grammar school by Sir Walter Mildmay, and the almshouses by Sir Thomas Mildmay); E.R.O. Mildmay Papers, D/DM Z3/ 1–5 (papers concerning the drafting and progress of the bill to allow barge navigation on the Chelmer River); Grieve, *The Sleepers and the Shadows*, 2:150–52.

6. (Papers on the proposed movement of the jail to the marketplace), E.R.O. Mildmay Papers, D/DM, F 28/ 1–3; (the Commons Committee reports on the jail hearings) *Journals of the House of Commons*, vol. 33, 1770–72, 6 May 1771, pp. 368–98.

7. E.R.O. Mildmay Papers, D/DM T33/29. (A receipt from the rector of St. Mary's Church for £200 that was left to the town in Sir William Mildmay's will for the repair of the pipes to the conduit, in the Chelmsford marketplace).

8. W.C.L. Mildmay Papers, 3:12 July 1752.

9. See the Mildmay Family Tree, appendix 2.

# Selected Bibliography

## Manuscripts

The Mildmay Papers, Series D/DM, The Essex Record Office, Chelmsford.

The Mildmay Papers, vols. 1-7, The William Clements Library, Ann Arbor, Mich.

The Leeds Papers, Egerton Add. Mss. Vols. 3416, 3456, 3458, The British Library, London.

The Newcastle Papers, Add. Mss. Vols. 32, 716, 32, 820, 32, 827, 32, 849, 32, 850, 32, 851, 32, 896, The British Library, London.

The Hardwicke Papers, Add. Mss. Vols. 35, 359, The British Library, London.

The Birch Papers, Add. Mss. Vol 4314, The British Library, London.

The Records of the Honourable Society of the Middle Temple Admissions to the House and Chambers (1695-1737), Vol. G, London.

*Ministere des Affaires Etrangeres,* The Public Archives, Ottawa, Canada.

*Correspondance Politique: Angleterre,* Vols. 429-39 (1720-55), The Public Archives, Ottawa, Canada.

MG5, A1, Microfilm Reels #12544–46, The Public Archives, Ottawa, Canada.

## Printed Primary Sources

Argenson, Marquis d'. *Journal and Memoirs of the Marquis d'Argenson.* 2 Vols. Edited by E. J. B. Rathery. Translated by Katherine Prescott Wormeley. Boston: Hardy, Pratt and Company, 1901.

Beatson, Robert. *Naval and Military Memoirs of Great Britain, from 1727–1783.* 2 Vols. London: Longman, Hurst, Rees and Orme, 1804.

Bedford, John, Duke of. *The Correspondence of John, Fourth Duke of Bedford.* 2 Vols. Edited by Lord John Russell. London: Longman, Brown, Green and Longman, 1842–46.

Bernis, Cardinal de. *Memoirs and Letters of Cardinal de Bernis.* 2 Vols. Introduction by C.A. Sainte-Breuve. Translated by Kathleen Prescott Wormeley. Boston: Hardy, Pratt and Company, 1902.

Bramstone, Sir John. *The Autobiography of Sir John Bramstone K.B. of Screens.* London: Camden Society, Vol. 32, 1845.

Brosses, Président de. *Lettres du Président de Brosses a Ch. -C. Loppin de Gemeaux.* Introduction by Yvonne Bezard. Paris: Firmin-Didot, 1929.

Clarke, J. C. D., ed. *The Memoirs and Speeches of James, 2nd Earl Waldegrave, 1742–1763.* Cambridge: Cambridge University Press, 1988.

Coxe, William. *Memoirs of the Administration of the Right Honourable Henry Pelham Collected from the Family Papers and other Authentic Documents.* 2 Vols. London: Longman, Rees, Orme, Brown, and Green, 1829.

———. *Memoirs of Horatio, Lord Walpole, selected from his Correspondence and Papers and Connected with the History of the Times from 1678–1757.* 2 Vols. London: Longman, Hurst, Rees, Orme, and Brown 1820.

Davenport, F. G., and C. O. Paullin, eds. *European Treaties bearing on the History of the United States and its Dependencies.* Vol. 3. Washington, D.C.: Carnegie Institute, 1917–37.

Dodington, George Bubb. *The Political Journal of George Bubb Dodington.* Edited by John Carswell and Lewis Arnold Dralle, Oxford: Clarendon Press, 1965.

Garrick, David. *The Diary of David Garrick: Being a Record of a Memorable Trip to Paris in 1751.* Edited by R. C. Alexander. New York: Oxford University Press, American Branch, 1928.

*Genealogical Memoranda Relating to the Family of Mildmay.* London: Taylor & Co., printers, 1871.

*The History, Debates and Proceedings of Both Houses of Parliament of Great Britain from the year 1743 to the year 1774.* 3 Vols. Great Britain: Parliament, 1779.

Historical Manuscripts Commission. *The Fifth and Seventh Reports of the Historical Manuscripts Commission.* London: Historical Manuscripts Commission, 1876.

Hoare, Sir Richard. *A Journal of the Shrievalty of Sir Richard Hoare, Esq. in the Years 1740 to 1741, printed from a manuscript in his own handwriting.* Bath: Richard Cruttwell, 1815.

House of Commons. *Journals of the House of Commons.* Vol. 26. Great Britain: Parliament, House of Commons.

House of Lords. *Journals of the House of Lords.* Vol. 27. Great Britain: Parliament, House of Commons.

Jeffreys, Thomas. *Remarks on the French Memorials concerning the Limits of Acadia, printed at the Royal Printing House at Paris and distributed by the French ministers to all the Foreign Courts of Europe.* London, 1756.

Johnson, Sir William. *The Papers of Sir William Johnson.* Edited by James Sullivan, Albany: University of the State of New York, 1921.

Keene, Sir Benjamin. *The Private Correspondence of Sir Benjamin Keene K.B.* Edited by Sir Richard Lodge, London: University Press, 1933.

King, Cyril L., ed. *Middle Temple Records: Minutes of the Parliament.* Vol. V (1703–1747). London: Inns of Court, 1970.

Lincoln, C. H., ed. *The Correspondence of William Shirley, Governor of Massachusetts and Military Governor of North America.* New York, 1912.

*Mémoires des Commissaries du Roi et ceux de Son Majesté Britannique sur la possessions et les droits respectifs des deux couronnes en Amerique, avec les actes publics et pièces justicatifs.* 3 Vols. Paris: *Imprimerie Royal, 1755.*

*Memorials of the English and French Commissioners concerning the Limits of Nova Scotia, or Acadia, and St. Lucia.* Vol. 1, Acadia; Vol. 2, St Lucia. London: His Majesty's Printing Office, 1755.

Mildmay, Sir Walter. *The Statutes of Sir Walter Mildmay Kt. Chancellor of the Exchequer and One of Her Majesty's Privy Councillors: authorised by him for the government of Emmanuel College founded by him.* Translated with an Introduction by Frank Stubbings. Cambridge: Cambridge University Press, 1983.

Mildmay, Sir William. *The Method and Rule of Proceeding on all Elections, Polls and Scrutinies at Common Hall and Wardmotes within the City of London.* 1741. Reprint, London: Thomas Harrison and William Johnson, 1768.

———. *A Fair Representation of His Majesty's Rights to Nova Scotia and Acadia briefly stated, with an answer to the objections contained in the French treatise entitled Discussion sommaire sur la Ancienne Limites de l'Acadie.* London: T. Harrison, 1756.

———. *The Police of France.* London: Edward Owen and Thomas Harrison, 1763.

———. *An Account of the Southern Maritime Provinces of France.* London: Thomas Harrison, 1764.

————. *The Laws and Policy of England Relating to Trade Examined by the Maxims and Principles of Trade in General and by the Laws and Policy of other Trading Nations*. London: Thomas Harrison, 1765.

————. "An Essay on measuring time at Sea." 1755. Ms. London: British Library, Ms. Birch Papers Vol. 4314, f. 33.

————. "A declaration of the rights of barristers and students assembled in various Parliaments in the Middle Temple. Presented to the Masters and Benchers by William Mildmay, Chairman of the Parliament, 1745." Ms., Essex Record Office: Mildmay Papers D/DM, f. 23.

Morant, Philip. *The History and Antiquities of the County of Essex*. 2 Vols. London: T Osborne, 1763–1768.

————. *The History and Antiquities of the County of Essex*. 2 Vols. 1763–1768. Reprint, East Ardsley, Eng.: E.P. Publishing Ltd., 1978.

Ogilby, John. *Britannia, or an Illustration of the Kingdom of England and the Dominion of Wales by a geographical and historical description of the principal roads thereof*. London: Christopher Wilkinson, 1689.

Ovington, John. *A Voyage to Surat in the Year 1689*. Edited by H.G. Rawlinson, Oxford: Oxford University Press, 1929.

Pitt, William. *Correspondence of William Pitt when Secretary of State with Colonial Governors and Military and Naval Commanders in America*. Edited by Gertrude Kimball, 2 Vols. New York: Macmillan, 1906.

Proulx, Gilles. *Between France and New France*. Toronto: Dundurn Press, 1984.

Reaney, H., and March Fitch, eds. *The Feet of Fines for Essex, 1423–1547*. Vol. 4. Colechester: The Society, 1963.

Smollett, Tobias. *The History of England from the Revolution of 1688 to the Death of George II*. London: R. Scholey, 1808.

————. *Continuation of the Complete History of England*. 2 Vols. London: Richard Baldwin, 1760.

Stock, Leo Francis, ed. *Proceedings and Debates of the British Parliaments Respecting North America*. 6 Vols. Washington, D.C.: Carnegie Institution, 1924– .

Sturgess, Herbert A.C. *The Register of Admissions to the Honourable Society of the Middle Temple from the Fifteenth Century to the Year 1944*. 2 Vols. London: Butterworth and Co., 1949.

Taylor, W. S., and J. H. Pringle, eds. *The Correspondence of William Pitt, Earl of Chatham*. Vol.1. London, 1838–1840.

Venn, J., and J. A. Venn, eds. *Alumni Cantabrigienses: A Biographical List of All Known Students, Graduates and Known Office Holders at the University of Cambridge.* 4 Vols. Cambridge: Cambridge University Press, 1922–54. Part I, Vol. 3, 1922–1925.Voltaire, François Marie Arouet de. *The Age of Louis XV, being the Sequel of the Age of Louis XIV, translated from the French of M. de Voltaire, with a Supplement Comprising an Account of all the private Affaires of France, from the Peace of Versailles, 1763, to the death of Louis XV, 1774.* 2 Vols., London: G Kearsly, 1774.

Waldegrave, James, Earl Waldegrave. *Memoirs from 1754–1758.* London: John Murray, 1821.

Walpole, Horace. *Horace Walpole's Correspondence with Sir Horace Mann. 1V, 15th November 1748–18th September 1756. The Yale Edition of the Correspondence of Horace Walpole.* Vol. 22, Edited by W. S. Lewis, Warren Hunting Smith, and George L. Lam, New Haven: Yale University Press, 1954– .

———. *Horace Walpole's Correspondence with the Rev. William Cole. 26 January 1776–7 November 1782, The Yale Edition of the Correspondence of Horace Walpole.* Vol. 2. Edited by W.S. Lewis and A. Dayle Wallace. New Haven: Yale University Press; London, H. Milford, Oxford University Press, 1937.

———. *Memoirs of the Reign of King George the Second.* Edited by Lord Holland, 2 Vols. London: Henry Colburn, 1846.

Wickham-Legg, L. G., ed. *British Diplomatic Instructions 1689–1789.* London: the Royal Historical Society, 1934.

Williamson, J. Bruce, ed. *Middle Temple Bench Book, being a Register of the Benchers of the Middle Temple from the earliest records to the present time.* 2nd Edition, London: Chancery Land Press, 1937.

Yorke, Philip C. *The Life and Correspondence of Philip Yorke, Earl of Hardwicke.* Cambridge: Cambridge University Press, 1913.

Young, Arthur. *Letters concerning the Present State of the French Nation.* London: W. Nicoll, 1769.

## SECONDARY PRINTED SOURCES

Alexander, Ryllis Clair, ed. *The Diary of David Garrick: Being a Record of His Memorable Trip to Paris in 1751.* New York: Oxford University Press, 1928.

Anderson, Fred. *Crucible of War: The Seven Years War and the Fate of Empire in British North America, 1754–1766.* New York: First Vintage Books, 2001.

Baker-Crothers, Hayes. *Virginia and the French and Indian Wars.* Chicago: University of Chicago Press, 1928.

Bamford, Paul. *Fighting Ships and Prisons: The Mediterranean Galleys of France in the Age of Louis XIV.* Minneapolis: University of Minnesota Press, 1973.

Barbier, Edmond. *Journal Historique et annecdotique du régne de Louis XV par Edmond Barbier.* Paris: Renourd, 1847–56.

Beattie, J. M. *Crime and the Courts in England 1660–1800.* Princeton: Princeton University Press, 1986.

Benhamou, Reed. "The Verdigris Industry in Eighteenth Century Languedoc: Women's Work, Women's Art." *French Historical Studies* 16 (spring 1990): 560–75.

Bernard, Leon. *The Emerging City: Paris in the Age of Louis XIV.* Durham, N.C.: Duke University Press, 1970.

Black, Jeremy. *Natural and Necessary Enemies: Anglo-French Relations in the Eighteenth Century.* London: Duckworth 1986.

Bluche, François. *Les Magistrats du Parlement de Paris au XVIIIe siécle.* 1960. Reprint, Paris: Economica, 1986.

Bosher, John. *French Finances 1770–1795: From Business to Bureaucracy.* Cambridge: Cambridge University Press, 1970.

Bromley, J.S. "The Decline of Absolute Monarchy." *France: Government and Society.* Edited by J.M. Wallace-Hadrill and J. McManners. London: Methuen, 1957.

Burke, Sir Bernard. *A Genealogical and Heraldic Dictionary of the Peerage, Baronage and Knightage of Great Britain.* London: H Colburn, 1893.

Chancellor, Frederick. *The Ancient Sepulchral Monuments of Essex.* Chelmsford: Edward Durrant and Co., 1890.

Dent, Julian. *Crisis in Finance: Crown, Financiers and Society in Seventeenth Century France.* New York: St. Martin's Press, 1973.

Drake, Samuel S. *A Particular History of the Five Years French and Indian Wars in New England and Parts Adjacent, from its Declaration by the King of France, March 15th 1744, to the treaty with the Eastern Indians, October 16th 1749, sometimes called Governor Shirley's War.* Albany, N.Y., 1870.

Eccles, William. *The Canadian Frontier, 1754–1760.* New York: Holt, Rinehart and Winston, 1969.

Edwards, A. C. *The account books of Benjamin Mildmay, Earl Fitzwalter,* London: Regency Press, 1977.

Egret, Jean. *Louis XV et l' opposition parlementaire 1715–1774.* Paris: *Libraire* Armand Colin, 1970.

Emmison, F. G. *Guide to the Essex Record Office.* Chelmsford: Essex County Council, 1969, Publication No. 52, Parts 1 and 2.

Fischer, Wolfram, and Peter Lundgreen. "The Recruitment and Training of Administrative and Technical Personnel." *The Formation of National States in Western Europe.* Edited by Charles Tilly. Princeton: Princeton University Press, 1975.

Ford, Franklin. *Robe and Sword: The Regrouping of the French Aristocracy after Louis XIV.* Cambridge, Mass.: Harvard University Press, 1953.

Forster, Robert. *The Nobility of Toulouse in the Eighteenth Century; a Social and Economic Study.* Baltimore: Johns Hopkins University Press, 1960.

———. *The Nobility of Eighteenth Century France.* Baltimore: Johns Hopkins University Press, 1960.

Fregault, Guy. *La Guerre de la Conquête* (Montreal: Fides, 1955), *Canada: The War of the Conquest.* Translated by Margaret M. Cameron. Toronto: Oxford University Press, 1969.

———. *François Bigot: Administrateur Français.* Montréal, L'Institut 1948.

Garden, Maurice. *Lyon et les Lyonnais au XVIIIe siècle.* 2 Vols. 1970. Reprint, Paris: Flammarion, 1975.

Grieve, Hilda. *The Sleepers and the Shadows: Chelmsford, a Town, Its People and Its Past.* 2 Vols. Chelmsford: Published by the Essex County Council in association with the Chelmsford Borough Council, 1988–94.

Hamilton, E. P. *The French and Indian War.* Garden City, N.J.: Doubleday, 1969.

Hampson, Norman. *The Enlightenment; an evaluation of its assumptions, attitudes and values.* 1968. Reprint, London: Penguin, 1984.

Hardy, James D. *Judicial Politics in the Old Regime; the Parlement of Paris during the Regency.* Baton Rouge: Louisiana State University Press, 1967.

Henretta, James A. *Salutary Neglect: Colonial Administration under the Duke of Newcastle.* Princeton: Princeton University Press, 1972.

Higonnet, Patrice. "The Origins of the Seven Years' War." *Journal of Modern History* 40 (1968): 57–90.

Hillairet, Jacques. *Dictionnaire historique des rues de Paris.* 7th Edition. Paris: *Editions de Minuit,* 1961.

Horn, D. B. *The British Diplomatic Service, 1689–1789*. Oxford: Clarendon Press, 1961.

———. *Great Britain and Europe in the Eighteenth Century*. Oxford: Clarendon Press, 1967.

———, ed., *British Diplomatic Representatives 1639–1789*. London: Offices of the Society, 1932 3rd Series, Vols. 46, 50.

Hufton, Olwen. *Europe: Privilege and Protest 1730–1789*. Ithaca, N.Y.: Cornell University Press, 1980.

Ilchester, the Earl of. *Henry Fox, First Lord Holland*. London: John Murray, 1920.

Koontz, Louis Knott. *Robert Dinwiddie in His Career in American Colonial Government and Westward Expansion*. Glendale, Calif.: Arthur H. Clarke Co., 1941.

Lee, Ralph Philip. *Sir Humphrey Mildmay: Royalist Gentleman, Glimpses of the English Scene 1633–1652*. New Brunswick: Rutgers University Press, 1947.

Lee, Sidney, and Leslie Stephen, eds. *Dictionary of National Biography*. Vols. 44, 52. London: Smith, Elder and Company, 1908–9.

Marion, Marcel. *Dictionnaire des institutions de la France aux XVIIe et XVIIIe siècles*. Paris: Auguste Picard, 1968.

McCloy, Shelby T. *Government Assistance in Eighteenth Century France*. Durham N.C.: Duke University Press, 1946.

McFarlane, Alan. *The Diary of Ralph Josselin 1616–1683*. London: Oxford University Press, 1976.

McLennan, J. S. *Louisbourg from its Foundation to its Fall*. London: Macmillan and Co. Ltd, 1918. Halifax: The Book Room Ltd., 1979.

Matthews, George T. *The Royal General Farms in Eighteenth Century France*. New York: Columbia University Press, 1958.

Mildmay, Henry A. St. John. *A Brief Memoir of the Mildmay Family*. London: privately printed, 1913.

Pargellis, Stanley, ed. *Military Affairs in North America 1748–1765: Selected Documents from the Cumberland Papers in Windsor Castle*. Hamden, Conn.: Archon Books, 1969.

Pease, Theodore C. *Anglo-French Boundary Disputes in the West 1749–1763*. Springfield, Ill.: United States Historical Library, 1936.

Peckham, Howard H. *A Guide to the Manuscript Collection in the William L. Clements Library*. Boston: 1978.

Penson, Lillian M. "The London West India Interest in the Eighteenth Century." *Essays in Eighteenth Century History from the English Historical Review*, 1–20. Arranged by Rosalind Mitchison. London: Longmans Green and Co., 1966.

Ravitch, Norman. *Sword and Mitre: Government and Episcopate in France and England in the Age of Aristocracy.* The Hague: Mouton, 1966.

Rémond, André. *John Holker, manufacturier et grand fonctionnaire en France au XVIIIme siècle 1719–1786.* Paris: M. Riviere, 1946.

Richardson, W. C. *A History of the Court of Augmentations 1536–1554.* Baton Rouge: Louisiana State University Press, 1961.

Riley, James C. *The Seven Years' War and the Old Regime in France: The Economic and Financial Toll.* Princeton: Princeton University Press, 1986.

Rogister, Rudolf. "The Crisis of 1753–4 in France and the Debate on the Nature of Monarchy and of the Fundamental Laws." *Herrschaftsvertrage, Wahlkaptulationen, Fundamentalgestze.* Edited by Rudolf Vierhaus, 105–20. Göttingen: Vandenhoeck and Ruprecht, 1977.

Savelle, Max. *The Diplomatic History of the Canadian Boundary 1749–1763.* 1940. New York: Russell and Russell, 1968.

Savelle, Max, and Margaret Anne Fisher. *The Origins of American Diplomacy: The International History of Angloamerica 1492–1763.* New York: The Macmillan Company, 1967.

Schutz, John A. *William Shirley, King's Governor of Massachusetts.* Chapel Hill: University of North Carolina Press, 1961.

———. *Thomas Pownall, British Defender of American Liberty.* Glendale, Calif.: Arthur H. Clarke Co., 1951.

Shennan, J. H. *The Parlement of Paris.* London: Eyre and Spottiswoode, 1968.

———. *Philippe, Duke of Orléans, Regent of France 1715–1723.* London: Thames and Hudson, 1979.

Stanley, George. *New France: The Last Phase 1744–1760.* Toronto: McClelland and Stewart Ltd., 1968.

Stock, Leo Francis. *Proceedings and Debates of the British Parliament Respecting North America*, Vol. 5, 1739–1754. Washington, D.C.: Carnegie Institution, 1941.

Stone, Bailey. *The Parlement of Paris 1774–1789.* Chapel Hill: University of North Carolina Press, 1981.

————. *The French Parlements and the Crisis of the Old Regime.* Chapel Hill: University of North Carolina Press, 1986.

Sutherland, Lucy. *The East India Company in Eighteenth Century Politics.* London; New York: Oxford University Press, 1952

Thompson, Mark. *The Secretaries of State 1681–1782.* Oxford: Clarendon Press, 1956.

Tilly, Charles. *The Contentious French.* Cambridge, Mass.: The Belknap Press, 1986.

————. "Food Supply and Public Order in Modern Europe." *The Formation of National States in Western Europe.* Edited by Charles Tilly. Princeton: Princeton University Press, 1975.

Van Kley, Dale K. *The Jansenists and the Expulsion of the Jesuits 1757–1765.* New Haven: Yale University Press, 1975.

————. *The Damiens Affair and the Unravelling of the Ancien Régime 1750–1770.* Princeton: Princeton University Press, 1984.

Voltaire. *The Age of Louis XV, being the Sequel to the Age OF Louis XIV, Translated from the French of M. de Voltaire.* London: G. Kearsly, 1774.

*The Victoria History of the County of Cambridge and the Isle of Ely.* Vol. 3 and Bibliography. London: Oxford University Press, 1979.

*The Victoria History of the County of Hampshire and the Isle of Wight.* Vol. 4. London: Constable and Company, 1911.

*The Victoria History of the County of Essex.* Vol. 4. Oxford: Oxford University Press, 1973.

Weinreb, Ben, and Christopher Hibbert, eds. *The London Encyclopedia.* London: Papermac Publications, 1983.

Williams, Alan. *The Police of Paris 1718–1789.* Baton Rouge: Louisiana State University Press, 1979.

Zysberg, Andre. "Galley Rowers in the Mid-Eighteenth Century." *The Deviants and the Abandoned in French Society; Selections from the Annales.* Vol. 4. Edited by Robert Forster and Orest Ranum, translated by Elborg Forster and Patricia Ranum. Baltimore: Johns Hopkins University Press, 1978.

# Index